We dedicate this book to our spouses,
Claudia and Dan, and to our children,
Jared and Shane McIntyre and Erica and Jonathan O'Hair,
in appreciation of their continued inspiration,
support, and patience throughout the project.

Contents

Chapter 2 The Communicator Role 49

Chapter 3   The Motivator Role 91

Chapter 4   The Manager Role 129

Chapter 5   **The Innovator Role 155**

Chapter 6   **The Counselor Role 195**

Chapter 7   **The Ethicist Role 223**

Chapter 8   The Professional Role 253

Preface

$\mathcal{T}$eaching is a multifaceted profession. As our world rapidly changes, teaching becomes even more complex as it gains additional facets or responsibilities. *The Reflective Roles of the Classroom Teacher* addresses the various roles or facets assumed by teachers and relates how these roles are related to each other and how effective teachers perform within each role. By examining classroom teacher roles, this book assists future and beginning teachers to relate theory and research to practice.

Most textbooks are very theoretical and mechanical in their approach to the teaching process. Teaching is not mechanical! Teachers must have the flexibility, creativity, and problem-solving ability to adapt their theoretical knowledge to any classroom situation. This book places theory in the classroom by consistently providing opportunities and activities for students to reflect about how their knowledge can be applied in classroom situations.

Appropriate both for undergraduate courses that incorporate field experiences and for general methods courses, this text is also applicable for alternative certification and induction programs. Preliminary testing found that this book is also effective with graduate courses that facilitate teachers' reflection of their own classroom behavior as it relates to teaching and learning.

The content of *The Reflective Roles of the Classroom Teacher* examines areas of teaching that many other texts ignore. Each chapter examines a specific role of the classroom teacher; for each role, research and best practice is related to actual classroom situations. Exercises are provided throughout that encourage readers to assess their knowledge of each role and, perhaps more important, to reflect on how they might perform within the role.

The roles included in this book are the organizer, the communicator, the motivator, the manager, the professional, the counselor, the ethicist, and the political. Chapter 10 examines how these roles are related to each other and how the teacher must mesh these roles in order to become effective.

To facilitate the readers' ability to reflect about their own attitudes and behavior, *The Reflective Roles of the Classroom Teacher* provides several unique features. First, the book is based on the Reflective Teaching Model, which helps the student link theory and practice. The model's key components are self-assessment, knowledge, coaching, and reflection. Self-assessment exercises are placed at the beginning of each chapter to help students assess the knowledge and attitudes they possess about each role before studying it. The knowledge, or experience, section of each chapter includes research, theory, and best practice related to each role. The coaching and reflection sections are designed for the beginning teacher to apply the skills, knowledge, and attitudes learned within each role.

Second, each chapter contains at least three Reality Bites, which are thought-provoking segments written by experienced teachers and administrators. These segments are designed to illustrate how roles are acted out in the school and community and to challenge beginning teachers to reflect upon "real" experiences of teachers and administrators.

Finally, the book encourages the development of collegial relationships, open dialogue, and shared decision making, all of which reduce teacher isolation. Most activities are designed to be practiced in a classroom with other beginning teachers or with cooperating experienced teachers. Again, the intent is for beginning teachers to relate the theoretical world of the textbook to the real world of the classroom.

Acknowledgments

This project would not have been completed without the support and guidance of many people. Suzanna Brabant, our first editor, provided both the initial motivation to begin the book and the enthusiasm to overcome any obstacles. Our current editor, Sabra Horne, has been most helpful in guiding us through the final stages.

We sincerely appreciate and are grateful to the authors of several chapters in this book: Sally Zepeda, University of Oklahoma, Chapter 4, The Manager Role; Angela McNabb Spaulding, Texas Tech University, Chapter 9, The Political Role; and Fredrick Hartmeister and Joseph Claudet, Texas Tech University, Chapter 10, The Legal Role. We want to thank Angela Spaulding also for her continued assistance and support throughout the project.

We also wish to express our sincere appreciation to the chapter consultants who provided valuable insights, comments, and suggestions for individual chapters as well as Reality Bites. The chapter consultants include both beginning and experienced teachers and administrators who helped ground the text in the realities of the classroom. All were enrolled in graduate classes at either Southern Illinois University at Carbondale or Texas Tech University: Severo Alvarado, Cynthia Bishop, Keith Bryant, Annette Campbell, Stacy Caviel, Lisa Cogswell, Caitlin Cole, Cheryl Cooper, Kim Cumby, Aaron Curtis, Tom Dickey, Sarah Dodson, Carl Donald, Mike Elkins, Judy Evrard, John Gatcia, Bob Hand, Karla Hankins, Holly Hursh, Rhonda Jones, Chuck Keating, Jan Kireilis, Corinne Lelievre, Cheryl

Martin, Janice Muller, Robert Nimtz, Tamra Peck, Joanie Prado, Alison Reeves, Marc Rich, Matt Seebaum, Diana Shackelford, Tara Stace, Barbara Tarro, Janice Thomas, Cindy Timms, Tresa Tolley, and David Worley. Dr. Lawrence Rossow provided valuable comments about Chapter 10, The Legal Role.

Finally, we would like to acknowledge the following reviewers who provided valuable comments throughout the writing process: Robert Alley, Wichita State University; Renee Clift, University of Illinois; Maureen Gillette, College of St. Rose; Carol A. Mullen, The Joint Center for Teacher Development, Ontario Institute for Studies in Education; Phillip Sciortino, University of Central Florida; and M. Kay Stickle, Ball State University.

About the Authors

D. John McIntyre is a professor in the College of Education and Director of Professional Education Experiences at Southern Illinois University at Carbondale. He earned his doctoral degree in curriculum at Syracuse University and has a continuing commitment to the development of effective teachers. He has authored or coauthored over 50 articles in the area of teacher education. A past president of the Association of Teacher Educators, he was named as one of the 70 Outstanding Leaders in Teacher Education by ATE in 1990. In addition, he received ATE's Distinguished Research in Teacher Education award in 1986.

Mary John O'Hair is an associate professor in the College of Education at the University of Oklahoma. She received her doctoral degree from New Mexico State University. Her areas of expertise are in educational administration, communication skills, and teacher education. Dr. O'Hair has authored or coauthored 5 books and over 20 articles. She has worked with many school districts in the area of improving communication for school restructuring. In addition, she has received research awards from the International Communication Association, American Educational Research Association, and the Rocky Mountain Educational Research Association.

Introduction

Learning to teach—like teaching itself—
is always the process of becoming; a time
of formation and transformation, of scrutiny
into what one is doing, and who one can become.

Deborah P. Britzman
Practice Makes Practice: A Critical Study of Learning to Teach

$\mathcal{T}$his quote reflects our philosophy about the process of becoming a teacher and is the philosophy that undergirds this book. Learning to teach is a growth process. Perhaps this explains why most teachers confront their field experiences, especially student teaching, with excitement, fear, confidence, uncertainty, and a myriad of other emotions and expectations. These conflicting feelings and expectations are not uncommon when one considers the extreme importance of the teaching profession. It is common for beginning teachers to question whether they can be effective, whether they can manage an entire classroom of students, whether they can be caring teachers, or whether they can deal with administrators and parents. In short, field experiences in teacher education are designed for beginning teachers not only to apply previously learned knowledge and strategies but also, and perhaps most important, to learn and to grow from the experience of working with students and in schools.

The purpose of this book is to assist you—a beginning teacher—with this growth process by examining various roles assumed by classroom teachers and by providing knowledge and activities that facilitate your ability to become a more reflective teacher within each of these roles. The roles discussed in this book are not exclusive; rather, they simply portray some of the many complex roles assumed by teachers: organizer, manager, counselor, communicator, professional, innovator, motivator, ethicist, political, and legal. Although each is discussed separately in this book, the roles are not discrete but occur within a dynamic structure of relationships. This holistic approach contributes to the complexity of the teaching–learning process (Heck & Williams, 1984).

Much of our approach evolves from the work of Van Manen's proposal of three stages of reflectivity (1977). At the first level, reflectivity focuses on the basic technical skills (instructional skills, classroom management skills, subject matter content) required to perform the act of teaching. During this level, the teacher is

1

concerned with the best way to reach an unexamined goal. Although this textbook will provide you with some technical knowledge, you will receive most of this knowledge in subject area and methods courses. During the second level, teachers critically analyze the basic rationale for the educational practices being utilized. In other words, the teacher is asking, "What should we learn?" and "What is the best way for each student to learn this material?" The third level finds teachers making the connection between what happens in the classroom and the wider moral and social structures, such as a community's moral, ethical, and political principles, that impinge on a classroom. During the course of this book, you will spend much time working on activities focusing on Van Manen's second level and will be introduced to thinking at his third level of reflectivity.

REFLECTIVE TEACHING

What is a "reflective teacher"? The term "reflective teaching" is subject to differing orientations. Some educators seek to engage teachers to become more thoughtful about the educational–social context, with aspirations that teachers should be agents of social change. Others seek to focus teachers' thoughts on the act of teaching in hopes that, through inspection, introspection, and analysis, teaching can be improved (Cruickshank & Metcalf, 1990).

For the purpose of this text, we have adopted Shulman's (1987) definition of reflective teachers as those who review, reconstruct, reenact, and critically analyze their own and their students' performances, and who formulate explanations with evidence. Reflective teachers view themselves not as passive but rather as proactive participants in the determination of curriculum and instruction decisions that impact on their students, school, and community. We believe that reflective teaching provides teachers with the willingness and ability to reflect on the origins and consequences of their actions and decisions, as well as on situations and constraints embedded within the instructional, curricular, school, and social contexts in which they work. Considering the moral, ethical, and social complexities of teaching, reflection allows teachers to think rigorously, critically, and systematically about educational practices and problems of importance in order to foster growth in self, students, and the system (Ayers, 1989). Schon (1987) asserts that although teachers gain some professional knowledge from traditional educational principles and skills, the bulk of their learning comes through continuous action and reflection on everyday problems.

Many beginning teachers have learned or have been "coached" to please their cooperating teachers and university supervisors for good grades. Teachers have learned or have been "coached" to please their administrators for positive evaluations and tenure. Although they have an "inner voice," or personal opinion, about teaching and its context, they have learned to withhold it (Canning, 1991). Reflective teaching gives rebirth to the teacher's "inner voice."

Zeichner (1983) suggests that teachers pose the following questions when carefully examining the origins and consequences of their actions and of the settings in which they work:

- What knowledge should be taught and to whom?
- How should a teacher allocate time and resources among different children?
- To what extent should personal knowledge that children bring to school be considered a legitimate part of the school curriculum?
- How much control do (and should) teachers exert in determining what is taught, how it is to be taught, and how it is to be evaluated? (p. 6)

FOUNDATION FOR REFLECTIVE TEACHING

The conceptual basis for reflective thinking can be found in the areas of cognitive psychology and experiential learning theory. Cognitive psychology provides insight into a teacher's thinking and decision-making processes. For example, studies of beginning and expert teachers indicate that expert teachers utilize a more complex schemata for approaching problems and making decisions. Berliner (1986) and Leinhardt and Greeno (1986) report that an expert teacher's schemata includes more categories, greater detail, and more relationships than schemata of beginning teachers. Expert teachers draw on a broader source of experiences and information and are thus able to make more appropriate decisions. Beginning teachers, with less experience and knowledge, produce fewer interpretations and alternatives when confronted with a problem.

For example, a beginning teacher might interpret a student's belligerent behavior as being a personal attack. Given this interpretation, the teacher might respond in a defensive and inappropriate manner by assuming the student has a behavior problem and must be disciplined firmly. Lack of experience and limited knowledge of student behavior may lead beginning teachers to inappropriate decisions and unfortunate consequences.

On the other hand, an expert, more experienced teacher may confront a similar situation with a completely different approach that includes a myriad of alternatives, such as the student might be experiencing some personal problems, might be having a problem at home, might be having difficulty with other students in class, or might be working late hours at an afterschool job. Expert teachers, with additional experience and knowledge, are able to draw on more alternatives and interpretations that will aid in their decision on how to address the student's needs.

It is important to note, however, that not all experienced teachers are experts or effective in the classroom, nor are all beginning teachers lacking experiences with students. Thus teachers must be aware of their wealth of personal experience and knowledge gained over the years. The expert teacher knows how to draw upon this knowledge and apply it to the decision-making process, but there are teachers that have been teaching for years who have not progressed beyond the "novice" stage and whose decision-making schemata remains immature.

This book is designed to increase the professional dialogue among teachers (beginning and experienced), university faculty, school administrators, students, and parents, and to focus the dialogue on the critical issues in education affecting curriculum, instruction, and student learning.

You may discover that you are never really satisfied with your teaching and are constantly searching for ways to improve. Hopefully, you have experienced and will continue to experience this "unsatisfied" feeling. Research reports that faculty in successful schools are *less* satisfied with regard to their teaching and student learning than are faculty in less successful schools. Also, successful schools are places where faculty members supervise and guide each other, plan courses together, and work in coordination (Glickman, 1993). A feeling of dissatisfaction may help improve rather than hinder your teaching performance.

In addition, you may begin to notice that teachers are giving up personal classroom autonomy in order to collectively gain school autonomy. As teachers gain school autonomy by working collaboratively with administrators to address shared school goals, we see a change in teacher attitudes and beliefs. Teachers begin to refer to classes as "our" class and "our" students rather than "my" class and "my" students. Glickman et al. (1995) refer to this concept as believing in a cause beyond oneself and in our school goals. It reflects a willingness to give up some of your personal classroom autonomy by working collectively toward a school vision and mission. At the core of improving teaching and student learning is adopting the philosophy of "a cause beyond oneself" and "beyond one's individual classroom." In order to become a part of the bigger picture and to adopt "a cause beyond oneself," you must first understand the "self."

This book is designed to help you understand, evaluate, and predict your success as a teacher, a professional, and an educational leader. In order to develop and enhance role competencies, you must be willing to take the risk of uncovering new knowledge about yourself. Specifically, this book helps you to identify your *self-concept* (knowing and understanding the self), *self-esteem* (evaluating the self), and *self-efficacy* (predicting success). Our focus begins with self-esteem or, as in the beginning of each competency, the assessment of self.

SELF-ESTEEM: ACCURATELY EVALUATING YOURSELF AS A TEACHER

Self-esteem is a common term that usually refers to how one thinks of oneself. It can be thought of as a set of attitudes that people hold about their feelings, thoughts, abilities, skills, behaviors, and beliefs. Although self-concept and self-esteem are often equated, a prevalent distinction exists between the notions. Self-concept refers to knowledge about self, whereas self-esteem refers to how one feels about that knowledge. Of course, the key to self-esteem is dependent on self-concept. If you do not know yourself, it is difficult to have an attitude about your "self." The self-concept is therefore formed first, and attitudes develop afterward. This book, through the reflective teaching model, is designed to help facilitate your teaching self-concept; in other words, to help you understand or know yourself as a teacher.

At this point, you probably can make accurate statements about your teaching. These statements reflect your self-concept. Whereas your self-concept is almost complete, you are still forming your self-esteem or attitudes about yourself as a teacher. How is your self-esteem formed? Do you have any control in developing a positive self-esteem? Feedback plays an important role in developing attitudes about yourself.

Feedback About Self

Because of the extensive contact you have with your university supervisor, cooperating teacher, other teachers, administrators, and students, you are constantly receiving information that provides a basis for self-evaluation. Information you receive about the self is called feedback, and it comes in many forms. Some types of feedback are positive, some are ambiguous, others are negative. You have received much feedback, both formal and informal, throughout your field experiences, and that feedback helps develop your attitudes about yourself as a teacher.

How you incorporate feedback into self-esteem depends on several factors. One of the most important is your *sensitivity level* to feedback. Research demonstrates that some individuals are highly sensitive to feedback, whereas others are largely unaffected by such information (Edwards, 1990). Presumably, people who are more sensitive to feedback are more susceptible and receptive to information about their abilities, knowledge, talents, etc., than are people with lower sensitivity to feedback. For example, when Rachel ignores suggestions that she include more student discussion in her lessons, she is being insensitive to feedback about her teaching performance.

Feedback, however, is a more complicated picture than that just painted. First, the type and source of feedback can make a big difference in how this information is viewed by high- and low-sensitive people. Edwards (1990) believes that low-sensitives may be susceptive, or open, to feedback from particular sources they find worthy, such as teachers, principals, university professors, etc. Their low sensitivity to feedback is a result of relying on only a *few* sources of feedback. High-sensitives, on the other hand, probably rely on many different sources of feedback. They look for feedback among students, parents, community members, teaching aides, friends, and neighbors. Furthermore, it is assumed that high-sensitives have a more fully developed self-schemata, or image of themselves, than low-sensitives (Baumgardner, 1990). Teachers who receive and interpret more feedback will assimilate more information about the self. The number of self-schemata will increase, resulting in a self-concept that is more vast (and probably more accurate) than that of low-sensitives. Sensitivity to feedback, therefore, has a positive effect on self-concept since people gain knowledge about self through this process.

REFLECTIVE INQUIRY

Stop for a moment and reflect on your sensitivity to feedback. As you begin your field experience, would you characterize yourself as a high-sensitive or low-sensitive? Answer these questions to help you get a better idea of your sensitivity to feedback.

- Do you ignore what other people say when they comment on your teaching, physical appearance, or success level?
- Do you seek out feedback in these areas of self from valued opinion leaders in your school? almost everyone at home and at school?
- Are you interested in learning what others have to say about you? Would you rather not know?
- Do you often wonder if the comments made about you by your cooperating teacher or university supervisor are really sincere?

There is a larger issue than feedback sensitivity. Assuming that even low-sensitive people receive some feedback about themselves, how do high- and low-self-esteem people react to feedback, regardless of their sensitivity level? Two possibilities exist. The first is termed *self-enhancing theory* (Sweeny & Wells, 1990) and refers to the notion that low-self-esteem people have a need to improve their view of self and seek information or feedback that is positive and favorable. They will react to such information more favorably than information that is less positive. According to this line of thought, low-self-esteem people are more likely to "enhance" their self by attributing positive information to self ("We won the tournament. I guess I am a great coach.") and attribute negative information to other sources ("We lost. I wish the team hadn't let us down."). As a beginning teacher, you may use self-enhancing theory to search for information that will build your self-esteem in teaching and instructional contexts. Do you seek out and want to talk to colleagues who enhance and reinforce you as a competent teacher?

The second way of viewing self-esteem and feedback is offered by *self-consistency theory* (Sweeny & Wells, 1990). According to this notion, teachers will be sensitive to information that is consistent with their existing self-esteem and resistant to information that contradicts their self-view. From this perspective high-self-esteem teachers will react favorably to information that supports their positive view of self as teachers, and they will ignore or disbelieve information that is inconsistent with their self-esteem. On the other hand, low-self-esteem people will maintain consistency by accepting information that confirms their poor view of self (i.e., negative information) and will react unfavorably to positive information that might contradict their low-self-esteem perspective ("I don't believe him when he says the lesson went well; he has to be positive because he is my university supervisor. If I am an unsuccessful teacher, it looks bad for the university.").

Regardless of which theory is correct, Shrauger (1975) suggested six different reactions or responses that individuals may have to feedback. As you read the list below, which reaction(s) do you usually have when hearing positive and negative feedback about yourself as a teacher?

1. Your initial reaction when hearing the information. Are you always optimistic? "I can count on my motivational skills in making learning exciting for students." Pessimistic? "I knew I could not handle student discipline."

2. Your assessment of the dependability and legitimacy of the person providing the feedback. "Does this person's opinion count?"

3. Whether you accept responsibility for the action or performance, or attribute it to something or to others. "Did I do this? There must be some mistake!"

4. Whether you feel satisfied with the feedback. "Finally, my hard work paid off." "If only I had reinforced the difficult concept with one more exercise."

5. Whether you change your behavior after hearing the feedback. "This didn't work. Let's try another approach." "I don't believe it. There must be something 'wrong' with these kids."

6. Whether you change your self-evaluation and expectations for yourself as result of feedback. "Well, this minor setback is simply an annoyance." "Oh well, that is just how I teach." "Thank goodness I found this out in time. Now I can begin work to improve."

SELF-CERTAINTY

Low self-esteem may result from an uncertain self-concept. Baumgardner (1990) proposes an idea that gets at the concept of uncertainty or ambiguity about self. Self-certainty simply refers to a strong sense of identity. Self-certainty is composed of strong self-attributes or ideas about self that are unaffected by adverse or competing information. Teachers with high degrees of self-certainty will be more likely to understand themselves and their abilities in various school situations.

Self-certainty could lead to successful outcomes for three reasons (Baumgardner, 1990). First, if you are certain that you can perform a task well, say for example, leading a class discussion or facilitating a small group, you will have more confidence going into those situations and are more likely to perform well. Second, when you are certain about your skills, you are more likely to seek out situations that are conducive to bringing out your competence. For example, you may search for opportunities that allow you to emerge as a team leader. Third, self-certainty is not necessarily tied to a high self-esteem. It pertains to negative self-esteem as well; that is, you might be certain that you do not have the temperament and patience to work with early elementary students. For example:

> Tom Murray, a well-respected sixth-grade teacher, decided to transfer to a school closer to his home. When he discovered that he had been assigned second grade, he had an uneasy feeling in his stomach. Tom had never worked with second-graders before and was a bit hesitant. He decided to accept the position and thought that perhaps it might even be fun. Unfortunately, it turned out to be a difficult year for him. Expecting longer student attention spans than he received, Tom found himself losing his temper often and leaving school each day feeling frustrated and unhappy. The following year, he moved to a sixth-grade opening and promised never to accept an assignment with younger children again.

As a beginning teacher, you, like Tom, would try to avoid those teaching environments where you might perform poorly and therefore would not have to endure confirmation of negative attributes. Unfortunately, beginning teachers usually receive the most difficult teaching assignments and may not be afforded many choices.

As this book reinforces, you can gain control of self by using self-certainty to control situations to your advantage, even if it means avoiding situations that afford you little opportunity to demonstrate your teaching skills. Problems emerge for beginning teachers who have not yet developed certainty about their abilities. The Reflective Teaching Model is designed to help increase self-certainty. Upon conclusion of your field experience, you will have an understanding of the teaching roles that you perform well and areas that you intend to improve.

Besides the fact that self-certainty allows you control over your life by searching for appropriate situations and avoiding inappropriate ones, self-certainty has the effect of improving your positive feeling for self. Even if you are not competent in some areas of your personal and professional life, the fact that you are certain of your abilities or inabilities allows you the control that was discussed earlier. Self-certainty gives you the control to know when to ask for help and when to continue to struggle. Most beginning teachers avoid asking for help for fear of appearing incompetent, whereas most experienced teachers avoid offering help and suggestions for fear of meddling. Knowing yourself and your competency level breaks down the fear barrier and allows you to seek help and guidance in improving instruction. When you know you have control, you are more likely to possess a positive opinion of self than when you feel out of control, even though you may be successful at many things. In other words, you do not have to demonstrate supreme competence in all areas of your persona and teaching; you need only possess good knowledge of your attributes and be certain of your opinions in these areas. Therefore, self-certainty leads to control, which leads to positive self-feelings, or esteem. Positive self-esteem improves teaching performance.

How can you become more certain about your knowledge, skills, and abilities in the classroom? One way is to complete this book. Completing the self-diagnostic inquiries, coaching, and reflection helps you gain a sense of how certain you are about what you know and how you feel about yourself. The Challenge on page 10 is designed to facilitate reflective critical thinking about yourself.

SELF-EFFICACY: PREDICTING SUCCESS FROM SELF-ESTEEM

This section explores the idea of self-efficacy as proposed by psychologist Albert Bandura. Self-efficacy is that part of your mental and behavioral system "concerned with judgments of how well you can execute courses of action required to deal with prospective situations" (Bandura, 1982, p. 122). Whereas self-certainty is the confidence you feel about your self-concept and self-esteem, self-efficacy is the ability to predict actual success from your self-certainty. Self-efficacy is the ability to view yourself and predict how competent you can be in specific teaching and learning situations. From an educational perspective, self-efficacy can predict your actual teaching competence by making use of your self-certainty about your knowledge and skills. Of course, the other side of this coin is that people can possess a low sense of self-efficacy because of an uncertain self or a negative view of self regarding their teaching abilities and skills. Two particularly important components of self-efficacy are *effort* and *coping* skills.

Self-Efficacy and Efforts

Your perceptions of self-efficacy guide which teaching and learning situations you seek out and choose to participate in. You are much more likely to avoid situations where you perceive low self-efficacy. Moreover, when you cannot avoid low-efficacy situations, your efforts to deal with the requirements of those situations are going to be much lower than in situations where you perceive high efficacy. For example, Erica is eight years old and extremely bright. She has been placed in advanced classes in reading and language arts; however, when it comes to math, Erica perceives a low level of self-efficacy. Because of her negative attitudes about math competency, she avoids practice and generally has a negative attitude about math and self. Erica will not even try to learn math. On the other hand, as a third-grader she reads at the seventh-grade reading level and gives maximum effort to reading and language arts. In fact, Erica never turns down a reading challenge (she has been reading restaurant menus since she was four). As a teacher, you may excel with advanced honors classes and avoid the challenge of basic or remedial classes

Challenge

Are You Certain?

The following inquiries are designed to reveal your certainty level of your teaching skills. Although you may feel that you know your ability levels and have an opinion about those abilities, you may not be confident or certain about those feelings. When you are more certain, you can exert more confidence in your teaching, making you more successful.

1. *Do you know when to ask for guidance about situations that make you feel uncomfortable?*

2. *Do you have concrete evidence about your ability as a teacher? listener? problem-solver? team member? novice teacher? leader?*

3. *How can you prove that you are* not *successful in some teaching and learning situations?*

4. *What courses of actions could you use to gain more certainty in some areas of your teaching competence?*

5. *In what types of teaching and learning situations do you feel especially confident?*

6. *How do you describe yourself as a teacher? a communicator? a motivator? an organizer? an innovator? a professional? an ethicist? a manager? a counselor? a legally and politically aware educator?*

because you hold negative attitudes that predict failure with lower-level classes. As a beginning teacher, your first teaching assignment will most likely involve teaching those classes you feel least confident with and may predict failure. Effort, in combination with mentoring, can help reduce and replace negative self-efficacy.

You may also know teachers who avoid school leadership opportunities because of low self-efficacy in teacher leadership situations. Even when they are encouraged strongly to participate in teams or small groups, they will often put in only a minimum of effort because they are resigned to the perception that they will not perform competently in teams under any circumstances. In other words, these reluctant teachers feel that even supreme effort would not convert them into competent group leaders, facilitators, or spokespersons. Experienced group leaders demonstrate that this perception could not be further from the truth. Instruction added to effort can produce positive results helping to break the cycle of low self-efficacy in teaming and working in small groups.

Before concluding the discussion of self-efficacy and effort, it should be pointed out that those with high efficacy may want to be careful about overconfidence. Bandura has also learned that those with very high levels of self-efficacy may withhold effort because of supreme confidence in their abilities. How many times have you seen athletes lose games or matches because their confidence superseded their effort level? Bandura recommends that people maintain a high level of self-efficacy with just enough uncertainty to cause them to anticipate the situation accurately and prepare accordingly to the demands of the situation. Effort must rise to the occasion in spite of how confident you feel.

Self-Efficacy and Coping

The other factor of self-efficacy is its effect on your ability to cope with failure and stress. Simply put, feelings of low efficacy may cause you to dwell on your shortcomings and failures more than your perceptions of high self-efficacy. A snowball effect occurs such that when you possess feelings of inadequacy and then fail at some event, your self-esteem is damaged, causing you to experience stress and negative emotional reactions. These feelings then give rise to a lower self-esteem, which lowers your self-efficacy level even further. High-self-efficacy individuals are less emotionally affected by failure, because they will usually chalk up their shortcomings to a "bad day." Their feelings of positive self-efficacy can counteract the experience of a temporary failure.

Short-term setbacks may make high-self-efficacy people even more determined to succeed next time. The bottom line for low-self-efficacy people is to (1) avoid situations that may cause stress until they have begun a program of improvement in those particular areas; (2) recognize that nearly all of their skills, abilities, and knowledge can be improved with instruction and practice, especially teaching and classroom management skills; and (3) recognize that there is always "another day." Few teachers in this world fail at every attempt. Effort will lead to occasional successes, and these experiences must be made a part of your self-efficacy level.

Self-efficacy is that part of the self that organizes how self-concept and self-esteem affect teaching performance. Self-efficacy is the intermediary between how you think of yourself as a teacher and how well you demonstrate teaching, that is, your *teaching performance*.

ORGANIZING THE GROWTH PROCESS

This text encourages teachers to examine, assess, build, and grow based on a reflective teaching model founded on John Dewey's equation of Experience + Reflection = Growth. According to Dewey, reflective thinking requires a teacher to "turn a subject over in the mind and give it serious and consecutive consideration." In order to enhance the growth process, the Reflective Teaching Model incorporates the elements of Assessment, Experience, Coaching, and Reflection (Figure 1).

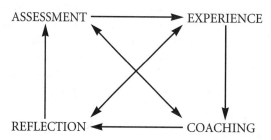

Figure 1   **Reflective Teaching Model**

The Reflective Teaching Model will serve as your road map throughout this text. Each chapter will begin with a scenario that provides you with a realistic school situation to consider and reflect upon throughout the chapter. The Assessment section will consist of questionnaires, role plays, and/or small group discussions designed to determine your level of understanding and/or ability within a specific teaching role. The process of reflection and growth begins here as you start to critically analyze your own perceptions, beliefs, knowledge, strengths, and weaknesses pertaining to any given role. The Assessment section is designed to provide baseline data from which you can assess your growth and understanding as you progress through a chapter. The Experience component will provide you with content from each of the roles. The knowledge gained about a specific teaching role facilitates the growth process by providing you with additional information based on research, theoretical studies, and experience so that you are better informed when making classroom decisions. The Coaching component contains exercises and simulations that can be used by cooperating teachers, university supervisors, or other expert teachers to help guide you in the growth process within each role. You may be asked to observe certain classroom situations, interview teachers or students, or conduct an action-research project in order to experiment and gain feedback in a school setting. Finally, the Reflection component facilitates your exploration of the new knowledge, attitudes, and beliefs pertaining to the teaching role. Its purpose is not only to allow you to gauge your understanding of this role but also to assess your growth as a beginning teacher. Do you have a different perception of the teacher as a manager or leader? Do you have a better understanding of the teacher's role as a communicator than you did prior to this experience? How does this new knowledge and understanding contribute to your growth as a teacher? The activities provided throughout this book are geared toward assisting you to become more reflective about yourself as a teacher.

SUMMARY

In 1983 the National Commission on Excellence in Education published *A Nation at Risk*. This report sounded an alarm about the quality of our schools, the students who graduate from them, and the teachers that teach in them. Other reform reports and critics painted a picture of schools with little direction, of students going through the motions, and of teachers with low expectations for student performance who do not engage their students much beyond the basic knowledge or memorization level in the classroom (Adler, 1982; Boyer, 1983; Goodlad, 1984, 1994; Sirotnik, 1981).

Obviously, our educational system and the way we think about teaching and learning must change. We believe that it is not sufficient to examine only the teacher's ability to teach a subject in isolation; rather, teachers of the twenty-first century must be deeply rooted in the complexities of teaching, which requires constant environmental assessment. Teachers must thus focus on the school as a complex workplace requiring them to be trained in reflectivity and critical perspectives. For example, many schools of the future will adopt a site-management approach to education. In these schools, teachers will need to become effective leaders who eagerly accept increased responsibility in the management of the educational program. As a result, it is important that teachers begin to acquire decision-making and reflective thinking skills early in their career. Teachers will need to accept the authority as well as the responsibility for student learning.

References

Adler, M. (1982). *The paideia proposal: An educational manifesto.* New York: Macmillan.

Ayers, W. (1989). Headaches: On teaching and teacher education. *Action in Teacher Education, 11* (2), 1–7.

Bandura, A. (1982). Self-efficacy mechanism in human agency. *American Psychologist, 37,* 122–147.

Baumgardner, B. (1990). To know oneself is to like oneself. *Journal of Personality and Social Psychology, 58,* 1062–1072.

Berliner, D. (1986). In pursuit of the expert pedagogue. *Educational Researcher, 15* (3), 5–13.

Boyer, E. (1983). *High school: A report on secondary education in America.* New York: Harper and Row.

Britzman, D. (1991). *Practice makes practice: A critical study of learning to teach.* Albany, NY: SUNY Press.

Canning, C. (1991). What teachers say about reflection. *Educational Leadership, 48* (6), 18–21.

Cruickshank, D., & Metcalf, K. (1990). Training within teacher preparation. In R. Houston (ed.), *Handbook of research in teacher education.* New York: Macmillan.

Edwards, R. (1990). Sensitivity to feedback and the development of self. *Communication Quarterly, 38,* 101–111.

Glickman, C. D. (1993). *Renewing America's schools: A guide for school-based action.* San Francisco: Jossey-Bass.

Glickman, C. D. et al. (1995). *Supervision of instruction: A developmental approach.* (3rd ed.). Needham Heights, MA: Allyn and Bacon.

Goodlad, J. (1984). *A place called school.* New York: McGraw-Hill.

Goodlad, J. (1994). *Educational renewal: Better teachers, better schools.* San Francisco: Jossey-Bass.

Heck, S., & Williams, R. (1984). *The complex roles of the teacher: An ecological perspective.* New York: Teachers College Press.

Leinhardt & Greeno, (1986). The cognitive skill of teaching. *Journal of Educational Psychology, 78* (2), 75–95.

National Commission on Excellence in Education. (1983). *A nation at risk: The imperative for educational reform.* Washington, DC: Government Printing Office.

Schon, D. (1987). *Educating the reflective practitioner.* San Francisco: Jossey-Bass.

Shrauger, J. S. (1975). Responses to evaluation as a function of initial self-perceptions. *Psychological Bulletin, 82,* 581–596.

Shulman, L. (1987). Knowledge and teaching: Foundations of the new reform. *Harvard Educational Review, 57* (1), 1–32.

Sirotnik, K. (1981). *What you see is what you get: A summary of observations in over 1000 elementary and secondary classrooms.* Arlington, VA: ERIC Document Service.

Sweeny, P. D., & Wells, L. E. (1990). Reactions to feedback about performance: A test of three competing models. *Journal of Applied Social Psychology, 20,* 818–834.

Van Manen, M. (1977). Linking ways of knowing with ways of being practical. *Curriculum Inquiry, 6,* 205–228.

Zeichner, K. (1983). Alternative paradigms of teacher education. *Journal of Teacher Education, 34* (3), 3–9.

Chapter 1

The Organizer Role

Chapter Objectives

After completing this chapter, you will be able to

- describe the various sources for school goals.
- identify your goals for teaching and reflect upon their impact on your role as teacher.
- describe the basic components of an objective.
- discuss the taxonomies of educational objectives.
- describe the criteria for selecting and sequencing instructional activities.
- identify your teaching strategy and reflect upon its impact on your role as teacher.
- discuss the variety of available instructional strategies.
- describe various approaches for grouping students.
- identify your preferences for grouping students and reflect upon their impact on your role as teacher.

*T*his chapter will give you an insight into James's problems. You may have studied some of the information included in this chapter in courses. However, now that you are teaching on a daily basis, please reexamine this knowledge in the context of your current teaching experience and in regard to your school community.

Imagine standing in front of a large audience. You are about to give an important speech but have no idea what you are going to say. You are totally unprepared! The audience is waiting patiently for your words of enlightenment, but you have no idea where to begin or what direction to take your remarks.

If you can imagine this speaker's sinking, empty feeling, you can imagine how an unorganized and unprepared teacher feels when presenting an unplanned lesson to a class. The importance of planning is illustrated by research data that reveals

The Case of the Unorganized Student Teacher

James Douglas began the school year with mixed emotions. He was excited about his student teaching assignment but worried about whether he would be ready to assume sole responsibility for the classroom. As the midsemester evaluation approached, it was clear to James and his cooperating teacher that he was having some difficulty with his sixth-grade class. After a series of observations, his cooperating teacher and university supervisor noted several items of concern. First, James's lessons seemed to lack a direction or focus. Although some activities were interesting, many were not related to each other or to a common theme. Second, his students did not appear to be challenged by the material. Many complained that all you had do in Mr. Douglas's class was to "repeat whatever he said during class to get a good grade." Third, James was commended for trying to use small groups during his instruction; however, the classroom often became chaotic during these times and students often seemed off task.

that teachers spend between 10 and 20 percent of their working time each week on planning activities (Clark & Yinger, 1979). Arends (1988) reports that educational research for the past three decades has consistently found that planning is the key to eliminating management problems. Teachers who are organized and plan well find they do not have to be strict disciplinarians, because their classrooms and lessons are characterized by a smooth flow of activities and ideas. This chapter will focus on three core competencies of the organizer role:

Competency 1: Goal Setting
Competency 2: Selecting Instructional Strategies
Competency 3: Grouping Students

■ *Competency 1* GOAL SETTING

ASSESSMENT

In this section you are asked to examine your goals and beliefs about schooling and your perception of the goals adopted by your school or school district. This information will assist you to better understand your own goals for schooling and will serve as a foundation for the remainder of the chapter.

Assessing 1.1 Assessing School Goals

Purpose: To assess the goals of a school district or content area.

Time required: 15 minutes

Procedure: Examine a school policy handbook or curriculum guide for your subject area. List the goals that relate to students' cognitive, affective, and psychomotor areas. What does this information tell you about the school district or your content area? What does this information tell you about the community? What are the expectations of the students? the teachers? Share your findings with another beginning teacher(s) or your cooperating teacher.

Assessing 1.2 What Are Your Basic Beliefs About Teaching and Learning?

Purpose: To examine your basic beliefs about teaching and student learning.

Time required: Varies

Procedure: Before you can assess your goals for teaching, you need to examine your basic beliefs about teaching and student learning. This activity should be completed with a group of your colleagues. It is important that you share your thoughts with each other. How do you describe your ideal teacher? What kind of relationship would your ideal teacher have with students? parents? administrators? What role would your ideal teacher play in the community? What expectations would your ideal teacher have for the students in the class? What would be the students' responsibility for learning in the classroom?

EXPERIENCE

Goals tend to be rather broad statements that reflect the needs of the learner, the needs of society, and the subject matter to be learned. Goals direct the long-range outcomes of instruction. If teachers are to be organized, they must be knowledgeable of the various sources for goals and must be able to express them in the planning process. Although goals are too broad for planning specific lessons, they are necessary for guiding a school's mission and environment and for determining the "kind" of educated student it wishes to produce. For example, goal statements such as "Students will practice principles of good citizenship" or "Students will acquire the basic skills of reading, writing, and mathematics" do not describe the specific skills that need to be mastered or how the skills or principles are to be attained. They do, however, inform the public, staff, and students of the school's general expectations.

Sources for Goals

Goals evolve from a variety of sources. In 1949, Ralph Tyler suggested that the sources for goals were the learners themselves, contemporary life outside of school, and suggestions from subject matter specialists. Other sources of goals are state and national administrative bodies (such as legislatures, state boards of education, U.S. Department of Education, etc.) and professional organizations.

Student Needs. Effective teachers know and understand their students. Whether you are a teacher at the preschool, elementary, secondary, or higher education level, understanding your students serves as a foundation for establishing your goals and objectives.

Gunter, Estes, and Schwab (1990) posed a series of questions that help teachers consider the learners' personal and skill needs when establishing goals.

1. Will the instruction fulfill any personal, social, or occupational goals the students may have?

2. Is the learning process (i.e., how they are asked to learn) appropriate to the students' present skill development? If not, what will they have to be taught, or what additional help will they need to ensure their successful learning?

3. How much do the students already know about the topic and how much can they be expected to learn? (p. 4)

While posing these questions for your own reflection, it is important to realize that students approach learning in a variety of ways. Dunn and Dunn (1978) explain that students are affected by their environmental, emotional, sociological, and physical needs, or stimuli. Within each of these stimuli, there are factors or preferences that influence a student's learning style. Table 1.1 illustrates the Dunns' approach to learning styles.

Table 1.1 **Elements of Learning Styles**

Stimuli	*Elements*
Environmental	Sound
	Light
	Temperature
	Design
Emotional	Motivation
	Persistence
	Responsibility
	Structure
Sociological	Peers
	Self
	Pair
	Team
	Adult
	Varied
Physical	Perceptual
	Intake (food)
	Time of day
	Mobility

Thinking about your own approach to learning helps to clarify the Dunns' approach to diagnosing learning styles. Some learners prefer a brightly lighted room for study, whereas others favor a dimly lit room. Some have a high tolerance for noise; others cannot concentrate with the slightest sound. Some are more awake and better prepared to learn in the afternoon; other learners prefer the morning. All these factors and preferences can influence a student's approach to learning.

By understanding that your students possess different approaches to learning, you know that they require different instructional approaches. The more you understand about your students' learning styles, the better you will be able to vary your instructional strategies to meet the myriad needs in your classrooms. As you gain more teaching experience, you will learn to effectively integrate lecture, discussion, small- and large-group work, independent work, cooperative learning, technology, field trips, etc., to meet the various learning styles of your classroom.

Society's Needs. One goal of education in the United States is to inculcate our students with the democratic values espoused by our society. We want our students to develop into good citizens. Of course, the dilemma is that a "good citizen" can be defined in different ways. What is your definition of a good citizen? How can your definition affect your approach to teaching and to students? Go back and examine your basic beliefs about teaching and learning. In your opinion, do they reflect society's needs?

Another example of goals being developed to meet society's needs can be found in subject matter being mandated into a curriculum. State and local agencies, local school boards, and individual schools often set broad goals that reflect societal and community needs. For example, until recently no curriculum included any information about AIDS education. However, within the past few years, state legislatures and boards of education have legislated that this subject be included in local curriculum to meet a societal need.

Subject Matter Specialists. Goals written for certain content areas are generally more specific than those previously mentioned. Professional organizations such as the National Council of Teachers of Mathematics, National Council of Teachers of English, National Council for the Social Studies, and National Middle School Association are among the learned societies that have adopted goals designed to guide teachers in these subject areas. We believe that it is important for all teachers to become involved in their content area's professional organization. This involvement can be a valuable resource.

The following case study describes a typical classroom and dilemma that could possibly confront a beginning teacher. It illustrates that not all teachers adopt the same goals for teaching nor do they have the same understanding of the principles of learning discussed in the preceding sections.

What would you say to Bill (see case study, p. 21) about his goals for teaching? How does he reconcile his goals with those of his cooperating teacher? What would you do if you were in Bill's situation?

Types and Levels of Objectives

Objectives are derived from goals and state specifically what students are to do as part of the curriculum. Hilda Taba states, "The chief function of objectives is to guide the making of decisions on what to cover, what to emphasize, what content

CASE STUDY

Bill Martin grew up in the suburbs of a mid-sized eastern city. During his freshman year in college, he decided he wanted to do something with his life that would benefit mankind. He selected the teaching profession because of the opportunities it provided for working closely with children. Bill was excited when he received his student teaching assignment to teach English at a junior high school in a low-income neighborhood.

Mr. Jefferies was assigned as Bill's cooperating teacher. He has been teaching at the same school for the past 15 years and believes that a teacher's only obligation to the students is to present subject matter and the students' responsibility is to learn it. Bill soon discovers that there are many students in his classes who cannot read beyond the third-grade level and who have low self-esteem and low motivation. Mr. Jefferies has cautioned Bill to place less emphasis on "being a friend" and more emphasis on teaching the basics. He told Bill, "It's impossible to reach every student, so you should just concentrate on those who want to learn." Midway through Bill's student teaching assignment, he begins to question his choice of teaching as a career. He seeks counseling from his university supervisor.

to select, and what experiences to stress" (1962, p. 197). Arends (1988) summarizes this important information about instructional objectives: First, objectives should be student based and should identify what the student is supposed to learn as a result of the instruction. This is normally accomplished by using precise words to identify learning outcomes. For example, a well-written objective is "The student will be able to identify the capitals of the Pacific Northwest." A poorly written objective is "Students will be introduced to the capitals of the Pacific Northwest." The first example describes what the student will do, whereas the second example describes what the teacher will do. Second, the objective should define the testing situation, such as "on a written essay test," "given a map . . . ," or " a test with the use of notes." Finally, the objective should describe the performance level that the teacher finds acceptable; for example, "The student can solve five linear equation problems within 40 minutes" is an example of a well-written objective. The following objective, however, is poorly written because it doesn't state how many problems the student should solve or in what time frame they should be solved: "The student can solve linear equation problems."

Teachers should be concerned with educating the whole child. Unfortunately, too much emphasis is often placed on the acquisition of knowledge and facts (cognitive domain), while excluding the students' attitudes, interests, and feelings (affective domain) and manipulative and motor skills (psychomotor domain).

These three domains—cognitive, affective, and psychomotor—have been categorized into taxonomies that describe levels of complexity from simple to more advanced. Some of your other courses probably discussed these taxonomies in detail. At this point of your teaching career, you can begin applying that knowledge to your students. For example, if you have an understanding of the *Taxonomy of Educational Objectives: Cognitive Domain* (Bloom et al., 1956), then you have a better grasp of writing objectives that attend not only to the students' need to gain knowledge but also to the students' need to operate at higher cognitive levels in order to become more complex thinkers and better problem-solvers.

Objectives serve as the foundations for your instruction. The ability to plan and write clear objectives will contribute greatly to how effective you will be in the organizer role. You know that a well-written objective is student based, specific, and describes the testing situation and expected performance level. You should also be familiar with the taxonomies that will assist you to write objectives for the whole child and to vary the complexity of your objectives.

This section discussed the mechanics required for a well-written objective. Perhaps the major requirement is that your objectives match the needs of your students. You must keep in mind, however, that your students have needs that go beyond the cognitive domain. The affective and psychomotor domains must also be considered. Simply said, if you are to be an effective teacher—one who is able to write objectives that guide instruction—you must *know* your students.

Relating Objectives to Instruction

A well-written objective informs the students of what is expected of them; however, if you do not relate your objectives to appropriate instructional strategies, your students are not as likely to master your objectives. For example, if your objective is to teach the students how to throw a baseball properly, you would not accomplish this by having them run around the track. The strategy does not match the objective.

A teacher who utilizes only one approach to instruction will be successful with only one type of student and at only one level of objectives. Your classroom will contain students with a variety of learning styles who need skill development at varying levels of the taxonomies. If lecture is your only instructional mode, you will reach only those students who learn best from a direct instruction model, and you will operate mostly at the knowledge level of the cognitive domain. As a result, many of your students will be at a disadvantage because their learning style does not match your teaching approach.

Your objectives should guide you in selecting the most appropriate instructional strategies. These objectives will tell you when it is most appropriate to utilize discussion, lecture, cooperative learning, individualized instruction, and so on. Thus it is important that you develop a broad repertoire of instructional strategies to employ in your classroom. Selection of instructional strategies will be discussed later in this chapter.

Reality Bite

The Beginning Organizer

I recently began my first teaching job at a small, rural high school in southern Illinois. I teach Spanish and world history. I love my job and my content areas and would not change either for all of the money in the world. Despite all the joys that come from teaching, I find my job a bit overwhelming at times. Each day I feel like an explorer charting new territory, because each day is a new experience. Some days I feel completely confident in what I am doing in the classroom; then, there are nights when I lie awake wondering if I have accomplished anything at all. No amount of teacher training could ever have prepared me for everything I encounter on a daily basis in my classroom.

It is said that good planning is vital to a good classroom experience for both teacher and students. For the past month I have tried to write good lesson plans and to look and plan ahead. I started writing plans before school even began. In fact, I am sure that if school never actually started, I would be exactly where I planned by the end of September. That is only wishful thinking, however, because the students came and threw everything out of sync. No matter how hard I try to stick to my lesson plans exactly as I have written, I cannot. Every Wednesday I am still trying to finish Monday's plans. Each night I have to rewrite my lesson plans for the following day. This makes me feel unprepared no matter how much I have prepared for the day. Because my plans are changing so often, I run into classroom management problems. It is difficult for me to keep my students on task, say something clever to buy myself some time, and figure out what I am going to say and do next. I trust the more experienced teachers when they say it will get easier. I only wish I knew when so I could look forward to that day.

Tara Stace, Beginning High School Teacher

COACHING

This section is designed for you to examine the different perspectives educators share regarding a school's curriculum. You also will be asked to predict future goals for schools. Working with your cooperating teacher, other beginning teachers, and/or expert teachers will help you to clarify your perceptions of curriculum and the future goals for schools. See how your views may differ from others. How do individual differences in perception of a school's curriculum and goals influence a school's continuity and effectiveness? How does your cooperating teacher or other expert teachers manage differing viewpoints within the school?

Coaching 1.3 Conflicting Conceptions of Curriculum

In 1974 Eisner and Vallance proposed two views of curriculum: (1) curriculum as subject matter and (2) curriculum as experience. Essentially, those educators who view curriculum as subject matter believe that the general purpose of schooling is to transmit our cultural heritage and to stress the knowledge of the subject matter. The knowledge that is generally accepted to be traditional to a subject area is thought to be important to pass on to the next generation.

Those who believe that curriculum is a set of experiences stress the process of learning rather than the subject matter itself. The subject matter is a means, not an end, for learning the process of critical thinking, creativity, or problem solving. The student is thought to develop into an "effective" citizen by participating in the experiences afforded by studying the subject matter.

Which view of the curriculum do you agree with? Is it possible to accept both views? Which does your school district appear to accept? How can you support your opinion? How will your view of the curriculum affect you as a teacher? Share your thoughts with other beginning teachers or your cooperating teacher.

REFLECTION

Reflecting 1.4 Assessing Lesson Objectives

Purpose: To be able to identify correctly written instructional objectives and to relate them to the appropriate instructional strategy(ies).

Time required: 20 minutes

Procedure: Complete this reflection task with one of your peers. Examine your instructional objectives for a specific lesson that you are going to teach or have taught already. With the other person, discuss your objectives relative to these questions:

1. Do your objectives include a specific verb that indicates the behavior or skill expected of the students?
2. Do your objectives include a testing situation and performance level?
3. Do your objectives address various levels of the taxonomies and various domains?
4. Are your objectives related to appropriate instructional strategies?
5. What are the sources for your objectives?
6. Based on your assessment of the lesson, would you add or eliminate certain objectives? Why?

Reflecting 1.5 Mr. Douglas and Objectives

Recall the problems that Mr. Douglas had with his teaching in the scenario at the beginning of the chapter. Which, if any, of his problems could be related to the planning of objectives for his lessons? If you were his cooperating teacher or university supervisor, what suggestions would you give him concerning objectives, and how could these suggestions improve his performance?

If you are going to build a house, you want to build it on a solid foundation. A house built on a weak foundation will soon show its cracks and strains. An effective lesson is no different. It must be built on a solid set of objectives that guide your instruction and evaluation processes. There is no substitute for good planning.

Competency 2 SELECTING INSTRUCTIONAL STRATEGIES

ASSESSMENT

After examining and establishing goals for yourself, students, and classroom, you need to think about the instructional strategies you are going to utilize in order to meet these objectives. The following exercise is designed for you to think about your teaching style and your personal preferences as an instructor. This knowledge gives you a better understanding of yourself as a teacher.

Assessing 1.6 Do You Know Your Teaching Style?

Purpose: To help teachers identify their teaching styles.

Time required: 10 minutes

Procedure: In 1967 Riessman proposed seven categories to describe the varying styles teachers exhibit in the classroom. This exercise is designed to stimulate thinking about your teaching style and should be completed in private. Rank in order the teaching styles that you believe are relevant to you. After completing this instrument, answer the following questions: What does this tell you about yourself? Do others perceive you this way? Do your students perceive you this way? Share your answers with other student teachers or beginning teachers.

_____ *Compulsive Type.* This teacher is fussy, teaches things over and over, and is concerned with functional order.

_____ *Boomer.* This teacher shouts out in a loud, strong voice: "You're going to learn." There is no nonsense in this room.

Source: Riessman, F. (1967) Teachers of the Poor: A Five Point Plan, Journal of Teacher Education, 18(3), pp. 326–336. Copyright by the American Association of Colleges for Teacher Education. Reprinted with permission.

_____ *Maverick.* This teacher raises difficult questions, presents ideas that disturb, and is loved by everyone, except perhaps the principal.

_____ *Coach.* Informal, earthy, and maybe an athlete, this teacher is physically expressive in conducting the class.

_____ *Quiet One.* Sincere, calm, but definite, this teacher commands both respect and attention.

_____ *Entertainer.* Relaxed and informal with children, this teacher will have lunch with them or play ball with them.

_____ *Academic.* The teacher is interested in knowledge and in the substance of the class.

EXPERIENCE

If goals or objectives are the proposed ends of an instructional unit, then selected instructional strategies and activities are the means to attain those ends. Moore (1989) suggests than an instructional strategy consists of two components: the methodology and the procedure. The methodology serves as the motivating event and "sets the tone" for the lesson. The most common instructional methods include lecture, discussion, inquiry, discovery, demonstration, role-playing, and simulation. Joyce, Weil, and Showers (1992) place these and other methodologies within four separate families that serve separate educational goals, objectives, and student needs: social interaction, information processing, personal sources, and behavior modification.

Specifically, the social interaction sources emphasize the relationship of a person to society or to direct relationships with other people; role-playing, simulations, and the jurisprudential teaching model are examples of this source. Information-processing sources focus on the ways students organize data and generate concepts and solutions for problems; examples include inquiry training and inductive reasoning. Personal sources share an orientation toward the individual student as the source of educational ideas. Nondirective teaching and classroom meetings are examples of personal sources. Finally, behavior modification is an attempt to sequence learning activities and shape behavior by manipulating reinforcements, as detailed in the operant conditioning model espoused by B. F. Skinner.

Criteria for Selecting Instructional Strategies

In order to select the appropriate instructional strategy, you should consider your strengths and experiences, your students' needs and experiences, the content and objectives, and the context and atmosphere.

You bring to the classroom your own unique strengths, weaknesses, experiences, abilities, and interests, which make your classroom different from any other. Teachers tend to use instructional strategies that have worked in the past or with which they feel most comfortable. All too often this leads to teacher stagnation and pupil boredom. Remember that students have a variety of learning styles, and as a result, you need to be able to implement a variety of instructional strategies that meet all of your students' needs.

A second criterion to consider when selecting instructional strategies is the students' needs, experiences, and maturity levels. With experience, you will know that some students learn better with direct instruction (lecture and recitation), others in a cooperative learning environment, and still others work best independently. Also, you will know that some students are ready to work at the synthesis and evaluation levels, whereas others need more work at the knowledge and comprehension levels. This knowledge of your students will help you select the appropriate instructional strategies.

A third criterion to consider when selecting instructional strategies is content and objectives. What are your specific objectives? What should your students do or know at the end of the lesson or unit? The instructional strategies you select must address these questions. Strategies that work best in the psychomotor domain may not be as successful in the cognitive areas. For example, you might choose a demonstration as your instructional strategy for teaching a particular laboratory experiment, but that same strategy might not be appropriate for teaching a lesson on values.

Finally, the setting and atmosphere influence your instructional strategies. This includes the classroom, school, and community. What resources are available to you? There may be some activities that you wish to implement that are impractical because of a lack of important resources. How much space and time do you have? If you know that there is going to be a school assembly in the afternoon, you may not choose to use certain strategies and activities because of time restraints.

Utilizing a Variety of Instructional Strategies

In 1971 Rosenshine and Furst reported that variability is one of the teacher qualities validated as promoting pupil growth. Effective teachers incorporate a variety of instructional strategies during lessons to help meet the various student needs and learning styles. A lesson may include a focusing event, lecture, questions, demonstration, and/or group work. Borich (1988) suggests that a lesson plan that includes some combination of lecture, discussion, question-and-answer, guided practice, and independent seatwork is generally preferable to one that exclusively emphasizes only one of these instructional alternatives.

Using a focusing event or attention-gaining device not only at the beginning of a lesson but also throughout the lesson can be very effective. Attention-gaining devices help students focus on the content to be covered during the lesson. They also serve as instructional cues that alert students to the importance of particular skills, behaviors, attitudes, and bits of information. These devices do not need to be spectacular in order to get the students' attention. Key questions, anecdotes, interesting dilemmas, videotapes, and demonstrations are among the options available to you.

We all like to be praised when we do things well; however, when we often hear the same words or observe the same type of praise for our actions, it soon loses its meaning. At this point, praise as an instructional strategy may turn sour. Teachers need to possess a variety of responses when praising or rewarding students. Responses may be verbal or nonverbal. A wink or a pat on the head or shoulder may be just as encouraging to some students as "Good job."

Using a student's idea or correct response is another instructional strategy. Students have a positive feeling when they know the teacher thinks enough of their ideas or answers to use them as examples of good effort or work. To put this instructional strategy into practice, you might begin a lesson by asking for students' opinions or ideas. Brainstorming is another strategy that can generate a lot of student response. The key to brainstorming is to accept all student ideas by writing their responses on the board or on newsprint. No value judgment is made on any of the student responses. The nonjudgmental environment generates many responses and encourages reluctant students to participate. Once you have all of the responses, you can discuss or assess them.

Another instructional strategy that can be utilized to promote growth is the use of questioning and probing. One way to ensure a variety of questions is to consult *Taxonomy of Educational Objectives: Cognitive Domain* (Bloom et al., 1956). The taxonomy can be used to structure questions at the various cognitive levels and encourages both convergent and divergent questions. Convergent questions are narrow in focus and tend to have one right answer; they promote lower-order thinking skills, such as those used at the knowledge and comprehension levels. On the other hand, divergent questions typically have several "correct" answers and promote the higher-order thinking skills of analysis, synthesis, and evaluation.

Borich (1988) states that although questions are tools for engaging students in the learning process, to be effective they must be administered flexibly and often. Questions should be followed up with probes that attempt to cut through the often superficial or inadequate responses initially given to a question. Probes are questions that follow initial questions and whose purpose is to expand or enrich an earlier response.

The following example illustrates questioning and probing techniques:

Teacher: How did the Vietnam War affect the people of the United States?

Student: Well . . . they thought that the war was wrong, and they marched in the streets to protest it.

Teacher: That's what those opposed to the war did at that time, but was that the only point of view held by the American people?

Student: I guess there were people who supported the war effort.

Teacher: That's right. Do you know why they supported the war?

Student: Some people believed you should always support your country.

Reality Bite

The Experienced Planner

Instructional strategies are very important. In knowing my strengths and weaknesses as a teacher, my students' needs, the objectives that must be met, and the classroom environment, I am able to select the most appropriate strategies for the lessons I teach. This is a lot to keep in mind while planning lessons, but my students greatly benefit from my efforts. I have students who are tactile learners, visual learners, and auditory learners. In order to teach effectively, I must plan lessons that meet all students' needs. I must also, on a continuous basis, reflect back on the way things went. If it didn't go well, adjustments need to be made.

Enthusiasm and motivation are two important factors that must be present in the classroom. If I display a positive and energetic attitude, so will my students. I try many different approaches and activities in the classroom. My students never know what to expect. These things make learning fun and exciting!

This section of the McIntyre and O'Hair textbook has made me more aware of the things I am doing and need to be doing in my classroom. I am here for the students. I want my classroom to be a place where students can get excited about learning!

Tamra Peck, Experienced Elementary Teacher

Teacher: Good! Were there any other reasons?

Student: Some people thought that if we didn't stop communism in Vietnam, it would spread through all of southeast Asia.

Enthusiasm is a teacher behavior that is often included on lists of strategies employed by effective teachers. Demonstrations of enthusiastic behavior include establishing eye contact with the students, gesturing, moving around the classroom, and varying the pitch and volume of your voice. A teacher who is stationary, who gazes at the floor and speaks in a monotone voice, will not generate enthusiasm in the classroom; on the contrary, such a teacher usually fosters unenthusiastic students and creates an atmosphere of boredom.

When organizing and planning your lessons, consider utilizing a variety of instructional strategies, such as attention-gaining devices, various modes of presentation, a mix of rewards and reinforcers, incorporation of student ideas, questions and probes, and teacher enthusiasm. All will contribute to the intellectual growth of your students.

Sequence of Activities and Content

Once you have developed goals and activities and planned your instructional strategies, you must sequence the lesson's activities and content. The material should be arranged to provide learning that is continuous and cumulative and that attends to previously learned skills and content. The subject matter that you teach often has its own substantive structure or logic. For example, history is often, but not always, taught in a chronological order.

Ornstein and Hunkins (1988) state that there are four basic methods for sequencing materials:

1. *Simple to complex.* Content is organized from its simple components to its more complex components. It is based on the premise that students will learn optimally when presented with easy, concrete content followed by more difficult, abstract content.

2. *Prerequisite learning.* This works on the premise that certain content must be learned before other content can be learned. Mathematics and science are often sequenced in this fashion.

3. *Whole to part learning.* Content is first presented in an overview (abstract) fashion to furnish students with a general idea of the information or situation.

4. *Chronological learning.* Content is sequenced as it occurs in the world. It is typically utilized in history, world events, and political science.

No matter which sequencing format you adopt for specific content, you must take into account the maturation, experience, interests, and learning styles of the students and the content itself before you sequence your material.

COACHING

Coaching 1.7 Instructional Strategies at Elementary and Secondary Grade Levels

Purpose: To examine the instructional strategies utilized in the elementary and secondary grades and to assess possible reasons for any differences.

Time required: Varies

Procedure: Observe in both an elementary and a secondary classroom. Note the specific instructional strategies used in each classroom. What are the similarities and/or differences? If there are differences, why do you think they exist? Ask the teachers in each classroom why they used certain instructional strategies. Do the

CASE STUDY

Mr. Kurt Cook was a first-year teacher at a rural high school in the Midwest. He was an avid student of history and looked forward to sharing his love for his subject area with his students. As a member of the college debate team, Kurt was an accomplished speaker who could motivate an audience.

In college, his methods instructor had introduced a variety of instructional strategies that could be used in the classroom. Kurt, however, had decided to adopt the teaching approach of his favorite history instructor. He was convinced that because he had learned so well from this teaching style, it also would be effective in his classroom.

Kurt began every lesson by announcing the learning objectives so that students understood what was expected of them. Next he would place a transparency of his lecture outline on an overhead projector. The students could then follow the outline as he proceeded through his "talk." At the conclusion of each lesson, Kurt would ask his students questions to determine if they understood the material. He followed this approach every day because he knew that it was successful for him as a student and believed that his students needed the same kind of routine.

After several weeks, Kurt was not pleased with the response he was getting from his students. Although he did not have any discipline problems, a portion of his students seemed to be bored and losing motivation. In addition, the students' performance on quizzes and tests were not up to his expectations. Kurt did not know what was causing his students' achievement problems. Kurt comes to you for advice.

responses of the elementary and secondary teachers differ? Share your thoughts with other beginning teachers.

Coaching 1.8 Variability and the Beginning Teacher

A research study by Emmer, Evertson, and Anderson (1980) revealed that experienced teachers who were flexible and showed variety in their instructional strategies were found to be more interesting to their students than were inexperienced teachers who had no knowledge of alternative teaching strategies. The case study above provides a glimpse of a beginning teacher's strategy.

After observing his class several times, what advice might you give Kurt? Share your advice with the other student teachers or beginning teachers in your class. What is Kurt's problem(s)? What steps can he take to remedy the problem(s)?

REFLECTION

Reflecting 1.9 What Is Your Enthusiasm Rating?

Purpose: To determine your enthusiasm in a classroom setting.

Time required: Varies

Procedure: The most effective method to gather this data is to videotape one or two lessons and rate yourself. If you do not have access to a videotape camera, ask a colleague (with a reciprocal agreement) to observe you. Repeated observations will allow you to obtain a more valid indication of your enthusiasm. Use the criteria in Table 1.2 to note your enthusiasm

Reflecting 1.10 Assessing Variability in the Classroom

Purpose: To determine the teacher's implementation of instructional variability in the classroom.

Time required: Varies

Procedure: There are two ways in which this reflectivity activity can be used. You may either videotape one (or several) of your lessons or observe another teacher's lessons. Review the videotape or observation records, and answer the following questions:

1. Was there a focusing event or attention-gaining device used during this lesson?
2. How many instructional strategies or modes of presentation were used in the lesson?
3. How did the students respond to the various strategies?
4. Was there a mixture of rewards and reinforcers used during the lesson?
5. Were student ideas incorporated into the lesson?

Reflecting 1.11 Mr. Douglas and Instructional Strategies

Recall the problems that were cited during the scenario featuring Mr. Douglas. What, if any, of his problems were related to instructional strategies? As his principal, what advice would you give him and how would it improve his ability to use instructional strategies?

Summary. Whereas goals and objectives serve as the guiding features of your lessons and curriculum, the instructional strategies are the means by which you will meet your objectives. A variety of instructional strategies that are planned to meet the potpourri of student needs in your classroom will contribute to your effectiveness as a teacher.

Table 1.2 **What Is Your Enthusiasm Rating?**

	DEGREE OF PERFORMANCE		
	Low (1) (2)	*Medium* (3) (4) (5)	*High* (6) (7)
1. Vocal delivery	Monotone, minimum inflections, little variation in speech, poor articulation	Pleasant variations of pitch, volume, speed; good articulation	Great and sudden changes from rapid, excited speech to a whisper; varied tone
2. Eyes	Looked dull or bored; seldom opened eyes wide or raised eyebrows; avoids eye contact; often maintains a blank stare	Appeared interested; occasionally lighting up; shining, opening wide	Characterized as dancing, snapping, shining, lighting up frequently, opening wide, eyebrows raised; maintains eye contact while avoiding staring
3. Gestures	Seldom moved arms out toward person or object; never used sweeping movements; kept arms at side or folded, rigid	Often pointed, occasional sweeping motion using body, head, arms, hands, and face; maintained steady pace of gesturing	Quick and demonstrative movements of body, head, arms, hands, and face
4. Body movement	Seldom moved from one spot, or from sitting to standing position; sometimes paces "nervously"	Moved freely, slowly, and steadily	Large body movements, swung around, walked rapidly, changed pace; unpredictable and energetic; natural body movements
5. Facial expressions	Appeared deadpan, expressionless or frowned; little smiling; lips closed	Agreeable; smiled frequently; looked pleased, happy, or sad if situation called for it	Appeared vibrant, demonstrative; showed many expressions; broad smile; quick, sudden change in expression
6. Word selection	Mostly nouns, few descriptors or adjectives; simple or trite expressions	Some descriptors or adjectives or repetition of the same ones	Highly descriptive, many adjectives, great variety
7. Acceptance of ideas and feelings	Little indication of acceptance or encourage-ment; may ignore students' feelings or ideas	Accepted ideas and feelings; praised or clarified; some variations in response but frequent-tly repeated same ones	Quick to accept, praise, encourage or clarify; many variations in response; vigorous nodding of head when agreeing
8. Overall energy level	Lethargic, appears inactive, dull, or sluggish	Appeared energetic and demonstrative sometimes, but mostly an even level	Exuberant; high degree of energy and vitality; highly demonstrative

Source: Collins, M. L. (1978). The effects of training for enthusiasm on the enthusiasm displayed by preservice teachers. *Journal of Teacher Education 24*(1), 53–57. Reprinted with permission of the author.

_____ ■ *Competency 3* GROUPING STUDENTS _____

ASSESSMENT

Forming small groups is one option you have for delivering instruction. Cooperative learning and other strategies using small groups have been related to gains in learning, as well as having provided social benefits to students. It is clear, however, that grouping students solely for the sake of using small groups will not result in great learning gains. There must be a definite purpose for using this strategy. In addition, you must be aware of the appropriate strategies available for assigning students to these groups in order to assure maximum benefits. This assessment exercise will help you determine your current knowledge of utilizing small groups.

Assessing 1.12 What Do You Know About Grouping Students?

Purpose: To assess your knowledge about grouping students in the classroom.

Time required: 5 minutes

Procedure: Choose the statements that are applicable to the proper grouping of students.

1. The teacher should demonstrate the ability to attend to more than one issue at a time.
2. The teacher should help students establish productive norms.
3. The teacher should establish group work only for the "good" students.
4. The teacher should assist the students in developing their social interaction skills.
5. The teacher must maintain the sole leadership role during group work.
6. The teacher must be able to manage more than one group at a time.
7. The teacher should allow the students to always select their own groups.
8. The teacher should recognize that peer group norms are powerful determinants of member behavior.
9. The teacher should force shy, withdrawn students to participate in group activities.
10. The teacher should understand that any type of small-group work will meet the lesson's goals.
11. The teacher should not afford group members the opportunity to discuss controversial issues.
12. The teacher should recognize that implementing small-group work takes less planning time than does whole-group instruction.

13. The teacher should recognize that the optimal size for a small group is five people.

14. Small-group instruction is prohibitive in some content areas.

15. The teacher should require that all students in a group be seated so that they can face each other. (Adapted from W. Weber, Classroom Management. In J. Cooper [ed.], *Classroom Teaching Skills.* Lexington, MA: Heath, 1986.) Reprinted with permission.

Answers: Statements 1, 2, 4, 6, 8, 13, and 15 reflect the strategy of grouping students accurately.

EXPERIENCE

Too often, teachers take for granted how they will group their students in order to meet their objectives. The most common approach to grouping is to place 25 to 30 students in a classroom by grade level. The same content is then taught to all students at the same time using the same method. This grouping format is acceptable if it meets the lesson's objectives and is compatible with the lesson's instructional strategies.

This section will discuss four approaches to grouping students: (1) *large-group instruction,* where the entire class is taught as one group; (2) *small-group instruction,* where the entire class is divided into subgroups according to criteria such as ability, learning style, or project; (3) *individualized instruction,* in which the individual student works alone on an individualized assignment; and (4) *cooperative learning,*

Large-Group Instruction

Teaching the entire class as a whole is probably the most traditional grouping pattern. Many educators believe that teachers adjust their instruction to the mythical "average student" on the assumption that teaching to this level will meet the needs of the greatest number of students.

During large-group instruction, the same content is usually taught to all students at the same time and in the same manner. The teacher, who is the central figure during large-group instruction, typically lectures, leads discussions, demonstrates problems, and distributes materials.

The large-group method is economical and efficient. If you need to teach the same skills, make an assignment, administer an exam, or make an announcement to all of the students, then large-group instruction is the best choice. Bringing members of the class together as one group enhances its cohesiveness and can help establish a sense of community and class spirit. However, teachers and students must realize that for large-group instruction to be successful, cooperation and respect must be fostered in the classroom.

For objectives other than those mentioned above, large-group instruction is not the proper format. There will always be a broad range of student abilities, needs, and learning styles. When you teach everybody alike, it is difficult to meet every student's needs and appeal to specific learning preferences. Differential student grouping is essential to meet all of your objectives and all of your students' needs.

Small-Group Instruction

Dividing the class into smaller groups permits more students to become actively involved in the learning process. It also allows the teacher to observe how students interact with each other and with the content. Although there is no absolute minimum or maximum number of students required for small groups, it appears that an optimal group size is between 5 and 7 students. When there are 4 or fewer students in a group, they tend to pair off rather than interact with all members. As the number approaches 15, student participation appears to decrease significantly.

Small groups can be used with any content or at any grade level. Ornstein (1990) lists seven criteria for use with small-group instruction. These criteria can help teachers expand small-group instruction beyond its typical use:

1. *Ability.* Grouping by ability reduces the problems of heterogeneity in the classroom.
2. *Interest.* Students have some choice in group membership based on special interests in a particular subject matter or activity.
3. *Skill.* The teacher forms groups in order to develop different skills in students or to have them learn to work with different types of materials.
4. *Viewpoint.* Students have some choice in forming groups based on feelings about a controversial issue.
5. *Activity.* The teacher forms groups to perform a specific assignment.
6. *Integration.* The teacher forms groups considering race, ethnicity, religion, or sex to improve human relations.
7. *Arbitrary.* Groupings are made at random or on the basis of alphabetical order, location in the room, or some other method not related to student or work characteristics.

Orlich et al. (1994) list the following purposes for using small groups. After reading these purposes, ask yourself how many topics in your discipline lend themselves to a discussion.

1. Arousing interest at the beginning of a new topic or the closing of one.
2. Identifying problems or issues to be studied, or suggesting alternatives for pursuing a topic under consideration.
3. Exploring new ideas or ways to solve problems, covering either the entire problem-solving cycle or just a phase of it.
4. Providing the opportunity to evaluate data, opinions, and sources of information, and structuring concepts for future application.

5. Allowing students to demonstrate individual strengths.

6. Promoting students to learn faster and better from each other.

7. Providing the opportunity to use the vocabulary of the discipline and to verbalize it in an appropriate context.

8. Developing cooperative work skills through practice in small-group discussion.

9. Learning and improving skills in leadership, organization, interaction, research, and initiative through discussion techniques.

10. Promoting defense of ideas so that they become more meaningful and personal.

11. Providing students (and the teacher) with opportunities for learning to accept and value other ethnic and/or cultural backgrounds.

Environment for Small Groups. It is your responsibility to establish the proper classroom environment for the implementation of successful small groups. In order to do this, you need to impress certain attitudes upon your students and establish an atmosphere of trust in your classroom. First, it is important that you have high expectations of your students. You need to believe that your students will succeed and that you can make a difference in their success. This is called *teacher efficacy.* If your students know that you believe in them, then you are more likely to get results. Second, you can show your students that you trust them by allowing them to make suggestions concerning their learning activities. Obviously, you will have the last word on suggestions, but if your students realize that you listen to their input, they will be more willing to work with you. Third, you can trust your students by allowing them to select a group leader and "run" their own small-group activities. These activities will need to be monitored, but students usually come through when trust is placed in them. In addition, this approach to small groups helps to develop leadership skills. Fourth, develop an environment where students are willing to take risks. Students should be willing to express their ideas and feelings without being "put down" by others. Great things can happen when students realize that they can take a chance, risk, or experiment in your classroom. Finally, it is more important to develop a "community" in your classroom that enhances both student-teacher and student-student relationships than to worry about adhering to a strict set of rules. Rules are necessary but should not be the focus during small-group work.

Types of Small Groups. There are several types of small groups that can be implemented in your classroom. Each type of small-group activity has a special instructional purpose and requires different levels of student discussion and teacher involvement skills. For example, if your goal is to facilitate creativity, use *brainstorming* to achieve your goal (Orlich et al., 1994). This type of small group should accommodate 5 to 15 students. Brainstorming begins when the leader states the problem under consideration. As students volunteer their suggestions, the teacher

*Reality Bite*

GroupSpeak

My approach to teaching geometric constructions by using a compass and protractor on the chalkboard was tedious and awkward for me and for my students. Some days I did the same construction ten times: once on the board and then with nine or more students. I knew that I had to try another approach, so I decided to put the students in small groups.

Individual learning strengths and abilities were instrumental in determining the makeup of each group of four students—one strong, one creative, one weak, and one average. Personality traits, how well they got along normally, and their levels of patience were other factors. The 25 constructions to be completed were placed in a folder along with a list of terms and definitions that the students would encounter during this project. The first 6 constructions had detailed instructions. Each member of a group had to present 3 constructions to the other members of the group. The remaining 7 were to be constructed as a group. The students were assessed both on the constructions and terms and on at least one of their presentations. They were also assessed on their participation in the group. This score was determined by whether the student asked questions, used correct terminology, or was helpful, considerate, and respectful to the other members of the group.

The students worked in their groups for two weeks. One day I looked up from observing one of the groups and noticed the English teacher from down the hall standing at my door. I walked over to her, "Are we too loud? I can close the door." She replied, "Listen to what they are saying." I stopped and listened. "What?" I was confused. The students were working on their constructions diligently. The English teacher snickered and replied, "They're speaking a different language, math." She smiled and walked away. I was not sure what to think, but I stood there for a while and listened—not very long because I was needed to assist in a group.

The next day I noticed the business teacher standing at my door. When I approached her, she waved and left. It was not long before the principal was at my door. He did not wait for me to move his way; he just came in and started walking around the room. He stopped at various groups asking, "What are you doing?" or "Why did you do that?" He looked at me, shook his head, and left. I could hardly wait to see him when class was over. Was I in trouble? "Good job, Mrs. Jones!" was the greeting I received when I found him.

"This was all right," "I learned a lot," "It wasn't as bad I thought," and "It was really kind of fun" were typical student responses during the first two years that I

used this method. Now they look forward to the construction project. Congruent, similar, radius, and vertex are terms that are part of the students' vocabulary after completing this project. The students not only speak mathematically, but they have had a successful, rewarding experience learning mathematics. They have learned to help each other as well as themselves. Grouping students into small groups can be a very rewarding experience for both teacher and students.

Rhonda Jones, Experienced Math Teacher

or a student writes the responses on the board or on a piece of newsprint. You must make it clear that all ideas need to be expressed and that the quantity of suggestions, rather than quality, is most important. All ideas are accepted without criticism or evaluation. Students should be encouraged to build upon each other's suggestions. After exhausting all suggestions, you can prioritize them or assess their contribution to the problem. Again, the emphasis is on creativity. You may be surprised that some of the most outrageous suggestions eventually result in the solution of the problem. Finally, remember that brainstorming is an initiating activity and must be followed by some other activity.

Small groups can also be used as a problem-solving–building technique. One such grouping is the *inquiry group,* which emphasizes problem-solving or discovery teaching and is ideal for six to ten students per group. The purposes of the inquiry group are to stimulate scientific thinking, to develop problem-solving skills, and to acquire new facts. A student who has good questioning skills and who understands the concepts under consideration is ideal for group leader. Since this is a more advanced type of small group, students should have already mastered the skills of observation, questioning, and inferring.

The inquiry group is most successful when real-life scenarios are used and are testable. Suchman (1966) suggests that students should first be presented with a real problem. Students then ask the teacher questions about the problem. Questions should require only "yes" or "no" answers. Based on the teacher's responses to the questions, the students propose and test their hypotheses.

Orlich et al. (1994) suggest that the student's ability to ask questions is the focal point for student evaluation. For example, did they ask higher-order questions that led to hypothesis making? Were the students able to make inferences or make cause-and-effect statements? The emphasis should be on the student's ability to interact at higher levels of thought.

One method to involve students in the evaluation process is to have students complete an evaluation form while watching a videotape of the small-group lesson. The videotape allows the students to replay any part of the tape where they may be uncertain about the level of the questioning. The evaluation process itself involves students in a higher-order function. The focus of student evaluation is not so much on the solution(s) to the problem but rather on the group process. Teaching students a basic problem-solving procedure is helpful because many are not adequately prepared to work in small groups.

The final small group is the *problem-solving* group. This is the most sophisticated of the small groups because it is best suited to students who are self-directed. The teacher is involved as an outside observer only. In a problem-solving group, students select a real problem, usually one that is student oriented. The problems should be selected before the formation of the groups. For example, students may choose to find the causes of and/or pose solutions to school vandalism, school truancy, pollution of a local stream, mass transportation, or any other problems that interest them. Students can now select their participation in a group according to their interests. As a result, the size of the groups may vary according to the interest, and the length of time may vary according to the complexity of the problem.

The problem-solving group encourages students to have a meaningful exchange of ideas on relevant problems. The student leader initiates the discussion and monitors the group so that it remains on task. The goal of the problem-solving group is to arrive at a conclusion(s) that can be presented to a "real" audience, such as teacher, principal, city council, etc.

Cooperative Learning

During the past decade, cooperative learning has become one of the most popular ways to group students. Chapter 4 discusses cooperative learning as a means of motivating students. This section examines it as an instructional strategy.

Johnson and Johnson (1984) state that cooperation fosters (1) positive and coherent personal identity, (2) self-actualization and mental health, (3) knowledge and trust of others, (4) communication, (5) acceptance and support of others, (6) wholesome relationships, and (7) reduction of conflicts. Cooperative learning encourages students to work together, to help each other, to praise and critique each other's work, and to receive a group evaluation score.

Robert Slavin (1988) has developed two of the most utilized cooperative learning arrangements: STAD (student team achievement divisions) and TAI (team-assisted instruction). In STAD, groups consist of four to five members who are balanced by ability, gender, and ethnicity. This arrangement consists of five steps:

1. The teacher presents the lesson to the entire class in one or two class periods.

2. Team study follows for one or two periods. Students who have mastered the material assist those who have not. The group is not finished with the assignment until *all* members score 100 percent on an exam.

3. Class quizzes are administered regularly to monitor student progress. Student scores are averaged into each group's score to encourage members to work together.

4. Groups with high averages are recognized weekly. Awards to individual group members are discouraged.

5. Groups are changed every five or six weeks, enabling students to work with members from the other groups.

The other cooperative learning arrangement, TAI, is similar to STAD except that more emphasis is placed on basic skills. Each student is pretested on the desired skill. Students who need assistance, according to the pretest, are helped by students who have already mastered the skill. No student can take the final exam until a score of 80 percent or higher is achieved on the pretest. Groups receive both achievement and improvement scores. Unlike STAD, TAI teams are grouped by ability and labeled "super teams," "great teams," or "good teams." Each day the teacher works with two or three groups who are at about the same point in the curriculum for 10 to 15 minutes.

Individualized Instruction

Perhaps the best approach for grouping students in order to meet their individual needs is individualized instruction. The various individualized instruction programs are similar in their approaches to maximizing individual learning by (1) diagnosing the student's entry achievement levels or learning deficiencies, (2) providing a one-to-one teacher-to-student relationship, (3) introducing sequenced and structured instructional materials (frequently accompanied by practice and drill), and (4) permitting students to proceed at their own pace (Ornstein, 1990).

Mastery Learning. One of the most popular forms of individualized instruction is mastery learning. Carroll (1963) declared that if students are distributed normally by ability and aptitude for subject areas and are provided appropriate instruction to meet their individual needs, then the majority will achieve mastery if given sufficient time.

The keys to mastery learning are that students' individual needs must be diagnosed, instruction must be prescribed in small "bits" tailored to meet these needs, and students must be given sufficient time to master the skills. The following techniques enhance mastery learning:

1. Diagnose each student's entry level by using criterion-referenced tests.
2. Based on test results, define instructional objectives behaviorally so students know what they must do to achieve mastery.
3. Focus instruction on the defined behavioral objectives.
4. Develop the instruction into small, discrete units. Instruction should utilize a variety of delivery systems to meet the student's learning style.
5. Provide immediate feedback to all learner responses. The more immediate the feedback, the more efficient the learning.
6. Provide the student with remediation if they fail to master a specific objective or skill.
7. Provide the student with sufficient time to accomplish mastery. (Cohen, 1977)

Mastery learning may not be for every teacher. It is not an easy system to implement in the classroom because you must adapt the instruction to the needs of each student rather than expect the student to adapt to the instruction. If you decide to implement mastery learning in your classroom, you may wish to "experiment" with one unit of instruction first before trying it with an entire content area.

Individually Prescribed Instruction. During the 1960s, the University of Pittsburgh developed an individualized instruction program called Individually Prescribed Instruction (IPI). An individual plan of instruction was prepared for each student based on a diagnosis of the student's ability. The teacher developed learning tasks for each student based on the diagnosis. The student's progress was monitored and evaluated continually.

Tracking Students

As mentioned previously, one of the ways to group students is by ability. This type of grouping students is often called tracking. In many schools, students are grouped into classes based on their ability; thus, the "high" group may be in one classroom, the "average" group in another classroom, and the "low" group in still another classroom. In other schools, students may be assigned to a heterogeneous class but then regrouped by ability into math groups, reading groups, etc.

This method for grouping students is very popular because the ability differences among students within the class are supposedly reduced greatly. One of the underlying assumptions behind tracking is the notion that tracking promotes overall student achievement. Some educators assume that students' academic needs will be better met when they learn in groups having similar capabilities or prior levels of achievement. Another assumption is that less-able students will suffer emotional damage from daily classroom contact with their brighter peers. Finally, most teachers and administrators contend that tracking greatly eases the teaching task and is, perhaps, the only way to manage students (Oakes, 1985).

Does tracking work? Students who are not in the top tracks—about 60 percent of the senior high students—seem to suffer clear and consistent disadvantages from tracking. It appears that the only group to reap any advantages from the tracking system is the "high-ability" student. The "low" group, in particular, seems to be at a great disadvantage with the tracking system. According to Oakes, tracking appears to reduce self-esteem, lower aspirations, and foster negative attitudes toward school among the lower-achieving students.

Oakes also states that the net effect of tracking may be cumulative because tracking placements tend to remain fixed throughout a student's schooling. Students placed in low groups in elementary school seem to remain in these tracks throughout junior high school into senior high school. We must ask ourselves, if tracking worked so well, wouldn't nearly all "lower" group students work their way into the "average" group eventually?

COACHING

The previous section discussed the research data regarding tracking. Did this data affirm or challenge your opinions about tracking students by ability-grouping? How do your colleagues feel about tracking? This coaching exercise encourages you and your colleagues to examine your beliefs about this issue. What are the alternatives to tracking?

Coaching 1.13 The Dilemma of Grouping

The issue of how to group students remains a problem. The research cited on previous pages makes it clear that tracking by ability-grouping does not work and, in fact, seems to penalize those who need the most assistance. Yet tracking remains the predominant method for grouping students in our schools.

On the other hand, cooperative learning, as an instructional strategy and grouping method, seems to produce higher levels of achievement and more positive feelings toward tasks and other students, generates better intergroup relations, and results in better self-images for students with histories of poor achievement. Yet cooperative learning is often difficult to find in a school system.

Form a group with other student teachers or beginning teachers to discuss the issue of grouping students. List the positive and negative attributes of tracking and cooperative learning. Discuss the possible reasons why cooperative learning is not used more widely in classrooms. How are students grouped in your classroom? What is the rationale for this grouping? Can the grouping patterns be changed in your classroom? Are the responses of the beginning and experienced teachers similar or different? If possible, solicit input from experienced teachers concerning cooperative learning.

REFLECTION

Reflecting 1.14 Classroom Sociogram

Purpose: To gain insight about how students form natural groups within the classroom and how the dynamics of this grouping can affect the classroom environment. Clark and Starr (1991) suggest that teachers can create a classroom sociogram in order to gain valuable information about their students, in-classroom interactions and relationships.

Time required: 1 hour

Procedure: To make a sociogram, follow these steps:

1. Ask the pupils to answer (in secret) such questions as: Which two students would you like to work with on a topic for an oral report? If we should change the seating plan, who would you like to sit beside? Or with whom would you most like to work on a committee?
2. Tabulate the choices of each pupil. Keep the boys and girls in separate columns.
3. Construct the sociogram.
   a. Select a symbol for boy and another for girl.
   b. Place the symbols representing the most popular pupils near the center of the page, those of the less popular farther out, and those of the least popular on the fringes. It may be helpful to place the boys on one side of the page and the girls on the other.
   c. Draw lines to represent choices. Show the direction of the choice by an arrow. Show mutual choices by a double arrow. Dislike may be shown by drawing jagged lines.
4. Evaluate the sociogram. What does this information tell you about the classroom environment? How can you use these natural relationships to encourage learning? How can you create new patterns of relationships?

Reflecting 1.15 Observing Classroom Grouping Strategies

Purpose: To gain insight into the strategies and rationale for grouping students in classrooms.

Time required: Varies

Procedure: Observe several classrooms at different grade levels or content areas. The following questions should guide your observations:

1. Can you determine how the students are grouped in the classroom? by ability? by interests? by learning style? by a cooperative learning format?

2. If grouping is by ability, is it obvious to you which groups are high and which are low? Why?
3. Do the students in the various groups act differently toward other groups? toward each other?
4. Does the teacher respond to the various groups differently?
5. Is the method of teaching similar for each group?
6. Is the content similar or different for each group?
7. Is the time spent on the content similar or different for each group?
8. What do your answers tell you about grouping students in this classroom?

Reflecting 1.16 Mr. Douglas and Grouping Students

Again, recall James Douglas's teaching problems cited in the Case of the Unorganized Student Teacher. What problems, if any, were related to the grouping of students? As his university supervisor, what advice would you give him concerning the grouping of students in his classroom? How would this advice help remedy his problem?

Summary

This chapter examined the various ways that teachers organize their lessons and their teaching. We discussed the importance of goals and objectives for establishing a foundation and direction for the curriculum and individual lessons. These goals and objectives direct the types of instructional strategies that you will select to meet the instructional, emotional, and physical needs of your students. Paramount to organizing your lesson is your understanding of your class as a whole and as individuals. Your students' learning styles, past experiences, and countless other variables will provide you with valuable information to meet their needs. Finally, we examined the role that grouping your students for instruction plays in the success of the classroom. The grouping alternatives available to you should be able to meet the needs of both you and your students.

Recommended Readings

Doyle, W. (1985). Effective teaching and the concept of master teacher. *Elementary School Journal, 86*, 27–34.

Gage, N. (1978). *The scientific basis for the art of teaching.* New York: Teachers College Press.

Good, T., & Brophy, J. (1988). *Looking into classrooms.* (4th ed.). New York: Longman.

Heck, S., & Williams, R. (1984). *The complex roles of the teacher: An ecological perspective.* New York: Teachers College Press.

Ornstein, A. (1990). *Strategies for effective teaching.* New York: Harper and Row.

Posner, G. (1989). *Field experience: Methods of reflective teaching.* (2nd ed.). New York: Longman.

Waxman, H., & Walberg, H. (1991). *Effective teaching: Current research.* Berkeley, CA: McCutchan.

References

Arends, R. (1988). *Learning to teach.* New York: Random House.

Bloom, B., Engelhart, M., Furst, E., Hill, W., & Krathwohl, D. (1956). *Taxonomy of educational objectives. The classification of educational goals. Handbook I: Cognitive domain.* New York: McKay.

Borich, G. (1988). *Effective teaching methods.* Columbus, OH: Merrill.

Carroll, J. (1963). A model of school learning. *Teachers College Record, 64,* 723–733.

Clark, C., & Yinger, R. (1979). *Three studies of teacher planning.* East Lansing: Institute for Research on Teaching, Michigan State University.

Clark, L., & Starr, I. (1991). *Secondary and middle school teaching methods.* (6th ed.). New York: Macmillan.

Cohen, A. (1977). Instructional systems in reading: A report on the effects of a curriculum design based on a systems model. *Reading World, 16,* 158–171.

Collins, M. L. (1978). The effects of training for enthusiasm on the enthusiasm displayed by preservice teachers. *Journal of Teacher Education, 24* (1), 53–57.

Dunn, R., & Dunn, K. (1978). *Teaching students through their individual learning styles: A practical approach.* Reston, VA: Reston Publishing.

Eisner, E., & Vallance, E. (1974). *Conflicting conceptions of curriculum.* Berkeley, CA: McCutchan.

Emmer, E. T., Evertson, C. M., & Anderson, L. M. (1980). Effective classroom management at the beginning of the school year. *The Elementary School Journal, 80* (5), 219–231.

Gunter, M., Estes, T., & Schwab, J. (1990). *Instruction: A model's approach.* Boston, MA: Allyn and Bacon.

Johnson, D., & Johnson, R. (1984). *Cooperative learning.* New Brighton, MA: Interaction Books.

Joyce, B., Weil, M., & Showers, B. (1992). *Models of teaching.* (4th ed.). Englewood Cliffs, NJ: Prentice-Hall.

Moore, K. (1989). *Classroom teaching skills: A primer.* New York: Random House.

Oakes, J. (1985). *Keeping track: How schools structure inequality.* New Haven: Yale University Press.

Orlich, D., Harder, R., Callahan, R., Kauchak, D., & Gibson, H. (1994). *Teaching strategies.* (4th ed.). Lexington, MA: Heath.

Ornstein, A. (1990). *Strategies for effective teaching.* New York: Harper and Row.

Ornstein, A. C., & Hunkins, F. P. (1988). *Curriculum: Foundations, principles and issues.* Englewood Cliffs, NJ: Prentice-Hall.

Riessman, F. (1967). Teachers of the poor: A five point plan. *Journal of Teacher Education,* 326–336.

Rosenshine, B., & Furst, N. (1971). The use of direct observation to study teaching. In R.M.W. Travers (ed.), *Second handbook of research on teaching.* New York: Macmillan.

Slavin, R. (1988). *School and classroom organization.* Hillsdale, NJ: Erlbaum.

Suchman, R. (1966). *Inquiry development program in physical science.* Chicago: Science Research Associates.

Taba, H. (1962). *Curriculum development: Theory and practice.* New York: Harcourt Brace.

Tyler, R. (1949). *Basic principles of curriculum and instruction.* Chicago: University of Chicago Press.

Weber, W. (1986). Classroom management. In J. Cooper (ed.), *Classroom teaching skills.* (3rd ed.). Lexington, MA: Heath.

Chapter 2

The Communicator Role

Chapter Objectives

After completing this chapter, you will be able to

- reflect on personal and others' perceptions of your communication inside and outside the classroom.
- evaluate the communication process with specific attention focused on accurately assessing barriers to effective communication.
- demonstrate successful small-group problem-solving.
- analyze the four basic communication styles people exhibit and discuss ways to make your style more flexible in order to successfully communicate with others.
- recognize and reduce communication anxiety and tension.
- reflect on your communication log and the Case of the Reluctant Teacher Communicator to develop strategies that
  a. identify communication problems,
  b. create flexible communication styles, and
  c. reduce negative reactions to stressful communication situations.

$\mathcal{R}$emember the case study on the following page as you read and react to the Competencies in the communicator role. In the Coaching and Reflection stages of each Competency, you will be asked to provide Tom Roberts with communication strategies and techniques to handle difficult communication situations successfully.

We begin our analysis of the communicator role by examining perceptions of ourselves as communicators. Why begin here? Aren't all teachers naturally good communicators? We believe that communication is the heart, if not the soul, of teaching. Some argue that teaching *is* communication, and that without communication, teaching and learning are impossible. In the communicator role, the teacher is expected

Case of the Reluctant Teacher Communicator

One early fall morning, Maria Martinez entered the classroom of Tom Roberts, a beginning history teacher at Glendale High School. She had called ahead and scheduled a conference with Mr. Roberts in hopes of identifying the problem her daughter Latisha and other honor students were having with him. Latisha had said that he disliked her, refused to answer her questions, and made her feel unimportant in class. When Latisha approached him before or after class, he acted too busy to talk to her and indicated that he would talk with her later. However, "later" never came. Latisha tried to participate actively in class discussions, but her input was usually dismissed by Mr. Roberts as being unrealistic and impractical. She demanded to know why her input was rejected and attempted to argue the issue with him, but he would change the topic before she could complete her argument. Latisha didn't think he even heard her anymore. Finally, out of frustration, she told her mother that she could not communicate with Mr. Roberts and really did not like him or his class. Feeling that Tish's reaction to the teacher was uncharacteristic, Mrs. Martinez decided to meet with Mr. Roberts to discuss the problem. She wanted to hear both sides but felt that the teacher's inexperience with honor students was probably to blame.

(Two minutes earlier . . .) Tom waited patiently in his classroom for Mrs. Martinez to arrive. He felt anxious and uncomfortable and wished he could somehow avoid the conversation with her. If she were anything like her daughter, she would be loud, opinionated, and very confrontational. He usually enjoyed talking to students in class and encouraged class discussions; however, whenever a student attempted to "take over" the class and threatened his authority, he reacted by reducing class discussion time to avoid confrontations. Didn't his university professor caution all beginning teachers about arguing with students in front of the class? According to his professor, the teacher usually ends up looking bad and the student benefits by having an audience. Tom despised direct confrontations and preferred to avoid conflict, hoping that it would "just go away." Usually, it did. Unfortunately, in the case of Latisha, the conflict had not disappeared. As Maria Martinez entered the classroom, he could not help but notice how confident she appeared. Fearing that he would sound incoherent, he took a deep breath and began: "Hello, uh, Mrs. Martinez. I'm Tom Roberts. Would you like, uh, please be seated."

to interact effectively with different people in many different formats and environments that characterize and define the school climate and culture. Specific formats include teacher–student, teacher–teacher, teacher–parent, teacher–principal, and teacher–community. The teacher must seek effective interaction in both interpersonal settings (i.e., one-on-one situations) and group settings (i.e., small-group and large-group situations). For example, the teacher who is operating under site-based management principles and modeling democratic governance must effectively interact in conferencing, interviewing, small-group problem-solving, team building, and public speaking.

It is no wonder that successful communication in all settings is difficult. Most of us take communication for granted until a problem arises; then, being interested in resolving the conflict or problem, we decide to look at the communication process. Have you ever caught yourself speculating on the outcome of a communication event? For example, you might say to yourself, "If only I had said *that,* then maybe she (the parent or student) would have said *this,* and I would have been more convincing." Whereas speculation and hindsight are unproductive for the moment at hand, strategic analysis of and reflection on the communication process itself can result in true understanding and change.

In order to examine communication, we must first understand the key elements involved. Unlike other professionals, teachers are often ill-equipped to evaluate successful and unsuccessful communication. Business colleges, medical schools, and law schools incorporate extensive communication training in their curricula, whereas colleges of education, often regulated by state departments of education, are limited in their communication offerings. In this chapter you are asked to assess, experience, be coached, and reflect on how you interact with students, parents, principals, and teachers. Rather than focusing only on the different communication situations teachers encounter, we choose to enhance your understanding of the communication process as applicable to *all* settings and situations. This type of focus allows you to analyze the situation critically and adopt the most appropriate communication strategy for success. Three core competencies of the communicator role are

Competency 1: Perceiving Yourself and Others
Competency 2: Adopting Flexible Communication Styles
Competency 3: Reducing Communication Anxiety

Competency 1 PERCEIVING YOURSELF AND OTHERS

ASSESSMENT

In this section you are asked to examine your interpersonal communication based on your own perceptions and those of three significant others: your students, your cooperating teacher, and your university supervisor. This information will serve as a foundation for critical analysis of you as a teacher communicator. The Assessment exercises are designed to help you analyze your communication behaviors. Keep in mind that the results are not absolutes. You are striving to *sketch* rather than *paint* an accurate picture of your communication behaviors. As you have time to experience, be coached, and reflect, the picture will develop more clearly.

Assessing 2.1 How I See Myself Inside and Outside the Classroom

Purpose: To help identify personal perceptions of communication within yourself.

Time required: 10 minutes

Procedure: Complete this exercise in private. Evaluate yourself on the following scales. Place an I in the space that most accurately describes you as an individual, and place a T in the space that most accurately describes you as a teacher. For example, sometimes you may feel out of control in your personal life but in control as a teacher.

happy	:	:	:	:	:	:	sad
weak	:	:	:	:	:	:	strong
quiet	:	:	:	:	:	:	talkative
slow	:	:	:	:	:	:	fast
brave	:	:	:	:	:	:	cowardly
disorganized	:	:	:	:	:	:	organized
reliable	:	:	:	:	:	:	unreliable
slow	:	:	:	:	:	:	fast
timid	:	:	:	:	:	:	aggressive
sure	:	:	:	:	:	:	unsure
cold	:	:	:	:	:	:	warm
decisive	:	:	:	:	:	:	indecisive
out of control	:	:	:	:	:	:	in control
leader	:	:	:	:	:	:	follower
reactive	:	:	:	:	:	:	proactive
caring	:	:	:	:	:	:	uncaring
boring	:	:	:	:	:	:	exciting

Questions: What did you learn about yourself as a person and as a teacher by doing this exercise? Do you see yourself differently in different roles (parent, teacher, student, etc.)? Which items are you most sure about? least sure about? Which items are most obvious to others? Why do you think so?

Assessing 2.2 How Others See Me in the Classroom

Purpose: To help identify communication within yourself as defined by others' perceptions.

Time required: 10 minutes

Procedure: Complete this exercise in private. Evaluate yourself on the following scales. Place yourself in the roles of a student in your class, your cooperating teacher, and your university supervisor. Place an S in the space that most accurately describes you as seen by your students, a C by your cooperating teacher, and a U by your university supervisor. You may have more than one response in each space.

happy	:	:	:	:	:	:	sad
weak	:	:	:	:	:	:	strong
quiet	:	:	:	:	:	:	talkative
slow	:	:	:	:	:	:	fast
brave	:	:	:	:	:	:	cowardly
disorganized	:	:	:	:	:	:	organized
reliable	:	:	:	:	:	:	unreliable
slow	:	:	:	:	:	:	fast
timid	:	:	:	:	:	:	aggressive
sure	:	:	:	:	:	:	unsure
cold	:	:	:	:	:	:	warm
decisive	:	:	:	:	:	:	indecisive
out of control	:	:	:	:	:	:	in control
leader	:	:	:	:	:	:	follower
reactive	:	:	:	:	:	:	proactive
caring	:	:	:	:	:	:	uncaring
boring	:	:	:	:	:	:	exciting

Questions: Did your scoring differ for the three groups (students, cooperating teacher, and university supervisor)? If so, in what way? Which of the three most closely resembles your impressions of yourself as analyzed in Assessing 2.1? Which of the three least resembles your impressions?

How might you follow up on the accuracy of others' perceptions of you in the classroom? How important are others' perceptions of you as a teacher? as an individual?

Accurate assessments of yourself as a teacher communicator allow you to identify personal strengths and weaknesses that affect the communication process. In the next section you will be asked to experience key components of the communication process and focus on barriers to successful communication.

EXPERIENCE

Communication Process

Before examining interpersonal communication and conversations, let's look at the very nature of the communication process. Communication is the process of individuals sharing ideas, beliefs, thoughts, and feelings with each other in common, understandable ways (Hamilton & Parker, 1993). Regardless of whether you are communicating with a student, a small group of teachers, or an auditorium full of parents, the same basic process evolves and the same misunderstandings can occur. It becomes increasingly important to know the elements of the communication process and the role each element plays.

The model in Figure 2.1 presents the basic communication process. The five key components are defined and analyzed through the following brief descriptions and examples. To synthesize and evaluate the key elements, please provide your own example for each. Use an interpersonal communication example from your school or other personal experiences, and examine the sender and receiver roles.

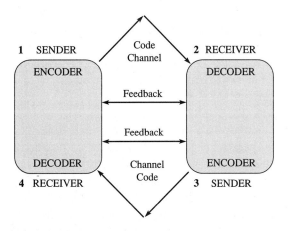

Figure 2.1   **Basic Communication Process**

1. Sender/Receiver. The sender is the source of the message; the receiver is the interpreter of the message. It is often difficult to delineate who is acting in which role whenever a conversation is really going. Remember, sending and receiving will occur simultaneously.

EXAMPLE

A beginning teacher (sender) looks across the classroom and establishes eye contact with two students (receivers) who are talking and are off task. The students (receivers) immediately stop talking and return to work. The students are sending the message that they are back on task.

2. Stimulation/Motivation. Each sender and receiver must have sufficient motivation and stimulation to send and receive a message. Sometimes a student may know the correct answer but simply not volunteer to answer because of a lack of motivation. The question asked is "What's in it for me?" This is true in most communication situations.

EXAMPLE

Consider the last university class meeting that you attended. Did the instructor ask a question that you could have answered? Why did you choose not to answer? Reasons may vary, but all stem from a lack of proper motivation or stimulation.

3. Encloding/Decoding. Senders process information internally, or *encode*, before sending a message; whereas, upon receiving a message, receivers interpret, or *decode*.

EXAMPLE

During a postobservation conference, a supervisor wishes to address the topic of improving classroom management and discipline in a beginning teacher's classroom. Before verbalizing the message, the supervisor considers several variables (e.g., the personality of the beginning teacher, the school's classroom management policy, the general discipline before the beginning teacher arrived, and the like) and chooses the best wording: "Sam, we need to develop a classroom management plan." Sam decodes the message to mean, "She is going to help me to improve discipline."

4. Code/Channel. The symbols that carry the message are the *code*. Two communication codes exist: verbal and nonverbal. Researchers have found that nonverbal codes, including paralanguage (the verbal elements that accompany spoken language, such as, tone volume, pitch, and rate), convey approximately 70 to 80 percent of a message, whereas language (verbal) codes convey 20 to 30 percent. In addition, as student populations become increasingly diverse, beginning teachers must increase their multicultural awareness. Culture greatly affects nonverbal behaviors, and understanding diversity requires emphasis on nonverbal communication (O'Hair & Ropo, 1994).

Reality Bite

Ethical and Moral Communication

Is the act of listening enough? Or, are we morally and ethically obligated to take action if our nonverbal behaviors suggest that we understand and support the speaker?

Communication with my principal is frustrating. He listens well, but avoids taking any action. You never see a problem resolved. If he disagrees with you, he never tells you. I leave his office feeling that he understood and supported me, but I never see any results. If he disagrees with me, why doesn't he tell me? I never know.

Experienced Elementary Teacher

What might you do in a similar situation? What communication styles does the principal demonstrate?

The *channel* is the medium by which a message is carried. Channels include face-to-face, letter, intercom, phone, fax, and e-mail. It is important to carefully analyze both the message and the message receiver in order to select the most appropriate channel.

EXAMPLE

One morning as you enter school and greet your cooperating teacher, he responds to your greeting by saying with a frown, "I'm doing great." Being a perceptive beginning teacher, you immediately focus on nonverbal communication and realize that your cooperating teacher is *not* having a great day. When a person's verbal and nonverbal behavior conflict, the nonverbal message is received and the verbal is forgotten.

5. Feedback. *Feedback* is the verbal and nonverbal acknowledgment of a message. Teachers may or may not be aware of their responses to messages. Feedback helps the sender know if the message has been received as intended.

EXAMPLE

A beginning teacher demonstrating a mathematics concept for the first time noticed that several students were frowning and looking confused. Rather than moving on to cover the next concept, the teacher chose to reteach the first concept based on student feedback.

Careful analysis of the communication process becomes even more difficult whenever communication barriers or breakdowns occur. In the next section, we will discuss communication failures in school settings and, specifically, where the communication process often shuts down.

Communication Barriers

Teachers no longer teach in a vacuum, isolated from peers, administrators, and community members. Rather, teachers are finding themselves with more real power to affect their own destiny and that of their students. Along with teacher empowerment come increased expectations from administrators, parents, and the community. Demonstrating effective communication in new settings is crucial for teachers. Let's examine communication issues and barriers that reduce the effectiveness of teacher communication: bypassing, inadequate preparation, vague instructions, poor listening, and tunnel vision. Each is briefly defined below and discussed in full during the Coaching and Reflection stages that follow.

Bypassing. It is important to remember that messages, not meanings, are transferable. For example, in Beverly Cleary's *Ramona the Pest,* a kindergarten teacher, on the first day of school, asks a child to sit in a particular chair for the present. The child interprets the statement to mean that the teacher is going to give her a present (gift) for sitting in the chair and is delighted with the prospect. However, the teacher means that the child may be moved later but for the time being is to sit in the chair. In this case, the message was misinterpreted completely because of different meanings for the word "present." This misinterpretation is often referred to as bypassing. Not only is it observed in child–adult communication, but it is prevalent in adult–adult communication as well. For example, a teacher may say to a parent, "I feel certain about the need to change your daughter's reading instruction. She will probably respond much better to the global reading technique." Examine the use of the words "certain," "probably," and "much better." For the teacher, the word "certain" holds an 85 percent chance of occurring, and "probably" and "much better" mean a 50 percent chance that the child will improve. A parent, on the other hand, may take the teacher's comments to mean a 100 percent chance of success and may be extremely disappointed, even hostile, whenever the child does not improve.

Most beginning teachers believe that bypassing rarely happens to them. Look briefly at the following terms, and give the percentage of certainty you feel when using the words in everyday situations. Ask your cooperating teacher and university supervisor to do the same.

_____	absolute	_____	sometimes
_____	little doubt	_____	we'll see
_____	definite	_____	maybe

_____ perhaps   _____ never

_____ slight chance   _____ looks promising

Compare your percentages with those of your cooperating teacher and university supervisor. Is there a discrepancy? Could this account for communication breakdowns? For instance, suppose you told your university supervisor that you would probably be ready to teach a lesson on Thursday. Your supervisor decides to plan a classroom visit based solely on your comment, believing that you would be teaching. Upon arrival, your supervisor discovers that not only are you not teaching but you are out of the classroom observing another teacher in the building. In actuality, you meant that there would be about a 50 percent chance that you would be teaching. Bypassing, involving talking past one another, has occurred. As noted by one communication specialist, "Communication does not consist of the transmission of meaning. Meanings are not transferable. Only messages are transmittable, and meanings are not in the message; they are in the message-user" (Berlo, 1960, p. 175).

Inadequate Preparation. Teachers need to prepare adequately and pay closer attention to details when communicating to colleagues, students, parents, principals, and community members. Communication is irreversible. In democratically governed schools, teachers participate as colleagues rather than subordinates of administrators and are actively involved in schoolwide decision making rather than making decisions that affect only their immediate classrooms. Often, however, teachers are uncomfortable when asked to assume unfamiliar leadership duties without adequate preparation. For example, teachers in democratic, site-base-managed schools are often asked to participate actively in teaming and small-group problem-solving. As a result of the lack of training in small-group dynamics, many teachers leave group meetings feeling unproductive and exhausted. In addition, many of these same teachers, if given a choice, would rather work alone than in a small group. Experts refer to this feeling as "group hate." Individuals reporting higher levels of hostility toward groups tend to be untrained in basic group problem-solving procedures. Why is training in small-group dynamics important? Because there are many advantages of group decisions over individual decisions, including the following:

- Resistance to change is reduced, and decisions jointly arrived at are usually better received since teachers serving as members are committed to the solution and are therefore more willing to support it.
- Decisions may be superior and more accurate since teachers with different viewpoints contributed input.
- Because decisions are better, they may be more readily accepted by others outside the group.
- Personal satisfaction and job enjoyment are greater.

- Hostility and aggression are significantly reduced.
- Productivity increases and occupational stress decreases.
- Responsibility for the decision is diffused, resulting in less risk for any group member. This is especially important when the solution is unpopular or unpleasant. (Bowen, 1981; Hamilton & Parker, 1993; Hatfield, 1972)

Not only will teachers benefit from training in small-group problem-solving, but students will benefit as well. Ineffective small groups are but one example of inadequate communication preparation. Inadequate preparation, whether by teachers or students, will decrease communication efficiency.

Vague Instructions. Even proper planning and preparation may not prevent vague instructions. As you find yourself working closely with teachers, counselors, principals, and other support staff, you may be effective in giving instructions to your students in the classroom but ineffective in giving instructions to adults. We often think that adults can understand our thoughts without our having to state them implicitly as we do for our students. Perhaps the lack of skills in giving instructions results from a lack of practice and confidence in assuming leadership roles within the school. Giving clear and concise instructions enhances your communication with adults and with students.

Some simple rules for giving instructions are listed below. Following this procedure can reduce misunderstandings and help others focus more on the message (content) and less on the procedure.

1. Begin with an overall picture.
2. Use a minimum number of words.
3. Use simple, easy-to-understand words.
4. Be specific.
5. Use simple comparisons.
6. Use repetition.
7. Number or "sign post" objects, steps, or sets of instructions.
8. Use good delivery techniques and watch for nonverbal signs of confusion.
9. Ask for feedback. (Lewis, 1973)

Poor Listening. Of the basic communication skills, listening is often the least developed. We listen before we learn to speak, read, or write. Unfortunately, our most basic communication skill is probably our least effective. Have you ever had an instructor, a peer, or your supervisor catch you not listening? Has anyone ever accused you of being a poor listener? Poor listening is common in both home and school environments. Research supports that listening is our most underutilized communication skill: During verbal communication time (including speaking, writing, and reading), elementary students listen 58 percent of the time; high school students listen 46 percent of the time; college students listen 42 percent of the time; older adults listen 42 to 55 percent of the time. Why does listening decrease as we grow older? Do we find more distractions?

Poor listening is responsible for many communication breakdowns. It can even lead to selective listening, sometimes referred to as tunnel vision.

Tunnel Vision. Teachers, principals, and parents with tunnel vision fail to examine new and innovative techniques to improve instruction and, ultimately, student learning. We can discover tunnel vision in ourselves and others whenever we hear these comments:

"That will never work."
"We tried that a few years back and it didn't work."
"Why fix it if it ain't broken?"
"I don't have the time to try it."

If we can avoid such language and attitudes and allow each other the opportunity to share ideas, we can accomplish much. Tunnel vision is a communication barrier that stifles the generation and implementation of ideas. Effective teachers cannot afford to have tunnel vision.

The communication process and the barriers impacting successful communication are complicated and often difficult to define. As discussed earlier, several variables may be responsible for communication failures. Correct identification and strategic action improve communication. The Coaching section presents opportunities for you to fine-tune your communication skills by reducing communication barriers often found in classrooms and schools.

COACHING

Both your cooperating teacher and university supervisor will play important roles in this section. In the exercises that follow, you will receive guidance, clarification, additional information, and support from experienced teachers. Remember, by becoming aware of the communication process and avoiding communication barriers, you will begin to perceive yourself and others accurately and thus improve communication.

Coaching 2.3 Analyzing Different Frames of References

In order to analyze different frames of references, follow these steps: (1) Select a person (student, teacher, principal, parent) with whom you have had several disagreements and/or misunderstandings. (2) Make a detailed list of this person's likes, dislikes, background, abilities, etc., until you have a fairly good idea about his or her frame of reference. (3) Complete a similar list about yourself. (4) Compare and contrast the two lists to determine frame-of-reference differences that could account for ineffective communication experiences with this person.

Coaching 2.4 Adopting a Basic Problem-Solving Procedure

Place in order the following steps of the small-group basic problem-solving procedure. Be ready to support your reasoning with examples.

1. Research and analyze the problem.
2. List possible alternatives.
3. Define the problem.
4. Evaluate each alternative.
5. Establish a checklist of criteria for use in evaluating possible alternatives.
6. Select the best alternative as your solution and discuss how to implement it.

(Correct order is 3, 1, 5, 2, 4, 6.) (Adapted from Hamilton & Parker, 1993.)

See the Appendix for a complete description of the Basic Problem-Solving Procedure (Hamilton & Parker, 1993).

How might this procedure improve communication in your school? From your own experience as a group member, would this process be helpful? Is it used often in groups? If not, how might you encourage its use?

REFLECTION

Reflecting 2.5 Case of the Reluctant Teacher Communicator

Reflect on the Case of the Reluctant Teacher Communicator that began this chapter. Identify the communication barriers that Tom Roberts and Latisha demonstrate. How might each barrier be reduced? Be specific in your recommendations. After evaluating the teacher-student barriers to effective communication, identify barriers that Tom Roberts and Maria Martinez face. How might each barrier be reduced? Again, be specific in your recommendations.

Correctly perceiving ourselves and others helps to reduce communication barriers and promotes successful communication. Becoming aware of verbal and nonverbal communication in the classroom and school settings allows us to change ineffective behaviors and practice relationship-building skills. Whether communicating in a dyad, small-group, or large-group setting, we can improve our communication perceptions through understanding, practice, and reflection on the communication process.

Competency 2   ADOPTING FLEXIBLE COMMUNICATION STYLES

ASSESSMENT

After developing a basic understanding of perceptions and the communication process, the next step involves assessing your communication style. You are asked to complete the Teacher Communicator Style Indicator, which is helpful in identifying both your predominant communication style and the style of communication you adopt under stress.

Assessing 2.6   Teacher Communicator Style Indicator*

Purpose: To help identify your general communication style.

Time required: 20 minutes

Procedure: Read each question carefully. Evaluate yourself on the following scale: Place an 8 on the line that "most closely" represents your feelings; a 4 on the line that "moderately" represents your feelings; a 2 on the line that "slightly" represents your feelings; and a 1 on the line that "least" represents your feelings. Remember to answer all questions based on your own feelings, not on what others may wish for you to do or what most people would do.

1. From your experience, what is the only realistic way to deal with other teachers?
    - _____ **a.** To get ahead, you must actively compete with other teachers. Try to stay one step ahead of everyone.
    - _____ **b.** You can't be too careful. The chances are that even your friends will try to take over your job if it means advancement for them.

*Adapted from the Survey of Communication Styles, Employee Tendency Indicator by Cheryl Hamilton and Cordell Parker, 1993. *Communicating for results: A guide for business and the professions* (4th.ed.), pp. 426–431.

_____ **c.** A friendly approach is best even if your personal opinions make it necessary for you to pretend friendship.

_____ **d.** A friendly but truthful approach works best; however, when a misunderstanding occurs, it is important to express your true feelings.

2. While your cooperating teacher is giving you instructions on how to complete a particular task, you realize that the instructions are wrong. What would you do?

_____ **a.** Question the teacher to make sure you didn't misunderstand the instructions; then, explain the problem as you see it.

_____ **b.** Errors such as this are typical, because a beginning teacher usually has the most recent knowledge and a new, fresh perspective. Press your advantage by pointing out the error.

_____ **c.** Pointing out an error to the cooperating teacher is a good way to receive lower evaluations. Do whatever the cooperating teacher tells you, regardless of what it is.

_____ **d.** If you point out the error, it could make the cooperating teacher feel uncomfortable and even ruin your standing with the teacher. Therefore, complete the task correctly, but say nothing.

3. During your postconference evaluation, your university supervisor criticizes you for something you feel is unfair. How would you respond?

_____ **a.** Accept the criticism quietly. Any comment on your part will only prolong the meeting.

_____ **b.** Unless it is a big issue, keep quiet about it. Otherwise, briefly disagree in a good-natured way; then drop it.

_____ **c.** Defend yourself. Let the university supervisor know that you feel that you are being treated unfairly. Insist that a different evaluation be submitted. Supervisors respect you more when you stand up for what you believe.

_____ **d.** Discuss the university supervisor's view until it is completely clear. Then offer your own opinion supported with facts and data. Debate the issue if necessary.

4. After receiving a detailed explanation of your classroom duties and responsibilities from your cooperating teacher, you still aren't clear on some of the instructions. What would you do?

_____ **a.** If you are a good teacher, you should be flexible and able to figure out what to do as you go along. There's probably a better way to complete the assignment anyway.

_____ **b.** Never ask questions. You only look stupid. If necessary, get help from a fellow beginning teacher.

_____ **c.** Ask questions of your cooperating teacher any time you aren't completely sure about an assignment.

_____ **d.** If your cooperating teacher believes that asking questions shows interest, ask for clarification. If not, pretend you understand and find out the missing information some other way.

5. Your university supervisor calls a meeting to evaluate the success of a new teaching method and asks for everyone's opinion. How would you respond?

_____ **a.** Listen carefully to everyone's comments. Openly agree with people when possible. However, if your experiences with the method differ from those being expressed, keep them to yourself.

_____ **b.** Inform those present about the success you've had in implementing the procedure and recommend that your method be adopted by the group.

_____ **c.** Don't volunteer any comments. Let the others do the talking. If the university supervisor specifically asks for your opinion, keep your answer general so you won't have any reason to regret what you have said.

_____ **d.** Participate actively in the discussion. Don't hesitate to express your experiences (both positive and negative) even if they differ from the experiences of the other employees.

6. Almost by accident, you discover an easier and faster way to grade papers. As a result, you can finish the other teaching duties of the day in a more relaxed manner. Would you tell anyone else of your discovery?

_____ **a.** Beginning teachers who can perform their duties better than others are the ones who get the high recommendations and good jobs. Therefore, the only way to get ahead is to keep such discoveries to yourself.

_____ **b.** If the cooperating teacher knew that grading papers could be completed in less time, you would be given additional tasks to do, and the smooth pattern of school life would be disrupted. Therefore, say nothing.

_____ **c.** Because it is everyone's responsibility to share job-related discoveries with each other, offer to do so. Then, if they are interested, tell them about the discovery.

_____ **d.** A discovery such as this gives you the perfect opportunity to prove that you are more capable than your fellow beginning teachers. If you can impress your cooperating teacher during a departmental meeting by presenting your discovery, then do so.

7. In a last-minute check of a rush job that is due immediately in the teacher's classroom, you discover a minor mistake that you have made. How would you handle it?

_____ **a.** If the error is small enough to pass by without notice, keep the problem to yourself. However, if the effort is sure to be noticed and could hurt your relationship with the cooperating teacher, mention the error in a joking manner and ask for extra time to correct it.

_____ **b.** Immediately go to see the cooperating teacher and explain that you have discovered an error in your work and will need to postpone delivery of the project.

_____ **c.** The best defense is a good offense. Because you did what the cooperating teacher told you to do, the mistake is obviously the result of the teacher's instructions. Point this out when you deliver the project.

_____ **d.** Keep quiet about the error and hope it passes unnoticed. Even if it doesn't, the decision to delay the project is now the cooperating teacher's responsibility.

8. You are aware of a situation that has the potential for creating a serious problem for your school or even the district. What would you do?

_____ **a.** It is the administrator's responsibility to be aware of potential problems. As a beginning teacher, it is not your responsibility to report on such things. Unless you could benefit by discussing your observations, keep quiet.

_____ **b.** Meddling in things that are none of your business is a good way to make enemies and fail to pass field experiences.

_____ **c.** Because administration depends on and should appreciate the input and observations of all teachers, don't hesitate to mention your observation to your principal and cooperating teacher.

_____ **d.** No one wants to hear negative things. Pointing out the problem will only make people unhappy. Also, if your observation is wrong, you will look like a fool. Therefore, just keep the information to yourself.

9. A serious conflict has arisen between you and a teacher in your department. How would you handle it?

_____ **a.** If you give in, the other person will lose respect for you, so try to win the argument. If no decision can be reached, select a person (such as your university supervisor) to serve as an arbitrator.

_____ **b.** Discuss the conflict in detail, making sure both of you get a chance to express your feelings. Honest discussion usually leads to a mutual agreement and an end to hostilities. In some cases, it may be necessary to compromise.

_____ **c.** Continuing the conflict will only bring you unwanted attention from others. Give in, if that's what it takes to end the conflict.

    _____ **d.** Continuing the conflict would permanently damage your friendship with this teacher. Do your best to smooth over the argument and regain a friendly footing with the person.

10. A curriculum writing team of teachers has failed to complete its assignment on time. The principal is starting to put pressure on your group and wants to know who's causing the slowdown. You know who the person is. What would you do?

    _____ **a.** Suggest that all members of the group meet to discuss the problem. If you find that the problem is caused by an unfair load distribution or some other group-related cause, try to find a workable answer.

    _____ **b.** Blaming the individual either personally or in front of others only creates a strain on the relationships in the group. The best thing to do is to blame circumstances; for example, you could say that the instructions weren't clear, there wasn't enough time, or someone outside the group was slow in supplying information.

    _____ **c.** Nothing is gained by keeping quiet. A single individual is making you and the entire group look bad. Put pressure on the person to admit causing the delays. If that doesn't work, tell the principal yourself.

    _____ **d.** Do nothing. It is not wise to volunteer this type of information.

11. While working on an extracurricular school project, a highly unusual problem arises that is not covered in your college textbooks or school policy manual. Even your cooperating teacher is uncertain about it. What would you do?

    _____ **a.** Postpone making a decision. If you put the decision off long enough, someone else will probably make it and any mistakes will be their responsibility.

    _____ **b.** Discuss the problem with your principal, your cooperating teacher, your university supervisor, and even knowledgeable people outside your school. Okay your final decision with your cooperating teacher before making it official.

    _____ **c.** Ask your cooperating teacher and teachers in your department to see what they would do. Base your decision on the majority opinion. That way no one can put the blame on you.

    _____ **d.** This is a chance to prove your ability. You don't need anyone else's opinion if you are a good teacher. Make the decision yourself.

12. How important is your cooperating teacher to your individual success?

    _____ **a.** Except for a few years of experience, you are as knowledgeable as or more knowledgeable than the cooperating teacher. Therefore, the teacher plays only a minor role in your success.

           _____ **b.** Extremely important. Without the cooperating teacher to tell you what to do, there could be no success.

           _____ **c.** Success depends on how happy the cooperating teacher is with what you do and how well he or she likes you. If the teacher is satisfied, you will be successful.

           _____ **d.** You and the cooperating teacher work as a team. Both are equally necessary for success.

Scoring: For all 12 questions, write the scores you selected for answers *a, b, c,* and *d* onto the score sheet below. Remember that each number puts your answers in an order different from the way you answered them. Total the numbers for each column.

	Open	Blind	Hidden	Closed
1.	d ( )	a ( )	c ( )	b ( )
2.	a ( )	b ( )	d ( )	c ( )
3.	d ( )	c ( )	b ( )	a ( )
4.	c ( )	a ( )	d ( )	b ( )
5.	d ( )	b ( )	a ( )	c ( )
6.	c ( )	d ( )	a ( )	b ( )
7.	b ( )	c ( )	a ( )	d ( )
8.	c ( )	a ( )	d ( )	b ( )
9.	b ( )	a ( )	d ( )	c ( )
10.	a ( )	c ( )	b ( )	d ( )
11.	b ( )	d ( )	c ( )	a ( )
12.	d ( )	a ( )	c ( )	b ( )
Totals	( )	( )	( )	( )

The two highest scores on the Teacher Communicator Style Indicator reflect your communication style. The highest score describes you whenever things are going well; the second highest score reflects your communication style when you are under stress. Notice that these surveys indicate only *tendencies* in your communication behavior.

Questions: What did you learn about yourself as an individual and as a teacher by doing this exercise? Do you like your communication style? Is it possible to change communication styles? Either in normal conditions or under stress, would you like to change or alter your communication style? If so, in what way?

EXPERIENCE

To be an effective communicator, teachers must have some understanding of themselves and others. Whereas all educators have some things in common, each teacher, principal, student, and parent is unique and different. How we communicate with others requires a close examination of our differences as well as our commonalities. Through careful analysis of other people's communication preferences, we become more flexible and adapt our communication style to meet their needs. Four basic communication styles exist: closed, blind, hidden, and open (Hamilton & Parker, 1993). Rather than operating exclusively in one particular style, teachers tend to utilize several styles based on personality, contextual, and situational variables. Most teachers do have a dominant communication style, however, and will often assume it under stress. For example, a beginning teacher whose basic style is open communication (i.e., is seen by others as trusting, friendly, and dependable; gives and receives criticism in a positive manner; is productive and a careful listener) may adopt a closed communication style (i.e., reserved, aloof, noncommunicative, and difficult to relate to) when experiencing stressful situations (e.g., unexpected performance evaluation, discipline problems, extreme amounts of extracurricular duties). In this section we will define the four communication styles, give examples and helpful hints for interacting effectively with individuals of each style, and evaluate strategies for making your style more flexible.

Communication Styles and Interactions in School Settings

Do you remember a teacher with whom you had difficulty communicating, just as Latisha had a difficult time communicating with Tom Roberts? Often the feeling of being unable to relate to another person is a result of incompatible communication styles. Remember, none of the styles is totally good or totally bad; each has a "best" and "worst" side (Hamilton & Parker, 1993). Let's examine the general characteristics of each style. In the Coaching section, we will discuss appropriate strategies for adapting styles in order to become more effective communicators.

Closed Style. The closed communicator is often referred to as someone who, like a turtle, tends to hide from others. Individuals operating under this style prefer less contact with others and rarely self-disclose or give feedback. They are often referred to as noncommunicators and appear reserved and uncaring. Closed communicators can be very productive if they are working alone. Rather than taking a risk or trying a new innovation, they prefer to keep the status quo. They find team meetings, small-group problem-solving sessions, and conferencing particularly difficult and avoid them whenever possible. Closed communicators have a low self-image, rarely assume leadership positions, and are highly apprehensive of situations involving interpersonal communication.

Reality Bite

Small-Group Decision Making: Can You Afford the Time?

Developing a collaborative work culture takes time. Group decision making is often time consuming. What should you do when challenged to make an independent and immediate decision? How should you handle the following situation? What are the advantages to group decision making that might help you?

You are currently serving as chair of the math department in your high school. You receive a phone call from a student's father, who is upset and wants to know your opinion on the new math curriculum. He also wants you to make immediate alterations in the curriculum. You have already assigned a math curriculum committee to study and make recommendations on the new curriculum. Should you state your personal opinion and take some specific action to alter the curriculum as requested by the parent, or should you wait until the committee completes its work? What should you communicate to the parent?

High School Math Teacher

Blind Style. Unlike the closed communicators, blind communicators are overconfident and often arrogant, believing that their way is always the right way. Rather than hiding from people and choosing to work in solitude, blind communicators enjoy people and often seek out and use others as an audience. Characteristics of blind communicators include talking more than listening, giving advice rather than seeking advice; and winning rather than losing an argument. They are very vocal in letting you know where you stand with them. They are also loyal, well organized, dependable, helpful to those who want to learn (as long as the help is appreciated), and not afraid to exercise authority (Hamilton & Parker, 1993).

Hidden Style. Hidden communicators are unable to disclose, keeping their opinions, ideas, and feelings to themselves. Hidden communicators like to interact with people and are concerned about others' successes and problems. They are often praised as being sympathetic listeners and tend to be viewed as well liked and fun to be around. These communicators are less concerned with quality of work and more concerned with keeping everything running smoothly. They often agree with others without carefully considering the problem or consequences. The hidden communicator is referred to as a "yes" person who is busy seeking a conflict-free environment, which may be viewed by some people as disloyal, manipulative, or two-faced (Hamilton & Parker, 1993).

Open Style. In contrast to the communicators who are afraid of people (closed), view others as uninformed (blind), and are suspicious of people (hidden), open communicators genuinely like and respect people. Open style encourages flexibility in giving and receiving feedback, and open communicators are well liked, productive, accept criticism well, and listen actively. When communicating with individuals of a different style, however, open communicators are viewed as free and easy liberals, making others feel uncomfortable with total openness. Also, open communicators become frustrated with time restraints and inflexible school systems.

COACHING

Now that you have a basic understanding of your own communication style, under both normal and stressful conditions, and can describe the four different communication styles, we would like for you, your cooperating teacher, and your university supervisor to supply hints for communicating successfully with individuals of different styles. Develop a list of strategies for successful communication with blind, closed, hidden, and open communicators. Remember, most individuals that you encounter on a daily basis (i.e., students, parents, principals, teachers) will have either a significantly or slightly different communication style from your own. Consider those students in your classes that you perceive as discipline problems. Analyze their motives and the characteristics that define their most dominant communication styles. Are their styles significantly different from your own? from your cooperating teacher's? If so, you need to find ways to bridge the communication gap between individuals with different communication styles.

Coaching 2.7 Helpful Hints for Success with Different Communication Styles

Now we will provide you with several hints for each basic communication style and ask that you and your cooperating teacher and university supervisor each supply an example of the communication style described in each hint. Your examples may come from observations and experiences inside or outside the school setting. Your cooperating teacher's and university supervisor's examples will provide you with interactions previously unexperienced by you in the classroom. Reflect on your own experiences and those of an experienced teacher. Discuss your examples with your cooperating teacher and university supervisor. Later, in the Reflection section, you will be asked to analyze and reflect on effective interactions with cooperating teachers, university supervisors, and other adults (principals, teachers, parents, staff, and custodians) encountered in school settings.

Communicating with Closed Communicators

HINT 1: PROCEED CAREFULLY AND STRATEGICALLY. DON'T THREATEN OR INCREASE A CLOSED COMMUNICATOR'S INSECURITY.

EXAMPLE: When communicating with her cooperating teacher, one beginning teacher noticed that her teacher was more receptive if introduced to new ideas gradually.

HINT 2: PUT CLOSED COMMUNICATORS IN ENVIRONMENTS WITH LITTLE INTERACTION WHERE THEY FEEL SAFE. THE "SHOCK TREATMENT" OF PLACING STUDENTS IN HIGHLY INTERACTIVE ENVIRONMENTS IS INEFFECTIVE.

EXAMPLE: When working in a cooperative learning environment, the teacher notices that one student, Tommy, refuses to participate with the group. He appears happy and comfortable working on the assignment alone. Rather than insisting that Tommy join the group and actively participate, the teacher encourages Tommy to complete part of the project on his own and report to the group.

HINT 3: BE AWARE THAT CLOSED STUDENTS ARE OVERLY CRITICAL AND HARD ON THEMSELVES.

EXAMPLE: In a peer tutoring situation, a teacher notices that Harvey is not improving in math. Most students involved in the peer tutoring math lab have made noticeable gains. After listening to Harvey, the teacher realizes that he is overly critical of himself, in part because of comments made by his student tutor ("You are the only one who still has trouble with this math. Let's get to work—you are really behind in math."). Although the comments were not meant to be overly critical, they made Harvey feel inferior and depressed. The teacher requests that the tutor give only positive and encouraging comments to Harvey and avoid any type of criticism.

HINT 4: DON'T EXPECT CLOSED STUDENTS TO OPENLY EXPRESS WHAT THEY FEEL OR DESIRE. YOU MUST ACTIVELY SEARCH FOR IT.

EXAMPLE: In language arts, Maria appeared frustrated and despondent. Her teacher tried to give her every opportunity to participate. Finally, after class one day the teacher stopped Maria and asked, "Is something bothering you in class? What can I do to help?" To the teacher's surprise, Maria responded to this direct approach, whereas she had been unresponsive to subtle inquiries.

Communicating with Blind Communicators

HINT 1: APPEAL TO THE STUDENT'S SELF-CONFIDENCE: "WE NEED YOUR HELP ON THIS TOPIC." BLIND COMMUNICATORS ARE EXTREMELY SELF-ASSURED.

EXAMPLE: John enjoys acting like an expert on any topic discussed in class. Often, it is obvious that John knows little about a topic, but his lack of knowledge rarely stifles his desire to communicate. While studying World War II, John's teacher asked him to research the types of aircraft used during the war and to prepare a report for the class. For his efforts, John received class recognition, new knowledge of the topic, and improved communication skills. John now understands that a competent communicator must be knowledgeable and have well-documented and accurate information.

HINT 2: STUDENTS WHO ARE BLIND COMMUNICATORS ARE RESPECTFUL OF TEACHER AUTHORITY BUT HAVE LITTLE RESPECT FOR TEACHERS WHO LACK CLASSROOM CONTROL.

EXAMPLE: A beginning teacher, experiencing discipline problems in an honors class, observes a well-behaved student turn into a chronic discipline problem. The student lost respect for the teacher because of her inability to maintain classroom control.

HINT 3: STUDENTS WHO ARE BLIND COMMUNICATORS ARE OFTEN ARGUMENTA-
TIVE AND TAKE SUGGESTIONS POORLY.

EXAMPLE: Sue, an eighth-grader, was considered a discipline problem by most
of her teachers. Often, she refused to follow directions, correct written assignments, or accept differing opinions. Recognizing Sue's argumentative blind
style and creative abilities, her English teacher began allowing Sue the opportunity to complete assignments according to her own format and style, provided
that Sue could convince her teacher that her approach was as good or better
than the suggested approach.

HINT 4: REVIEWING PREVIOUSLY LEARNED SKILLS WILL PROBABLY INSULT THE STU-
DENT WHO IS A BLIND COMMUNICATOR, UNLESS HE OR SHE IS CALLED ON TO PRO-
VIDE CORRECT EXAMPLES FOR OTHER STUDENTS.

EXAMPLE: Mrs. Reynolds, a third-grade teacher, notices that Raymond refuses
to participate in the daily language arts review session. Only after she encourages him to become a student tutor and to assist her in the review session does
he participate.

HINT 5: BE AWARE OF HOW IMPORTANT SOCIAL EVENTS ARE FOR BLIND COMMUNI-
CATORS. THEY FREQUENTLY SERVE AS ORGANIZERS OF PEP CLUB ACTIVITIES,
SCHOOL DANCES, SPORTING EVENTS, AND THE LIKE.

EXAMPLE: Sam seldom participates in class, but if an extracurricular activity is
being discussed, he is the first to volunteer. He is distracted easily from classroom
activities and chooses to do only the accepted minimum for class assignments.

Communicating with Hidden Communicators

HINT 1: HIDDEN STUDENTS KEEP THEIR FEELINGS AND CONCERNS TO THEMSELVES.
THEY MAY BE NODDING THEIR HEADS TO MEAN "YES" WHEN THEY ACTUALLY
DISAGREE.

EXAMPLE: Rachel, agreeing in class with her group's solution to a problem,
later said to her teacher that the solution would not work.

HINT 2: HIDDEN COMMUNICATORS ARE SUSPICIOUS OF OTHERS' MOTIVES. AWARE-
NESS OF THIS GENERAL LACK OF TRUST SHOULD ENSURE THAT COMMUNICATIONS
WITH THESE STUDENTS ARE EXTREMELY EXPLICIT.

EXAMPLE: Jackie is suspicious of her friend Julie's motives for volunteering for
a special science project. The science teacher, Mrs. Riley, is also the cheerleader
sponsor. Jackie believes that Julie volunteered in order to have a better chance
at becoming a cheerleader.

HINT 3: ENCOURAGE TWO-WAY COMMUNICATION. HIDDEN COMMUNICATORS ARE
GREAT LISTENERS BUT RARELY DISCLOSE INFORMATION.

EXAMPLE: After talking at length to Bill about his failure to turn in his art homework, the teacher realizes that she has done all of the talking. Bill had listened intently but still did not state why he was not turning in his homework. The next day, Bill's teacher broke the one-sided communication ritual by asking him to draw a picture of what he did after school each day. This activity stimulated discussion of the problem.

Communicating with Open Communicators

HINT 1: BE PREPARED FOR OPEN STUDENTS TO MAKE "BLUNT" COMMENTS IN CLASS. THESE STUDENTS ARE OFTEN VIEWED AS BEING "TOO OPEN."

EXAMPLE: In describing her social studies assignment, Suzie stated that she did not have enough information to prepare adequately for the assigned report. Rather than becoming defensive and disagreeing with Suzie, her teacher allowed her to explain what specific information would have been useful. Suzie was then allowed to collect the information to use for her report.

HINT 2: ALLOW OPEN STUDENTS TO HAVE PLENTY OF TIME TO DEVELOP CREATIVE IDEAS. OPEN STUDENTS OFTEN BECOME FRUSTRATED WHEN FACING TIME RESTRAINTS.

EXAMPLE: Mrs. Ellis allows student input in designing time limits for projects. As long as the time seems reasonable and students are engaged actively in learning, she feels that students adopt an ownership concerning time limits, strive to complete projects on time, and exhibit greater creativity in their work.

HINT 3: OPEN COMMUNICATORS ARE USUALLY THE MOST POPULAR STUDENTS IN CLASS. THEY SHOULD BE VIEWED AS OPINION LEADERS.

EXAMPLE: Tired of picking up trash and straightening desks after fifth period, Mr. Smith, a beginning history teacher, asks Rick, a popular student, to help him monitor the problem. The next day Mr. Smith observes students picking up their own trash and leaving the room tidy for the first time all year. All of his preaching to the class about cleanliness did not compare to one opinion leader's actions.

HINT 4: OPEN COMMUNICATORS ARE FLEXIBLE IN USING COMMUNICATION STYLES. EVALUATE AN OPEN COMMUNICATOR'S FLEXIBILITY IN A DIFFERENT COMMUNICATION CONTEXT. OBSERVE THEIR ABILITY TO ADAPT TO THE NEEDED STYLE OF COMMUNICATION. BECAUSE OF THIS FLEXIBILITY, OPEN COMMUNICATORS MAKE EXCELLENT LEADERS IN SMALL- AND LARGE-GROUP SETTINGS. NOT ONLY ARE THEY PRODUCTIVE, BUT OPEN COMMUNICATORS ALSO ENCOURAGE PRODUCTIVITY IN OTHERS.

EXAMPLE: Mrs. Hunter is a very authoritarian teacher in the classroom. Consequently, Joseph, who is an open communicator, adopted a more hidden style in order to deal effectively with her.

REFLECTION

Reflecting 2.8 Communication Styles and the Case of the Reluctant Teacher Communicator

Reflect back to the Case of the Reluctant Teacher Communicator. Describe Tom Roberts's communication style, and suggest ways in which he could adapt his style to communicate effectively with Latisha and her mother. After analyzing your communication style, place yourself in Tom's classroom and assume his role. Examine the communication styles of Latisha and her mother. How would you adapt your style to communicate effectively with them? Is it difficult to adapt your communication style? Why do you think so?

Effectively adapting a basic communication style to meet the needs of the situation is a challenge not only for beginning teachers but for all professionals. Individuals who are the most successful in education, business, and other professions are those who understand diversity in communication styles. Successful professionals adapt effectively to diversity and continuously monitor the communication process.

■
Competency 3 REDUCING COMMUNICATION ANXIETY

The third communication Competency involves managing communication anxiety. Many beginning teachers experience some form of communication anxiety in school settings. Whether speaking to a classroom of students, a hostile parent, or a university supervisor, beginning teachers often feel excessive anxiety, fear, stress, or worry associated with one or several communication events. Whereas some stress is positive and may actually be helpful in improving your performance, negative anxiety or stress that serves to reduce or hinder your teaching and professional performance, left unchecked, may lead to physical and mental health problems. Let's begin by discovering which communication situations are stressful for you.

ASSESSMENT

Assessing 2.9 Identifying Anxious Situations

Purpose: To help beginning teachers identify stressful communication experienced in school settings.

Time required: 5 minutes

Procedure: On a scale of 1 to 4 (with 4 being the highest level of stress and 1 being the lowest) rate your degree of stress for the following communication situations.

_____ leading a group discussion

_____ demonstrating leadership skills

_____ arguing with your cooperating teacher

_____ requesting a favor

_____ disagreeing with another teacher

_____ persuading your university supervisor

_____ making an excuse for a mistake

_____ explaining your actions

_____ discussing your performance evaluation

_____ confronting a hostile parent

_____ challenging someone's point of view

_____ presenting a report to a small group

_____ answering questions in a meeting

_____ giving a formal presentation to the faculty

_____ refusing to grant a request

_____ leading a PTA program

_____ giving a media interview

_____ giving someone bad news

_____ telling jokes in a group session

_____ responding to backtalk from a student

_____ speaking up in a hostile group

_____ negotiating a better deal

Scoring: As you examine your ratings, you may notice that some situations produce more stress for you than others. Examine closely your ratings for items you marked 3 or 4. Divide these high-stress items into three settings: interpersonal (one-on-one), small group, and large group. This should give you some idea of which context produces the greatest communication anxiety for you.

EXPERIENCE

Communication anxiety management refers to an individual's ability to control communication apprehension, or nervousness. *Trait* and *state* are the two types of communication apprehension. Beginning teachers who experience a great deal of trait anxiety feel apprehensive in all communication situations, whether school related or not. This section focuses on beginning teachers who for the most part experience state communication apprehension; in other words, those who experience stress only in specific communication contexts or situations. Until you understand what causes state communication anxiety in school settings, you will be unable to achieve successful anxiety management and reduction.

Causes of Communication Anxiety

In the Beginning. Beginning teachers report two overriding factors that contribute to communication anxiety: unfamiliarity or novelty of the situation and student misbehavior. Upon closer examination of each contributing factor, a "feedback gap" emerges. For example, beginning teachers are constantly focusing on their own behaviors, or in terms of the communication model, they are keying only on the encoding process. They overlook decoding, which requires the sender to look for message understanding and send appropriate feedback. This lack of feedback (or constant student monitoring) has a negative effect on student learning and performance in the classroom. Because beginning teachers are concerned solely with their own behavior or performance, feedback from students is often ignored. Until beginning teachers are able to attend to decoding student messages and adapt instruction based on student feedback, classroom management and discipline problems will continue. The example in the case study on the next page may be familiar to you.

Natalie probably felt communication anxiety in communicating to a large group; thus, she eliminated a very important phase of the lesson cycle: modeling and guided practice. Natalie is not alone. Many beginning teachers and even some experienced teachers experience stress or anxiety at the prospect of modeling or guiding students, especially if the material and situation are new. Effective modeling and guidance require that teachers understand students and their environment. The teacher must rely on student feedback to constantly monitor how meaningful their instruction is for students and how students can apply new information to immediate environments. If students are unable to see immediate applications, learning is reduced, instruction becomes meaningless, and discipline problems usually increase. Taking a proactive response is thought to be more stressful at first than waiting for problems to occur and trying to solve them retrospectively. In reality, teachers who do not lay the proper framework (i.e., provide not only clear, meaningful instruction based on adjusting instruction based on student feedback

CASE STUDY

Natalie is considered a promising secondary education major. During her early field experiences she assisted Mrs. Langley, one of the most respected math teachers in the district. After three weeks in Mrs. Langley's classroom, Natalie realized that the students who behaved perfectly while Mrs. Langley was teaching were becoming increasingly rude and disruptive during Natalie's lessons. She approached Mrs. Langley with her problem.

Mrs. Langley had also noticed the change in student behavior when Natalie was teaching. Rather than appear to lack confidence in Natalie and offer advice on classroom management, she had decided to wait until Natalie asked for help and had remained quiet until Natalie recognized the difference in student behavior.

Mrs. Langley had observed Natalie teach many times and had discovered early on a very basic communication problem. Like so many beginning teachers, Natalie was focusing only on her own speech and presentational skills and forgot to examine student reactions and feelings to her instruction. After presenting the lesson, Natalie would assign the independent practice without providing the modeling, guidance, and assistance her students needed to thoroughly understand the lesson. Natalie said that she felt uncomfortable speaking to the class as a large group and would rather instruct her students independently, or one-on-one. The problem with Natalie's approach to instruction occurred when everyone seemed confused and needed immediate assistance. Unfortunately, Natalie could not help 20 students at once.

but also modeling and guidance for students) tend to react to problems. Reactive responses produce more communication anxiety and stress than proactive responses. In other words, anticipating potential problems provides you the opportunity to think about and practice your communication strategies rather than be surprised and caught off guard.

After Five Years. After you become comfortable communicating with students in your class, you may discover that communicating with adults is an even greater challenge—and one that is enhanced as school renewal and change occurs. Teachers with five or more years of classroom experience report that communicating with principals, parents, and colleagues produces greater stress than communicating with students.

In the past, traditional schools were places where teachers worked in isolation, rarely discussing or debating important issues that impacted the educational environment of all students. They made decisions that affected only their own classrooms and were largely unaware of what occurred in other classrooms. As a result, left alone and isolated to teach as they pleased, faculty tended to cancel each other's efforts. This type of traditional school still exists, but change is occurring rapidly. As school renewal and change occurs, teachers and principals in restructured schools are discovering that developing new working relationships is not easy and may often be stressful. Teachers are no longer treated as subordinates of administrators, but rather as colleagues, and are expected to participate as equals in making schoolwide decisions. These new expectations may be very stressful for many teachers.

Changing roles in restructured schools require that principals and teachers share decision making; maintain responsibility while giving up individual authority; develop interpersonal communication skills; and build trust through collaborative working relationships among teachers, principals, and parents. Research on the changing roles of teachers and principals concludes that educators in restructured schools are "having difficulty accepting changing roles and responsibilities, fearing the loss of power, lacking skills, lacking trust, and being afraid of the risks" (Duttweiler & Mutchler, 1990, p. 23). As a result, communication anxiety often occurs.

Communication Anxiety Contexts

Let's examine some communication contexts that are responsible for communication anxiety for both beginning and experienced teachers. First, perhaps the most anxiety-producing situation is the performance evaluation. Research has found that teachers prefer principals who are less authoritarian and more democratic during the evaluation cycle (O'Hair & O'Hair, 1992). Often, these teacher preferences are not met. In many cases, principals in traditional schools remain authoritative, unyielding, and insensitive to teachers' communication expectations. Consequently, teachers experience communication anxiety. The subordinate status in which teachers find themselves (especially during performance evaluation) often makes teachers feel intimidated and uncomfortable. In addition, situations in which we feel that much is at stake (such as performance evaluation) increase communication anxiety.

Second, communicating with parents and community members causes communication anxiety. Ideally, teachers should seek parents as partners in the educational process. Many teachers desire and seek parental support and are sad when discovering the unavailability of such support. Some teachers remember a few bad experiences with hostile parents and become anxious during all parent conferences.

Third, teacher communication with other teachers can produce anxiety. It is only recently that teachers have reported increased anxiety when communicating with peers. Competitive environments created by state-mandated systemic change,

Reality Bite

Changing Roles of Principals and Teachers

"My goal this year is to not make a decision. The role (of principal) is much, much more facilitative—working with everyone rather than owning decisions. The day is long gone that the autocratic administrator says This is what we are going to do!"

Mark Taft, Principal, Academy School
Brattleboro, Vermont

What might you expect Mr. Taft's communication style to reflect? As a teacher at Academy School, what might you observe regarding school communication and governance? Describe how the teacher's role is changing.

such as career ladders, merit pay, and curriculum and program alignment, have strained teacher peer communication.

In summary, changing roles of teachers and principals, novelty, lack of feedback, lack of interpersonal skills, communication style, subordinate status, unfamiliarity, past experiences, and evaluation all contribute to communication anxiety. The Coaching section examines ways to manage this anxiety.

Effects of Communication Anxiety

Several effects of communication anxiety are immediately observable. When teachers are afraid to communicate, they unconsciously send negative messages to others. Teachers and principals often view communication-apprehensive teachers as being shy, unprepared, and withdrawn. Students view them as uncaring and uninterested, just as Latisha viewed Tom Roberts as being uninterested in her point of view. Effective teacher verbal and nonverbal communication behaviors that, according to research, impact student learning are reduced greatly. Consequently, teachers who suffer high levels of communication anxiety receive lower performance evaluations and less recognition and are not considered for leadership positions in the school. As school renewal continues to occur and traditional schools become the exception rather than the norm, teachers who suffer high levels of communication anxiety and prefer isolation to collaboration may not fit into the restructured democratic school environment. These teachers may need to seek career alternatives outside the education discipline.

COACHING

It is important to remember that being nervous or anxious in certain situations is perfectly normal and is often useful if channeled properly. Research supports three successful methods for managing and reducing communication anxiety: cognitive restructuring, systematic desensitization, and participant modeling. It is difficult to change behavior that has existed for many years. Careful attention to reflection, modeling, and coaching is needed in order to alter how we think about stressful situations and produce meaningful changes. Cooperating teachers and university supervisors are valuable resources in helping you identify and reduce communication anxiety.

Coaching 2.10 Cognitive Restructuring

Cognitive restructuring (CR) focuses on the mental process involved in an individual's anxiety and has been very effective in both public speaking situations and interpersonal situations. In examining thought processes before, during, and after a stressful situation, research indicates that people constantly process negative self-statements (labels) (Krayer, O'Hair, & O'Hair, 1984). For example, a parent requests a conference with a teacher. The teacher begins by thinking, "This parent believes that I am not doing all that I can to help Johnny" or "Johnny's dad thinks that I'm a poor teacher." The constant barrage of negative self-statements produces communication anxiety. These self-statements involve three factors:

1. Anxious teachers prelabel stressful speaking situations and the corresponding behavior associated with them.
2. The label becomes reality and the corresponding behaviors are reinforced.
3. Teachers are inclined to continue to behave according to these labels.

CR helps beginning teachers reduce communication apprehension by following these simple steps:

1. **Self-Awareness:** Become cognizant of the negative statements you make to yourself before, during, and after a stressful communication event, and recognize the destructive nature of negative self-statements.
2. **Replacement Strategy:** Replace negative self-statements with positive, realistic self-statements called coping statements. The two types of coping statements are
   a. *task statements,* which emphasize immediate ways to calm down that are within the individual's ability (e.g., slow down; breathe deeper; pause); and

    b. *context statements,* which emphasize the nonstressful aspects of the situation ("I'm doing better than last time. She liked my example.").

3. **Reinforcement:** Beginning teachers need lots of practice in identifying and reducing negative self-statements and in producing task and context coping statements. Cooperating teachers and university supervisors may serve as reinforcers by encouraging beginning teachers to develop coping statements.

An excellent tool to use for reinforcement and reflection purposes is the Teacher Communication Log (Figure 2.2). In order to complete each log entry, you must focus on a communication situation by examining feelings before, during, and after the stressful event. In addition, you are responsible for generating coping statements (both task and context) before, during, and after the event.

To make the most of CR, you must commit some time to practice this method of anxiety reduction. Try keeping a Teacher Communication Log for one week. Begin your log by making five copies of Figure 2.3 and placing them in a folder or binder. Choose one situation each day to enter in your log. After one week with five entries, share your experiences with your cooperating teacher and university supervisor. Both may choose to join you in keeping a log. CR works best if used consistently for four to six weeks or until the process of replacing negative self-statements with coping statements is internalized and applied automatically to stressful communication events. Once your level of self-awareness is increased, you will discover many situations to include in your log.

Coaching 2.11 Systematic Desensitization

Before you can control anxiety, you must first understand and experience complete relaxation. Systematic desensitization (SD) is a relaxation process designed to calm you during stressful communication events. It increases your ability to physically control nervousness or tension and provides a way of imposing a state of complete relaxation during stressful events. SD utilizes mock and imaginary situations to help you learn new responses to control stress. The intent is that these newly learned responses will carry over to real situations. Remember, unlearning destructive, conditioned responses to stress is difficult and requires deep individual commitment. O'Hair and Friedrich (1992) provide a step-by-step process for using SD:

1. Assume a relaxed position.
2. Take several deep breaths.
3. Become as relaxed as possible. Focus on this feeling and remember for future reference.
4. Conduct progressive relaxation in the following manner:
   a. Select a muscle group (legs, neck, shoulders),
   b. tense the muscles and hold for 2 seconds,

Situational Description:

Two boys in my fifth period class constantly disrupt class.

Negative Self-Statement	**Coping Statement**

Before I dread seeing Sean and Michael

During I am losing my temper. I hate being out-of-control.

After I'm not a very good teacher if I can't manage two 8th graders.

Context I'll try a new approach today.

Task Take a deep breath, smile, and greet all students

Context Other students are on task

Task Slow down, relax, and then speak.

Context I'm beginning to understand and reach them.

Task Relax. Don't expect too much in one day. Be patient

Figure 2.2 Sample Teacher Communication Log

Situational Description:

_____

_____

Negative Self-Statement

Before _____

_____

During _____

_____

After _____

_____

Coping Statement

Context _____

_____

Task _____

_____

Context _____

_____

Task _____

_____

Context _____

_____

Task _____

_____

Figure 2.3 **Teacher Communication Log**

      c. relax the muscles, and

      d. concentrate on the relaxed state you experience.

5. Go through all of the basic muscle groups to the point where you are completely relaxed.

6. After complete relaxation has been achieved, envision a pleasant scene (mountains, beach, party, etc.) and associate the relaxation with the image.

7. Concentrate on a speaking situation that is not anxiety producing and relate this to your relaxation.

8. Progressively think of different speaking situations that cause anxiety.

   a. Start with ones that cause mild anxiety (talking to a parent; making a point in a discussion); then,

   b. think of increasingly anxious speaking situations* (confronting your cooperating teacher on disagreement; discussing your performance evaluation with your university supervisor; making a presentation to a team of teachers).

9. In each case, relate the relaxation you felt earlier with the scene you are envisioning.

10. If anxiety is felt during any of the images, return to the pleasant scene and take deep breaths. Tense and relax affected muscles if necessary.

11. Finally, return to the original relaxed state through deep breathing and imaging pleasant scenes.

SD is a technique that beginning teachers can use to reduce communication anxiety. It not only allows you to relax before the stressful situation (deep breathing and muscle relaxation), but provides a frame of reference for assessing and evaluating the situation. Reflecting on the situation allows you to reduce tension and change your performance for the next similar situation.

Coaching 2.12 Participant Modeling

Participant modeling (PM) may best be described as role-playing. However, PM involves more than just playing a role. The role must reflect real-world experiences for the participants. PM focuses on the dialogue that occurs following each role-playing activity. This dialogue is designed to encourage reflectivity and analysis, identify strengths and weaknesses, and provide a path for future improvement. The principles of PM are the following:

1. Select realistic school situations that produce communication anxiety.

2. Role-play the situation in which you experience communication apprehension. Ask your cooperating teacher or university supervisor

*Your cooperating teacher may assist you in developing a list of increasingly anxious teaching situations.

to serve as your coach and to assume the role of the person with whom you experience communication apprehension. (This person could be a principal, parent, teacher, student, custodian, etc.) Remember to role-play the situation without prior discussion. Handle it as you have in the past or as you would probably handle a situation not yet encountered.

3. Upon completion, discuss the situation and the communication strategies used. Focus on your strengths, and outline exact ways to improve.

4. Once you have developed a complete outline of strategies for improvement, switch roles (the coach becomes the teacher and you assume the role of the other person). This allows you to witness the outlined strategies in action. Your coach (cooperating teacher or university supervisor) serves as a mentor and models effective strategies. Hopefully, you will not only see effective strategies but will also develop an understanding of how the other person may feel in the situation (i.e., understand different frames of reference).

5. Discuss the role reversal.

Coaches and beginning teachers are encouraged to apply the principles of PM to the following situations, which were selected based on case studies that identify occupational stressors for beginning teachers.

Situation 1: I have one student who continually acts defiant in class. He uses back-talk to undermine my authority and control. I dread third period each day because I know that I will be confronted by him. He seems to want an audience and to make me look bad in front of the class. I have tried threats, punishments, and rewards, but the results have been short-term at best. I continue to experience frustration when communicating with him.

Situation 2: I need help with my fifth grade class. The students in that class have a wide range of ability levels; consequently, I invariably bore some students while losing others. The teacher next door has students very similar to mine and appears to be successful with them. Without appearing insecure, I would like to find out what she is doing that works so well. I don't want the reputation of being incompetent or unprepared. How can I seek help without looking helpless?

Situation 3: Freddy, in my fourth period, is failing my class (and other classes, according to lounge talk). Other teachers have commented on his family life and how hostile his father can be in parent–teacher conferences. The father's attitude reflects the belief that the school is responsible for Freddy's achievement, and if Freddy is failing, it must be the school's fault, namely the teacher. I have just found a note in my box that Freddy's father has requested a meeting with me. How can I ensure a productive parent conference and reduce my anxiety over having to communicate with this man?

REFLECTION

Reflecting 2.13 Communication Anxiety and the
Case of the Reluctant Teacher Communicator

Reflect back to the Case of the Reluctant Teacher Communicator and analyze Tom Roberts's anxiety when Maria Martinez entered his classroom. Discuss ways to reduce his anxiety. If you were Tom, or found yourself in a similar situation, what would you do to reduce your anxiety? Be specific.

Effective communication requires that we monitor, manage, and reduce communication anxiety. At one time or another, we have all experienced it, but successful teachers learn how to manage it while working to reduce or eliminate it. Some anxiety is based on the novelty of the situation alone, and as the novelty wears off, so does the apprehension. Other experiences, however, require a conscious effort on the teacher's part to reduce communication apprehension. Cognitive restructuring, systematic desensitization, and participant modeling serve as mechanisms to help the beginning teacher successfully reduce communication apprehension and focus on effective communication.

CONCLUSION

As educators are involved in school change and renewal, teachers and principals in restructured schools tell us that communication is the key to success. Without effective communication, school will remain marginal and fail to meet the needs of students and their parents. The communicator role encourages beginning teachers to become aware of the basic communication process, to carefully examine the communication styles and the barriers to successful communication, and to adopt flexible communication styles. Special attention is focused on the beginning teacher's feelings of communication anxiety in the school environment. In quest of communication competency, awareness alone is not enough. Beginning teachers must internalize, experience, adapt, and reflect on the concepts and skills demonstrated in the communicator role.

Recommended Readings

Burgoon, J. K., Buller, D. B., & Woodall, W. G. (1989). *Nonverbal communication: The unspoken dialogue.* New York: Harper and Row.

Goss, B., & O'Hair, D. (1988). *Communicating in interpersonal relationships.* New York: Macmillan.

Hamilton, C., & Parker, C. (1993). *Communicating for results: A guide for business and the professions.* (4th ed.). Belmont, CA: Wadsworth.

Himstreet, W. C., Baty, W. M., & Lehman, C. M. (1993). *Business communication: Principles and methods.* (10th ed.). Belmont, CA: Wadsworth.

O'Hair, D., & Friedrich, G. (1992). *Strategic communication for business and the professions.* Boston: Houghton Mifflin.

O'Hair, D., O'Rourke, J., & O'Hair, M. J. (in press). *HarperCollins' handbook for business communication.* New York: HarperCollins.

O'Hair, M. J., & Wright, R. (1990). Application of communication strategies in alleviating teacher stress. In D. O'Hair and G. Kreps (eds.), *Applied communication and research.* Hillsdale, NJ: Erlbaum.

References

Berlo, D. (1960). *The process of communication.* New York: Holt, Rinehart and Winston.

Bowen, W. (1981). How to regain our competitive edge. *Fortune, 103,* 74–90.

Duttweiler, P. C., & Mutchler, S. E. (1990). *Organizing the educational system for excellence: Harnessing the energy of people.* Philadelphia: Research for Better Schools.

Hamilton, C., & Parker, C. (1993). *Communicating for results: A guide for business and the professions.* (4th ed.). Belmont, CA: Wadsworth.

Hatfield, F. C. (1972). Effect of prior experience, access to information and level of performance on individual and group performance ratings. *Perceptual and Motor Skills, 35,* 19–26.

Lewis, C. (1973). Clear interpersonal communication. In J. Stewart (ed.), *Bridges not halls: A book about interpersonal communication.* New York: Random House.

O'Hair, D., & Friedrich, G. (1992). *Strategic communication for business and the professions.* Boston: Houghton Mifflin.

O'Hair, M. J., & O'Hair, D. (1992). A model of strategic principal communication during performance evaluations. *Journal of Research for School Executives, 2,* 13–22.

O'Hair, M. J., & Ropo, E. (1994). Unspoken messages: Understanding diversity in education requires emphasis on nonverbal communication. *Teacher Education Quarterly, 21* (3), 91–112.

Chapter 3

The Motivator Role

Chapter Objectives

After completing this chapter, you will be able to

- synthesize key components of student motivation.
- identify unsatisfied needs of students and target motivational strategies to meet those needs.
- develop and implement motivational strategies designed to increase student participation.
- assess teacher stress and burnout.
- demonstrate techniques that reduce teacher stress and increase personal motivation.
- analyze the Case of the Unmotivating Teacher and apply specific strategies to increase student motivation.

*T*hroughout the three competencies in this chapter, you will have the opportunity to identify more specifically the motivational problems facing Kathy Westin and her students. During the Reflection stage in each competency you will be asked to analyze her problem in greater depth.

Motivating students in the twenty-first century may prove to be a challenge for teachers and administrators. After surviving the first waves of school reforms of the 1980s and early 1990s, schools, for the most part, have changed very little. Real and meaningful change requires time. Whereas schools remain essentially the same, students have changed drastically from ten or even five years ago. Change factors involve, to a great extent, an increase in single-parent homes, minority–majority communities, AIDS, teenage pregnancy, teenage crime, poverty, and child abuse. Understanding and motivating young people today requires more than the old bag-of-tricks approach used by teachers in the past.

Case of the Unmotivating Teacher

Kathy Westin is a new teacher in the Brickwall School District, a large urban school district in the Midwest. She is assigned to David Corbin, an eighth-grade history teacher, who will serve as her mentor during her first teaching year. True to the middle school concept, they will serve on a team of teachers. Although she and Mr. Corbin teach different subjects, both teach the same group of students throughout the year. Kathy's assignment includes three basic English and two reading enhancement classes.

A recent graduate of Ivory Tech University, Kathy completed her student teaching assignment in a wealthy suburban school district only six miles from her hometown. She felt very fortunate to be assigned Mrs. Harvey, a highly successful middle school English teacher, as her supervising teacher. During student teaching, Kathy was allowed to incorporate many new instructional practices with her eighth-grade honors students, and she experienced few discipline or motivational problems. She spent her summer developing new and exciting instructional materials for her new assignment at Brickwall.

After inservice and the first week of school, Kathy decided that she had a problem. First, the students in her classes did not behave and respond like those she had become accustomed to during student teaching. These students appeared bored and preferred to stare out the window or talk to a neighbor rather than participate. Second, her new activities were not well received, and she felt hurt and frustrated after spending hours developing them. Instead of being eager-to-learn students, Brickwall students almost had to be forced to respond. She felt underpaid and unappreciated. She experienced difficulty sleeping, often reliving some negative portion of her school day.

Like many new teachers, Kathy tried to handle the problem herself. She did not want other teachers or Mrs. Lyon, the principal, to know she was having problems. In the third week of school during her morning planning period, Kathy decided to visit David Corbin's second-period class and see how he motivated these hard-to-motivate students. She was amazed at what she observed. Surely these students could not be her students. David's class appeared excited about the lesson. Students raised their hands eagerly to respond to questions and participated cooperatively in small groups. David related his topic of city government to the city of Brickwall, and they were actually discussing specific people and locations in the city.

Descriptions of the nature of schooling give clues to why students appear unmotivated and foster negative attitudes and why teachers feel unproductive and frustrated. Brophy (1987) describes the nature of schooling:

> Schools are set up to benefit students themselves (as well as society at large, of course); the facts that attendance is compulsory and that performance will be graded tend to focus students' attention on the problem of meeting externally imposed demands, rather than on the personal benefits that they might derive from education. Second, teachers confronted with classes of 20–40 students cannot meet each individual student's needs optimally, so many students are frequently bored and many others are frequently confused or frustrated. Third, classrooms are public settings, so failure often means not only personal disappointment but public embarrassment before the peer group. Finally, even in classrooms where fear of failure, test anxiety, and concern about avoiding ambiguity and risk are minimized, both teachers and students can easily settle into familiar routines that become "the daily grind" as the school year progresses. (p. 202)

To be successful in the motivator role, a teacher must understand how to gain student participation through meeting individual needs, reinforcing internal benefits, avoiding personal disappointments and public embarrassment, and breaking boring routines. Key to operating in this role is the premise that one cannot motivate others without first motivating oneself. For many teachers self-motivation requires managing stress and avoiding burnout. Specifically, the motivator role will address the following Competencies:

Competency 1: Understanding Motivation
Competency 2: Gaining Participation
Competency 3: Managing Stress

■ *Competency 1* UNDERSTANDING MOTIVATION

ASSESSMENT

Assessing 3.1 Motivation and the First-Year Teacher

Purpose: To identify and reduce student motivation problems described in the Case of the Unmotivating Teacher.

Time required: 15 minutes

Procedure: After careful analysis of the case study, develop two lists. In the first, compare and contrast Kathy Westin's student teaching experience with her first-year teaching assignment. In the second list, provide suggestions for her based on your own experience and understanding of motivation. Strive for five items per list.

Reality Bite

Showing Interest in Students

Between class changes at my high school, I usually stand by the door to greet the students as they enter the room. I try to make positive comments to them in order to make them feel special. Such comments as, "Hope you're having a good day," "I like your new hair cut," "Great sweater," or "You played an excellent game last night" can make students feel that others care about them. Consequently, they often have a more positive and motivated attitude in the classroom. Sometimes their motivation comes about because the comment was something they needed to hear to brighten their day.

Judy Evrard, High School Math Teacher

EXPERIENCE

Understanding motivation requires examination of the basic concepts involved in the development of motivation. The study of motivation is the search for answers to perplexing questions about human nature.

What Is Motivation?

Motivation is a complex process. Any teacher or parent will concur that motivation is one of the most important prerequisites for learning. The term "motivation" has little practical meaning by itself; the real question becomes *motivation to do what?* (Slavin, 1988). When Kathy Westin describes her classes as lacking in motivation, she means that they are not motivated to learn about English grammar as much as they are motivated to pursue other activities. Good and Brophy (1990) define motivation as a hypothetical construct used to explain the initiation, direction, intensity, and persistence of goal-directed behavior. It incorporates concepts such *as need for achievement* ("I want to do well on the test"); *need for affiliation* ("I want to work with my friends"); *incentives* (reward or punishment) and *habit* ("I never do my homework until after my snack"); *discrepancy* ("How could I, a good person, have cheated on the assignment?"); and *curiosity* ("That seems like a good idea, but I wonder if it will work").

Motivation is simply an individual's willingness to act. A student's willingness to act is dependent upon the action's ability to satisfy some need for the student. Need refers to a physiological or psychological deficiency that makes particular

outcomes appear attractive. Robbins (1984) notes that unsatisfied needs cause tension in the individual, which in turn stimulates drives. These drives generate a behavior search to find particular goals that, if obtained, will satisfy the need and lead to the reduction of tension. This cyclical pattern of motivation occurs within students in our classrooms. Students who have unsatisfied needs are in a state of tension. In order to relieve this tension, students initiate behavior searches to find particular goals that, when obtained, will satisfy the needs and lead to the reduction of tension. The greater the tension, the more activity students need to bring about relief. Therefore, when we see students working hard or not working at some

Reality Bite

Professional Perspective

Students are either intrinsically or extrinsically motivated. Some students accomplish tasks, involve themselves in activities, and strive for perfect scores because it makes them feel good. Other students manage to meet their learning responsibilities because of some type of reward they are given for doing so. Knowing the difference between intrinsic and extrinsic motivation; recognizing and discovering the cues that inform you of a student's motivational preference; using those cues to discover a student's motivational preference; and using all that knowledge to provide appropriate feedback on an individual basis is the key that unlocks a student's incentive for learning.

Cynthia M. Bishop, Communications Instructor

activity, we conclude that they are driven by a desire to achieve some goal that they perceive as having value to them. For example, David Corbin's students were motivated to learn about city government because he made the topic relevant to them by focusing on a familiar locale, their hometown. He increased their tension level, which in turn required more activity or motivation to learn. This motivation was what Kathy Westin observed.

COACHING

When reflecting on knowledge and experiences about motivating young people, it is important to remember not to deal with theory in a vacuum or discuss practice issues in a cookbook format. Rather, the intent should be to integrate theory with practice and avoid separating the two. Cohen, Emrich, and deCharms (1976–1977) point out that acquiring knowledge of motivation is insufficient by itself to promote student motivation. Educators argue that teachers need to develop process skills that would enable them to choose and implement appropriate motivational strategies for individual students (Cohen, 1986; Rohrkemper, 1985). Classroom teachers are asking for pertinent information to answer this question: "What can I do on Monday morning to motivate my students? Don't give me anything that sounds like theory. Just give me techniques and methods that will help me motivate my students." However, giving teachers methods without a sound theoretical background leads to overuse or even misuse of motivational strategies. It is crucial to know why, how, and when to use instructional strategies for motivating students. In this section, we reflect on these issues by relating them to the improvement of students' self-esteem, the breaking away from existing mind sets, going the extra mile, and the creation of a supportive and positive environment.

Read each exercise carefully and reflect on what you know about motivating students based on your experiences, methods classes, and human nature. Ask your cooperating teacher and university supervisor to serve as coaches.

Coaching 3.2 Improving Students' Self-Esteem

After reflecting on general methods to improve students' self-esteem, ask your coaches for assistance in focusing on the following concepts. Utilizing each concept, describe ways to improve the self esteem of students. How might each concept be related to student motivation?

participation	planning
peers	feedback
achievement	caring
culture	assessing

Coaching 3.3 Breaking Away from Existing Mind-Sets

A school district recently adopted a new schoolwide reading program to replace the existing reading programs used by individual teachers. A 30-minute videotape was presented to the teachers, followed by a short discussion of the new program. Most teachers left the inservice confused about the details of the program and concerned about implementation. Because of the ambiguity resulting from insufficient training as well a general reluctance to change, most of the teachers involved in the new program went back to their old ways of teaching reading within the first month of the program's inception. The teachers found it extremely difficult to change their mind-sets on reading programs.

Teachers are no different from 99 percent of the general public when it comes to change. However, effectively motivating students to learn requires teachers to be flexible not only in their teaching styles but also in the instructional methods they use. Flexible teachers tend to have an internal locus of control. Teachers who refuse to change in order to meet student needs will find that many of their students seem unmotivated and reluctant to learn.

Demonstrate your ability to assume an internal, flexible mind-set by completing this exercise: Fold an 8½-×-11-inch piece of paper lengthwise; then fold it twice toward the middle. You should end up with your paper having six sections (see Figure 3.1). Rather than numbering each section 1, 2, 3, 4, 5, and 6, devise a method of numbering using only the numeral 3. For example, to replace number 1,

$\dfrac{3}{3}$	

Figure 3.1   **Sample Form for Breaking Mind-Sets**

you might choose 3/3 because that equals 1. Now decide what equals 2 using only the numeral 3, and so on. This exercise is designed to help you break away from doing things the same old way and to consider new ways of thinking.

Discuss the idea of adopting flexible mind-sets with your coaches. How might breaking a mind-set improve your teaching and motivate students? Ask your coaches for specific examples and illustrations pertaining to increased self-esteem and motivation. Design a new approach to teaching an old concept.

Coaching 3.4 Going the Extra Mile

Going the extra mile may include history teachers dressing as historical characters to gain and focus students' attention on a particular era and English teachers sponsoring Renaissance fairs when studying Shakespeare. The philosophy of going the extra mile should permeate everyday classroom life. We do not suggest that teachers dress in costumes every day but rather that they go the extra mile in determining the needs of students and, once determined, provide each student with the opportunity for success. For example, integrate a factor of success into each assignment for all students. Level or degree of success will vary, but all people have a need to feel personally competent and successful. Consider a typical day in your classroom.

What are some ways to break up the routine or go the extra mile to increase motivation? Ask your coach to help identify ways that create an opportunity for success for all students. What might be involved in implementing the idea? How might you evaluate the outcome? Are you creating an atmosphere of success for all students?

Coaching 3.5 Creating a Supportive and Positive Environment

After reflecting on his college career and his instructors, a college senior recalled one particular professor who influenced him most. His immediate memory of the first day of class with this professor was of walking into class and being addressed by name. Confused, he had quickly looked around at the other students, who also looked surprised that this teacher knew not only their names but something about each of them. It is obvious that this professor took the time to research each student in her class before the first class meeting. This is but one example of creating a positive and supportive environment. As teachers, we must make concerted efforts to produce positive environments, without which student success and motivation are minimal at best.

With the aid of your cooperating teacher, select one of your classes in which to construct a positive environment. Write each student's name on a piece of paper. Beside each name list one or two positive ways to motivate the student. Grouping students with similar motivators is acceptable. Be specific and remember that each successful motivation technique requires a deep understanding of the student's needs and personality. If you have difficulty with certain students, write ways to gather additional information about them.

REFLECTION

Reflecting 3.6 Recommendations for Ms. Westin

We would like you to analyze the Case of the Unmotivating Teacher. Based on personal experience, knowledge, understanding, and coaching, develop an action plan for Kathy Westin. To facilitate the development of an action plan, answer the following questions:

1. Describe specific variables affecting Kathy's classroom situation.
2. How many of her problems are related to the context in which she is teaching?
3. What recommendations would you make to her? Be specific.
4. How many of Kathy's motivational problems are probably faced by other first-year teachers? What could school districts do to help first-year teachers motivate their students?
5. Is Brickwall's mentor teacher program a success? How might it be improved?

Reality Bite

Purpose of Education

Students at Spade High School were asked to participate in "Project Real World," in which they were to undertake a real-world issue and, through problem-solving techniques and special student cadres, look for solutions. They chose to focus their energies on the increasing dropout rate. In a partnership effort with Lubbock Christian University, they developed a video that depicted an Hispanic boy making two different choices and showed the consequences of those choices. The students from Spade High School received national recognition for the making of the movie.

John D. Gatica, Principal at Spade High School

In conclusion, we must evaluate the motivation process by recognizing individual needs, such as those for achievement and affiliation. We must also recognize that other key factors such as incentives, habits, discrepancy, and curiosity affect student motivation. Student motivation is most effective when teachers break away from existing mind-sets, improve student self-esteem as learners, go the extra mile, and create a supportive and positive environment.

Competency 2 GAINING PARTICIPATION

We have already defined motivation in general terms, applying pertinent theory to support choices of particular methods to motivate students. In this section, we will narrow the topic to focus on how to increase participation and activate student learning.

ASSESSMENT

Assessing 3.7 To Participate or Not to Participate

Time required: 10 minutes

Procedure: On a scale of 1 to 5, record how you feel about the following statements:

Strongly Disagree	Disagree	Neutral	Agree	Strongly Agree
1	2	3	4	5

_____ Most of the time my students are too shy and inexperienced to take charge of their own learning.

_____ Allowing students to make major decisions about class policies and instruction is too time consuming.

_____ Many students avoid participating in the discussion because they are not interested in the topic.

_____ Most students aren't ready to handle additional responsibility.

_____ Even with sufficient effort, some students will not succeed.

_____ I avoid asking extremely shy students to speak in front of the class.

_____ Often students lack the prior knowledge and experience needed to participate in a class discussion.

_____ When students are encouraged to participate in the development of class rules and policies, they tend to develop lenient ones.

_____ Often, students become too noisy if encouraged to participate.

_____ Total

Scoring and Interpreting: After totaling your responses to the items above, your score will fall into a range between 9 and 45. Each item represents one of the commonly used reasons, or excuses, for not seeking student participation. Those reasons include lack of interest, lack of skill, choosing the easy way out, shyness or communication apprehension, time constraints, lack of control, lack of cooperation, and the lack of responsibility on the part of students. The more strongly you personally support any of these reasons, the less likely you will increase participation and activate student learning in your classroom. In the Experience section, we suggest some techniques to avoid this faulty reasoning. It is our goal to turn arguments against increased participation into reasons for gaining participation.

EXPERIENCE

Two successful approaches to gaining student participation are discussed and incorporated into the motivator role: Expectancy X Value and responsibility training. Both are successful techniques for improving student participation and, ultimately, student learning.

The Expectancy X Value Model

Before describing specific approaches to gaining participation, we will describe a model that will help you understand the "why" factor for choosing certain approaches. In describing the Expectancy X Value model, Brophy (1987) states, "the effort that people will be willing to expend on a task will be a product of (1) the degree to which they *expect* to be able to perform the task successfully if they apply themselves (and thus the degree to which they expect to receive the rewards that successful performance of the task will bring); and (2) the degree to which they *value* those rewards. Investment of effort is viewed as the product rather than the sum of the expectancy and value factors, because it is assumed that no effort at all will be invested in a task if either factor is missing entirely, no matter how strongly the other factor may be present" (p. 207).

Students do not participate and invest time and effort on tasks if they feel there is little chance for success or if they see little value or purpose in doing the task. Students may seem unresponsive and uninterested in a topic if they feel there is no chance for success or see no real-world value (as applied to their world) in participating. A reasonable conclusion is that teachers need to help their students recognize the value in learning different content areas and to make sure that each student, when appropriate effort is applied, can succeed at the task. Even shy students can improve their participation in class discussions. Teachers must take time to build self concepts of shy students by increasing their expectations of performing the task successfully. This is accomplished in several ways:

1. Pair shy students together when working on presentations. This approach presents an aggressive student from taking over completely and allows some comfort in working together.

2. Give shy students previews of what will be expected the next day in terms of class participation. Often, shy individuals feel more secure if having prepared responses in advance.

3. Strive for small successes in terms of class participation. Best results occur when peers acknowledge correct responses.

Responsibility Training

The second technique we recommend for increasing class participation involves responsibility training. Fred Jones, a clinical psychologist, has been studying student motivation and discipline in effective classrooms for the past 20 years. Jones (1987) maintains that a teacher's duty is to encourage students to become responsible for their own learning. In other words, students must be active participants in learning. Dr. Jones was faced with a situation similar to that of Kathy Westin. He was hired as a consultant by the Los Angeles Unified School District to help teachers work with students who are difficult to motivate and discipline. In the first class he observed, all the children were out of their seats: some were hiding inside the coat closet, others were sitting on top throwing spit wads at those hiding. The teacher, red-faced with embarrassment, stated he would simply wait until every student was seated before beginning class. It occurred to Jones that the teacher could wait until Christmas and still not see the children return to their seats! The children were never seated in that classroom.

After lunch, Jones visited a second classroom. He noted an entirely different climate—an excitement for learning and active participation. Students were raising their hands and responding eagerly to questions. Jones was surprised to recognize many of the students who were in the coat closet earlier in the day. They were now behaving as highly motivated, well-disciplined students. Immediately after class, he approached the teacher and asked her to explain exactly what she was doing and if

Reality Bite

Motivating Activity

Last year I tried an activity that motivated students to learn. It was homecoming week at our school, and the student council was raising money by selling Tootsie Roll Pops. A group of underachieving students tried to escape an algebra lesson by licking Tootsie Roll Pops to see how many licks are necessary to get to the center. As a mathematician, I was delighted with the opportunity to introduce data collection and analysis. The students licked their candies to their hearts' content, and I tied each moment into graphing results, figuring measures of central tendencies, researching other sources that resulted in similar situations, and drawing conclusions. At the end of the activities, the students were amazed at the mathematics they had learned. They also were surprised to find that data collection and analysis is a useful tool that is used every day.

Rhonda Jones, High School Math Teacher

she knew that her students were sitting on the coat closet throwing spit wads earlier in a different class. She looked at him as if he were crazy. When asked specifically how she gained participation with these difficult students, the teacher responded that they had always acted that way in her classroom and could not give Jones any specific techniques she used.

A key element apparent in both classroom situations (David Corbin's and the second teacher Jones observed) is that students have been taught to cooperate, and this cooperation increases positive participation in class. The most important teacher response in training for responsibility involves the answer to the student question, "Why should I cooperate with you?" Jones (1987) outlined three management options for obtaining cooperation: (1) teach well and reward well; (2) nag, threaten, and punish; and (3) lower one's standards and make peace with the fact that cooperation will not be forthcoming. Of course, the first option is preferred. Without the systematic use of incentives, teachers will get cooperation only from those students who feel like giving it; without complete cooperation, teachers will either become punitive or lower their standards. Both result in lower levels of student participation and, ultimately, student learning.

COACHING

O'Hair and Harmon (1990) surveyed over 100 students in grades two through six in terms of what motivates students to participate in class and discovered that similar needs or desires were restated throughout the various grade levels. Analysis of the students' comments on participation, motivation, and learning disclosed the following concerns: incorporating interest, teaching beyond the textbook (making learning relevant), communicating success, and incorporating technology. In addition to discussing the student-generated topics, we will reflect on cooperative learning and cultural awareness as means to gain student participation.

Coaching 3.8 Incorporating Interest

Students surveyed by O'Hair and Harmon (1990) offered many suggestions for creating interest in a subject or lesson; for example, including art or drawing as part of the lesson, increasing subject matter games, and adding additional field trips or guest speakers. These are only a few methods that children are asking teachers to use. We can increase student motivation and learning by using a wide range of strategies that directly incorporate students' interests into the curriculum (Jones & Jones, 1990). The following list is a composite of available methods and is by no means complete. Take some time to brainstorm with your coach and come up with additional interest gainers.

1. Early in the school year, have students build a list of things they would like to learn. This provides you with valuable information regarding both student interests and their prior knowledge in each curriculum area. After completing the lists, students feel excitement about learning based on their input into the learning process. Remember, it is important that you actually *do* some of the things that students list.

2. When beginning a unit, allow students to draw and write about what they wish to learn about. Students enjoy not only creative drawing and writing but sharing their work with the class. Teachers have been criticized in the past for not specifically trying to motivate students as they introduced new learning tasks. Brophy (1987), in one long-term investigation that included over 100 hours of classroom observations, discovered that only nine instances were recorded of teachers specifically trying to motivate students when introducing new material.

3. Create a unit on biographies. Students are asked to choose a person about whom they would like to know more. Students then dress up like the person they have researched and make presentations to the class as that person (Jones & Jones, 1990).

4. Invite guest speakers (including parents) to speak to the class on topics of interest. One interesting example involves an Iowa fifth-grade class that was studying

World War II. The class became interested in the Pacific Ocean crash of a plane carrying World War I flying ace Eddie Rickenbacker and his crew. All were rescued after 21 days at sea. The fifth-graders researched the incident and discovered that four of the five crew members were still alive. They tracked down and invited each man to visit their school. All four men were delighted to come for a reunion. This project, which involved each class member, will be remembered always by the students and the flight crew.

5. Induce curiosity and suspense. Begin a lesson with a riddle or unsolved mystery about the topic to be studied. This produces a need in students to obtain more information.

6. Appear enthusiastic. Through verbal and nonverbal channels, teachers need to project enthusiasm for the topic. Remember, students are very adept at decoding messages sent by the teacher. Enthusiasm breeds enthusiasm.

7. Include subject matter games, videos, and puzzles when appropriate to enhance the topic. It is important for teachers to capitalize on their students' natural interests in games, videos, and puzzles for instructional purposes. Allow students to help create these activities.

Coaching 3.9 Teaching Beyond the Textbook

Many content area reading experts argue that a teacher's responsibility in motivating students involves teaching students to read on, between, and beyond the lines of a textbook. In other words, a teacher's responsibility involves reducing students' uncertainty by helping them to use background knowledge, raise questions, and make predictions about what they will be reading and learning. The teacher must help the students comprehend, process, and analyze new information by connecting it to old information. We will reflect on two strategies that will motivate students to read beyond the lines of a textbook or assignment: creating frames of reference and exploring concepts visually.

Creating Frames of Reference

This strategy refers to activating and building background knowledge in students. More specifically, a frame of reference reflects the schemata that students need to relate new information to existing knowledge. Students need to recognize how new material "fits" into the conceptual frameworks that they already have already established (Vacca & Vacca, 1989). With this in mind, we emphasize motivational strategies involving analogies, graphic organizers, and guided imagery.

Analogies. Analogies are defined as the establishment of a relationship between concepts that are familiar to the student and unfamiliar concepts that are presented by the teacher. For example, students may compare what they already know about snakes to new information concerning different types, habitat, hibernation, and reproduction.

We recommend that you use the following guidelines when preparing analogies:

1. Construct an analogy for difficult-to-understand material only.

2. Devise the analogy so that it reflects the main ideas in the lesson or textbook to be assigned. Make sure that these ideas are prominent and easily identifiable in the analogy.

3. Use real-life incidents, anecdotes, familiar examples, or illustrations to which learners can relate. These devices serve as a basis for comparing or contrasting what learners know already about unfamiliar material.

4. Raise a question or two in the analogy that will engage students in thinking about the upcoming lesson. (Vacca & Vacca, 1989)

Examine the analogy in Figure 3.2. It was designed for an intermediate level study skills lesson on Survey, Question, Read, Recite, and Review (SQ3R). The hamburger serves as a visual image to help students connect new information, SQ3R, to a familiar concept. Ask your coach to describe additional sample analogies.

Graphic Organizers. Graphic organizers are diagrams that organize main and subordinate ideas to be presented in the lessons. Students begin to discover how concepts interrelate and coexist with previous mastered concepts. Graphic organizers should always relate prior knowledge to the new concepts to be learned. The graphic presentation of old material helps to review and reinforce previously learned concepts. In addition, graphic presentations help students develop important links between prior knowledge and new knowledge required for lasting learning to take place. Here are some suggestions on constructing a graphic organizer.

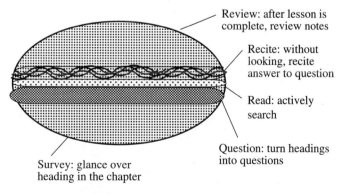

Review: after lesson is complete, review notes

Recite: without looking, recite answer to question

Read: actively search

Question: turn headings into questions

Survey: glance over heading in the chapter

(Begin here and move counterclockwise)

Figure 3.2   **SQ3R Analogy: Building a Hamburger**

1. Analyze the lesson, and list the important concepts or words to be learned.

2. Arrange the list by choosing the word that represents the most inclusive concept. Organize the words that fall under the first concept, those that fall under the second, and so on.

3. Add to the organizer vocabulary list terms that the students will understand.

4. Discuss the learning task. Discussion is the key to success in this step. Encourage students to relate the words they understand to the new words crucial to understanding the new material to be covered.

5. After discussion, modeling, and guided practice with the new material to be learned, both students and teacher evaluate the graphic organizer and review new words in addition to relating additional information where appropriate. This serves as an excellent tool for reviewing lessons and discussing new ideas conceived after the task is completed. See example in Figure 3.3.

Guided Imagery. Guided imagery, or exploring concepts visually, is not new. Few teachers, however, take the time to use this approach to increase student participation. Guided imagery has been used for many different instructional purposes, such as a fear reduction device, memory aid, and method of relaxation. Guided imagery increases motivation by allowing students to visually explore concepts. Samples (1977) recommends guided imagery for

- building an experience base for inquiry, discussion, and group work;
- building self-image;
- exploring and stretching concepts;
- solving and clarifying problems;
- exploring history and the future; and
- exploring other lands and worlds. (p. 189)

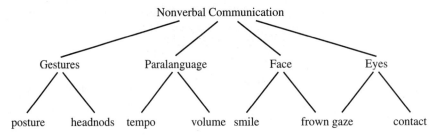

Figure 3.3   **Graphic Organizer**

According to Samples, the teacher begins the imagery process by guiding the students in a daydream; however, the teachers use "words to get into the process—but once there, images take over" (p. 188).

Read the following illustration of guided imagery provided by Vacca and Vacca (1989), then close your eyes and try doing it:

> Close your eyes . . . tell all your muscles to relax. You are entering a space capsule ten minutes before takeoff. Soon you feel it lift off. You look over at your companions and check their reactions. Now you are ready to take a reading of the instrument panel. As you relay the information to ground control, it is eleven minutes into the flight . . . you settle back into your chair and tell your fellow astronauts about your thoughts . . . about what you hope to see when the vehicle lands . . . about what you might touch and hear as you explore the destination. Finally, you drift off to sleep . . . picturing yourself returning to earth . . . seeing once again your friends and relations. You are back where you started. . . . Tell your muscles to move. . . . Open your eyes. (p. 141)

After visualizing the scene, always have students discuss their "trips" either orally or in written form. Discussion helps students understand the feelings and thoughts of others and results in a more thorough understanding of new concepts and situations. Develop a guided imagery to introduce a new topic or concept. Practice the guided imagery on other beginning teachers or family members. What was their reaction to the guided imagery approach? How might you improve?

Analogies, graphic organizers, and guided imagery help students understand difficult material, which in turn improves class participation and motivation to learn. All three techniques relate to students on a personal level, help students develop an ownership in their learning, and model participatory learning while encouraging success.

Coaching 3.10 Communicating Success

It is not enough merely to encourage success in your students. You must communicate success in everything you say and do as a teacher. In the O'Hair and Harmon (1990) survey of second-graders, they discovered that most were motivated by a teacher who "acted and talked nice" to them. Earlier in the chapter we discussed the importance of responsibility training in terms of student participation and learning. Now let's explore a specific communication strategy—Praise, Prompt, and Leave—that helps motivate students to participate while providing success in learning.

Praise, Prompt, and Leave

This strategy was developed by Fred Jones, a clinical psychologist. Jones (1987) bases his approach on the fact that "initial instruction as well as reinstructing through corrective feedback might best be defined as the process of taking students from where they are to where you want them to be *one step at a time*" (p. 49). This strategy was developed for students who do not pay attention or participate during the presentation of the lesson. During independent practice, such students raise their hands for help and look thoroughly confused and helpless. They have been pulling this routine since kindergarten and have always been successful in gaining the teacher's undivided attention, which results in a private mini-lesson just for them. Let's label these students the "dazed and confused." You may be feeling sorry for this group of students and thinking "hurray" for individualized instruction. However, what is really occurring is not individualized instruction but rather "spoon feeding," which results in lazy, unmotivated, irresponsible students. Teachers may begin the year with five "dazed and confused" students and by Christmas notice an additional five. This cycle perpetuates and multiplies itself until the teacher's time is monopolized by "dazed and confused" students. As these students enter middle school and high school, they are labeled "slow learners" and are generally placed in remedial classes. This is unfortunate because they are no less able to learn than any other student; they have simply been conditioned to be dependent on the teacher or, in many cases, on other students. What might we do as teachers to break the "dazed and confused" cycle?

One of the best strategies confirmed by teachers is the Praise, Prompt, and Leave (PP&L) method. Jones (1987) refers to it as positive helping interaction and reminds teachers to "always be brief—10 to 30 seconds on the average—and always positive. In fact, it cannot generate a failure experience" (p. 47). The PP&L method looks relatively simple on paper but is difficult for teachers to put into action without considerable practice. Difficulty occurs because old teaching habits are hard to alter and change. Now, let's go through the steps of the Praise, Prompt, and Leave approach.

Praise. Our notion of giving praise is usually to say something nice to the student; for example, "Johnny, I like your drawing. It's very colorful." In the PP&L model, we must go one step further and tell the student *exactly* what he or she has done right so far. For example, "Johnny, I like your drawing. It is very colorful and describes the main character in the story very well. I can see that the character is running. Who is chasing him? How will you draw the main character's face? Is he happy? sad? afraid? angry?"

The key is remembering to focus on what you want to teach in your praise. It is often difficult for teachers to focus on what is right rather than what is wrong. When we look at a half-filled bottle of water do we say that it is half-empty or half-full? It is so easy to spot the student's error first and focus only on the problem. This type of feedback is negative and works to lower a student's self-confidence; hence, producing a dazed and confused, unwilling-to-take-a-risk student. The most logical reaction would be to review what the student has done right just before the error (from now on let's call the error "new learning"). In other words, if a student missed step 5 on a math problem, then reviewing steps 3 and 4 would be the best starting point for new learning. After praise, which consists of review and focus, the teacher will give the student a prompt.

Prompt. A prompt is a clear, concise verbal statement that tells the student exactly what to do next. Give the student the next step only in solving the equation or completing the assignment. Many teachers feel that it is better to quickly describe all the remaining steps. This tends to be confusing and denies the student the opportunity for independent success with the remainder of the problem. To be an effective prompter, the teacher must remember to Keep It Short and Simple (KISS) and to communicate clear and concise directions.

Leave. Probably the most difficult step involves leaving the student alone to complete the work. Teachers would rather look over the student's shoulder "just to be sure" the student understands. Those who refuse to leave the student often end up reteaching the entire lesson. Jones (1987) describes the interaction this way: The teacher says to himself or herself, "I need to help Bill, and I feel good that I was able to give him the help he needed." Bill, in contrast, may say to himself, "I *still* can't do this, even though the teacher helped me. I really must be *dumb*." The Praise, Prompt, and Leave strategy requires most teachers to break existing mind-sets and begin developing motivated, responsible students.

With your coach's assistance, try the PP&L strategy. First, role-play a realistic situation involving a student who lacks motivation and relies solely on the teacher for help. Discuss the role-playing. Next, try the same strategy with a student in one of your classes. Were you effective in encouraging the student to become more self-reliant and to gain active rather than passive class participation? Which step of the PP&L strategy is the most difficult for you to implement? Which is easiest? Why do you think so?

Coaching 3.11 Incorporating Technology

Most of our students will grow up with technology in their homes. They have been around advanced technology since birth, and most thrive on using some facet of it daily. They not only watch regular television programs but use the TV for many other purposes, such as games, movies, and recording. Most children begin using a computer as early as kindergarten and continue throughout school. Several studies have shown that individuals achieve mastery of desired objectives 25 to 40 percent faster with computer-based training than with traditional instructor-led training programs (Madlin, 1987; Wehr, 1988).

In addition to computer-based training, an exciting and revolutionary new technology called laser videodisc is available. This technology has actually been around since 1978 when MCA Disco Vision made it available to the public. Videodiscs, in contrast to 16mm films, are easy to play, never need rewinding or maintenance, and do not wear out. Best of all, the total cost of a videodisc player and monitor is roughly equal to the price of a 16mm film projector (Van Horn, 1987). Videodisc technology has opened up to education a whole new world called image processing. "Image processing promises to be to education what data processing is to business" (p. 697). Imagine being able to talk to President Lincoln about the Civil War or maneuver the Amazon in a boat while observing the jungle.

What is the problem then? It appears that children like new technology and are motivated to participate by using advanced technology in the classroom. The children are not the problem. A major barrier to computer-based training, laser videodiscs, and image processing in public school classrooms involves preservice and inservice for teachers and administrators. Let's reflect on this training barrier along with the positive features of computer-based training that all teachers must keep in mind when seeking to increase class participation and interest.

Recently, a professor at a large southwest university teaching a senior-level reading practicum course for elementary majors asked her students to complete a diagnostic reading report on the elementary child that they had been tutoring through the semester. She asked her students to use a computer. The purpose behind the assignment was not to teach students to use a computer but rather to have the reports on disc to provide quick access if the child returned to the center for future tutoring. The professor assumed incorrectly that most education majors in the 1990s were computer literate. This assignment was viewed by the elementary majors as the most difficult and stressful hurdle faced in their college careers. The professor provided training sessions for those in need; however, the majority opted for paying another student (usually from outside the college of education) to do the word processing required to complete the assignment. When asked on course evaluations if they would ever use the computers in their own classrooms, the majority responded emphatically "no." One student stated that if she had known that learning to use a computer was prerequisite to being an effective teacher, then she would never have entered the profession.

We in education have known for several years that our older teachers feel uncomfortable using computers in the classroom. Studies have found that older teachers refuse to use technology in any form in their jobs and consequently report higher levels of stress due to the increasing paperwork, often referred to as job overload (O'Hair & Bastian, 1993). Educators thought the problem would resolve itself as older teachers retired and younger, computer literate teachers replaced them. However, many of our younger teachers appear to be just as computer apprehensive as their older colleagues.

If teachers are to become computer literate and to use computers in the classroom, they must be convinced of the advantages for students and themselves, such as these:

1. Students progress at their own pace without being held back by slower class members.

2. Students have the capability of performing simulated practice of the objectives as many times as is necessary to gain mastery.

3. Learning can be designed to force mastery before the learner may progress to more difficult material. This both motivates and keeps students' from getting in over their head.

4. Slower learners are not embarrassed by their performance in front of others.

5. Faster learners do not need to wait for the rest of the class to catch up. They can skip modules they already know.

6. Deficiencies are automatically diagnosed, and remediation is provided as needed.

7. In networked systems, software can be updated as soon as new information relevant to the training becomes available. This is a key element in computer-based training (CBT) programs (Granger, 1989; Huber & Gay, 1985; Madlin, 1987; Schwade, 1985; Wehr, 1988).

After discussing the advantages that computers bring regarding motivation and increased participation, reflect on what preservice and inservice teachers may do to improve computer literacy in the teaching profession. Are you computer literate?

Perhaps the first step is to have access to a computer, whether personally owned, rented, or borrowed. Having your own computer helps make the computer instruction offered at the university more meaningful. Rather than simply completing unrelated assignments in a required educational technology class, it makes more sense to use a computer daily for word processing needs and spreadsheets for grading and accounting purposes. What else could you do to become computer literate? First, with the aid of your coach, develop an action plan that incorporates the use of technology in the classroom. Second, survey beginning and veteran teachers regarding their use of technology in the classroom. Ask for their input concerning your action plan. Evaluate their input. Are there any differences between beginning and veteran teachers' attitudes about using technology?

Coaching 3.12 Encouraging Cooperative Learning and Cultural Awareness

As teachers become more and more aware of students' individual learning styles, they discover that children are individuals and learn differently. When we ask students which classes they like most, we usually hear PE, band, art, journalism, debate, etc. Do you recognize a pattern? In most of those classes, students are encouraged to work cooperatively to accomplish objectives. Glasser (1990), among others, has described the importance of restructuring our schools so that cooperative learning can take place in *all* classrooms. Roy Smith, a junior high English teacher in Massachusetts with 22 years of experience, describes cooperative learning as "placing the responsibility for learning where it belongs: on the students. Second, it increases achievement and improves students' attitudes toward school, toward learning, and toward classmates. Third, it makes both teaching and learning more fun. . . . A workshop (ten years ago) on cooperative learning changed my entire approach to teaching; I think it even kept me from leaving the profession"

(p. 663). Students participating in a cooperative learning environment are enthusiastic and motivated participants in learning.

Cooperative learning takes on new meaning when we examine multicultural learning issues. *Culture* refers to the ways in which different groups of people organize their daily lives within national or ethnic groups, urban neighborhoods, companies and professions, and other settings (Trachtenberg, 1990). Like it or not, cultural diversity is synonymous to national survival. Minority subcultures such as Hispanics and African-Americans are becoming the majority in many states. Educators must renew the commitment on which this country was founded—to provide quality education for *all* students. For years we have ignored special learning needs of minorities. Trachtenberg states that "white middle-class Americans can empathize with a resident of Barcelona—especially if he or she is a creator or consumer of high culture—more easily than they can empathize with a U. S. citizen whose grandparents emigrated from Mexico or Cuba" (p. 611). Unless teachers, administrators, and parents strive harder to make a difference in the education that minorities are receiving, our international rivals may be correct in believing that Americans are not prepared to compete in the global marketplace. How can teachers make a difference? They are the spark that can either ignite the flame or extinguish the love of learning for many minorities. Teachers can use cooperative learning and cultural awareness to make a difference!

Let's reflect on the collective instructional model and examine how this approach increases participation and motivation for all children. Students working collectively in small groups discover the following advantages. Try to think of others.

1. Greater pool of knowledge and information than when working alone.
2. Greater number of approaches to a problem. Individuals may get into ruts in their thinking, but group members can avoid this by multiple inputs.
3. Participation in problem-solving increases acceptance of the solution. Members tend to support decisions arrived at collectively.
4. Better comprehension and working knowledge of the problem.
5. Groups make riskier decisions than do individuals. This is known as the "risky-shift phenomenon."

Although the advantages to group work generally outweigh the disadvantages, it is important to recognize some of the liabilities:

1. **Social pressure.** Group members want to be accepted and may not present contradictory information if the leader(s) have already decided on a solution. This phenomenon is "GroupThink" (Janis, 1972), which refers to selecting a solution without exploring all possible alternatives. Rather than argue for the best alternative, group

members may support inferior alternatives in order to be perceived positively by others in the group.

2. **Individual domination.** A group member may dominate the discussion, making it difficult to accomplish the task.

3. **Time.** Group decisions generally take longer than individual decisions.

Can you or your coach think of any other disadvantages of cooperative learning? How might these disadvantages be turned into advantages? Consider ways to implement cooperative learning in your classroom. Develop an action plan to encourage cooperative learning.

Here are some suggestions for enacting cooperative learning in your classroom. Generate additional ideas with your coach. Discuss the implementation of each suggestion.

1. Help students become aware of the need for cooperative communication skills (sharing, recognizing others' ideas as important, listening without interrupting others, brainstorming, etc.) and gain a clear understanding of each skill. Describe the three patterns for interacting: cooperation, competition, and independent work. Relate each new cooperative learning behavior to the skills of reading, writing, speaking, listening, and thinking (Smith, 1987).

2. Always demonstrate and model the procedures you wish your students to follow in group work. Without teacher and student training, cooperative learning can result in a nightmare for the teacher. As a consequence, the teacher will decide the approach failed and never use cooperative learning again. (See the basic problem-solving procedure in Chapter 2, Coaching 2.4, and the Appendix.)

3. Begin by having your students use brainstorming techniques. Suggested guidelines include (a) setting a time limit (usually 5–10 minutes); (b) designating a student as group recorder (may also use a tape recorder); (c) generating as many ideas as possible within the time limit; and (d) avoiding evaluation, criticism, and all forms of judgment (good or bad) until time is up. The purpose behind this exercise is to give students situations in which they can practice cooperative learning skills. Remember, it is important that you give each student feedback on his or her performance of the skill. Through this feedback students are better able to fine-tune and develop social skills. Continually remind students that "*None* of us is as smart as *all* of us."

When students were asked to share their views of cooperative learning, the most-mentioned advantage was the opportunity it provides for sharing ideas and seeing material from a different point of view. One ninth-grader stated that "Group learning not only allows me to share something that no one else may have thought of, but I also get two or three times as many ideas as I started out with on my own" (Smith, 1987, p. 666).

REFLECTION

Reflecting 3.13 Teacher Interview

Interview a teacher that you believe has excellent student participation (such as David Corbin or Dr. Jones's afternoon teacher). Ask the teacher what strategies he or she uses to increase student participation in class. Make your own form to reflect the model shown in Figure 3.4, and record responses in the appropriate boxes. If unsure where to place a comment, begin a separate box. If the teacher you choose does not provide information for one or more of the boxes, ask if she or he feels it is important to increase participation. Discuss the results of your interview with other beginning teachers.

Reflecting 3.14 Gaining Participation and the Case of the Unmotivating Teacher

After carefully examining the strategies for gaining student participation that are provided by this textbook, your cooperating teacher, your university supervisor, and/or other beginning teachers, analyze Kathy Westin's situation and offer her suggestions for improving student participation. Be specific and conclusive.

Effective teachers use a variety of methods and strategies to increase student participation. Exerting the effort required to use different strategies effectively suggests that the teacher is motivated and concerned about student learning. Unless the teacher is highly motivated to impact learning, student motivation and participation are impossible. In the next Competency, we will discuss teacher stress and burnout and how, if left unchecked, it will ultimately reduce student motivation and achievement.

■ *Competency 3* MANAGING STRESS

The final competency of the motivator role is managing stress. In order to successfully motivate others, you must first motivate yourself. Motivating yourself may be hindered by negative stressors in your professional as well as personal life. Teaching is rapidly becoming one of the most, if not *the most,* stressful occupations in the United States. Teachers surveyed report approximately twice the stress level experienced by other professionals; as a result, somewhere between 10 and 20 percent of all teachers have reached the burnout level (Farber, 1984; Litt & Turk, 1985). Burn-

Incorporating Interest	Teaching Beyond the Textbook
Communicating Success	Incorporating Technology
Cooperative Learning	Cultural Awareness

Figure 3.4   **Gaining Participation**

out is extremely difficult to recover from and is linked to low pupil–teacher rapport (Petrusich, 1966), pupil anxiety (Doyal & Forsyth, 1973), poor classroom management (Kaiser & Polczynski, 1982), and low pupil achievement (Forman, 1982).

ASSESSMENT

Before discussing how to minimize or avoid harmful stress, let's assess your current personal stress level using the Social Readjustment Rating Scale (Table 3.1).

Assessing 3.15 Measuring Personal Stress

Purpose: To determine your personal stress level at this time. Keep in mind that in a month or a year from now your score and ability to cope with stress may change.

Time required: 30 minutes

Procedure: Check each item in Table 3.1 that applies to you. Add up the numbers you checked to determine your total score.

Table 3.1 **The Social Readjustment Rating Scale**

Rank	Event	Value	Score
1.	Death of a spouse	100	_____
2.	Divorce	73	_____
3.	Marital separation	65	_____
4.	Jail term	63	_____
5.	Death of a close family member	63	_____
6.	Personal injury or illness	53	_____
7.	Marriage	50	_____
8.	Fired from work	47	_____
9.	Marital reconciliation	45	_____
10.	Retirement	45	_____
11.	Change in family member's health	44	_____
12.	Pregnancy	40	_____
13.	Sex difficulties	39	_____
14.	Gaining a new family member (birth adoption older child moving back)	39	_____
15.	Business readjustment (merger, bankruptcy, reorganization)	39	_____
16.	Change in financial status (much worse off or much better off)	38	_____
17.	Death of a close friend	37	_____
18.	Change to different line of work	36	_____
19.	Change in number of marital arguments	35	_____
20.	Taking on a mortgage or loan for a major purchase (home, business, etc.)	31	_____
21.	Foreclosure of mortgage or loan	30	_____
22.	Change in work responsibilities (promotion, demotion, etc.)	29	_____
23.	Son or daughter leaving home	29	_____
24.	Trouble with in-laws	29	_____
25.	Outstanding personal achievement	28	_____
26.	Spouse begins or stops work	26	_____
27.	Starting or finishing school	26	_____
28.	Change in living conditions (remodeling, building a new home)	25	_____
29.	Revision of personal habits (dress, manners, friendships)	24	_____

Table 3.1 **The Social Readjustment Rating Scale (continued)**

Rank	Event	Value	Score
30.	Trouble with boss	23	_____
31.	Change in work hours, conditions	20	_____
32.	Change in residence	20	_____
33.	Change in schools	20	_____
34.	Change in recreational habits	19	_____
35.	Change in church activities (much more or much less than usual)	19	_____
36.	Change in social activities	18	_____
37.	Taking on a mortgage or a loan for a lesser purchase (car, TV, stereo)	17	_____
38.	Change in sleeping habits	16	_____
39.	Change in number of family gatherings	15	_____
40.	Change in eating habits	15	_____
41.	Vacation	13	_____
42.	Christmas season	12	_____
43.	Minor violation of the law (traffic, tickets, jaywalking, etc.)	11	_____
		TOTAL	_____

Source: Minor revisions made of the original Social Readjustment Rating Scale developed by Holmes and Rahne, 1967. *Journal of Pscyosomatic Research, 2,* 213–218.

Scoring and Interpretation

Score of less than 150:   37 percent chance of illness during next two years.
Score of 150 to 300:   51 percent chance of illness during next two years.
Score of 300 or more: 80 percent chance of illness during next two years.

1. Whereas we often associate stress with major life tragedies, such as the death of a spouse or being fired, most people do not associate stress with positive life events, such as marriage, outstanding personal achievement, or holidays. How many of the items that you checked on the scale are positive events in your life? Why might these events be stressful?

2. As you examine closely the items you checked, try to remember a coping mechanism you used with each. How successful would you rate your coping skills in minimizing stress?

3. If you checked an item not work related, did you think about the item while at school? If so, did your feelings concerning the item affect your work performance? Describe.

In the next section, we will discuss ways to reduce harmful stress. Teachers suffering from burnout, the ultimate result of stress, are hurting not only themselves but also students. Can beginning teachers suffer from burnout? If so, what options are available for them?

EXPERIENCE

Teacher stress is multidimensional in that three components interact to produce above-normal stress levels in both beginning and veteran teachers: environmental, personal, and organizational stressors. Each component is described briefly, but our focus centers on organizational factors that contribute to teacher stress. In the Coaching and Reflecting sections, you will identify organizational stressors and develop coping strategies for stress reduction.

Environmental Stressors

Environmental stressors are conditions outside the classroom and school setting that produce stress for teachers. Prime examples include changing demographics (e.g., single parenting, divorce rates, crime and violence, declining rural and increasing urban settings); financial considerations (e.g., decreasing purchasing power); and negative public attitudes about education (e.g., declining parent and community support, demand for accountability, lack of trust). During the last decade, the lack of public goodwill toward the teaching profession has significantly increased teacher stress.

Personal Stressors

Personal stressors involve individual characteristics, personality, and ideology factors. We do not all respond to specific events in the same way. What causes great amounts of stress for some may be only a minor cause of stress for others. Researchers have published some interesting findings concerning the following personal factors.

Age. Teachers age 31 to 44 report higher levels of stress than teachers under 30 or over 45. Perhaps one viable explanation is that individuals in the 31-to-44 age range experience major problems involved with teenage children, career choice, and marriage (Eskridge & Coker, 1985).

Gender. Both males and females report high stress levels; however, the origins for stress appear different. Females report high levels of stress regarding *role conflicts* (pressures to continue performing functions that society has placed on women, such as cleaning house, preparing meals, and entertaining guests) and *male-dominated administration* (especially in secondary schools and in administration, i.e., superintendent). In general, high stress levels among males are the result of basic authoritarian orientation. Males are reported to be more authoritarian in their leadership styles than their female counterparts, and authoritarian teachers and principals are characterized as experiencing more stress and tension than nonauthoritarian teachers and principals (Calabrese & Anderson, 1986; Harris, Halpin, & Halpin, 1985; O'Hair & O'Hair, 1992).

Experience. Beginning teachers report greater stress levels than experienced teachers. The greatest stressor for beginning teachers involves classroom management (Eskridge & Coker, 1985).

Professional Preparation. Beginning teachers who completed teacher education programs that emphasized early field experiences report lower stress levels than teachers completing programs void of early field experiences (O'Hair & Housner, 1989).

Student Population. Teachers working with special populations (ESL and special education) experienced higher levels of stress than regular education teachers. Special education teachers seem to share the frustrations experienced by their students (Horwitz, Horwitz, & Cope, 1986).

Organizational Stressors

Organizational stressors are conditions in the workplace that produce teacher stress. Many organizational factors have been reported by teachers as being stressful, such as the lack of clear role definitions, heavy workloads, incompetent administration, student discipline, and negative student attitudes toward school. The highest stress levels for teachers appear to be in the area of interpersonal relationships that involve teachers' relationships with supervisors, colleagues, and students (Eskridge & Coker, 1985). The five major organizational stressors for beginning teachers are the following:

1. Professional Inadequacy. Often, beginning teachers experience stress resulting from inadequacies in the teaching profession. Inadequacies include an inadequate salary, parents who are indifferent about school problems, unrealistic expectations (i.e., being expected to do the same job as an experienced teacher), and lack of recognition for good teaching.

2. Group Instruction. Group instruction involves working with students in the classroom. This includes maintaining classroom discipline and teaching groups of children with wide ability ranges. Beginning teachers with fewer than five years' classroom experience tend to report that maintaining discipline in the classroom is the single most stressful factor. Teachers ranked continual student misbehavior as a major contributor of tension and stress, stating that tension is more often caused by one or two students who chronically misbehave than by a general lack of discipline among all students in the classroom or school.

Reality Bite

Managing Stress

As a beginning teacher, I find that the single most stressful factor in my professional life is classroom management. I try so hard to come up with possible solutions to my classroom problems; some days I feel successful and others I do not. There are times when I feel as though I have no control in my classroom. As I begin my fourth month of teaching, however, I believe I have control about three days a week, and it is getting better all the time. The experienced teachers at my school tell me it will get easier and I know it will—I just wish I knew when. I am getting tired of waiting!

Another stressful aspect of my job is working with the special education students in my classes. In one of my classes 8 of the 23 students are in special education. This is very difficult for me because I have no training in special education, and it is difficult to ensure that they are learning. I am lucky that there is a wonderful special education teacher at my school who helps me a great deal. However, I worry about these students constantly, and I wonder if they are learning anything at all and, if not, is it my fault? My teacher preparation classes never taught me how to deal with the special needs learners.

I am lucky that my principal has been very helpful and concerned about me as I embark on my first year. His help and understanding makes my job easier. I have found relations with the other teachers at my school to be more stressful than those with the principal. When I was first hired, I did not feel supported by the other teachers at all. No one welcomed me to the school, informed me of procedures and shortcuts that only the teachers know about, or even offered me any advice as the "new kid on the block." This was very hard for me because teaching is a very lonely profession. Being with students all day long is hard enough, but knowing that the teachers were not there for me made it even more difficult. This was very stressful for me, in a different way than the classroom management problem.

I am lucky that classroom management is improving and that the teachers at my school have finally accepted me a bit more. My stress level is going down, which has made me a happier person both professionally and privately.

Tara Stace, High School Teacher

3. Principal–Teacher Interaction. Both teachers and principals have stressful jobs. Most beginning teachers wonder what the principal does all day, and they feel that principals fail to support them concerning discipline cases. This perceived lack of administrative support tends to escalate the interpersonal problems between teachers and administrators. Conversely, principals report interactions with teachers to be the most stressful part of their jobs. In a large survey, 1,200 school principals were asked to rate 48 events in order of stressfulness: 4 of the top 5 stressors were teacher related. In order of occurrence, the top 5 were (1) forcing the resignation or dismissal of a teacher, (2) dealing with unsatisfactory performance of professional staff, (3) involuntary transfer to another principalship, (4) preparing for a teachers' strike, and (5) refusal of a teacher to follow policies (Koff, Laffey, Olson, & Cichon, 1980). Principals often feel stress when interacting with teachers. As a result, teachers, who sense the principal's tension, respond in a like manner creating a reciprocal relationship.

4. Teacher–Teacher Interaction. Peer interaction among teachers has been reduced greatly due to several factors. First, many state reforms have included merit pay and master/expert status for teachers. These reforms have served to increase teacher competition for dollars and status rather than promote collaboration among teachers. Second, as special school populations increase (i.e., ESL, special education, etc.), beginning teachers working with these students feel isolated from the regular education teachers. As a result, effective communication between teachers is greatly reduced. Finally, any meaningful interaction requires time and commitment from the participants. Teachers lack time on the job to interact with each other. How often do teachers observe colleagues in the classroom? The lack of time makes it increasingly difficult for them to go and observe innovative and new ideas being used by colleagues. It is not surprising that many beginning teachers find teaching to be a lonely profession.

5. Job Overload. Last, but not least, job overload is a major stressor for teachers. Beginning teachers are often amazed at how time consuming and exhausting teaching can be. Experienced teachers often complain of the amount of paperwork associated with new state guidelines and reforms; as a result, many older teachers seek early retirement and relief from the noninstructional stressors.

COACHING

Coaching 3.16 Teacher Occupational Stress Questionnaire

Purpose: The purpose of this activity is to encourage reflective analysis on job-related stressors. You and your coach are asked not only to assess what causes stress at school but also to examine and compare coping tactics.

Time required: 20 minutes

Procedure: Read carefully each of the statements in Figure 3.5, and rate your job-related stress in the following way:

1. Assign values from 0 to 10 to each item listed, adding others not listed.
2. Indicate whether you have control (C), no control (NC), or limited control (LC) over the situation.
3. Discuss with your coach how to cope with each stressor you rated 5 or above (i.e., would you avoid it or discuss it?).

Coaching 3.17 Developing and Implementing Coping Strategies

Analyze your stress reduction strategies. Over the next two weeks, identify *one* or *two* major organizational stressors (e.g., discipline, teacher appraisal, planning, instruction, etc.). Ask your cooperating teacher, university supervisor, or fellow teacher to help you (1) generate a list of contributing factors, (2) identify root causes, (3) develop realistic solutions, and (4) implement solutions. You may wish to switch roles and serve as a coach to your cooperating teacher, university supervisor, or colleague. Developing an action plan to reduce occupational stress is as helpful to experienced teachers as it is to beginning teachers.

REFLECTION

Reflecting 3.18 Managing Stress and the Case of the Unmotivating Teacher

After evaluating stressors experienced by you and by experienced teachers, what advice might you give Kathy Westin about the management and reduction of stress? Be specific and detailed.

Summary

In this chapter, we presented a number of important strategies that can guide you in becoming a more successful and motivating teacher. We began the chapter with a discussion of why motivating students of today may prove challenging. Understanding the nature of schools gives us clues to why teachers feel unproductive and why students demonstrate negative attitudes toward schooling. Understanding motivation requires that we first examine the basic concepts involved in the development of motivation—need for achievement, need for affiliation, incentives, habit, discrepancy, and curiosity. After evaluating these concepts, we examined

Stressors	Value	Control (C), No Control (NC), Limited Control (LC)
1. Trying to motivate students who do not want to learn.		
2. Feeling my salary is not equal to my duties and responsibilities.		
3. Feeling there is a lack of administrative support for teachers in my school.		
4. Working in a school where there is an atmosphere of conflict among teachers.		
5. Having students in my class who talk constantly.		
6. Having to do school work at home to meet what is expected of me.		
7. Feeling my principal lacks insight into classroom problems.		
8. Feeling some teachers in my school are incompetent.		
9. Feeling too many parents are indifferent about school problems.		
10. Feeling my opinions are not valued by my principal.		
11. Feeling there is competition among teachers in my school rather than a team spirit of cooperation.		
12. Having to tell my students the same thing over and over.		
13. Having insufficient opportunity for rest and relaxation.		
14. Having to little clerical help.		
15. Working for an inadequate salary.		
16. Feeling that cliques exist among teachers.		
17. Feeling I do not have adequate control of my students.		
18. Feeling I never catch up with my work.		

Source: Adapted from Clark, E. (1980). An analysis of occupational stress factors as perceived by public school teachers. Doctoral dissertation, Auburn University. Dissertation Abstracts International.

Figure 3.5 **Teacher Occupational Stress Questionnaire**

motivational techniques and strategies used to increase student participation. Successful strategies include incorporating interests, teaching beyond the textbook, communicating success, incorporating technology and cooperative learning, and increasing cultural awareness. Unless we are able to motivate ourselves, motivating others is impossible. Reducing teacher stress and burnout allows beginning teachers to become effective motivators.

Glickman (1993) summarizes the intent of the motivator role very well when he stresses "if our schools were to focus on the main goal of citizenship and democracy and show students how to connect learning with the real issues of their surroundings, then more students would learn how to write cogent compositions, would learn basic skills, would use higher-order thinking, would learn aesthetic appreciation, would excel in academics, and would graduate. . . . The reason why many of our students do not do better in schools is not that they are deficient, or that their teachers are incompetent or uncaring; the reason is that these students do not see the relevance of such learning to altering and improving their immediate lives in their communities" (p. 9).

Recommended Readings

Berger, C. (1985). Social power and interpersonal communication. In M. L. Knapp & G. R. Miller (eds.), *Handbook of interpersonal communication*. Beverly Hills: Sage.

Brophy, J. E. (1987). On motivating students. In D. G. Berliner & B. V. Rosenshine (eds.), *Talks to teachers*. New York: Random House.

Good, T. L., & Brophy, J. E. (1987). *Looking in classrooms*. (4th ed.). New York: Harper and Row.

Goodlad, J. I. (1984). *A place called school*. New York: McGraw-Hill.

Johnson, D., & Johnson, R. (1987). *Learning together and alone: Cooperative, competitive, and individualistic learnings*. (2nd ed.). Englewood Cliffs, NJ: Prentice-Hall.

Jones, F. H. (1987). *Positive classroom instruction*. New York: McGraw-Hill.

Jones, V. F., & Jones, L. S. (1990). *Comprehensive classroom management: Motivating and managing students*. (3rd ed.). Boston: Allyn and Bacon.

O'Hair, M. J., & Odell, S. J. (eds.). (1995). *Educating teachers for leadership and change*. Newbury Park, CA: Corwin.

O'Hair, M. J., & Wright, R. (1990). Application of communication strategies in alleviating teacher stress. In H. D. O'Hair & G. Kreps (eds.), *Applied communication theory and research*. New York: Erlbaum.

Slavin, R. E. (1987). *Educational psychology: Theory into practice*. (2nd ed.). Englewood Cliffs, NJ: Prentice-Hall.

Slavin, R. E. (1987). *Student team learning*. (2nd ed.). Washington, DC: National Education Association.

References

Brophy, J. E. (1987). On motivating students. In D. G. Berliner & B. V. Rosenshine (eds.), *Talks to teachers*. New York: Random House.

Calabrese, R., & Anderson, R. (1986). The public school: A source of stress and alienation among female teachers. *Urban Education, 21* (1), 30–41.

Clark, E. (1980). An analysis of occuptional stress factors as perceived by public school teachers. *Dissertation Abstracts International.* Auburn University.

Cohen, M. W. (1986). Research on motivation: New content for the teacher preparation curriculum. *Journal of Teacher Education, 37* (3), 23–28.

Cohen, M. W., Emrich, A. E., & deCharms, R. (1976–1977). Training teachers to enhance personal causation in students. *Interchange, 7,* 34–39.

Doyal, G., & Forsyth, R. (1973). Relationship between teaching and student anxiety levels. *Psychology in the Schools, 10,* 231–233.

Eskridge, D., & Coker, D. (1985). Teacher stress: Symptoms, causes, and management techniques. *The Clearing House, 59,* 387–390.

Farber, B. (1984). Teacher burnout: Assumptions, myths, and issues. *Teachers College Record, 86,* 321–338.

Forman, S. (1982). Stress management for teachers: A cognitive-behavioral program. *Journal of School Psychology, 20,* 180–187.

Glasser, W. *The quality school.* New York: Harper and Row.

Glickman, C. D. (1993). *Renewing America's schools.* San Francisco: Jossey-Bass.

Good, T. L., & Brophy, J. E. (1994). *Looking in classrooms.* (6th ed.). New York: HarperCollins.

Goodlad, J. I. (1984). *A place called school: Prospects for the future.* New York: McGraw-Hill.

Granger, R. E. (1989). Computer-based training improves job performance. *Personnel Journal, 68* (6), 116–120.

Harris, K., Halpin, G., & Halpin, G. (1985). Teacher characteristics and stress. *Journal of Education Research, 78,* 346–350.

Holmes, T. H., & Rahne, R. H. (1967). The social readjustment rating scale. *Journal of Psychosomatic Research, 2,* 213–218.

Horwitz, E., Horwitz, M., & Cope, J. (1986). Foreign language classroom anxiety. *The Modern Language Journal, 70,* 125–132.

Huber, V. L., & Gay, G. (1985). Channeling new technology to improve training. *Personnel Administrator, 48,* 49–57.

Janis, I. L. (1972). *Victims of groupthink: A psychological study of foreign-policy decisions and fiascoes.* Boston: Houghton Mifflin.

Jones, F. H. (1987). *Positive classroom instruction.* New York: McGraw-Hill.

Jones, V. F., & Jones, L. S. (1990). *Comprehensive classroom management: Motivating and managing students* (3rd ed.). Boston: Allyn and Bacon.

Kaiser, J., & Polczynski, J. (1982). Educational stress: Sources, reactions, preventions. *Peabody Journal of Education, 10,* 127–134.

Koff, R., Laffey, J., Olson, G., & Cichon, D. (1980). Stress and the school administrator. *Administrator's Notebook, 28,* 1–4.

Litt, M., & Turk, D. (1985). Sources of stress and dissatisfaction in experienced high school teachers. *Journal of Educational Research, 78,* 178–185.

Madlin, N. (1987). Computer-based training comes of age. *Personnel, 64* (11), 64–65.

O'Hair, M. J., & Bastian, K. (1993). Physiological measurement of principal vocal stress in urban settings. Paper presented at the University Council of Education Administration, Houston, Texas.

O'Hair, M. J., & Harmon, S. (1990). Elementary students rank what motivates them to learn in the classroom. Unpublished manuscript.

O'Hair, M. J., & Housner, L. (1989). Differences between traditional and nontraditional education students. Paper presented at the annual American Educational Research Association, San Francisco.

O'Hair, M. J., & O'Hair, D. (1992). A model of strategic principal communication during performance evaluations. *Journal of Research for School Executives, 2,* 13–22.

Petrusich, M. (1966). Separation anxiety as a factor in the student teaching experience. *Peabody Journal of Education, 14,* 353–356.

Robbins, S. P. (1984). *Essentials of organizational behavior.* Englewood Cliffs, NJ: Prentice-Hall.

Rohrkemper, M. (1985). Motivational coursework in teacher education. In M. K. Alderman & M. W. Cohen (eds.), *Motivation theory and practice for preservice teachers.* (Teacher Education Monograph No. 4). Washington, DC: ERIC Clearinghouse on Teacher Education.

Samples, R. (1977). *The wholeschool book.* Reading, MA: Addison-Wesley.

Schwade, S. (1985.). Is it time to consider computer-based training? *Personnel Administrator, 46,* 25–35.

Slavin, R. E. (1988). *Educational psychology: Theory into practice* (2nd ed.). Englewood Cliffs, NJ: Prentice-Hall.

Smith, R. A. (1987). A teacher's views on cooperative learning. *Phi Delta Kappan, 68* (9), 663–666.

Trachtenberg, S. J. (1990). Multiculturalism can be taught only by multicultural people. *Phi Delta Kappan, 71* (8), 610–611.

Vacca, R. T., & Vacca, J. L. (1989). *Content area reading.* (3rd ed.). Glenview, IL: Scott, Foresman.

Van Horn, R. (1987). Laser videodiscs in education: Endless possibilities. *Phi Delta Kappan, 68* (9), 696–700.

Wehr, J. (1988). Instructor-led or computer-based: Which will work best for you? *Training and Development Journal, 42* (6), 18–21.

Chapter 4

The Manager Role*

Chapter Objectives

After completing this chapter, you will be able to

- envision a classroom environment in which you attend to the task of learning as a result of having developed a classroom management platform.
- distinguish the elements necessary to construct classroom rules and develop classroom procedures.
- construct beginning-of-the-year rules and procedures in order to successfully "kick off" a school year.
- develop intervention systems for students who will not or cannot follow the rules and procedures.
- formulate, communicate, and implement student behavior expectations so they can "save face."
- specify strategies that are appropriate for the beginning and ending of classroom sessions.

$\mathcal{T}$he roller coaster stuggles of student and beginning teachers have been chronicled over time, and common themes have emerged that describe these struggles (Borko, 1986; Cruickshank, Kennedy, & Myers, 1974; Dropkin and Taylor, 1963). First-year teachers often encounter difficulties with the transition from student/scholar to a professional capable of managing the learning environment (Bullough, 1987; Brown & Willems, 1977; Kane, 1991; Ryan, 1979). It is interesting to note that there have been very few shifts in the problems experienced by first-year teachers during their induction into the teaching profession. Even more interesting is that discipline, the development of classroom routines and procedures,

---

* Chapter 4 was written by Sally Zepeda, The University of Oklahoma.

The Case of the Missing Management

It was the third week of the school year, and Nick was discussing the rowdiness of his students with Luke, a trusted colleague in the English department at Bruckenbary High School. Since this was Nick's first teaching position, he was not sure about either the "type" of students at Bruckenbary or the types of classroom management techniques that could assist him in getting his classroom under control. Luke offered to observe Nick in his classroom environment, and the next morning, saw the following:

As the warning bell rang (students had three minutes to get to class), Nick was sitting at his desk organizing papers, flipping through a textbook, and trying to stack a set of handouts. Students were milling about the room, standing at the doorway, and talking about the events of the day. When the late bell rang, students were still at the doorway and milling around the room. Nick took his position behind the podium and began calling off names. His voice was muffled by talking, giggling, and the sound of books dropping to the floor. Nick continued calling off names. A student hall guard walked into the room looking for a student for one of the deans. Nick stopped calling names and loudly announced, "Another one bites the dust." At this point, students began jeering and chanting "Another one bites the dust."

After four minutes, Nick began lecturing about the novel The Scarlet Letter. *Students were looking for their study guides, flipping through pages, and still talking among themselves. After a few more minutes, Nick asked students to take out their notebooks so they could "catch a few major ideas." As students were readying themselves by pulling out notebooks, looking for pen and paper, and asking each other what was just said, a student in the back of the room got out of his seat and walked across the room to borrow a pen. Nick exploded and screamed, "Don't you remember? I told you to come to class prepared to work." The student responded by asking Nick, "When?" The rest of the class began talking even more loudly asking, "When, where, what date?" In total exasperation Nick assigned an extra chapter of reading for the next day. He then turned to the student who was still by another student's desk looking for a pen and said, "Hey, quit being a clown and sit down. If you don't sit down, I'll write a detention slip or push the panic button."*

Nick's attempts to gain the attention of the class did not work. Students began mumbling, putting their books down, and mimicking him and the student—"Sit down, clown, or he'll push the button, and the dean will get you out of here."

In another attempt to gain attention, Nick again began lecturing and instructed students to pull out their worksheets on The Scarlet Letter. *More shuffling and talking occurred. A student asked, "Did the first settlers have religious ceremonies on the boats?" Nick stopped lecturing and walked to his desk to look for the answer in an American literature textbook. While Nick was doing this, students were talking among themselves.*

Seventeen minutes had passed since the bell rang, and Nick was still attempting to begin class. The rest of the period followed pretty much the same format, with Nick stopping to correct students who were not focused. With four minutes left to the class, Nick announced the period would be ending soon. Students started packing up their books and belongings and talking among themselves. In exasperation Nick announced, "Pop quiz—pull out a sheet of paper." Students began ripping sheets of paper from their notebooks as Nick posed the first question, "In The Scarlet Letter, *explain the symbolism of the title of the book." Students were turning around in their seats asking each other if they understood the question. Nick asked another question, then another, in rapid succession.*

When the change-of-class bell sounded, students were still trying to figure out what the quiz questions were. Several students picked up their books and walked out of the room. Although half of the class had left the room, Nick was still collecting quiz papers, and he quickly assigned yet another assignment for the next day while reminding students about the extra chapter they had to read.

Luke, a veteran teacher who had once been the English department chair, left the room and began to plan a feedback conference. Luke decided that he needed to engage Nick in a discussion about student management, classroom control, and the development of organized procedures so future classes could begin promptly and end in a more purposeful manner. Moreover, Luke thought it imperative to focus on the interactions he had witnessed between Nick and his students.

and interaction with students continue to plague those entering or about to enter the classroom (Borko, 1986; Bullough, 1987; Dropkin & Taylor, 1963; McDonald & Elias, 1982; Smith, 1950; Veenman 1984; Wey, 1951).

In addition. research reveals that good classroom instruction, the management of students, and the development of procedures within the learning environment complement one another (Brophy, 1983; Good & Brophy, 1991; Kounin, 1970). Although this chapter will not address instruction directly, it does focus on the development of clearly defined classroom rules and procedures, the lack of which can and will impede the instructional effectiveness of any teacher, regardless of the amount of experience.

This scenario will be used to illuminate some of the common problems that beginning teachers experience when assuming the role of professional educator. It will also be used to analyze these problems to enable you to use a problem-solving approach in the development of classroom procedures to enhance the learning environment. This chapter will focus on the following three competencies:

Competency 1: Developing a Classroom Management Platform

Competency 2: Developing Rules and Procedures That Set the Stage for Learning and Instruction

Competency 3: Developing Beginning and Ending Classroom Procedures

Competency 1 DEVELOPING A CLASSROOM MANAGEMENT PLATFORM

ASSESSMENT

This section will engage you in a self-reflection activity and a discussion about the development of a classroom management platform with your cooperating teacher and university supervisor. Your classroom management platform basically is a statement of your beliefs and attitudes regarding the management of student behavior. Many experienced teachers believe that learning cannot occur until students know the types of behavior acceptable within the learning environment; that is, learning and, in fact, teaching cannot occur until classroom procedures are developed, explained, and implemented by the teacher. This sounds simple, but you really cannot set rules and procedures and consequences for infractions until you develop a classroom management platform. In a sense, the platform you develop will guide you in achieving the other two competencies in this chapter.

Assessing 4.1 The Classroom Management Platform

Purpose: To help you develop a classroom management platform.

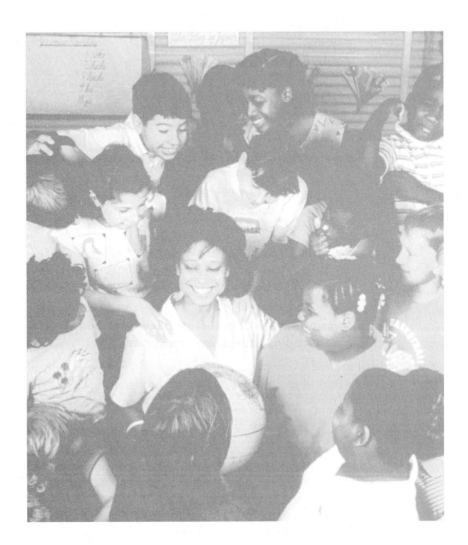

Time required: Varies

Procedure: This exercise should be completed privately. Study the following questions and begin clarifying your responses. There are no right or wrong answers, but your responses should assist you both in gaining insight about your views of an organized learning environment and in developing a classroom management platform.

  1. I learned the most in a classroom where the teacher
     a. was in control and guided student learning.
     b. developed clear rules of behavior, explained the rules, and enforced the rules consistently and fairly.
     c. had no clearly defined rules and procedures.
     Elaborate on your choice.

2. I believe classroom rules and procedures are
    a. necessary and fulfill a function.
    b. unnecessary.
    c. both necessary and unnecessary.

    Elaborate on your choice.

3. What are the most important aspects of developing rules and procedures?

4. Reread the Case of the Missing Management. From the glimpse of Nick's classroom environment, can you identify classroom procedures? If so, what are they?

5. From your perspective, what classroom procedures does Nick need to develop?

6. Is it too late for Nick to change his procedures?

7. What will be your classroom management platform? Sketch the major beliefs that will guide you as you move into the classroom.

Assessing 4.2 Discussion/Interview with Cooperating Teacher and/or University Supervisor

Purpose: To assist you in developing a classroom management platform by opening lines of communication with your cooperating teacher and/or your university supervisor.

Time required: 20 to 30 minutes

Procedure: Engage your cooperating teacher in a discussion about discipline, classroom control, and the development of procedures. These questions are intended to get you started and should guide your discussion: What guides your thinking about classroom procedures? What are the most important attributes of an effective learning environment relative to establishing procedures, clarifying student behavior and expectations, and developing consequences?

Assessing 4.3 What Are You Thinking?

Purpose: To assist you in clarifying and solidifying your own thoughts after your interview in 4.2, thereby helping you further develop your classroom management platform.

Time required: Varies

Procedure: After you have reflected about your classroom management platform and interviewed your cooperating teacher and university supervisor, elaborate on the following questions: What are the most important attributes of an effective learning environment? How does a teacher put these attributes into practice? What is your platform? If you were discussing your own platform with Nick, what would you want to communicate to him?

EXPERIENCE

The Assessment activities provided you with an opportunity to examine your own predispositions toward a classroom management plan. This section is designed to discuss the important elements necessary for developing an effective platform.

Considerations for a Classroom Management Platform

Defining your classroom management platform is critical regardless if you are a student teacher, beginning teacher, or veteran teacher. Without this platform, routines, procedures, and consequences will become "knee-jerk," will appear to be capricious, and will be reactive rather than proactive. Developing a management plan is not simple, because you first need to develop a sense of style and personality.

Consider the "types" of teachers you have had as a student, such as the "drill sergeant," and the "buddy, buddy—I'm your friend." Many preservice and first-year teachers do not really have a defined style and experiment as they progress. This experimentation is both positive and problematic: It allows one to develop a "best fit," but it can send mixed messages to students. Students often view beginning teachers as being primarily inconsistent. Consider Nick's explosion when the student walked across the room to get a pen. From the details of the scenario, we can only surmise that Nick has behaved this way before. How do you think that Nick responded in similar and prior episodes? Do you think that he consistently reacts in the same manner?

COACHING

This section will underscore the three key concepts inherent in developing a classroom management platform: (1) the necessity of having a classroom management plan so you can move on to developing beginning-of-the-year procedures that set the stage for learning and instruction, (2) the importance of defining your classroom management style, and (3) the pitfalls inherent in each of these two areas. You will be guided by your cooperating teacher or university professor as you begin to solidify your platform.

Coaching 4.4 The Classroom Management Platform

Answer the following questions and discuss them with your coach.

1. What is involved in developing a classroom management platform?

—— *Reality Bite*

First-Year Frustration

As a first-year teacher, I was plagued by discipline problems. In an effort to be nice and well liked by my students, I waited until situations were out of hand before I intervened. This resulted in mostly negative reinforcement. My classroom was out of control, and I hated my job. Student behavior was so poor that my best-planned lessons went awry. When I compared my students to those students of other teachers, I told myself that the other teachers had the better classes. I was afraid to ask them how they were managing their classes for fear of being viewed as incompetent.

The day I asked a colleague for advice about classroom management was a turning point in my teaching career. She came to visit while my students were supposed to be napping. They were getting up and talking noisily, and I was reprimanding them loudly—without results. Susan started walking around the room and praising the few students who were behaving appropriately. Once the students quieted, she carefully explained the appropriate behavior for a nap. The results were miraculous. Almost every student got quiet immediately, hoping she would notice them. On this day, I realized that I was the one responsible for the atmosphere of my classroom, an empowering position. This incident caused me to analyze my classroom, to realize that by making expectations clear and reinforcing positive behaviors that it was within my grasp to change things, and to begin doing so.

It took a few weeks to regain control of my classroom. I am quite sure that I would have left teaching if I had not asked for help and realized that I was responsible for the climate in my classroom

Allison Reeves, Experienced Early Childhood Educator

2. Why is a classroom management platform essential for beginning teachers?

3. What function does this platform play in the development of more specific types of procedures in the classroom?

4. If a first-year teacher does not have a platform, what will be the consequences?

Coaching 4.5 Things to Consider While Developing a Classroom Management Platform

Excerpts from Nick and Luke's discussion are found in Reflecting 4.6. Review them, focusing on Nick's description of his classroom and instructional style, and answer these questions:

1. How does a classroom management style affect a beginning teacher in the development of a platform?
2. Is there a "perfect" style or is one better than another?
3. The styles that you reflected upon earlier included the "drill sergeant" and the "buddy, buddy—I'm your friend." Identify the strengths and weaknesses found in each.

REFLECTION

Reflecting 4.6 The Scenario Revisited: What Style Will You Adopt?

Luke met with Nick after school on the day of the observation. The following exercises contain excerpts from their discussion.

Purpose: In order to further explore the development of a classroom management platform, you must first be aware of the "type" of classroom manager and teacher you are. This exercise will help you explore and clarify your style.

Time required: Varies

Procedure: Read each of the following excerpts from Nick and Luke's discussion, and then respond to its accompanying set of questions.

Excerpt #1

Luke: Thanks for letting me visit your classroom today. I have some insights that might assist you in developing some classroom and student management procedures. First, however, let's talk about what's important. What's your style as a teacher? That is, how do you perceive yourself?

Nick: I want to be their buddy. . . . I want to understand them. . . . I'm not much older than they are. . . . It's tough to know what to say and do.

Questions: What are the consequences of being a buddy-type teacher relative to classroom management? Is it impossible to be a buddy and still be effective? Elaborate.

Excerpt: #2

Nick: I was strict at the start, but I got lax way too soon. I lost them—I
lost them [students] on two levels: discipline and curricularly. I
wasn't enforcing the rules I started the year off with. There weren't
any consequences—the consequences I laid out for my students I
didn't follow through.

　　　If the atmosphere in the class isn't conducive to learning, then
they're not going to learn. We accomplished little because things
were so out of control. They couldn't even regurgitate stuff covered
in class on a quiz or a test because they never heard it said—Johnnie
was talking so Mary couldn't follow along with the discussion.

Questions: What is the relationship between learning and classroom management?
Consistency plays an integral part in the development of a classroom management
style. How does Nick's style interfere with teaching? learning? development of rapport with students?

Excerpt #3

Nick: Everything was herky-jerky. Every time I developed a procedure, something or someone threw me a curve ball—a pep rally, a shortened schedule, a fire drill. I would try something new, and it worked for a few days, then "bang"—everything fell apart. I wasn't as consistent as I should have been. I wanted to be my students' friend. I wanted them to like me. They [students] thought my kindness was a sign of weakness—they were partially correct.

Questions: How might Nick answer these questions: What are the external factors that can impede a beginning teacher from developing a classroom management style? What can a beginning teacher do to prevent these external factors from interfering with the development of a classroom management style?

Excerpt #4

Nick: It started with little things that I tolerated—I tolerated too much. My threshold for the things that were going on in the classroom was too high. I put up with things—I let things go.

Questions: Nick talks about his "threshold" being too high. To a large extent, your style will determine your threshold. What would be the threshold for the "drill sergeant"? for the "buddy, buddy—I'm your friend"?

■ *Competency 2* DEVELOPING RULES AND PROCEDURES THAT SET THE STAGE FOR LEARNING AND INSTRUCTION

The beginning of the school year is perhaps the most crucial time—especially for beginning teachers. Some veteran teachers believe this is the most critical stage of the year because during this period they set not only the expectations for academic work but also the procedures and expectations for student behavior. Many teachers believe that the tenor of the student–teacher relationship is established during these first few days. Most agree that every class has its own personality and that this personality continues to develop throughout the school year. To this extent, the old adage "First impressions are lasting ones" seems to apply. Research, past and present, appears to support these notions (Brophy, 1983; Emmer, Evertson, Sanford, Clements, & Worsham, 1989; Good & Brophy, 1991; Kounin, 1970).

With a classroom management platform thoughtfully developed, now is the time for teachers to communicate, model, and reinforce not only the rules and procedures but also the student expectations relative to rules and procedures. Coupled with these objectives, it is critical for the teacher to have developed intervention systems for students who cannot follow the rules and procedures, and to be able to reinforce them consistently.

No teacher, especially a beginner, can walk into a classroom on the first day and expect a program to unfold. A great deal of attention directed toward developing rules and procedures *before* the first day is required. It takes time to develop rules, practices, and procedures that fit both the context and climate of the classroom and school. Beginning teachers sometimes develop rules and procedures that are both inappropriate and in conflict with schoolwide rules; for example, setting "time-out in the hall" as a consequence for disruptive behavior when the school does not want unsupervised students in the hall. Moreover, sending a student out of the room for less than compelling reasons merely rewards the unacceptable behavior—the student gets out of class.

Differentiating Between Rules and Procedures

Rules typically identify primary expectations or standards set by an authority (Emmer, Evertson, Sanford, Clements, & Worsham, 1989). For example, common rules at elementary, middle school, and secondary levels include "No running in the hallways" "Be in your seat when the bell rings" "No jackets or coats allowed in the classroom" and "No chewing gum in the classroom" Set standards and expectations tell the students what behaviors are acceptable or not acceptable in the classroom.

Procedures communicate expectations for a different kind of student behavior. They usually apply to a specific activity and are directed at accomplishing something rather than prohibiting some behavior or defining a general standard (Emmer, Evertson, Sanford, Clements, & Worsham, 1989). To this extent, classroom procedures are typically developed to facilitate instructional activities such as discussions, small group work, transitions, and the general smooth running of a classroom from the beginning to the end of class (Good & Brophy, 1991). Procedures may include "Class begins as soon as the bell rings" "Quizzes will come about three times a week, possibly more frequently. Most quizzes are unannounced, so be ready when you walk into the classroom" and "Makeup quizzes are always in the morning at 7:15 and by special arrangement only."

ASSESSMENT

Assessing 4.7 Differentiating Between Rules and Procedures

Purpose: To review the definitions of rules and procedures in order to examine the Case of the Missing Management and identify those present in Nick's classroom.

Time required: 20 minutes

Procedure: You have been reading quite a bit about the classroom environment and the role that teachers plays in developing a climate conducive for learning. Together, a classroom management platform and a set of beginning-of-the-year rules and procedures set the stage for learning and instruction. After rereading the scenario and reviewing the definitions of terms, answer the following questions:

1. Identify the classroom rules that are present in Nick's classroom. What evidence do you have to support your perceptions of the rules that he has established for his classroom?

2. Are Nick's rules appropriate?

3. Identify classroom procedures evident in Nick's classroom and provide support for your observations.

4 Are Nick's procedures appropriate?

EXPERIENCE

When developing rules and procedures, it is critical to remember that each school and thus each classroom has its own context—that is, no two classrooms are identical. Developing classroom rules and procedures is critical, however, to maintaining an effective learning environment and enforcing classroom management. The Effective Schools Research (Edmonds, Mortimore, & Rosenshine, 1981) makes a strong case for the development of rules and procedures. Relative to classroom management and student behavior, the proponents of effective schools research postulates that the effective teacher is (1) well organized and thus prevents problems from occurring; (2) selects and directs classroom activities; (3) monitors student progress by asking questions and circulating around the room; (4) encourages positive behavior and controls negative behavior; and (5) does not permit interruptions of class activities or demonstrations of negative behavior (Edmonds, Mortimore, & Rosenshine, 1981).

Setting Rules

Classroom contexts vary. Rules must take into account student age (elementary, middle, or high school), the type of school (private, sectarian, public), and the philosophical culture of the school. Other variables include the ability of the teacher to enforce rules, the types of support the teacher will get from administration when referring a student, and the degree of support and cooperation the teacher will receive from students' parents while enforcing the rules.

Hence, this section will discuss only general guidelines for the development of classroom rules. These guidelines for developing rules come from the field of experience and are supported by research (Good & Brophy, 1991; Emmer, Evertson,

Sanford, Clements, & Worsham, 1989). Effective classroom management rules have seven common characteristics :

1. Rules are introduced and explained early. Many teachers introduce and explain their classroom rules, expectations for student behavior, and classroom procedures on the very first day of the school year. As a result, students know immediately what behaviors are expected. The rationale for each rule should be included in the explanation. By explaining the rationale, the teacher and the rule become more credible as the rule takes on an importance and value. Through role-playing and discussion, rules and behaviors can be modeled by both the students and the teacher.

2. Rules are specific. For example, rules should state the positive behaviors that are expected of students in the classroom.

3. Rules are limited. Many beginning teachers walk into the classroom on the very first day with 20 to 30 classroom rules. Although there is no magic number of rules, veteran teachers believe they can effectively manage a class of students with a minimal number of rules. Because rules typically identify general expectations or standards (Emmer, Evertson, Sanford, Clements, & Worsham, 1989), 4 or 5 carefully crafted rules can set the expectation for desired student behavior within the classroom.

4. Rules are presented in positive and proactive terms. For example, this rule is presented in negative terms: "Class ends when I say it does." A more proactive approach might be "Class will be dismissed by the instructor and not the bell."

5. Rules are consistent with the context of the school setting. Classroom rules should not conflict with schoolwide rules. Establishing rules that are in opposition to schoolwide rules or norms of behavior sends mixed messages to students. In addition, teachers can face even tougher standards, such as censure by administrators, if classroom rules are incompatible with schoolwide rules.

6. Rules are simply stated. Rules that are too long and convoluted are cumbersome to explain, difficult for students to understand, and open to too many interpretations.

7. Rules are reflected upon. Developing a set of classroom rules is a continuous process that takes time to perfect. Many seasoned teachers are comfortable and confident enough to revise and adjust classroom rules throughout the year. It is probably wise for beginning teachers to take the no-fair-changing-rules-in-the-middle-of-game approach in order to maintain consistency. However, first-year teachers can and should revise rules for the next year based on the first year's experiences of what was or was not effective.

Regardless of the rules you set, it is important to note that rules, if they are to be effective, need to be fairly, firmly, and consistently upheld in the classroom. More-over, you need to have set consequences in mind for students who do not follow the rules, and regardless of the consequence, you *must* maintain consistency on a day-to-day basis. Student teachers and beginning teachers tend to be inconsistent and thus do not send the same message to students on a daily basis. This inconsistency can result in classroom and student management problems reaching a point beyond teacher control. Once lost, teacher control of the classroom is tough to get back.

Setting Procedures

The work of Kounin (1970) identifies five techniques that can assist teachers in developing effective classroom management procedures. The coupling of instruction and student management are inherent in these techniques:

1. "Withitness"
2. Overlapping
3. Signal continuity and momentum in lessons
4. Group alerting and accountability in lessons
5. Variety and challenge in seatwork

"Withitness." If teachers are "with-it," they are able to "nip problems in the bud" and prevent escalation. "Withitness" is achieved by the teacher actively participating in what is happening in the classroom on a regular and continuous basis. The teacher is not glued to one spot, such as the podium or desk. The teacher uses close physical proximity, walks up and down the aisles, and maintains eye contact with students. When student behavioral problems emerge, the teacher handles the problem promptly, and gives immediate feedback about the inappropriate behavior. In addition, the teacher must be aware of positive behavior so that it can be reinforced in the classroom.

Overlapping. By overlapping, the teacher is able to attend to many activities at the same time. With the acceptance and implementation of the cooperative learning model and other such instructional methods, overlapping is critical. It is achieved through intensive preparation before class to ensure that materials, such as handouts and overheads, are ready for use. As a result of this preparation, the teacher is freed from accomplishing these tasks during class time and can circulate around the room. Continual circulating fosters a check on student or group progress, allows for teacher interaction with students individually or in groups, and still allows the teacher to maintain order in the classroom.

Signal Continuity and Momentum in Lessons. This technique is closely tied to preparation in that the teacher knows in advance what is to be taught (content) and what activities will be used to help students achieve content mastery. Thus the common trap of "dead time," or downtime, does not occur. During dead time, students are not engaged in positive tasks and are more likely to engage in inappropriate activities. Through planning, momentum from one topic (or aspect of a topic) or activity, coupled with planned transitions, helps keep students on task. In order to facilitate the signaling of continuity and to achieve momentum in teaching, some veteran teachers identify a "barometer"—a student who is generally responsive to learning. By observing this student, you can determine if concepts are being absorbed. If this student appears confused, then other students might be confused. When large numbers of students are having difficulty with the material, you must be ready to switch gears to get students back on track.

Group Alerting and Accountability in Lessons. Delivery of instruction is varied with the use of question-and-answer sequences, in which students are called upon randomly in order to maintain attention. The answer that a particular student offers is often used as a springboard in another question for another student. Thus students are naturally drawn into the discussion because they have to pay attention not only to the questions but also to the answers that their classmates offer.

The carefully planned question-and-answer sequences, coupled with a clear instructional plan of activities for the class session, assist the teacher in remaining on task and ensure that the learning objectives set by the teacher can be met.

Variety and Challenge in Seatwork. The idea here is "no more mindless busy work." The teacher who consistently schedules the last ten minutes of class for students to answer the questions at the end of the chapter is looking for classroom management problems. Seatwork should provide a challenge, and students should see a reason for the work. Seatwork that allows students to extend their knowledge by independently applying the content of the lesson or activity assists in keeping students engaged in learning.

It is interesting to note the interrelatedness of the techniques discovered by Kounin (1970) and then later more fully developed by Good & Brophy (1983, 1991). The teacher who is alert to students and the classroom environment, who has planned instruction carefully and has organized all materials and made them accessible, who engages students in the planned lecture through the use of activities or question-and-answer sequences, and who can reinforce learning through meaningful and challenging seatwork is a successful manager of students and their learning. Each of these techniques builds upon the others and thus has a scaffolding effect on both instruction and classroom management.

Developing Intervention Systems

With a classroom management platform developed, specified rules and procedures formulated and in place, and consequences for failure to follow rules and procedures established, the teacher must now think about intervention techniques for students who elect not to follow classroom rules. As the instructional leader, you are responsible not only for imparting knowledge but also for assisting students in learning and in behaving appropriately in the classroom. To this end, you will need

Reality Bite

Professional Perspective

Students need structure in their educational experiences. Structure in both class-room management and curriculum are mandated. Since I am a fairness-cen-tered educator, I believe that rules and procedures, as well as consequences for not following the rules and/or procedures, ought to be set forth from the begin-ning of the school term. In order to create a comfortable and safe environment for effective learning, I clearly state—and reinforce in writing—the rules and procedures for expected student behaviors in my classroom. While in class, I use positive feedback to reinforce appropriate behaviors and enforce consequences for inappropriate behaviors. As part of my first quiz, I include questions about rules, procedures, and consequences. In doing so, I accomplish three goals: (1) I reinforce the importance of positive classroom behaviors in the students. (2) I assess to what degree each student takes the rules and procedures to heart. (3) I ensure a manageable classroom dynamic for myself. Effective classroom man-agement techniques are not unlike loving discipline provided by parents—both foster a sense of responsibility and good citizenship in the leaders of tomorrow. Without them, anarchy reigns.

Cynthia Bishop, Experienced Speech Communicator

to deal with students who refuse to follow rules or procedures or who just "forget" about the behavioral expectations of the classroom.

The teacher who lets others hold students accountable for not following rules and procedures loses credibility in the eyes of the students. It is only after the teacher has worked repeatedly with a student that one should be referred to a coun-selor, psychologist, or administrator.

The first step in an intervention system is a proactive approach through moni-toring, or "withitness," that permits the teacher to prevent problems from escalat-ing. It is too idealistic, however, to believe that *every* student will follow the rules and procedures that have been introduced, explained, modeled, and reinforced. Therefore, you need to develop a plan for working with students who just will not or cannot follow through with the established rules and procedures.

The following approaches, derived from the field of practice, are meant to be a starting point as you work with students:

1. Model appropriate behavior.
2. Use physical proximity and eye contact.
3. Reinforce appropriate behavior through praise.
4. Direct questions to wandering students.
5. Give subtle reminders about rules and procedures.
6. Give feedback to students who do not follow the rules by stating what behavior is not acceptable.
7. Meet with offending students after class or school.
8. Reexplain rules and procedures and then ask the students to explain what the rule or procedure means to them.
9. Communicate that you will hold the students responsible for their behavior.
10. Hold firm on established rules and procedures.
11. If behavior continues to go against established rules and procedures, consider developing a contract with the offending student that spells out in writing rules, procedures, consequences, and rewards.
12. Follow through with consequences. For each infraction of the same rule or procedure, increase the severity of the consequence. The punishment for an infraction of the rule the first time should not be the same for the fourth or fifth infraction of the same rule.

Of course, if a student's behavior is disruptive to the entire class and jeopardizes the learning of others, then assistance should be sought from other school personnel. You might want to consider getting the student's parents involved before calling for assistance from other school personnel.

If infractions are not dealt with immediately and if students see that they can "get away from the rules," then you are giving an open invitation for more blatant types of behavioral and classroom management problems. Students will continually test the rules and your tolerance of infractions, so be prepared to be fair, firm, and consistent as you plan and implement classroom rules and procedures.

COACHING

Coaching 4.8 Setting Rules and Procedures

Purpose: In Assessing 4.7 you were to read the scenario and discuss the rules and procedures in the teaching segment. Now, in order to look at what you found in Nick's classroom and to put into practice the information about setting rules and procedures covered in the Experience section, you will develop a set of classroom rules and procedures for Nick.

Time required: Varies

Procedure: Imagine that you now know what to expect if clear classroom rules and procedures are not developed before the first day of school. Develop a set of rules and procedures that you will present to a classroom of students on the very first day of school.

Coaching 4.9 Setting Rules and Procedures

Purpose: To work with Kounin's (1970) techniques for developing classroom procedures.

Time required: Varies

Procedure: Show that you have used Kounin's techniques in the procedures you developed in the first two experiences, and predict how you will apply each of the five techniques when you finally put your classroom procedures into practice.

1. "Withitness"
2. Overlapping
3. Signal continuity and momentum in lessons
4. Group alerting and accountability in lessons
5. Variety and challenge in seatwork

REFLECTION

Reflecting 4.10 Developing Intervention Systems for Students Who Cannot Follow Rules and Procedures

Purpose: Teachers, no matter how experienced, will have students in their classrooms who will not or possibly cannot follow rules and procedures. The purpose of the exercise is to examine ways to deal with students who are blatantly out of control.

Time required: 40 minutes

Procedure: Focus on the segment of the Case of the Missing Management where the student in Nick's classroom walked across the room to borrow a pen. Examine the way Nick responded.

Questions:

1. Did Nick set himself and the student up for a no-win situation? Elaborate.
2. What could Nick have done differently so that he:
   a. would not establish an adversarial situation with the student?

      b. could have handled the responses of the class differently?

      c. could have regained control of situation?

3. How important is it for students to be able to save face in front of class members?

4. What choices could Nick have offered to this student?

5. Imagine that you are Nick, and asked the student to see you after school. What would you want to communicate to this student?

6. Pretend that you and the student met after school. How will you interact with this same student the next day?

Competency 3 DEVELOPING BEGINNING AND ENDING CLASSROOM PROCEDURES

In Competency 2, we examined the development of beginning-of-the-year rules and procedures that set the stage for the year. However, teachers set the stage for learning *every single day*. Each period of the day has two critical times—the beginning and the end. The first few minutes sets the stage for what will unfold during the period in terms of objectives, content, activities, and transferring learning from the previous day. Moreover, beginning-of-class procedures that are established and consistently maintained enable the teacher to attend to the typical "house maintenance activities" such as taking attendance, collecting work, and returning student work.

Equally important are the last few minutes of the period—the time that teachers establish closure for the day. Bringing closure can be meaningful in that teachers recap the activities of the class period, indicate how these activities help achieve the overall objectives of what is being studied, and establish a link or preview to what will transpire the next day. Like beginning-of-period procedures, end-of-period procedures can be developed systematically or they can be haphazard.

ASSESSMENT

Assessing 4.11 Types of Beginning and Ending Procedures

Purpose: To get you thinking about the types and kinds of beginning- and ending-of-class activities that are necessary to ensure an orderly learning environment.

Time required: 20 to 30 minutes

Procedure: Answer the following questions and give examples from your own experiences as either a student or beginning teacher.

1. What types of activities usually occur during the first five minutes of a class period?

2. How long do you think it should take to begin a class; that is, how long should it take a teacher to begin the activities of the period?

3. Is it possible for a teacher to attend to a multitude of tasks simultaneously at the beginning of a class period? How? Why?

4. What do you suppose some of the traps are in the ways in which teachers begin and end a class period?

5. Do you think there is a magic number of minutes that it takes to begin and end a class period? Elaborate.

EXPERIENCE

Since each school, grade level, and classroom has its own context, no absolute formulas for developing beginning- and ending-of-class rules and procedures exist. There are, however, certain procedures and rules that veteran teachers and administrators believe to be effective in beginning and ending class. Before examining the first few beginning and ending minutes of Nick's classroom, let's look at established beginning and ending practices.

Beginning-of-Class Procedures

1. Organize materials before students enter the classroom. You should have materials ready for easy access once class begins; otherwise, you will spend time trying to ready these materials instead of focusing on students and other procedures that typically have to be accomplished within the first few minutes of class. If you are not prepared, you create a dead time in which students can begin wandering off task as you organize class materials.

2. Weave in and out of the classroom a few minutes before class begins. This way you can, through physical proximity, encourage students to get into the classroom before the last few seconds before the bell rings. Your movement will cue students to get seated and ready for the beginning of class.

3. Have some organizing directions written on the blackboard. Indicate specific instructions, e.g., "Books out—page 36"; "Quiz—no paper needed"; "Get into your groups"; "Essays due. Be ready to turn in at the bell."

4. Have attendance slips as filled out as possible (period, section, date, signature, etc.)

5. Develop a seating chart. Some teachers begin taking attendance before the bell; this technique communicates that it is important to be seated early.

6. Keep an eye on traffic patterns—students lined up at the pencil sharpener, back-of-the-room groupings, and other suspect activities.

7. Develop a "makeup" folder for students returning from an absence, and keep it in a designated place on a bookshelf. If handouts were given on a day when a student was absent, he or she can go to the folder and retrieve materials. This technique can assist you in organizing materials in advance and thus you will not have to stop monitoring in order to find materials.

8. Use time before the bell to begin returning corrected assignments and quizzes and distributing handouts.

9. If there are an inordinate number of "housecleaning" activities, such as mandated quarterly attendance reports or census reports that occasionally have to be completed, have sponge activities ready—a question or two to answer, a problem to solve, a short reading. Use anything that relates to the day's learning objective and that will keep students focused for the amount of time you need to complete the forms or reports.

10. Use general comments such as "Let's have a seat folks," "Two minutes to the bell," and "Check the board for directions" in order to give gentle reminders to get situated for the class.

11. Be available for questions before the final bell sounds. If students have the opportunity to ask questions before the bell, you will be able to delve into the activities of the day immediately following the bell. It is not beyond students to deliberately ask inane questions as a distraction.

12. Squelch noise after the bell with a question such as "Are we ready?" If students persist with disruptive behavior, get very specific with questions: "Mary, are you ready?"

13. Give clear and concise directions so that students can get started on tasks and instruction and/or activities will not be interrupted with questions that could be clarified within the instructions. Notice how these instructions are short and provide a rationale for taking notes: "Pull out a sheet of paper and pen. We're going to begin reading the book *The Scarlet Letter,* and you need some information to help you understand tonight's reading assignment."

Ending-of-Class Procedures

Like the beginning of a class period, the ending can be problematic if certain procedures are not developed. The following practices from the field are offered as a beginning point.

1. Allow three to four minutes for closure activities. These activities might include recapping the highlights of the period, reviewing specific content, assigning work to be completed at home, checking for understanding, or highlighting the direction of the next class session. Engage students in the recap process by asking questions and encouraging extended answers.

2. Avoid dead time or the "I just ran out of materials, so read or write" syndrome. Some teachers will skillfully use the last ten minutes of the period to get students started on a homework assignment. This can serve as a form a closure and can allow students to ask clarifying questions about the content of the assignment, especially if the homework is a direct outgrowth of what was discussed and analyzed in class.

3. Avoid giving mindless busywork that has no real bearing on the work under study. Students will soon recognize that this busy work has no meaning, does not relate, and is therefore not important to accomplish.

4. Avoid group activities during the last few minutes of class because group activities can be a source of noise, talk, and confusion.

5. Establish a rule that class does not end until you give the dismissal signal; otherwise, students will get up and leave.

6. Similarly, establish a rule that students cannot begin packing up their materials and bookbags until the very moment the bell rings and you dismiss the class. Imagine the noise level of papers and books being packed while you are engaging students in closure questions.

Remember that rules and procedures need to be (1) introduced and explained early, (2) specific, (3) limited, (4) presented in as positive and proactive terms as possible, (5) consistent with the context of the school setting, (6) simply stated, and (7) reflected upon.

COACHING

Coaching 4.12 What Classroom Rules Are Important to You?

Purpose: To help you identify what rules are most important to you in the development of a set of beginning- and ending-of-period rules and procedures.

Time required: 30 minutes

Procedure: In the Case of the Missing Management, identify Nick's behaviors that caused problems at both the beginning and ending of his class. Then, develop some basic beginning- and ending-of-class procedures that Nick can implement to bring order to the learning environment.

After you have analyzed the scenario, identified the problem areas, and begun developing beginning- and ending-of-class procedures for an effective classroom environment, answer the following questions: Are the rules and procedures realistic? Can you readily implement these rules and procedures? Are they specific? limited? presented in positive and proactive terms? consistent with the context of the school setting? simply stated?

Coaching 4.13 Clarifying Your Rules and Procedures

Purpose: To help you clarify the beginning- and ending-of-period rules and procedures you developed in 4.12.

Time required: Varies

Procedure: Share and discuss with either your cooperating teacher or colleague the list of rules and procedures you developed for both the beginning and ending of your classroom period. As you are discussing your rules and procedures, ask for assistance in trying to present them to a class of students. Your cooperating teacher or university professor will help you envision what these rules will be like in actual practice.

REFLECTION

Reflecting 4.14 A Final Look at the Case of the Missing Management

The following excerpt is from a discussion between Nick and his colleague Luke.

> *Nick:* There is just so much to keep you busy. It's just so complex to know how and when and where to start and end. To know what to do on any particular day at a specific time are difficult things to deal with.
>   If I came up short at the end of the period, I would just give some work. My students eventually figured out that they didn't have to do the work. They just sat and talked away the last few minutes of the period—even with threats. They just blew me off.

The thoughts expressed by Nick are not uncommon to student teachers and beginning teachers. What can you as a beginning teacher do to avoid the pitfalls detailed in both the scenario and the above excerpts?

SUMMARY

Although classroom management can be problematic for beginning teachers, the rules and procedures set forth in this chapter will assist in the development of a classroom environment that is conducive to learning. Remember though, rules and procedures will not ensure an orderly learning environment. It is the approach of the teacher that is of utmost importance. Rules that are consistently and fairly enforced, rules that serve a specified purpose, and rules and behavior that are modeled by the instructor will yield more positive results.

Recommended Reading

Curwin, L., & Mendler, A. N. (1988). *Discipline with dignity.* Alexandria, VA: Association for Supervision and Curriculum Development.

Emmer, E. T., Evertson, C. M., Sanford, J. P., Clements, B. S., & Worsham, M. E. (1989). *Classroom management for secondary teachers.* (2nd ed.). Englewood Cliffs, NJ: Prentice-Hall.

Good, T. L., & Brophy, J. E. (1991). *Looking in classrooms.* (5th ed.). New York: HarperCollins.

Harmin, M. (1994). *Inspiring active learning: A handbook for teachers.* Alexandria, VA: Association for Supervision and Curriculum Development.

Ornstein, A. C. (1990). *Strategies for effective teaching.* New York: HarperCollins.

Sprick, R. S. (1985). *Discipline in the secondary classroom: A problem-by-problem survival guide.* West Nyack, NY: Center for Applied Research in Education.

References

Borko, H. (1986). Clinical teacher education: The induction years. In J. V. Hoffman & S. A. Edwards (eds.), *Reality and reform in clinical teacher education.* New York: Random House.

Brophy, J. E. (1983). Classroom organization and management. *The Elementary School Journal, 83* (4), 265–285.

Brown, M.A., & Willems, A. L. (1977). Lifeboat ethics and the first-year teacher. *The Clearinghouse, 51,* 73–75.

Bullough, R. V. (1987). First-year teaching: A case study. *Teachers College Record, 89* (2), 219–237.

Coates, T., & Thoressen, C. (1978). Teacher anxiety: A review with recommendations. *Review of Educational Research, 51* (2), 159–184.

Cruickshank, D. R., Kennedy, J. J., & Myers, B. (1974). Perceived problems of secondary school teachers. *Journal of Educational Research, 68,* 154–159.

Dropkin, S., & Taylor, M. (1963). Perceived problems of beginning teachers and related factors. *Journal of Teacher Education, 14,* 384–389.

Edmonds, R., Mortimore, P., & Rosenshine, B. (1981). *Teacher and school effectiveness: Leader's guide.* Alexandria, VA: Association for Supervision and Curriculum Development.

Emmer, E. T., Evertson, C. M., Sanford, J. P., Clements, B. S., & Worsham, M. E. (1989). *Classroom management for secondary teachers.* (2nd ed.). Englewood Cliffs, NJ: Prentice-Hall.

Fox, S. M., & Singletary, T. J. (1986). Deductions about supportive induction. *Journal of Teacher Education, 37* (1), 12–15.

Good, T. L., & Brophy, J. E. (1991). *Looking in classrooms.* (5th ed.). New York: HarperCollins.

Kane, P. R. (ed.). (1991). *The first year of teaching: Real world stories from America's teachers.* New York: Walker and Company.

Kounin, J. (1970). *Discipline and group management in classrooms.* NY: Holt, Rinehart and Winston.

McDonald, F. J. & Elias, P. (1982). *The transition into teaching: The problems of beginning teachers and programs to solve them. Summary Report.* Berkeley, CA: Educational Testing Service. ETS Document Reproduction Contract No. 400-78-0069.

Ryan, K. (1979). Toward understanding the problem: At the threshold of the profession. In K. R. Howey & R. H. Bents (eds.), *Toward meeting the needs of the beginning teacher— Initial training/induction/inservice.* Minneapolis: Midwest Teachers Corps Network.

Smith, H. P. (1950). A study of the problems of beginning teachers. *Educational Administration and Supervision, 36,* 257–264.

Stout, J. B. (1952). Deficiencies of beginning teachers. *Journal of Teacher Education, 3,* 43–46.

Tate, M. W. (1943). The induction of secondary-school teachers. *School Review, 51,* 150–157.

Veenman, S. (1984). Perceived problems of beginning teachers. *Review of Educational Research, 54* (2), 143–178.

Wey, H. W. (1951). Difficulties of beginning teachers. *School Review, 51* (1), 32–37.

Chapter 5

The Innovator Role

Chapter Objectives

After completing this chapter, you will be able to

- describe the areas of concern regarding change and innovation.
- describe steps for implementing change at both classroom and school levels.
- identify the elements of an effective school.
- identify the instructional behaviors related to teacher effectiveness.
- determine the uses for direct and indirect instructional strategies.
- describe various approaches for teaching higher-level thinking skills.
- describe the similarities and differences among critical thinking, problem-solving, and creative thinking.
- describe the use of questions for teaching higher-level thinking.
- describe the guidelines for conducting an effective discussion.

*T*his chapter provides information about the types of knowledge, strategies, and skills required of teachers who wish to become more innovative and creative in the classroom. These same strategies are the ones necessary to facilitate students' abilities to be creative, innovative thinkers.

One dictionary defines an innovator as one who begins or introduces something new. To a beginning teacher, the idea of being an innovator may seem an unrealistic expectation. We know that most beginning teachers are more concerned with making it through the day and surviving that first year of teaching than they are with being innovative. Attempting something new or unfamiliar is often the last thing considered by a new teacher.

However, the role of innovator is important to all successful classroom teachers. Effective teachers have a realistic grasp of their strengths and weaknesses; are aware

155

Challenge

The Case of the Innovative Teacher

Jamie is halfway through her second year of teaching English to eighth-graders at the local junior high school. The new principal at her school has been encouraging teachers to become more innovative and creative in their approaches to instruction. Jamie would like to become more innovative but doesn't believe that she has enough experience or knowledge to venture beyond the basic teaching strategies she observed as a student. Although her students do well in her classes, none appear to be motivated or challenged to be innovative.

Given the principal's push toward innovative practices, Jamie believes that her tenure could be in jeopardy if she does not change her approaches to instruction. With the goal of gaining a broader repertoire of instructional strategies, she enrolls in a graduate course in advanced teaching methods at the local university.

that students need varied approaches to learning and are able to incorporate a wide variety of strategies and activities to meet these needs; and create a community of learners by challenging students to become independent problem-solvers and thinkers. Perhaps most important, innovative teachers are open to new ideas and are willing to modify their behavior in order to better meet the needs of all students.

Competency 1: Changing Teacher Behavior and Attitudes

Competency 2: Linking Research and Practice

Competency 3: Encouraging Higher-Level Thinking

Competency 1 CHANGING TEACHER BEHAVIOR AND ATTITUDES

ASSESSMENT

Assessing 5.1 Tuchman's Teacher Characteristics

Purpose: To determine your disposition toward being a creative, dynamic, organized and warm teacher. Understanding your inclinations within these characteristics can help guide your actions.

Time required: 15 minutes

Procedure: The following instrument contains 28 bipolar items on which you will rate yourself on a continuum. Place a check (✔)on the line that most closely reflects your behavior. For example, line 3 asks you to choose between cold and warm. If you believe that you are warm and friendly toward your students, mark the line that best illustrates that behavior.

1.	Original	___	___	___	___	___	Conventional
2.	Patient	___	___	___	___	___	Impatient
3.	Cold	___	___	___	___	___	Warm
4.	Hostile	___	___	___	___	___	Amiable
5.	Creative	___	___	___	___	___	Routinized
6.	Inhibited	___	___	___	___	___	Uninhibited
7.	Idiosyncratic	___	___	___	___	___	Ritualized
8.	Gentle	___	___	___	___	___	Harsh
9.	Unfair	___	___	___	___	___	Fair
10.	Capricious	___	___	___	___	___	Consistent
11.	Cautious	___	___	___	___	___	Outspoken
12.	Disorganized	___	___	___	___	___	Exacting
13.	Unfriendly	___	___	___	___	___	Friendly
14.	Resourceful	___	___	___	___	___	Dull
15.	Reserved	___	___	___	___	___	Purposeful
16.	Imaginative	___	___	___	___	___	Straight
17.	Erratic	___	___	___	___	___	Systematic
18.	Aggressive	___	___	___	___	___	Passive
19.	Accepting	___	___	___	___	___	Critical
20.	Quiet	___	___	___	___	___	Bubbly
21.	Outgoing	___	___	___	___	___	Withdrawn
22.	In control	___	___	___	___	___	On the run
23.	Flighty	___	___	___	___	___	Conscientious
24.	Dominant	___	___	___	___	___	Submissive

25.	Observant	_____	_____	_____	_____	_____	Preoccupied
26.	Introverted	_____	_____	_____	_____	_____	Extroverted
27.	Assertive	_____	_____	_____	_____	_____	Soft-spoken
28.	Timid	_____	_____	_____	_____	_____	Adventurous

Source: Adapted from Tuckman, B. (1985). *Evaluating Instructional Programs.* Boston: Allyn and Bacon.

- A *creative teacher* is imaginative, experimenting, and original; a *noncreative* teacher is routine, exacting, and cautious.
- A *dynamic teacher* is outgoing, energetic, and extroverted; a *nondynamic teacher* is passive, withdrawn, and submissive.
- An *organized teacher* is purposeful, resourceful, and in control; a *disorganized teacher* is capricious, erratic, and flighty.
- A *warm teacher* is sociable, amiable, and patient; a *cold teacher* is unfriendly, hostile, and impatient.

What kind of teacher are you? Are there any behaviors that you need to change?

EXPERIENCE

Understanding Change

Once teachers understand the characteristics of effective teaching and effective schools and are able to implement instructional strategies that facilitate students' thinking skills, they find it easier to become innovative. However, innovation often requires modifying teachers' actions and attitudes. Desirable human change originates from people who are open to life and growing, who view life with limitless possibilities. Teachers with that attitude share their vision and commitment with their students and create a learning environment where they can grow in confidence and competence (Drummond, 1964).

Change and innovation are often uncomfortable for many people. People do not change their behavior and/or attitudes unless they are convinced that the change is for their betterment. Neagley and Evans (1980) state that teachers are often fearful of giving up familiar practices. They often believe that they lack the necessary skills to implement the change or that too much work and time is required to do so. Hord et al. (1987) discovered several assumptions regarding change:

1. *Change is a process, not an event.* Change is not simply inheriting a new program; rather, it is a process that occurs over a period of time, sometimes several years. Recognizing that change is a process one undergoes is a prerequisite to successful innovation.

2. *Change is accomplished by individuals.* Innovation affects people, and their roles in the process are extremely important. Therefore individuals, not the program, must be the focus of attention. School change occurs only when the teachers have absorbed the innovation; simply mandating a change will not make it happen.

3. *Change is a highly personal experience.* Each teacher will react differently to change. Change is most successful when its support is geared to the individual needs of the teachers. Different responses and interventions will be necessary when dealing with a teaching staff. Expecting that all teachers or students will react to an innovation in the same way can create a roadblock to change.

4. *Change involves developmental growth.* As teachers gain experience with a new program or innovation, they demonstrate growth in terms of their feelings and skills. As they become more experienced, they become more confident and can express this confidence in their attitude toward the change.

Ethical Dimension

If we educators are going to be agents of change, or innovators, we must keep in mind why we are doing the changing. Our moral and ethical responsibilities must always be to do what is best for our kids, not just what might make our own institutional lives easier.

Karla Hankins, Elementary School Counselor

5. *Change is best understood in operational terms.* Teachers will relate to an innovation or change in terms of what it means to them or how it will affect their current practice. They will consider the changes required in their own and/or students' behavior, values, and beliefs. They will consider the amount of preparation time that the innovation will require of themselves and their students. These concerns must be addressed in order for the change to be implemented successfully.

6. *The focus of change should be on individuals, innovations, and the context.* Most people mistakenly view the product of an innovation as the change itself. For effective change to take place, the emphasis must be on those who implement that change, not the ultimate product of the change. If the teachers cannot be convinced that the innovation is good for them and for their students, they will not implement the product to its full capability.

Having read the aforementioned assumptions about change, you will realize that Jamie's principal must not only consider individual teacher's reactions to change but also be knowledgeable of the process of change itself. The principal cannot encourage the teachers to become more innovative without first considering the impact on the students, the teachers themselves, and the school as a whole.

Concerns About Change and Innovation

As mentioned previously, teachers will have individual concerns about change and their involvement in it. In 1979, Hall developed a model (Table 5.1) that reflects the stages of the concerns of individuals involved in change. The model describes six stages of concern as the individual passes through three dimensions, or focuses, on self, task, and impact.

Table 5.1 **Stages of Concern: Typical Expressions of Concern About the Innovation**

	Stages of Concern	*Expressions of Concern*
6	Refocusing	I have some ideas about something that would work even better.
5	Collaboration	I am concerned about relating what I am doing with what other instructors are doing.
4	Consequence	How is my use of the innovation affecting students?
3	Management	I seem to be spending all my time getting material ready.
2	Personal	How will using it affect me?
1	Informational	I would like to know more about it.
0	Awareness	I am not concerned about the innovation.

Let's assume that Jamie's principal's program for classroom innovation entails an entire school devoted to the teaching of thinking skills that will enable students to be better critical and creative thinkers and better problem-solvers. At what stage of concern is Jamie? She is at a point where she wishes to become more proficient at teaching thinking skills and so has enrolled in a university course designed to teach higher-level thinking skills. Thus she is most likely at Stage 1, Informational.

Facilitation of Change and Innovation

As stated previously, it is important to account for individual concerns about any planned innovation, whether that of students or staff. Hord et al. (1987) respond to the stages of concern with suggested interventions that will help implement innovations. The following recommendations address school reform, but you should apply many of the same principles to any innovation you plan for your classroom.

During the first stage, *Awareness Concerns,* all teachers should be involved in discussions and decisions about the innovation and its implementation. Information that arouses interest but doesn't overwhelm should be shared. It is important to realize that some people will be unaware of the innovation, so all questions regarding it should be welcome. Remember, when people are unsure or afraid of change, rumors can surface that can doom any innovative effort.

During the second stage, *Informational Concerns,* clear and accurate information should be provided to the entire staff. One strategy for sharing information is to invite others who have already successfully implemented the innovation to talk to the staff. Another is to have teachers visit a site(s) where the innovation has been implemented. This stage should help teachers understand how the innovation relates to their practices.

The third stage, *Personal Concerns,* legitimizes and attends to the personal concerns of the staff. Emphasize that concerns about change are natural. Teachers need to know that the innovation will be implemented sequentially rather than in one big step. This expectation allows teachers to get a handle on the change without feeling overwhelmed by it.

During the fourth stage, *Management Concerns,* the specific how-to issues should be addressed in order to alleviate management concerns. Immediate demands and concerns of the innovation should be discussed rather than issues about what will be or could be in the future. Teachers should be helped to sequence specific steps and time lines for implementing the innovation.

The fifth stage, *Consequence Concerns,* addresses concerns that teachers might have about the impact of the innovation on their students or themselves. Again, these teachers should be provided with the opportunity to visit other schools where the innovation has been implemented successfully. Their concerns must be addressed directly; otherwise, the innovation may never be implemented fully.

The sixth stage, *Collaboration Concerns,* provides interested parties with opportunities to work collaboratively to develop the innovation. This may include teachers, administrators, parents, students, and others who can be used to provide technical assistance to those who need it. Collaboration should be encouraged but never forced.

Finally, the *Refocusing Concern* respects and encourages the interest some might have for finding a better way. These people should be helped to channel their ideas in ways that will be productive rather than counterproductive. It is possible that these people may modify or significantly alter the innovation.

The preceding steps take into account that all people may have different concerns about change and innovation. If the concerns are not addressed, then the innovation's chances of being implemented are diminished. Students, too, will have concerns when change and innovation are proposed for the classroom. Your role is to attend to those concerns so that students not only understand the innovation but also accept it. Implementing a curriculum that emphasizes higher-level thinking skills can cause concerns in students who are not used to thinking beyond the knowledge or comprehension levels. They will be concerned both about their ability to answer the different types of questions and problems and about how they will be assessed in this new curriculum. Failure to address these concerns will only heighten their anxiety and possibly doom the innovation.

Reality Bite

Positive Outlook

Innovative teachers who meet challenges and strive to be creative and motivated should also be aware of those factors that unconsciously have a negative effect on innovation. Listening to teachers who seemingly always have negative comments about the students or the curriculum can have an overpowering effect if you allow their viewpoints to influence your teaching style.

Seek out teachers who seem motivated and have a more positive outlook. After grading a test that covers a unit or chapter over which much time and energy were spent preparing and presenting, the challenged teacher should not take low test scores personally but instead should see areas that need more attention and focus on them. When a particular method, idea, or entire unit is not meeting its objectives, don't think it must be carried out until the end. The innovative teacher will immediately see the need for change, make the necessary changes, and then try again. Being innovative means taking risks, and that is what makes teaching exciting.

If beginning teachers can perceive each day as a mystery waiting to unfold, they can bring much motivation into the classroom with a natural ease.

Judy Evrard, Experienced Mathematics Teacher

School Reform

Jamie's principal is attempting to introduce an innovation that will require teachers and administrators to change their ways of thinking about instruction and evaluation of learning. In short, the principal is attempting to help facilitate school reform. This is no easy task even when the reform effort is supported with grant money from the state or national government or from a foundation. Orlich (1989) lists several conclusions that have been discovered about school reform and the successful implementation of innovation:

1. Innovations take hold best when the objectives and techniques are few and sharply defined.

2. Larger changes seemed to take place when the specific purposes of the project were agreed to at the outset of the program. Programs with broad purposes produced few measurable outcomes.

3. Projects that were most effective and sustained momentum were those whose directors were present at the planning stage and remained through the implementation, evaluation, and adaptation phases.

4. Innovation and change require the broadest possible commitment of intellectual and financial resources.

5. Universities, as institutions, seldom functioned as a force for improving elementary and secondary schooling, although individual faculty members worked in schools and with teachers.

6. The less complex a school system's structure, the more easily innovations were introduced and accepted. However, smaller schools were more likely to abandon an innovation if external funding was diminished.

7. The most lasting innovations seemed to occur in mid-sized suburbs, communities small enough to avoid divisive debates among powerful special interest groups.

Change is inevitable but it does not need to be a scary proposition. If it is to be successful, you must be committed to the change. You must be able to communicate your vision and passion for the direction of your classroom and for the expectations of your students if your innovative practices are to take hold.

COACHING

Coaching 5.2 Levels of Use of an Innovation

Purpose: To examine the stages that teachers use to incorporate an innovation into their classrooms.

Time required: 15 minutes

Procedure: Visit with several teachers who are involved with some innovative project in the school. Where did the innovation originate? What are the attitudes of the teachers toward the innovation? What are the attitudes of the teachers toward the change process? At which of the following levels would you place the various teachers?

Level 0—Non-use: The individual has little or no knowledge of the innovation, has no involvement with it, and is not planning future involvement.

Level I—Orientation: The individual has acquired or is acquiring information about the innovation and/or has explored its value orientation.

Level II—Preparation: The user is preparing for the first use of the innovation.

Level III—Mechanical Use: The user focuses on short-term, day-to-day use of the innovation with little time for reflection. The user is primarily engaged in an attempt to master tasks required to use the innovation. These attempts are often disjointed.

Level IV-A—Routine: The use of the innovation is stabilized. Little thought is given to improving the innovation.

Level IV-B—Refinement: The user varies the use of the innovation to increase its impact on students. Any variations are based on knowledge of short- and long-term consequences.

Level V—Integration: The user combines own efforts to use the innovation with related activities of colleagues to achieve a collective impact on students within their common sphere of influence.

Level VI—Renewal: The user reevaluates the quality of the use of the innovation, seeks major modifications of, or alternatives to, present innovation to achieve increased input on students. (Adapted from Hord, S., Rutherford, W., Huling-Austin, L., & Hall, G. [1987]. *Taking charge of change.* Alexandria, VA: Association for Supervision and Curriculum Development.)

REFLECTION

Reflecting 5.3 Core Values for Implementing Change

Purpose: Using Patterson's (1993) list of basic core values, assess the ability of a school or school district to nurture change.

Time required: 30 minutes

Procedure: With several colleagues, answer the questions regarding the following core values. How do your responses compare? If there are differences, why? What do your collective responses reveal about your school or school district?

1. **Core Value: Empowerment**
   To what extent does your school or school district:
   a. value empowering staff throughout the school/district to assist in achieving the mission of the school/district?
   b. value equal access by all staff to support information and resources?
   c. value all staff as equally important members of the organization?

2. **Core Value: Decision Making**
   To what extent does your school or school district:
   a. value placing decision making as close to the point of implementation as possible?
   b. value the opportunity for input in districtwide decisions?
   c. value decisions being made by those who are directly affected by them?

3. **Core Value: Belonging**
   To what extent does your school or school district:
   a. value commitment to the development of the individual within the district?
   b. value treating all individuals as significant stakeholders in the organization?
   c. value a "we" spirit and feeling of ownership in the organization?

4. **Core Value: Trust and Confidence**
   To what extent does your school or school district:
   a. believe that staff act in the best interest of students and the organization?
   b. value staff as having the expertise to make wise decisions?
   c. value investing in the development of staff?

5. **Core Value: Diversity**
   To what extent does your school or school district:
   a. value differences in individual philosophy and practices?
   b. value differences in perspectives?
   c. value schools and children within them celebrating their distinct character?

6. **Core Value: Integrity**
   To what extent does your school or school district:
   a. value honesty in words and actions?
   b. value consistent, responsible pursuit of what we stand for?
   c. value the unwavering commitment to ethical conduct?

7. **Core Value: Student Success**
   To what extent does your school or school district:
   a. value students as inherently curious learners?
   b. value doing whatever it takes to achieve student success?
   c. value students being meaningfully engaged in work that has personal value to them? (Adapted from Patterson, J. [1993]. *Leadership for tomorrow's schools.* Alexandria, VA: Association for Supervision and Curriculum Development.)

■ *Competency 2* LINKING RESEARCH TO PRACTICE

ASSESSMENT

Assessing 5.4 What Do You Know About Successful Teaching and Schools?

Purpose: To assess your knowledge of the components of successful teachers and successful schools.

Time required: 10 minutes

Procedure: On a sheet of paper, make two columns. Label one column Successful Schools; the other, Successful Teachers. List all the behaviors and characteristics that you believe describe successful teachers and successful schools. After completing this chapter, compare your list with what you have learned about successful teachers and successful schools.

EXPERIENCE

Successful Schools Research

Most of us have attended more than 15 years of school. As a result of this experience, we believe that we know the characteristics required of a successful school. But what is a successful school, and what are the characteristics that determine one? Among the major researchers in school success are Rutter (1979) and Goodlad (1984). Although the findings of each study vary slightly, all appear to have some common threads. One major thread is what Glickman (1994) refers to as teachers within a school adhering to a philosophy of "a cause beyond oneself." These teachers view themselves as part of a higher pursuit, not just as isolated individuals each carrying out tasks within their own classrooms.

The majority of schools commonly considered to be successful display each of the following ten characteristics to a greater or lesser degree.

1. *Opportunity to learn.* Providing students with the opportunity to learn means that teachers create ways for maximizing the amount of time devoted to academic learning. This includes beginning class on time, staying on task, and making smooth transitions between activities. In addition, optimizing students' opportunity to learn requires school policies that protect instructional time from unwarranted interruptions. Teachers in successful classrooms tend to cover more material than in other classrooms.

2. *Tightly coupled curriculum.* Arends (1988) explains that a curriculum in a successful school is closely connected, or tightly coupled, to the goals, objectives, and evaluation procedures. Successful schools make curricular decisions based on a set of sequential goals and objectives. Also, teachers know what teachers at other grade levels are teaching and build upon or work toward what is being taught in other grades.

3. *Direct instruction.* Direct instruction refers to instruction where teachers ensure that goals are clear to students, learning time is protected, and well-planned instructional presentations utilize a variety of teaching methods, including discussions, demonstrations, and discovery learning approaches.

4. *Academic focus and mission.* A successful school continuously emphasizes student achievement for *all students* as its primary objective. This objective is shared with and believed in by teachers, administrators, parents, and students. The goal of academic excellence is consistently communicated to the community; for example, a school that provides rewards for academic achievement is telling students and parents that it is a priority.

5. *Monitoring student progress.* In successful schools, administrators and teachers employ systematic procedures for monitoring students' progress. Homework is required and checked regularly by teachers (Arends, 1988). Feedback is provided to students in order to appraise them of their strengths and areas needing improvement.

6. *Staff development.* Successful schools incorporate a staff development program that is structured around the school's mission, goals, and objectives; solicit teacher input; and ensure that the content of the staff development program will be implemented in the curriculum. These programs are relevant to the needs of teachers and students, and they promote teacher growth.

7. *Strong teacher leadership.* Rather than the fate of a school depending solely on the strengths or weaknesses of one individual—the principal, successful schools promote shared leadership. Teachers and principals work collaboratively as colleagues, model democratic beliefs and principles for students, and critically study the school and their individual practice.

8. *High expectations.* High expectations refer to a school environment where teachers and administrators expect the students to do well, believe that all students can perform well, and believe in their own ability to facilitate student achievement. Accordingly, teachers and administrators are held accountable for student achievement. As a result, all school activities, both academic and social, are developed around these expectations.

9. *Safe environment.* Similar to the belief in high expectations, successful schools also share a belief in the basic rules of conduct. The school is safe in regard to absence of physical harm, and rules are enforced consistently and fairly. Teachers and students alike share a responsibility for enforcing the code of conduct.

10. *Sense of community.* An effective school breeds a sense of community where parents and other members of the community become involved in the school's programs. An open-door policy to the school promotes a sense of ownership and pride in the school and its programs. Tutoring, talent shows, and fund-raisers are among several methods for promoting a sense of community.

Research by Epstein and Dauber (1989) indicates that parents of all races and social classes want their children to succeed in school and want to help. Lueder (1989) found that parent involvement programs resulted in positive results at both grade and school levels. What can you do to involve parents in your class?

Systemic Reform

Fullan (1993) calls the decade of the nineties the "systemic reform" period of the school reform movement. Systemic reform refers to the change process of linking together assessment, curriculum and instruction, staff development, and personnel selection and promotion for the purpose of improving the whole system—in this case, the school system. The theory behind systemic reform is that change cannot occur within the system if it is piecemeal; for the system to change, all aspects must be attended to by the innovators.

Unfortunately, there are limitations to the systemic strategy (Fullan, 1993). First, many reformers greatly underestimate the complexity of the system and the nuances involved with each particular system. Second, systemic reforms that occur in one place cannot necessarily be transported to another system. Each school system, like any other community, has its own dynamics that are acute only to that system; consequently, duplicating the circumstances that supported an innovation in one school may be difficult in another location.

Teacher Effectiveness Research

What is effective teaching? A teacher is effective to the extent that he or she causes students to learn what is intended that they learn (Dunkin & Biddle, 1974). It is important to note that there is a difference between "good" teaching and "effective" teaching. Good teaching tends to be a subjective term that relies on a person's preference for a particular teaching style. Effective teaching, on the other hand, is based on research that links certain teacher behaviors or variables with gains in student learning.

Perhaps the most often cited list of teacher behaviors related to student achievement is that compiled by Rosenshine and Furst (1973) following their analysis of over 40 correlational studies. Clarity, enthusiasm, use of multiple teaching methods, and the ability to keep students on task appear to most consistently affect student learning.

Clarity. How clear are the teacher's presentations, directions, instructions, questions, and overall organization? In order for students to learn, they must be able to understand what is being communicated to them and what is being asked of them. Students who are unsure of the skills or knowledge they are to learn, the directions they are to follow, or the questions they are to answer will not perform as well or learn as much as students having well-organized teachers who give clear presentations.

There are several means of assessing your ability to communicate clearly. Videotape or audiotape your teaching, or invite a colleague to observe your classroom. Then ask the following questions: Do you communicate the objectives of your lessons clearly? Do students consistently ask you to clarify your stated objectives? Do they consistently ask you to restate important points that you make throughout your lesson? Do your lessons have an introduction and conclusion? Do you spend a lot of time repeating or rephrasing questions? Do you use a lot of vague expressions?

Enthusiasm. Today's teachers must compete with the MTV generation. You therefore need to develop a teaching style that communicates enthusiasm for teaching, for your students, and for your subject matter. Teachers who are enthusiastic in the classroom are more likely to have students who likewise are motivated and more inclined to pay attention. As a result, those with enthusiastic teachers are more apt to learn their material.

Again, certain mannerisms help determine teacher enthusiasm. In general, enthusiastic teachers can be observed moving around the classroom monitoring student behavior and performance, using gestures coupled with voice tone and volume to emphasize key points, displaying a sense of humor, and smiling at their students.

Use of Multiple Teaching Methods. Throughout this text we have discussed the various roles that teachers assume in the classroom as well as multiple instructional approaches employed with students. Research indicates that the systematic utilization of a variety of instructional techniques results in higher student achievement than does the reliance on any one strategy (Rosenshine & Furst, 1973; Good & Brophy, 1987).

Why does this occur? A teacher who uses a variety of teaching methods sustains student attention and motivation more than the teacher who stresses only one approach, even a good one. Students soon learn what to expect when a teacher uses the same instructional approach for each class period. The use of lectures, small-group activities, demonstrations, different types and levels of questions, discussions, field trips, etc., not only keeps the students' interest but also appeals to the wide variety of learning styles and abilities found in any classroom.

Ability to Keep Students On Task. During the 1980s there was much discussion about increasing the length of the school day and school year. Many people believed that merely increasing the length of time students spend in school would increase achievement proportionally. We have discovered, however, that the time allocated for learning is not as related to achievement as is the time students' spend engaged in learning tasks. An effective teacher will ensure that students spend an appropriate amount of time actually engaged in learning activities.

It is impossible to expect that *all* students will be attentive at *all* times. Everyone has moments of daydreaming and inattentiveness. Good and Brophy (1987) estimate that an effective teacher should be able to create a learning environment in which 80 to 90 percent of the students are engaged in learning at any given moment. Several techniques are used for monitoring student engagement in the classroom (Good & Brophy, 1987; Arends, 1988):

1. When the teacher gives directions, how many students watch?
2. When the teacher completes the directions, how many students begin to work?
3. How many students ask questions in order to complete a task?
4. When students are assigned seatwork, how many are writing or reading?
5. When the teacher works with a small group, what percentage of the remainder of the class is actively working?
6. How frequently does the teacher need to reprimand students for inappropriate behavior during an assigned task?

Arends (1988) states that the following management and interaction behaviors maximize student engagement and, as a result, increase student achievement:

1. Accurately *diagnosing* student skill level.
2. *Prescribing* appropriate tasks.
3. Conducting *substantive interaction* with students. (This differs from social, disciplinary, or procedural interaction.)
4. Providing *academic feedback* to students, especially when correcting a student error.
5. *Structuring* the lesson and providing directions for on-task procedures.
6. Creating a *learning environment* in which students take responsibility for their work and cooperate on academic tasks.

Perhaps the bottom line on this issue, according to Arends, is that a teacher must value student achievement and establish meaningful goals.

Direct Instruction

Direct instruction can be defined as academically focused classrooms that employ sequenced and structured learning materials. Rosenshine (1979) states that direct instruction refers to instruction where goals are clear to students, time allocated for learning is sufficient, coverage of content is extensive, performance and behavior of students are monitored, and questioning strategies are thoroughly planned and implemented effectively. Although the classroom is teacher directed and structured, successful direct instruction is not authoritarian but takes place in a positive, supportive environment.

Lecture. Since direct instruction is most often utilized to communicate facts or rules to students, the lecture method is the typical vehicle. Although some educators tend to criticize lecturing as a noncreative approach to teaching, it remains one of the most direct and efficient ways for communicating large amounts of information. A successful lecture includes not only extensive amounts of time spent presenting information but also interaction with students in the form of questions and answers and review and practice.

Rosenshine and Stevens (1986) cite four basic steps to conducting a successful lecture: First, you must be clear about your objectives and main points. State the objectives at the beginning of the lecture, focusing on one piece of information at a time, and avoid digressions and ambiguity. Second, you should present the content sequentially and in small steps. You may need to present an outline if the material is complex. Third, you should be specific and concrete. Provide models, concrete examples, and explanations to support your statements. Finally, you should monitor your students' understanding. For example, make sure students understand one point before proceeding to the next; ask questions to monitor their comprehension of what has been presented; have students summarize the main points in their own words; and reteach the segment of the presentation that the students have difficulty understanding.

Academic Focus. Effective teachers maintain a strong focus on academics while spending less time on nonacademic activities. Research indicates that teachers who spend more time on activities in a content area (i.e., reading, mathematics) have students with higher achievement rates than teachers who spend a lot of time in activities involving games, group time, or arts and crafts (Stallings & Kaskowitz, 1974). Teachers also maintain academic focus by emphasizing regular homework, giving weekly tests or quizzes, marking and grading students' assignments, and requiring students to be attentive in class.

Questions. It is estimated that teachers ask 350 to 400 questions a day. Research indicates that for students to learn facts and rules, the teacher must ask a higher proportion of factual, single-answer questions. These questions are typically derived from the knowledge and comprehension levels of Bloom's *Taxonomy of Educational Objectives: Cognitive Domain* (see Chapter 1). Asking a high percentage of higher-order questions, such as those derived from the analysis, synthesis, and evaluation levels of the taxonomy, appears to be negatively correlated to the learning of facts. Of course, this makes sense because questions of a higher order are designed to require students to do more with information than merely recall facts. As a result, students will perform better at higher levels of thinking when asked higher-order questions.

Reality Bite

Diversity

A great need exists in education today for children to participate in activities that span the cultures. Many children lack awareness of cultures different from their own. In today's society, it is critical that children be exposed to a variety of multicultural experiences, starting at an early age. A rich cultural understanding and awareness can give them a competitive edge when they enter the job market of the twenty-first century.

Teachers as innovators and change agents should be willing and motivated to take the initiative to incorporate multicultural activities into daily instruction. Teachers with the drive and initiative to expose children to a variety of cultures give their students an advantage that they will use throughout their lives. In some schools, new teachers who take it upon themselves to present multicultural lessons will at first be met with resentment from other teachers in the school, especially if the culture being presented has very little representation on that campus. In time though, the resentful teachers usually come around and begin to incorporate multicultural lessons into their own teaching as well. They do this because they have observed the success that the innovative new teacher has had by implementing multicultural teaching into daily routine. The end result is that new teachers, through their innovative thought and motivation, have set a standard for the rest of the school to follow.

A good way to expose many children to a new culture is for new teachers to get to know the community that their school serves. They are then able to make many contacts with members of different cultures, many of whom may be willing to come to school and give talks about their particular culture. By asking community members to come to a school to give cultural demonstrations, the innovative new teacher is setting a standard for other teachers to follow. This not only teaches children about a new culture but fosters community involvement as well.

Matthew Seebaum, First-Year Elementary Teacher

It is important to remember that lower-order questions are most appropriate when testing factual knowledge. At a later point in this chapter, we will discuss the appropriateness of asking higher-order questions.

Direct Instruction Versus Indirect Instruction

Too often, teachers read the research linking aspects of direct instruction to gains in achievement and believe that those are the only strategies useful in the classroom. While direct instruction strategies are ideal for learning factual material, it is the indirect instruction strategies that are appropriate for teaching the higher-level skills of problem-solving, inquiry, discovery, and creativity. Indirect strategies also appear to be more successful for increasing students' independence and for fostering more favorable attitudes toward school and learning. Whereas direct instruction is typically related to teacher-directed instructional strategies, indirect instruction is often characterized by a more open style that includes flexibility of space, student choice of materials and activities, variety of learning resources, integration of the curriculum, and more individual and small-group instruction (Horwitz, 1979). Peterson (1979) believes that educators should provide opportunities for students to be exposed to both approaches.

COACHING

Coaching 5.5 Observing Classroom Behavior

This section of the chapter discusses behaviors that have been linked to successful teaching and successful schools. Arrange with one of your peers to conduct a series of exchanged observations where you can observe each other teaching in actual classroom situations. For each of the observations, select one or two of the successful teaching behaviors included in this section of the chapter. For example, focus on your colleague's enthusiasm or clarity. Note examples of the enthusiastic or nonenthusiastic approach to teaching. Also note examples of your colleague's clarity (or lack of) in giving directions or explanations. Another method for gathering this data is to videotape your teaching and, at different times, assess several different teaching behaviors.

REFLECTION

Reflecting 5.6 Dimensions of Successful Schooling

Purpose: To examine the dimensions of effective schools and to apply these dimensions to your school.

Time required: 15 to 20 minutes

Procedure: Mackenzie (1983) listed three dimensions that have been related by research to effective schools—leadership, efficacy, and efficiency—and listed core and facilitating elements of each (Table 5.2).

Table 5.2 **Dimensions of Successful Schooling**

LEADERSHIP DIMENSIONS	
Core Elements:	Positive climate and overall atmosphere Goal-focused activities toward clear, attainable, and relevant objectives Teacher-directed classroom management and decision-making Inservice staff training for effective teaching
Facilitating Elements:	Shared consensus on values and goals Long-range planning and cooperation Stability and continuity of key staff District-level support for school improvement

EFFICACY DIMENSIONS	
Core Elements:	High and positive achievement expectations with a constant press for excellence Visible rewards for academic excellence and growth Cooperative activity and group interaction in the classroom Total staff involvement with school improvement Autonomy and flexibility to implement adaptive practices Appropriate levels of difficulty for learning tasks Teacher empathy, rapport, and personal interaction with students
Facilitating Elements:	Emphasis on homework and study Positive accountability; acceptance of responsibility for learning outcomes Strategies to avoid nonpromotion of students Deemphasis of strict ability; interaction with more accomplished peers

EFFICIENCY DIMENSIONS	
Core Elements:	Effective use of instructional time; amount and intensity of engagement in school learning Orderly and disciplined school and classroom environments Continuous diagnosis, evaluation, and feedback Well-structured classroom activities Instruction guided by content coverage
Facilitating Elements:	Opportunities for individualized work Number and variety of opportunities to learn

Source: Adapted from Mackenzie, D. (1983). Research for school improvement: An appraisal of some recent research trends. *Educational Researcher, 12* (4), 4–17.

Apply each of the elements within the three dimensions to your school. How does your school rate for each of these elements? For example, is there a positive climate and atmosphere? Are any of the three dimensions stronger or weaker than others? What strategies can be used to improve these elements and dimensions? Compare your results and perceptions with your mentor or with another teacher in your school.

■ *Competency 3* ENCOURAGING HIGHER-LEVEL THINKING

ASSESSMENT

Assessing 5.7 Identifying Higher-Level Thinking Skills

Purpose: To assess your knowledge of higher-level thinking skills.

Time required: 5 minutes

Procedure: The following questions require students to respond by using either lower- or higher-order thinking skills. For each question, mark L for lower order or H for higher order. You might want to review Bloom's *Taxonomy for Educational Objectives: Cognitive Domain* in Chapter 1. Remember that the terms lower and higher do not reflect a value judgment but refer to complexity of the thought process required to address a question or problem.

_____   1. What does *mañana* mean?

_____   2. How would a map of the United States look if the South had been victorious in the Civil War?

_____   3. What is the definition of a noun?

_____   4. What do you think will happen when I mix this dye with the water?

_____   5. What ways can you group these items other than by size?

_____   6. Who discovered the Pacific Ocean?

_____   7. How do the characters in the movie *The Firm* compare to those in the novel?

_____   8. How many animals are there in this picture?

_____   9. How would you rate Dave's performance in the school play?

_____   10. What is the difference between fact and opinion in journalism?

(*Answers:* 1-L, 2-H, 3-L, 4-H, 5-H, 6-L, 7-H, 8-L, 9-H, 10-H)

EXPERIENCE

The direct instruction strategies discussed in this chapter are important to master if you are to become an effective teacher. However, as previously stated, total reliance on direct instruction strategies often leads to classrooms that emphasize the learning of facts and operate solely at the knowledge level of the cognitive domain. Students in these classes do very well with factual knowledge but are not as proficient in problem-solving or critical thinking; in other words, they are not as adept at manipulating these facts within new situations in order to solve problems or arrive at creative solutions. As a result, it is important that teachers master both direct and indirect instruction strategies so that their students can not only recall facts but also be able to manipulate this data in order to solve problems.

Beyer (1987) believes that schools should be consciously and systematically attending to improving students' thinking skills, because skillful thinking must be valued, taught, and nurtured—it does not just develop on its own. He lists four reasons why the teaching of thinking skills in classrooms is particularly important: First, becoming a skillful person is not a natural process. It neither occurs through experience nor is the product of a particular academic area. Skillful thinking requires deliberate, continuing instruction, guidance, modeling, and practice. Second, the teaching of thinking skills is important to student survival in school. Students are continually confronted by situations where they are assessed on the products of their thinking. Students who are not instructed to be skillful thinkers have more difficulty when asked to solve problems, to synthesize or evaluate materials, or to develop a creative product. Third, teaching thinking is important for what it can do for teachers and schools. Various reform reports of the 1980s decried the thinking skills of United States students. As a result, several state legislatures mandated the teaching of thinking skills in the curriculum, and testing agencies have begun to produce standardized tests that include an emphasis on complex thinking skills. Finally, our world is changing so rapidly that students need to be skillful thinkers if they are to cope with the unknown situations and problems of the future. For example, in 1970 information was doubling every ten years. During the 1990s, however, information is doubling every 20 months. So much of what we taught just a few years ago is now obsolete in several academic areas. Students must become skillful thinkers if they are to adjust to a rapidly changing world.

Teaching Critical Thinking

The term "critical thinking" has been used to describe any type of thinking that is beyond factual recall. This uncertainty of definition has caused some confusion. Critical thinking is neither problem-solving nor a creative process. According to Ennis (1962), it is judging the authenticity, worth, or accuracy of something. Unfortunately, critical thinking has often become synonymous with negative comments about the worth or value of something. Instead, as Beyer (1987) relates, critical thinking is objective and value-free and often results in positive and affirmative comments. Table 5.3 illustrates some of the differences between ordinary thinking and critical thinking.

Critical thinking operations typically involve both analysis and evaluation skills. Students must first examine the data to determine what is applicable to the problem at hand and then assess the data to determine what is necessary to solve the problem. Teachers must provide students with numerous opportunities to analyze, apply, and evaluate information; allow students to argue opposing sides of an issue; and challenge students to provide rationale or data to support an answer. Teachers must be skilled at asking appropriate questions, at probing and challenging students' responses, at leading invigorating discussions, and at organizing the classroom in order to facilitate critical thinking. Perhaps most important, teachers themselves must be critical thinkers. Ennis (1985) divided critical thinking into four components: First is *defining and clarifying*. This includes identifying conclusions and stated and unstated reasons, identifying and handling irrelevance, and seeing similarities and differences. The second is *asking appropriate questions* to clarify or challenge student thinking. Third is *judging the credibility of a source*. The fourth component is *solving problems and drawing conclusions*. This includes the ability to deduce and judge validity, induce and judge conclusions, and predict probable consequences.

Teaching Problem-Solving

Teaching students to solve problems may be one of the most important tasks assumed by teachers. Students who develop problem-solving skills are able to apply these skills to novel and unique situations that may confront them in the future.

Table 5.3 **Ordinary Thinking Versus Critical Thinking**

Ordinary Thinking	*Critical Thinking*
Guessing	Estimating
Preferring	Evaluating
Grouping	Classifying
Believing	Assuming
Inferring	Inferring logically
Associating concepts	Grasping principles
Noting relationships	Noting relationships among relationships
Supposing	Hypothesizing
Offering opinions without reasons	Offering opinions with reasons
Making judgments without criteria	Making judgments with criteria

Source: Adapted from Lipman, M. (1988). Critical thinking—what can it be? *Educational Leadership,* 46, 38–43.

Table 5.4 illustrates one approach that is widely used to teach problem-solving to gifted and talented students. Developed by Sidney Parnes (1967), this is a structured method to problem-solving that emphasizes consideration of multiple alternatives before implementing a solution. During Step 1, you should develop or select exercises to lead students, both individually and as a group, through a process of discovering the known and unknown facts and information about a situation. In Step 2, develop or select exercises to assist students, both individually and as a group, in focusing the problem. Encourage them to use verbs that provide a more solvable statement of the problem. During Step 3, encourage the students to generate as many ideas as possible. Do not criticize any of the students' suggestions, because you will be discouraging participation. Remember that some of the most off-the-wall ideas sometimes are the best! At Step 4, assist the students to develop criteria for evaluating the ideas. Finally, in Step 5 the students develop a plan of action using the ideas generated by the class. They also need to develop a strategy(ies) that will enable them to sell the plan to the appropriate audience.

Table 5.4 **Parnes's Creative Problem-Solving Process**

Step 1. Fact Finding:	Collect information about the situation. Find what is known from what needs to be known. Observe carefully and objectively.
Step 2. Problem Finding:	Look at problem from several viewpoints. Restate the problem.
Step 3. Idea Finding:	Generate many ideas and possible solutions. Defer judgment until all ideas are considered. Brainstorm for ideas or alternative solutions; strive for quantity. List as many ideas as possible.
Step 4. Solution Finding:	Develop criteria for evaluating solutions. Objectively apply criteria to selected ideas. Choose alternatives with greatest potential. Evaluate alternatives.
Step 5. Acceptance Finding:	Develop a plan of action. Consider all audiences. Brainstorm ways to gain acceptance of plan.

Teaching Creative Thinking

Often, teachers and students confuse creative thinking with critical thinking. Although related because both attempt to facilitate higher-level thinking skills, they are different. Beyer (1987) points out the differences between the two approaches:

> Whereas creative thinking is divergent, critical thinking is convergent; whereas creative thinking seeks to generate something new, critical thinking seeks to assess worth or validity in something that exists; whereas creative thinking is carried on often by violating accepted principles, critical thinking is carried on by applying accepted principles. (p. 35)

Creative thinking attempts to create something new. This "creation" can take many forms, such as a poem, musical lyrics, a painting, a new fuel injection system for automobiles, or a novel approach to a mathematics, chemistry, or physics problem. Students who think creatively are often a challenge to teachers who are comfortable only with "right" answers, because these students approach typical school situations and problems in an atypical fashion. However, like other modes of higher-level thinking, creative thinking needs to be encouraged and facilitated by teachers.

Torrance (1962) discovered that the growth of creativity, as defined by test performance, increases from age three to age four then begins to drop, rising again to drop at fourth grade. He also found that many fifth-graders scored higher in creativity in the first grade than they did in the fifth grade. The reasons for the drop in creativity vary but often find their roots in the classroom and the home. Some

Reality Bite

Problem-Solving

Providing problem-solving experiences in the classroom can be both challenging and time consuming, but the payoff is worth it!

Eighth-graders in our junior high school were learning about the solid-waste problem in their community. We wanted to create an awareness about the problem, and we wanted the students to think about ways in which the problem could be addressed.

Using a problem-solving process, the students collected information about local landfills and recycling programs, brainstormed several ideas to address the problem, and decided to produce their own video that would encourage younger students to recycle at home and at school. They planned the production, worked as scriptwriters, actors, and researchers, and did the filming. When they finished the video, they spoke to elementary students about the importance of recycling and then showed the video to increase interest.

Through the video production process, the students learned how to clearly identify a problem, how to utilize local resources for possible solutions, and how to work together as a team. This project enabled the students to gain both creative thinking skills and problem-solving skills.

Annette Campbell, Cooperative Extension
Madeline Meadows, Experienced Middle School Teacher

teachers discourage creativity because it does not result in the "right" answer or accepted mode of thought, or because they are not familiar with strategies that facilitate creative thinking. Some parents do not encourage creativity because they do not want their child to be "different." Thus it is important for the teacher to create an environment that encourages creativity and experimentation.

Williams (1982) has suggested the following guidelines for establishing a supportive environment for creative thinking:

1. Establish a responsive and expressive climate.
2. Provide encouragement for self-resourcefulness.
3. Recognize, respect, and give emotional support.
4. Expect and allow for comfortable regression in growth patterns.

5. Allow and provide some balance between interpersonal and intrapersonal experiences.

6. Establish well-defined standards of discipline and conduct.

7. Establish an achievement-oriented climate.

8. Establish an attitude of basic trust.

You should integrate the teaching of creative thinking throughout the curriculum by including it in your objectives, activities, questions, and evaluation. Remember, it will be creative thinkers who will provide us with art, music, literature, and solutions to future problems.

Indirect Teaching Strategies

Indirect teaching strategies are the ones utilized to teach the higher-level thinking skills of critical thinking, problem-solving, and creative thinking. Indirect instruction involves the teaching of concepts, abstractions, and patterns. Unlike direct instruction where the teacher is the purveyor of all knowledge, indirect instruction requires the teacher to be more of a facilitator—to guide students to an answer or answers that go beyond the recitation of facts. Indirect teaching strategies incorporate students' experiences and problems into the lessons and encourage them to become more involved in the evaluation of their own and their peers' ideas and products. Although indirect strategies can be employed in a large group setting, they are often utilized in many small-group arrangements or in individualized learning situations (see Chapter 1).

Inductive and Deductive Thinking. Both inductive and deductive thinking are important for student learning. Inductive thinking is more appropriate for stimulating students' thinking, whereas deductive thinking is more appropriate for delivering information.

Inductive thinking occurs when a set of data or a situation is presented to students and, after a process of investigation, they are asked to make a generalization or develop a pattern of relationships from the data. In many ways, inductive thinking is related to discovery learning.

Borich (1988) provides several examples of inductive thinking:

1. You notice rain-slick roads are causing accidents on the way to school, so you reduce speed at all the remaining intersections.

2. You get an unsatisfactory grade on a chemistry exam, so you study six extra hours a week for the rest of the semester in all of your subjects.

3. You see a close friend suffer from the effects of drug abuse, so you volunteer to disseminate information about substance abuse to all of your acquaintances.

4. You get a math teacher who is cold and unfriendly, so you decide to never enroll in a math course again.

In each case, the student was presented with some data and proceeded to infer a broader conclusion or generalization. For example, the student received data regarding a math teacher, interpreted or investigated it, and then made a generalization to all future math courses. In the classroom, a teacher might introduce information at the beginning of the lesson and then, later in the lesson, relate it to other examples for students to understand the relationships or patterns between the two sets of examples.

Deductive thinking states a rule or generalization and then expects the learners to apply it to specific instances. Teachers can utilize three steps when presenting deductive thinking:

1. *Advanced Organizer.* An advanced organizer provides students with a preview of what is to come during the lesson. In essence, it helps provide a road map to the lesson for the students. For example, consider a lesson about metaphor and simile. To use an advanced organizer, the teacher would begin the discussion by defining the parts of speech.

2. *Progressive Differentiation.* At this stage, the content is divided into its more complex ideas. The teacher would define and provide examples of a metaphor and simile.

3. *Integrative Reconciliation.* Finally, students are helped to understand similarities and differences between the concepts. The teacher would discuss the relationship between metaphor and figure of speech (vertical reconciliation) and metaphor and simile (lateral reconciliation).

Questioning Skills. A large portion of a teacher's day is devoted to asking and responding to questions. An effective teacher understands that there are different types of questions designed for soliciting different kinds of information from students. Essentially, lower-level questions emphasize memory and recall of facts; higher-level questions seek to solicit more complex and abstract thinking.

Although the intent of asking higher-level questions is to facilitate students' ability to think at higher levels, research does not provide adequate support that students do, in turn, engage in higher-level thought processes when responding to these questions. Beyer (1987) asserts that a question requiring a student to analyze information may still result in the student answering on the basis of recall and be judged to be correct. Although the intent of the question clearly is to encourage higher-level thinking, the result may sometimes be a lower-level response. He states, however, that questions that require more than simple recall are *essential* for stimulating higher-level thinking.

Three types of questions—convergent, divergent, and evaluation—can be posed to students. *Convergent questions* are restricted in scope and usually require the student to arrive at a correct answer. For example, "If the radius of a circle is 10 feet, what is the circumference of the circle?" The question may require a lot of thinking in the beginning but, once thought out, has only one correct answer. Convergent questions typically focus on the knowledge and comprehension levels of the cognitive domain. These questions require the teacher to dominate the teacher–student interaction and are not designed to stimulate the higher-level thought processes.

Divergent questions are open-ended. No one can predict exactly what the answer will or should be. Divergent questions are designed to make students think or speculate. For example, "What steps might the United States government take to reduce the budget deficit?" As you can see, this question requires cognitive thinking strategies and focus on the application, analysis, and synthesis levels of the cognitive domain. Divergent questions require the teacher to ask for diversity in student responses and allows and encourages more interaction between students.

Evaluation questions require the student to place a value on something and/or make a value judgment or choice between several alternatives. These are a special type of divergent questions since, as a rule, values are very subjective. For example, "Should Clarence Thomas have been confirmed as a Supreme Court justice? Why or why not?" Evaluation questions focus on the analysis and evaluation levels of the cognitive domain.

Each of these types of questions are important for students' cognitive development. The learning and recall of factual information is important not only for the purpose of learning important information but also for applying that information during higher-level thought processes. An effective teacher will use a combination of convergent, divergent, and evaluation questions.

In addition to asking different levels of questions, Beyer (1987) suggests that there are at least three other things teachers can do to engage students in thinking. The first is for teachers to use their responses to student answers to encourage thinking. For example, you might ask a student to clarify or elaborate on his or her answer; you might ask another student to respond to the answer; or you might challenge the student's answer. These responses can help students to think at a higher level.

Another strategy involves the amount of time you wait until you respond to the student's answer. This is called "wait time." Teachers usually wait only one second before responding to the answer. Costa (1985) discovered that if teachers wait a minimum of three seconds, then students will give longer responses and will provide more evidence to support their answers. In addition, increased "wait time" seems to increase the numbers of unsolicited responses and questions asked by students.

Another strategy for engaging students in thinking is to utilize questions designed to elicit specific types of thinking. The use of divergent, convergent, and evaluative questions elicits different types of thinking from your students. Your lesson planning should carefully incorporate all three types of questions in order to facilitate different types of thinking. Arends (1988) suggests that one approach to questioning is to begin by asking recall (convergent) questions to see if students understand the basic information, then ask divergent questions in order to view the material more analytically, and conclude with evaluation questions about the content and about the students' own thinking processes.

Finally, you can teach students how to ask their own questions. Beyer (1987) suggests a strategy: The first step is to provide the students with a topic or allow them to select their own, individually or in groups. After selecting a topic, the students should brainstorm a series of ten or more questions that will help them learn more about the topic; evaluate each question to determine the level of thinking (low or high) required of them; and ask if the question is focused on the topic or goes beyond it. After assessing the questions, the students should select the ones most useful for obtaining the needed information and should consider limiting the number of low-order questions. Upon selecting the questions, the students should answer them and develop additional questions if they are unable to acquire the needed or desired information. Finally, the students should reevaluate the questions to determine whether the questions succeeded in helping them obtain the needed information. If necessary, they should modify the questions in order to gain the information.

Developing skill in preparing and utilizing questions requires attention to both planning and detail. The following guidelines may assist you in formulating questions. Questions should

- be clear, understandable, and when written, readable.
- be used to stimulate thinking and to produce extended answers.
- not contain or suggest the answer.
- not contain complex qualifiers.
- rarely call for a simple yes or no answer, except when used to develop or elicit specific information or skills.
- lead students toward the development of concepts, generalizations, and principles.
- be related to the level of learning and thinking being sought.
- have simple structure and logical organization.

Developing good questioning skills requires knowledge of content and student skills, careful planning, and a lot of practice. Once mastered, these skills will greatly enhance the learning environment in your classroom and contribute to your students acquiring productive thinking skills.

Discussions. Much of what teachers consider to be discussions in their classrooms are actually recitations, activities in which students provide short answers in response to knowledge-based questions. Typically, there is no discussion about the merit or rationale of the answer or about alternative answers. A discussion should serve an instructional purpose and is utilized for students to examine an issue from a variety of viewpoints. Successful discussions typically include 5 to 15 students; discussions with larger groups are difficult to conduct because it is hard for everyone to participate. Different discussion formats are included in Chapter 1.

Good questioning skills are not enough to conduct successful discussions. Several additional strategies are suggested by Passe (1984): First, you should be knowledgeable of the subject or issue. This will allow you to get to the "heart of the issue" rather than discussing too many points tangential to the matter. Second, begin the discussion with some type of motivating event. You might ask an intriguing question, relate a personal experience, or ask a student to relate a personal experience. This approach helps to grab the students' attention and draws them into the discussion. Third, establish a positive learning environment in which students feel safe to offer an opinion. *The class should be relaxed and free of embarrassment*—perhaps the most important point for the discussion strategy. Fourth, keep the discussion moving. Often times, students and, sometimes, teachers will begin talking about points that are tangential to the discussion at hand. Although these might be interesting, they do not contribute to the discussion, and you will need to guide it back into focus. In addition, a student may begin to monopolize a discussion because of personal interest in the topic. You may need to call on students with raised hands. If students are not permitted to speak unless called upon by the teacher, you have better control over the session. Of course, this subtracts from any source of spontaneity. Fifth, reword or help students reword ambiguous comments. This helps students reconstruct their thoughts and present their views more clearly. Finally, use humor judiciously. Depending on the topic, some discussions can become intense. A humorous comment by the teacher can often lessen the tension and help continue the discussion.

Discussions are good strategies for assessing students' knowledge, for facilitating higher-level thinking, and for determining whether students can apply or assess that knowledge. You must be mobile during a discussion so that you can monitor student behavior and involvement. Also, you should involve all students without embarrassing anyone. You will find that the discussion method is exciting but that it requires a lot of planning and structure.

Use of Student Ideas. Incorporating students' ideas, experiences, and feelings into the lesson is a strategy for increasing student interest and motivation, organizing content around student problems, and fostering positive attitudes toward the subject (Borich, 1988). However, these goals are difficult to achieve unless the teacher provides the underlying organization.

How can you incorporate student ideas into the lesson? Encourage students to use personal experiences and to relate them to the topic. By relating and reinforcing the students' experiences, you make the subject matter "come alive" to them. They begin to understand the feelings and motives of characters in literature, "view" the terrain of a faraway country, or better understand some abstract concept.

Another use of student ideas is to reintroduce a particular student's contribution to the discussion. For example, early in a class discussion, Colleen related her experience of being left alone at home for the first time. Several minutes later, at an appropriate point in the discussion, the teacher might relate, "Remember what Colleen said about her first experience at being alone at home? How were her feelings similar to those of the character in the story?" By reintroducing a student's ideas or contribution to class, you are telling the students that you value their input and that what they have to say is related to what they are learning. This strategy helps build bridges between you and the students and between the students and the subject matter.

Technology

Technology in the schools has been touted as an innovation for many years. Opaque and overhead projectors were once innovations for teaching; more recently, the computer has been praised as the latest innovation that will revolutionize the teaching–learning process.

Peck and Dorricott (1994) cite that teachers utilize computers for creating puzzles, delivering instruction, assessing student progress, and producing reports. They discovered that teachers who implement the computer for these tasks find that it actually increases their workload rather than reduces it and that consequently the computer spends more time turned off than on.

In contrast, teachers who move beyond this stage ask how computers and other technology can contribute to a more powerful educational experience and new ways of thinking. Students in their classrooms use Internet and E-mail to communicate with other students. They also use computers to improve their writing skills, CD-ROMs and laserdiscs to put thousands of images at their fingertips, and software to improve their thinking skills. Using these tools of the Information Age helps students prepare for the future.

Technology can play an important role in your classroom. What have you done to improve your awareness and skills in these new technological arenas? Are you prepared to incorporate technology in your classroom? Are you prepared to keep up-to-date on the rapidly changing world of technology?

Innovation is a complex task. It requires an open mind and willingness to change, knowledge of the change process itself, and knowledge and skill in the strategies necessary to be an effective teacher and leader. This is a process that you will either welcome or be confronted with throughout your teaching career. Your attitude toward and knowledge about change will contribute greatly to your professional stress level.

COACHING

Coaching 5.8 Divergent Thinking Index

Guilford (1967) describes four attributes of divergent or creative thinking: fluency, flexibility, originality, and elaboration. A divergent thinker is one who generates many ideas (fluency), is able to break with conformist or set ideas (flexibility), suggests ideas that are new in the present context (originality), and contributes details that extend or support the ideas beyond a single thought (elaboration).

Think about the students in your classroom. Do many exhibit these four attributes of divergent thinking? What about your approach to teaching? Do you incorporate teaching strategies that facilitate divergent thinking? What types of strategies could you implement that would encourage your students to become more divergent thinkers?

Coaching 5.9 Systematic Observation of Higher-Level Questions

Many of us believe that we are exhibiting certain teaching behaviors when, in fact, we are not. For example, we may think that we are praising student responses when data might indicate that we only accept their answers and then ask another question. The same is true for asking higher-level questions. Our perception might be that we ask a high percentage of higher-level questions when we actually don't.

One method for gathering accurate data about your specific teaching behaviors is to conduct systematic observation. On a sheet of paper, write columns for each of the levels of the cognitive domain: K = Knowledge, C = Comprehension, Ap = Application, An = Analysis, S = Synthesis, E = Evaluation. Invite another novice teacher or a colleague to observe your teaching, or audiotape a lesson. Ask your assistant to make a mark beside the appropriate level each time you ask a question that is applicable to that level. After completing the lesson, determine the percentage of questions within each level. Another approach is to mark L = Lower-Level Questions (Knowledge and Comprehension) and H = Higher-Level Questions (Application through Evaluation). Mark them and calculate the percentages in the same manner as the previous approach.

Given the lesson's objectives, do you believe that you asked an appropriate percentage of lower- and higher-level questions? How could you have modified your questions to increase the percentage of higher-level questions?

REFLECTION

Reflecting 5.10 Good Thinking Versus Poor Thinking

Purpose: To examine your own and your students' approaches to thinking.

Time required: 10 minutes

Procedure: Table 5.5 lists the traits of a good thinker and those of a poor thinker. Which apply to you and which apply to the majority of your students? Given the information in this chapter, what strategies could you use to improve your own and your students' approaches to thinking?

Reflecting 5.11 How Thoughtful Are Your Classrooms?

Purpose: To reflect upon your school's effectiveness for developing thinking skills.

Time required: 10 minutes

Table 5.5 **Approaches to Thinking**

	Good Thinker	*Poor Thinker*
General Traits	• Welcomes problematic situations and is tolerant of ambiguity	• Searches for certainty and is intolerant of ambiguity
	• Is sufficiently self-critical; looks for alternate possibilities; seeks evidence on both sides of issues	• Is not self-critical; satisfied with first attempt
	• Is reflective and deliberative; searches extensively when appropriate	• Is impulsive, gives up easily, and is overconfident in the correctness of initial ideas
	• Believes in the value of rationality and that thinking can be effective	• Overvalues intuition, denigrates rationality; believes thinking won't help
Goals	• Is deliberative in discovering goals	• Is impulsive in discovering goals
	• Revises goals when necessary	• Does not revise goals
Possibilities	• Is open to multiple possibilities and considers alternatives	• Prefers to deal with limited possibilities; does not seek alternatives to an initial possibility
	• Is deliberative in analyzing possibilities	• Is impulsive in choosing possibilities
Evidence	• Uses evidence that challenges favored possibilities	• Ignores evidence that challenges favored possibilities
	• Consciously searches for evidence against possibilities that are initially strong, or in favor of those that are weak	• Consciously searches only for evidence that favors strong possibilities

Reality Bite

Technology and Assessment

Technology and assessment are two growing areas in education today. Everywhere we look, we see technology being used in schools in many ways. It lends itself easily to the evaluation and assessment of students.

I teach at the elementary level and use portfolio assessment with my students. Portfolios can include many items, such as samples of students' written work, audio recordings of students reading or speaking, videotaped footage of student performances and interactions, and computer-produced writings. By using the technologies of audio recorders, camcorders, and computers, a teacher can assess students in a much more effective and authentic manner. These assessments not only help teachers; they also help parents to see and hear where their child's strengths and weaknesses lie. The parents I know clearly prefer this type of assessment over letter grades on report cards.

Matthew Seebaum, First-Year Elementary Teacher

Procedure: Using the 14 criteria below, rate your school's effectiveness in developing thinking skills. Circle the appropriate rating for each question.

	Degrees of Effectiveness				
	HIGH				**LOW**
1. Does your community and staff value thinking as a primary goal of education?	5	4	3	2	1
2. Does the staff believe that human intelligence can continue to grow throughout life with appropriate intervention?	5	4	3	2	1
3. Have you reached consensus on or adopted some model of intellectual functioning?	5	4	3	2	1
4. Are students aware that intelligent behavior is an objective of instruction?	5	4	3	2	1
5. Does teachers' language (questioning and structuring) invite students to think?	5	4	3	2	1
6. Do teachers' response behaviors extend and maintain higher levels of thinking?	5	4	3	2	1

7.	Are learning activities arranged in order of increasing complexity and abstraction?	5	4	3	2	1
8.	Do the materials of instruction support higher cognitive functioning?	5	4	3	2	1
9.	Is adequate instructional time devoted to thinking?	5	4	3	2	1
10.	Does instruction provide for differences in modality strengths?	5	4	3	2	1
11.	Are concepts and problem-solving strategies encountered repeatedly throughout, across, and outside the curriculum?	5	4	3	2	1
12.	Do students and teachers discuss their own thinking?	5	4	3	2	1
13.	Do evaluation measures assess intelligent behavior?	5	4	3	2	1
14.	Do significant adults model intelligent behaviors?	5	4	3	2	1

Recommended Readings

Baron, J., & Sternberg, R. (1989). *Teaching thinking skills: Theory and practice.* New York: Freeman.

Beyer, B. (1987). Common sense about teaching thinking skills. *Educational Leadership, 41* (3), 44–49.

Costa, A. (1985). *Developing minds: A resource book for teaching thinking.* Alexandria, VA: Association for Supervision and Curriculum Development.

Fullen, M. (1993). *Change forces: Probing the depths of educational reform.* Bristol, PA: Falmer Press.

Fullan, M., with Stiegelbauer, S. (1991). *The new meaning of educational change.* New York: Teachers College Press.

Joyce, B., Wolf, J., & Calhoun, E. (1993). *The self-renewing school.* Alexandria, VA: Association for Supervision and Curriculum Development.

O'Hair, M. J., & Odell, S. J. (1995). (Eds.). *Educating teachers for leadership and change.* Newbury Park, CA: Corwin.

Raths, L. et al. *Teaching for thinking: Theories, strategies and activities.* (2nd ed.). New York: Teachers College Press.

Rosenshine, B. (1986). Synthesis of research on explicit teaching. *Educational Leadership, 43* (7), 60–69.

Sarason, S.B. (1993). *Letters to a serious education president.* Newbury Park, CA: Corwin.

Sarason, S.B. (1990). *The predictable failure of educational reform.* San Francisco: Jossey-Bass.

Smith, W., & Andrews, R. (1993). *Instructional leadership: How principals make a difference.* Alexandria, VA: Association for Supervision and Curriculum Development.

Wetherall, C. (1984). *The gifted kids guide to creative thinking.* Minneapolis, MN: Wetherall.

Williams, L. (1983). *Teaching for the two-sided mind.* Englewood Cliffs, NJ: Prentice-Hall.

References

Arends, R. (1988). *Learning to teach.* New York: Random House.

Beyer, B. (1987). *Practical strategies for the teaching of thinking.* Boston: Allyn and Bacon.

Borich, G. (1988). *Effective teaching methods.* Columbus, OH: Merrill.

Brandt, R. (1989). On parents and schools: A conversation with Joyce Epstein. *Educational Leadership, 47* (2), 24–27.

Drummond, H. (1964). Leadership for human change. *Educational Leadership, 23* (8), 626–629.

Dunkin, M., & Biddle, B. (1974). *The study of teaching.* New York: Holt, Rinehart and Winston.

Ennis, R. (1962). A concept of critical thinking. *Harvard Educational Review, 32* (1), 81–111.

Ennis, R. (1985). Logical basis for measuring critical thinking skills. *Educational Leadership, 43* (2), 44–48.

Epstein, J. L., & Dauber, S. L. (1989). Teacher attitudes and practices of parent involvement in inner-city elementary and middle schools. Report 33. Baltimore: Center for Research in Elementary and Middle Schools, Johns Hopkins University.

Fullan, M. (1993). Innovation, reform, and restructuring strategies. In G. Cawelti (ed.), *Challenges and Achievement of American Education. The 1993 ASCD Yearbook.* Alexandria, VA: Association for Supervision and Curriculum Development.

Glickman, C. D. (1993). *Reviewing America's schools: A guide for school-based action.* San Francisco: Jossey-Bass.

Good, T., & Brophy, G. (1987). *Looking into classrooms.* (4th ed.). New York: Harper and Row.

Goodlad, J. I. (1984). *A place called school: Prospects for the future.* New York: McGraw-Hill.

Guilford, J. P. (1967). *The nature of human intelligence.* New York: McGraw-Hill.

Hall, G. (1979). The concerns-based approach to facilitating change. *Educational Horizons, 57* (4), 202–208.

Hord, S., Rutherford, W., Huling-Austin, L., & Hall, G. (1987). *Taking charge of change.* Alexandria, VA: Association for Supervision and Curriculum Development.

Horwitz, R. (1979). Effects of the open classroom. In H. Walberg (ed.), *Educational environments and effects: Evaluation, policy and productivity.* Berkeley, CA: McCutchan.

Lipman, M. (1988). Critical thinking—what can it be? *Educational Leadership, 46* (1), 38–43.

Lueder, D. (1989). Tennessee parents were invited to participate—and they did! *Educational Leadership, 47* (2), 15–17.

MacKenzie, D. (1983). Research for school improvement: An appraisal of some recent research trends. *Educational Researcher, 12* (4), 4–17.

Neagley, R., & Evans, D. (1980). *Handbook for effective supervision.* (3rd ed.). Englewood Cliffs, NJ: Prentice-Hall.

Orlich, D. (1989). Education reforms: Mistakes, misconceptions, miscues. *Educational Leadership, 70* (7), 512–517.

Parnes, S. (1967). *Creative behavior guidebook.* New York: Charles Scribner's Sons.

Passe, P. (1984). Phil Donahue: An excellent model for leading a discussion. *Journal of Teacher Education, 35* (1), 43–48.

Patterson, J. (1993). *Leadership for tomorrow's schools.* Alexandria, VA: Association for Supervision and Curriculum Development.

Peterson, P. (1979). Direct instruction reconsidered. In P. Peterson & H. Walberg (eds.), *Research on teaching: Concepts, findings and implications.* Berkeley, CA: McCutchan.

Rosenshine, B. (1979). Content, time and direct instruction. In P. Peterson & H. Walberg (eds.), *Research on teaching: Concepts, findings and implications.* Berkeley, CA: McCutchan.

Rosenshine, B., & Furst, N. (1973). The use of direct observation to study teaching. In R. M. Travers (ed.), *Second handbook of research on teaching.* Chicago: Rand McNally.

Rosenshine, B., & Stevens, R. (1986). Teaching functions. In M. C. Wittrock (ed.), *Handbook of research on teaching.* (3rd ed.). New York: Macmillan.

Rutter, M. (1979). *Fifteen thousand hours.* Cambridge, MA: Harvard University Press.

Soar, R. (1973). *Follow through classroom process measurement and pupil growth (1970–71): Final report.* Gainesville, FL: College of Education, University of Florida.

Stallings, J., & Kaskowitz, D. (1974). *Follow through classroom observation evaluation, 1972–73.* Menlo Park, CA: Stanford Research Institute.

Torrance, E. (1962). *Guiding creative talent.* Englewood Cliffs, NJ: Prentice-Hall.

Tuchman, B. (1985). *Evaluating instructional programs.* Boston: Allyn and Bacon.

Wagner, T. (1993). Systemic change: Rethinking the purpose of school. *Educational Leadership, 51* (1), 24–29.

Williams, F. (1982). Developing children's creativity at home and in school. *GCT, 24,* 2–6.

Chapter 6

The Counselor Role

Chapter Objectives

After completing this chapter, you will be able to

- describe teachers' roles and functions as counselors.
- describe the attitudes necessary for successful counseling.
- be aware of the situations appropriate for student counseling.
- recognize and begin practicing effective communication skills that are basic to counseling.
- describe the phases for establishing a helping relationship.

*W*hat would you do if you were in Mr. White's position? Amanda's problem—the breakup of her parents' marriage—is not uncommon. Student problems frequently have their roots outside of the school but are manifested in the classroom. An inexperienced teacher may not be able to identify the source of the problem and, consequently, may respond inappropriately to the student. Some teachers believe that it is not their responsibility to become involved in a student's private life outside the classroom; however, effective teacher-counselors recognize that their responsibility is to the whole child and realize that emotional health is as important as academic achievement.

There is a clear link between counseling and teaching, because interpersonal relationships are at the heart of both activities. Throughout the school year, you will be confronted with situations that require you to give counsel or provide advice to students. For most of these occasions, your assistance will be adequate. During others, a student's problem(s) will be so severe or complicated that you will feel unqualified or inadequate to provide these services. In such cases, you might refer your student and/or the student's parents to a person or agency better equipped to deal with the problem.

The purpose of this chapter is not to train you to become a school counselor but to provide you with basic knowledge and skills to assist you in the role of

◆ *Challenge*

The Case of the Withdrawn Student

Mr. White observed Amanda carefully as she entered his classroom. He was hoping he would catch a glimpse of the bubbly, outgoing freshman that used to come in with a smile and a word of greeting. Amanda had been not only an excellent student but was also active in extracurricular activities—a model student. However, her behavior and performance changed after the Christmas holidays.

As the new year began, Amanda withdrew from her friends and stopped partici- pating in class. Soon she stopped doing her homework, and her test scores and grades declined dramatically. Mr. White noticed that Amanda would sit alone in the cafeteria during lunch and would walk home alone. There were rumors that Amanda's father and mother were seeing a marriage counselor. Mr. White wanted to help but was afraid that he would be interfering in Amanda's personal life. As a new teacher, he wasn't sure that he had enough experience to help Amanda even if she was willing to talk to him.

teacher as counselor. The responsibility for guiding students through their cogni- tive and emotional development is enormous. Much like professional counselors, teachers who are effective in their role as counselor demonstrate the characteristics of empathy, spontaneity and genuineness, and nonpossessive warmth (Hamblin, 1974). These personal qualities are essential in establishing the interpersonal rela- tionships necessary for successful counseling.

> Competency 1: Advising and Counseling Students
> Competency 2: Promoting Student Self-Concept
> Competency 3: Learning Cooperatively

■ *Competency 1* ADVISING AND COUNSELING STUDENTS

ASSESSMENT

Assessing 6.1 Effective Listening Skills

Purpose: One of the keys to being an effective teacher-counselor is good listening skills. This activity helps you to assess your listening skills.

Time required: 5 minutes

Procedure: For each of the following statements answer either Yes, Sometimes, or No. Tally the results for each of the three responses in the spaces provided.

1. I feel comfortable when listening to others on the phone.
   Yes   Sometimes   No

2. It is often difficult for me to concentrate on what others are saying.
   Yes   Sometimes   No

3. I feel tense when listening to new ideas.
   Yes   Sometimes   No

4. I have difficulty concentrating on instructions others give me.
   Yes   Sometimes   No

5. I dislike being a listener as a member of an audience.
   Yes   Sometimes   No

6. I seldom seek out the opportunity to listen to new ideas.
   Yes   Sometimes   No

7. I find myself daydreaming when others seem to ramble on.
   Yes   Sometimes   No

8. I often argue mentally or aloud with what someone is saying even before he or she finishes.
   Yes   Sometimes   No

9. I find that others are always repeating things to me.
   Yes   Sometimes   No

10. I seem to find out about important events too late.
    Yes   Sometimes   No

Number of times I answered Yes   _____

Number of times I answered Sometimes   _____

Number of times I answered No   _____

If you answered Yes or Sometimes on less than three questions, you perceive yourself to be a good listener. If you answered Yes or Sometimes on three to six questions, you are an average listener. If you answered Yes or Sometimes on seven or more questions, you need immediate improvement of your listening skills.

Source: Hamilton, C., & Parker, C. (1987). *Communicating for results: A guide for business and professions.* Belmont, CA: Wadsworth Publishing, p. 110. Adapted from Wheeless, L. (1975). An investigation of receiver apprehension and social context dimensions of communication apprehension. *The Speech Teacher,* 261–263. Reprinted with permission of Wadsworth Publishing Company.

EXPERIENCE

Munter et al. (1988) explain that there is an important distinction between teachers acting as advisers and as counselors. Advising is typically a problem-solving activity occurring when the absence of information causes a problem for a student and the teacher's access to the information can solve the problem. Most of the problems you encounter with students will be of this nature. For example, a student may not be aware of available resources in the community that can supplement a history project. Another may be interested in applying for admission to one of the service academies but not be aware of the procedure, or one may seek advice about the courses or experiences required by certain professional schools. In these cases, you may be able to provide the appropriate information or be able to suggest where this information can be found. However, advising does require the teacher to be more directly responsible for the student's decision making.

Counseling, on the other hand, is a kind of problem-solving wherein feelings, not lack of information or facts, are the issue and the student possesses the information. Feelings can produce problems in self-esteem, behavior, relationships, and performance. Counseling helps you to identify and work with the student's feelings. Unlike advising, however, counseling requires more of a collaborative effort with the student. The solution to the problem arises from the student being willing to share information about feelings and the teacher's willingness to listen. Thus there is a mutual responsibility for the decision-making process.

Defining the Teacher's Role and Function as Counselor

In many cases, teachers provide support and participate with a trained school counselor; however, on-site counselors are not found in all schools, especially elementary and middle schools. In these situations, the teacher assumes more responsibility for counseling and advising students. Whatever the circumstances, it is important to recognize the role and function of the classroom teacher in the counseling process. Gibson and Mitchell (1990) have defined six roles that teachers can anticipate assuming in the classroom as part of their counselor role.

Listener-Adviser. No other adult, except parents, spends as much time with children and young adults as do teachers. In some elementary schools, teachers average spending as much as 7 hours per day with their students for 180 days each year. In other cases, especially secondary schools, a teacher spends 45 to 50 minutes per day for 180 days per year per student. This staggering amount of time offers the teacher the best opportunity to get to know each student well. Teachers who are able to establish a relationship of trust and respect in their classrooms are likely to be more aware of potential problems in students' academic and personal lives.

Referral and Receiving Agent. Teachers are typically most, and often first, aware of a student's counseling needs; consequently, they are the primary source of student referrals to the school counselor. The teacher not only must refer the student to the counselor but also may need to actively encourage the student to seek counseling services. In addition, the teacher's responsibility does not end after the referral. They also play the role of receiving agent by "receiving" the student back into the classroom and by reinforcing the outcome of the counseling sessions. It is important that the teacher be as supportive as possible of the student during and after the counseling sessions.

Human Potential Discoverer. Since teachers spend so much time with students, they have the opportunity to identify those with special talents. For example, a student might exhibit a special interest or skill in film production. To whom would you refer the student for career advice in this field? The teacher who does not have expertise in a certain field can recommend the student to the counselor or some other specialist/expert for guidance. As a result, the teacher not only assists the school counseling program but also helps meet the individual needs of students.

Career Educator. The role of career educator is closely related to that of the human potential discover. It is important that the classroom teacher integrate career education into the curriculum as much as possible. Gibson and Mitchell (1990) state that teachers must promote positive attitudes to education and its relationship toward career preparation. Students must also develop positive attitudes and respect for honest work and have the opportunity to examine and test concepts, skills, and roles and to develop values appropriate to their future career planning.

Human Relations Facilitator. Classroom teachers should develop classroom environments that promote positive human relationship experiences. Students should be made to feel that they are valued and that they are not at risk, physically or emotionally. Later in this chapter we will discuss how teachers can help students develop positive self-esteem.

Counseling Program Supporter. Teachers can be especially helpful in influencing how students view and participate in a school's counseling program. The responsibility for ensuring that teachers understand the goals and role of that program rests both with the individual teacher and with the counselor. If you have not been prepared or had experience in counseling, you may be unaware of the services the program can provide. It is very important that you become knowledgeable about not only the counseling program available in your school or district but also the services available in your community.

Counseling Attitudes for Teachers

As stated previously, the objective of this chapter is not to prepare you to become a school counselor but to help equip you with the attitudes and skills to provide advice and counsel for students when appropriate. You will need to advise and counsel students in many situations, but you should always refer to a specialist any serious student problems that you do not feel adequately prepared to handle.

Munter et al. (1988) state that the purpose of training teachers as counselors is not to train counselors but to help teachers develop a "counseling attitude." This requires teachers to listen more than to tell and to pay more attention to feelings than to facts. The most effective counselors are warm and accepting of students' feelings. These teachers have an unconditional positive acceptance of the student and are not judgmental in their reactions to the student's problem(s).

Effective counselors are also genuine—they are in touch with their own feelings. Teachers may or may not share these feelings with students, but they must know themselves if they are to be truly helpful in a counseling or advising role.

Finally, effective counselors have empathy for their students. Empathy is the ability of the teacher to sense what the student is feeling and to communicate that perception to the student. If the students believe that the teacher understands their problems, then they are more likely to accept suggestions or advice given by the teacher. Warmth, genuineness and empathy are traits that we hope all teachers possess. These attitudes, which help define a caring teacher, also allow the teacher to be an effective counselor.

Appropriate Situations for Counseling

As this point, you might accept and understand the counseling roles assumed by classroom teachers and might also believe that you possess the attitudes necessary to become an effective counselor. Despite these perceptions, however, you might still be unsure of *when* it is appropriate to offer advice or counsel.

Munter et al. (1988) suggest several situations that potentially require counseling. First, students who continually break rules in school eventually need to explore their feelings about themselves, about their behavior, and about their relationships. Sometimes misbehavior is the result of frustration and unhappiness with relationships at home or at school. Other times, students' misbehavior may be an attempt to call attention to themselves because of their feelings of inferiority or insecurity. If the problem is serious, it may require professional assistance from an outside agency. The important first step, however, is to understand the underlying cause for the misbehavior.

Second, the depressed student who is always fatigued, is quiet and withdrawn, does not have many friends, and/or does not perform academically or athletically as well as expected may be a candidate for counseling. When these signs begin to accumulate, you may need to discuss your concerns with the student, urging that feelings be explored or discussed.

Third, occasionally you will have a student whose academic performance has markedly declined over time. The student will need to understand the reason for the drop in grades in order to improve performance. The reason may be pressure from home, too many outside interests, problems within relationships, or illness, for example. Understanding the reason not only benefits the student but also assists you in helping the student to deal with the problem.

Reality Bite

Adoption

After giving a powerful speech on adoption, a student came to my office to ask me if I thought adoptive children should attempt to locate their biological parents. After I listed some of the advantages and disadvantages of the issue, she told me that she was adopted and was considering initiating a search. Because I was not well versed on the subject, I accompanied her to the library where we conducted an extensive search of adoption literature. In addition, I suggested she seek professional advice from a counselor. In the ensuing weeks, we spent time reading articles and discussing our findings. The student was ultimately able to make a well-informed decision.

Marc Rich, Experienced Speech Teacher

Fourth, students who cope well—perhaps too well—with a serious loss or change in personal life may be keeping their real feelings inside. They may act as if a divorce, illness, or death has not affected them and that they are able to cope with this tragedy. They may not be "permitted" to show emotion by other family members or may be trying to protect others. Their need for privacy may not be as essential as their need for support in order to cope with the problem. The teacher and/or counselor can help students confront their feelings in order to keep more serious emotional problems from developing.

This list of possible situations is certainly not exhaustive. You must always be attentive and alert to your students' needs. As Munter et al. (1988) state, "... by the time it is clear that a student needs counseling, a sense of helplessness and failure has already developed, probably in both the teacher and the student, as well as in the parents" (p. 16). Whatever the problem(s) underlying student behavior, the teacher must always offer a supportive environment where students feel safe to share thoughts and feelings.

Communication Skills

Most counseling and advising that you do will be with individual students about relatively minor issues and will take little of your time. Some students, however, will bring serious problems with them to your classroom. They will challenge your ability as an effective teacher-counselor and, sometimes, will require you to refer them to a more skillful and knowledgeable professional counselor.

There are many counseling approaches available to the professional counselor. The chosen approaches are often related to the particular theories of psychology adopted by the counselor and require extensive training. It is unlikely that you will be utilizing these approaches with your students. Those students who need assistance through the use of these models will usually exhibit problems beyond your area of counseling expertise and will need to be referred to a professional counselor. There are, however, universal counseling skills that you must apply if you are to be successful with the types of student problems you will encounter in the classroom.

Verbal Skills. A prerequisite to effective communication and counseling skills is listening. This may appear to be odd since we are talking about verbal communication, but effective listening skills allow counselors to adapt their verbal behavior to the needs of the students and to the situation. Listening skills are closely identified with *attending behavior,* behavior that communicates to the student that "I am listening to you and interested in what you are saying." Attending behaviors not only communicate that you are listening to the student ("I understand," "I see") but can also encourage the student to continue responding ("Please explain that," "Please tell me more about that").

Another communication skill is feedback—the verbalization of your reactions and perceptions to the student's feelings and behaviors. It allows the student the opportunity to provide feedback about the teacher-counselor's perceptions and advice. Feedback also allows both the teacher and the student to determine the accuracy of their perceptions of what the other is saying during this process. It is important that both clearly understand each other before moving on in the counseling process.

Effective questioning is another type of verbal communication strategy utilized in the counseling process. Gibson and Mitchell (1990) believe that skillful questioning involves timing, wording, and type of questions. It is important not to interject questions that will alter or stop the process; instead you should ask questions that will keep the discussion moving ("Why do you think they behaved that way toward you?"), that will clarify ("What do you mean?") and validate ("Give me an example of that behavior").

When deciding the type of question to ask the student, you should consider the desired outcome. If you want the student to elaborate on feelings or to provide greater detail, then you should ask open questions; for example, "How do you feel about that?" Open questions allow the student to express feelings with greater detail and may provide you with better insight. A closed question, on the other hand, will result in a specific answer rather than a rambling reply. "Will you express your feelings to Sandra?" is an example of a closed question. Again, the questions you ask should be directed by the type of information needed from the student.

Nonverbal Skills. Hamilton and Parker (1987) define nonverbal communication as all intentional and unintentional messages that are neither written nor spoken. Gazda et al. (1977) have identified four modalities of nonverbal behavior:

1. *Nonverbal Behavior Using Time*

   Recognition: Promptness or delay in recognizing the presence of another or in responding to another's communication

   Priorities: Amount of time one is willing to spend communicating with another

2. *Nonverbal Behavior Using the Body*

   Eye contact: Looking at student/teacher; looking down; looking defiantly at student/teacher; frequency of looking at student/teacher

   Posture: Slouching, slumping, tired-looking; arms crossed as if to protect self; crossing legs; sits facing the person; hangs head, looks at floor; body positioned to exclude others from the group

   Facial expression: No change in expression; frowning; smiling, laughing; biting lip

   Repetitive behaviors (often interpreted as signs of nervousness): Tapping foot; drumming fingers; fidgeting, squirming; trembling; playing with button

   Signals or commands: Snapping fingers; pointing; holding fingers to lips for silence; shrugging shoulders; nodding in recognition or agreement; winking

   Touching: To get attention; affectionate; poking finger to chest; slapping on back; belittling pat on head

3. *Nonverbal Behavior Using Vocal Media*

   Tone of voice: Flat, monotone, absence of feelings; vivid changes of inflection; strong; confident; weak; hesitant; faltering

   Rate of speech: Fast; medium; slow

   Loudness of voice: Loud; medium; soft

   Diction: Precise versus careless; regional differences; consistency of diction

4. *Nonverbal Behavior Using the Environment*

   Distance: Moves away when another moves toward; moves toward when the other moves away; distance widens gradually; distance narrows gradually

   Arrangement of physical setting: Neat, well-ordered, organized; untidy; casual versus formal; warm versus cold colors; soft versus hard materials; expensive taste versus shabby

   Clothing: Bold, stylish versus unobtrusive and nondescript

   Position in the room: Positions desk or table between self and other person; sits in the middle of the room; moves about the room;

moves in and out of other person's territory; stands when the person sits or gets in a higher position

Each of the nonverbal behaviors cited above presents a different message to the receiver of those messages. If you are serious about being an effective teacher-counselor, you need to be aware not only of countless possible nonverbal messages but also of how they might be interpreted by your students; therefore, improving your skills in sending and receiving nonverbal messages is important. Hamilton and Parker (1987) suggest the following steps for improving nonverbal communication: (1) Develop awareness of nonverbal differences; (2) try to become more open-minded; (3) do not assign nonverbal meanings out of context; and (4) practice. Knowledge and skill in nonverbal behavior can be an important tool for improving your ability as a teacher-counselor.

Phases of a Helping Relationship

Having the skills to provide effective counseling and advice to students is necessary, but knowing the steps or phases a counselor would utilize to help a student is also crucial. Basically, there are three phases for developing a helping relationship with students: developing a good relationship, self-exploration, and implementing a plan of action (Gazda et al., 1977).

The first phase, developing a good relationship with the student(s), is crucial for both effective teachers and effective counselors. Establishing a good, solid relationship with your students requires *empathy, respect,* and *warmth.* Carkuff (1969) believes that empathy is the most important element for establishing a trusting relationship with another person. If you cannot understand—empathize with—the feelings of a student, then you will not be able to provide helpful counsel or advice. Respect means that you trust the students to be able to help solve their own problems. You can show your respect by the verbal and nonverbal attending behaviors you exhibit with them. Warmth means that you care for your students. It is unlikely that students will approach you for help or allow you to help them if they do not believe that you care for them. Establishing a good relationship with your students is paramount to being an effective teacher and an effective counselor.

The second phase of the helping relationship is self-exploration. If you are truly going to help students, you must help them help themselves. During this phase, the teacher-counselor helps the students to accurately label their feelings and experiences. Allow the students to talk about what is bothering them, or encourage them to relate the events that have preceded a specific problem. It should be apparent that if you have not established a relationship of respect and trust with your students, they are not likely to share their feelings and experiences with you in an honest and open manner. If you are unable to get students to discuss problems beyond vague and general terms, or if they relate to you in a superficial or phony manner, then you may need to seek assistance from a professional counselor.

The final phase—action—is often considered the most important. It is during this phase that a plan of action must be developed by both the student and teacher-counselor. You must be willing and able to help develop a plan that will resolve the problem. If the problem is too serious or complicated, you may need the assistance of the school counselor. Carkuff (1969) suggests seven stages for implementing the action phase: (1) Define and describe the problem area(s); (2) define and describe the direction and/or goals dictated by the problem areas; (3) analyze the critical dimensions of this direction(s)/goal(s); (4) consider alternative courses of action; (5) consider the advantages/disadvantages of the alternative courses; (6) develop physical, emotional-interpersonal, and intellectual programs for achieving; and (7) develop progressive gradations of the program.

All three phases for developing a helping relationship with your students are important. The teacher-counselor who consistently exhibits empathy, respect, and warmth helps students *explore* themselves and their problems. As this relationship builds and the teacher-counselor helps to explore the problem, the students *understand* themselves and their problems. Once this has been accomplished, the teacher-counselor and students can begin developing a plan of action to deal with the problem. On the other hand, if you show empathy, respect, and warmth for your students but are unwilling to get involved in developing a solution to the problem, you will not be an effective teacher-counselor.

COACHING

Coaching 6.2 Nonverbal Communication

Purpose: To help you become familiar with effective and ineffective instances of nonverbal communication in establishing a helping relationship with your students.

Time required: 30 to 60 minutes

Procedure: (1) Observe how teachers in your school relate to students nonverbally. How do the students react to this communication? How effective are these observed behaviors in establishing a relationship of trust and respect? (2) Video-tape one or more of your classes. Observe the nonverbal communication you use with your students. How good are you at implementing effective nonverbal communication? What steps can you take to improve your nonverbal communication?

REFLECTION

Reflecting 6.3 Shadowing School Counselor

Purpose: School counselors have been trained to advise and counsel students in need, and they are an important source of support for the classroom teacher. This exercise can help you learn valuable counseling techniques and strategies.

Time required: 1 to 2 hours

Procedure: Shadow a school counselor for one or two class periods. What types of student problems or situations are encountered during the day? What behaviors and strategies are employed while working with students/parents? What phases of the helping relationship are used with the students/parents? How can you use these skills to improve your effectiveness as a teacher-counselor?

Reflecting 6.4 Advising and Counseling Amanda

Purpose: To implement knowledge and skills regarding counseling and advising students.

Time required: 30 minutes

Procedure: Recall the Case of the Withdrawn Student at the beginning of this chapter. With the assistance of two or three colleagues or peers, develop a plan for helping Amanda with her problem. Use the phases of developing a helping relationship. How would you help Amanda confront her problem(s)? How would you develop a plan of action to deal with the problem? What would Amanda's role be in the development of the plan?

Competency 2 PROMOTING STUDENT SELF-CONCEPT

ASSESSMENT

Assessing 6.5 In Touch with Your Own Self-Concept

Purpose: To examine your perceptions of your self-concept. If you are going to help others, you must be aware of your own self-concept, your own strengths and weaknesses.

Time required: 10 minutes

Procedure: List as many adjectives as possible that describe *you*. These adjectives can describe aspects of your personality, appearance, intelligence, work habits, etc. How many adjectives are positive and how many are negative? When you review your responses, what kind of picture do you get of yourself? That picture is a little glimpse of your self-concept.

EXPERIENCE

To define self-concept as your concept of *your self* is probably too simplistic; however, all of your positive and negative experiences, especially those from early childhood, combine to form the kind of person you are and the kind of person you perceive yourself to be. For example, repeated exposure to negative responses from parents can result in a child believing that "I'm bad." Once your self-concept is established, it is difficult to change it. New experiences that are inconsistent with your self are typically ignored or rejected.

A child's self-concept is quite well formed by the time he or she enters school. The beliefs and attitudes about ourselves then influence our reactions to learning, to the physical, emotional, and social climate of the classroom, and to our school successes and failures. For example, Wattenberg and Clifford (1962) examined the relationship between self-concept and reading success with kindergarten students. They discovered not only that a child's concept was predictive of reading success

Reality Bite

Promoting Self-Esteem

Since kindergarten, Kevin attended a small private school where I was principal and part-time teacher. During that time, he had been a student in my science classes and had always done well academically; in fact, he had a flaire for science in particular. However, he never fit in with the other students. He had few social skills and spent recesses by himself, seemingly content to play in an obscure corner. He came to school unwashed and ungroomed. Often other students withdrew in disgust from his odor and commented on it to each other and to teachers. This rejection was epitomized by the fact that although Kevin invited his entire class to his twelfth birthday party, no one attended. His mother was understandably angry and complained to me. Kevin was crushed and withdrew all the more. His self-concept was evidently poor and was declining as his social awareness increased. I was caught in between since I wanted to guard Kevin from additional scarring but had no grounds to require my other students to be Kevin's friends. Friendship cannot be forced, although it can be encouraged.

I knew his parents well enough to know that problems existed in the home that were evidenced by Kevin's bedwetting and withdrawal. I did not know the nature of these problems, but I suspected they were much deeper than I might imagine. Whatever the details, I was sure that Kevin's self-concept problems had roots in his home life as well as his school experience. His mother played the peacekeeper while his father stayed quiet when they were approached about Kevin's difficulties.

I was struggling with what I could or should do to help Kevin. After reflection, I decided to begin building Kevin's self-esteem directly. I looked for ways to compliment him on a job well done. I talked with him nonconfrontatively about paying more attention to his appearance when he came to school. At one point, when I noticed that he was working independently on a small machine using simple electrical principles he had learned in science, I asked him to explain to the class how he had built the machine. At another point, during his seventh-grade year in my class, I showed Kevin his achievement scores (which were impressive) and explained to him what a fine intellect he possessed. I made sure he received recognition for his achievements at our annual year-end awards ceremony.

Did I help? I'm not sure, since self-concept is, as the term implies, self-controlled as well as being deeply entrenched. At times, Kevin seemed to improve, and then old patterns would emerge. The one thing I do know is that whenever I see Kevin, even to this day, he always has a warm smile and friendly greeting for me. I know that he knows I tried to make a difference. Maybe that is the best we can ask for in some cases.

David Worley, Former Elementary Principal

but also that it was more predictive than IQ. Children with a poor concept did not learn to read as well as those with a good concept.

Principles for Promoting Student Self-Concept

Canfield and Wells (1976) suggest several principles for promoting the self-concept of your students:

1. *Provide a safe and supportive environment.* Students must trust fellow students and the teacher if they are express their feelings openly without ridicule. A supportive environment will help students understand that they are valued and will receive support from others. Without a supportive environment, all of your work to enhance student self-concept will be for naught.

2. *Teachers affect students' self-concept every day.* Teachers have a tremendous impact on students. Many of us decided to become teachers because of a teacher(s) that we had during our schooling. These people had a positive impact on our self-concept. Unfortunately, some teachers routinely criticize and humiliate students; these teachers obviously have a negative impact on their students' self-image. How you influence your students is *your* choice!

3. *Changing a student's self-concept takes time.* Do not expect sudden, dramatic improvement in your students' self-concept. It will take time and may be imperceptible at first.

4. *Efforts should aim at the student's central beliefs.* Canfield and Wells (1976) believe that you should emphasize a child's central beliefs. For example, if you can help students realize that they are capable of learning, you are dealing with a central belief. If you help a mischievous boy view himself as polite and caring, then you have made a big difference in his life. You need to realize that central beliefs are crucial to attend to but harder to change.

5. *Peripheral experiences are helpful.* Any type of success can help improve a student's self-concept. Don't hesitate to call attention to anything positive the student does in or out of the classroom. Sometimes just calling on students by their names or complimenting them on their attire can contribute to their viewing themselves more positively.

Strategies to Promote Self-Concept

How do you help students who have a low self-concept? Frey and Carlock (1984) and Meggert (1989) suggest that there are four phases in the process of intervening to build students' self-concept: (1) identity, (2) strengths and weaknesses, (3) nurturing, and (4) maintenance.

The purpose of the identity phase is for the student to gain knowledge and understanding of self. At this point students should become aware of their feelings not only about themselves but also about their family and friends. There are several specific activities that are useful during this phase.

Simon, Howe, and Kirschenbaum (1972) have developed a series of "values exercises" designed to help students identify what they believe. One activity is *What's in Your Wallet?* All students are asked to pull out two or three articles from their wallet, purse, or pocket and to then talk about the importance of these articles in their lives. The purpose of this activity is to help students learn what they value in their daily lives.

Another values activity is *Personal Coat of Arms.* Students are asked to create their own personal coat of arms that will depict several aspects of themselves. Meggert (1989) suggests that students might identify their greatest personal achievement or failure, their family's greatest achievement, their personal motto, or one thing each would like to accomplish by age 65.

Learning to trust self and others is another aspect of the identity phase. "Trust exercises" are designed to encourage this aspect of a student's self-concept. The *Blind Walk* is an excellent example of this type of exercise. Each student has a partner; one of them is the "blind" person while the other is the leader responsible for showing the blind person what the world is like. After the walk is completed, the partners change roles.

The *Trust Fall* is another possible exercise to be used during this phase. Students form a small circle. A student, with hands and arms clasped, falls backward and is caught by members of the group and passed around the circle. One variation is to blindfold the student who is being caught.

Once students have become more aware of their self, they can move into the second phase and learn about their strengths and weaknesses. It is important to provide specific, nonjudgmental feedback about positive and negative behaviors with a 5:1 ratio of positive to negative feedback. Meggert (1989) asserts that feedback statements should be phrased in behavioral terms rather than evaluative judgments. In addition, it is important for the student receiving the feedback to filter out inappropriate statements.

Managing Your Pig is an activity designed for students to discover parts of themselves that they like or dislike. Students are asked to list things about which they get down on themselves. Then, on a 5-point scale, they identify their willingness to change each of these things in their lives. Students set goals for change and assess the reality of these plans.

Personal descriptions are also useful for this phase. Each student writes a description about another person, describing only positive aspects. These descriptions are placed into a hat, and each student selects one and reads it with everyone guessing the student it describes.

COACHING

Coaching 6.6 Assessing Students' Self-Concept

Purpose: To assess the self-concept of your students. The technique used in this exercise helps students describe their feelings about themselves and also helps you have a better understanding of your students and their feelings.

Time required: 30 to 45 minutes

Procedure: In Assessing 6.5, you were asked to provide a picture of yourself that was intended to help you better understand your self-concept. Now, ask your students to participate in a similar exercise. Each student should list as many personal descriptive adjectives as possible. These adjectives can describe aspects of personality, appearance, intelligence, work habits, etc. After they have listed these words, ask them to count how many are positive and how many are negative. When you review their responses, what kind of picture do you get of your students? That picture is a glimpse of the individual and collective self-concept of your students.

REFLECTION

Reflecting 6.7 Bolstering Amanda's Self-Concept

Purpose: To implement skills and knowledge for promoting students' self-concept.

Time required: 30 minutes

Procedure: In Reflecting 6.4, you were asked to develop a plan for counseling and advising Amanda. Considering that plan, discuss with your peers a strategy that will help improve Amanda's self-concept. How do your strategies for improving Amanda's self-concept differ from those of your classmates?

■ *Competency 3* LEARNING COOPERATIVELY

ASSESSMENT

Assessing 6.8 What Are Your Attitudes Toward Cooperative Learning?

Cooperative learning can be used to meet a variety of learning objectives. This approach can also be utilized to meet various social needs of your students. In order to successfully implement small groups or cooperative learning, you need to feel comfortable about this strategy. As you think about your experiences as a student in the elementary and secondary grades, how did you feel about working in groups? How much did you participate in the group? What was the nature of your participation? Were you a leader or a follower? Did working in groups help you feel differently about some of your classmates? If so, in what ways? How might your attitude about working in small groups affect your ability to implement this approach in your classroom?

EXPERIENCE

Earlier chapters examined small groups and cooperative learning in relation to instructional strategies and classroom management. However, an effective teacher realizes the need to plan activities that attend not only to students' academic needs but also to their social and psychological needs. Educators long have argued that group work could be the foundation upon which strong democratic communities could be established and maintained. For example, Clark states (1973) that small groups are useful for several purposes in addition to academic learning, such as providing students with opportunities to learn social skills and to develop good social attitudes as a result of give-and-take, providing students with leadership opportunities, and promoting self-reliance and self-direction. By working in groups, students can learn about others as well as about themselves.

Arends (1988) has discussed the advantages of working in cooperative settings as opposed to the competitive situations that often exist in many classrooms. He reports that students who are rewarded for their group success develop a strong motivation to complete tasks, a considerable friendliness among group members, and a highly effective communication process that promotes maximum generation of ideas.

Group Process Skills

Whether your goals are academic or social, students often need to be instructed how to function in the various roles associated with group interaction. This can be accomplished by role-playing the various roles assumed by students working in groups. Instruction in group skills must take place over time, thus the incorporation of group work into the curriculum should occur often throughout the school year.

Jarolimek and Foster (1989) suggest that the following skills need to be taught and learned in connection to group efforts:

1. *Contributing to group planning:* providing suggestions, evaluating proposals, suggesting alternatives, and compromising on points of difference.

2. *Defining problems:* raising questions, suggesting which questions are relevant, and respecting the views of others.

3. *Organizing to achieve a defined task:* deciding on a plan of action, suggesting subtasks, suggesting specific assignments, and deciding what materials will be needed.

4. *Working as a committee member:* knowing and carrying out specific responsibilities, assisting with planning, cooperating and working with others rather than in isolation, supporting the leadership of the chair, and working responsibly toward the achievement of group goals.

5. *Assuming the leadership of groups:* developing plans cooperatively with group members, respecting the suggestions and contributions of group members, moving the group toward the achievement of its goals, delegating responsibility as needed, serving as spokesperson for the group, and maintaining democratic rather than autocratic relationships with group members.

When beginning group work, it is better to give a specific task with clear directions. At the elementary level, you might want to begin with one small, closely supervised group. While this group is working on its task, the other students can be working on a class assignment. Gradually, all students should be given the opportunity to work in groups. This slow induction to group work allows younger students to learn the various roles and expected behaviors of group work while also allowing them to accomplish their task.

How do you assign students to cooperative learning groups? Webb (1987) suggests that equal numbers of boys and girls should be assigned to a group as well as equal numbers of students from low-, medium-, and high-ability groups.

Improving Self-Concept

It is clear that self-concept can be modified, either positively or negatively, by experiences at school. Cooperative group work can improve a student's self-concept. It has been found that students working in cooperative teams have a better understanding of themselves than do students in traditional classes (Good, Mulryan, & McCaslin, 1992). These students report that they both like and feel liked by the other members of the group more often than do students in traditional classroom settings. Liking and being liked by others are obvious components of feeling good about oneself.

It also appears that students are more successful in their school work when they work in cooperative groups (Slavin, 1986). This success leads to an increase in self-concept. Students who have a cooperative, supportive environment in school appear to be less likely to become withdrawn or antisocial.

Improving Relations with Other Students

In addition to improving a student's self-concept, working cooperatively in groups can help improve student-to-student relationships. For example, status or difference in status can play a major role in group interaction. If some students believe that other students are not as smart as they are or as capable of contributing to a group project, they will not want to participate with them during group work. Cohen (1986) believes, however, that providing all group members with experiences in different assigned roles can change expectations for low-status students. It is important that these roles be rotated so that all members can be the facilitator, the reporter, and the checker who determines that all students have completed their work. If you do not consciously place all students in these roles, high-status students will typically assume all of the leadership positions and the status quo will remain the same.

Purposely placing students in specific roles within cooperative learning groups also helps improved relations between students from different cultures, races, and ethnic groups. Working interdependently and through the use of cooperative rewards, students learn to appreciate each other. In fact, DeVries, Edwards, and Slavin (1978) discovered that students working in cooperative groups had more friends from different ethnic groups than did students in traditional classrooms.

It appears that working cooperatively in groups also helps to improve the interaction between nonhandicapped and handicapped students. Johnson et al. (1979) reported that when students classified as trainable mentally retarded were placed on bowling teams with nonhandicapped students, they received three times the number of positive interactions from nonhandicapped students than those students who did not work cooperatively.

It is important that you realize the affective and social benefits of learning cooperatively in the classroom. As stated earlier, if you are to be an effective teacher-counselor, you must create an environment of trust and respect in your classroom. It appears that classrooms that incorporate a cooperative approach are more likely to promote self-concept and understanding of others than classrooms that operate on a more traditional approach.

COACHING

Coaching 6.9 Giving and Receiving Help in Groups

Webb (1987) has reviewed the research on helping behaviors that contribute to successful learning in cooperative groups. She reported that it is important to differentiate between giving help and receiving help in groups as well as to distinguish between different kinds of help. For example, a student whose explanation consists

Reality Bite

Sexual Orientation

I had not been a teacher long when I discovered that there is more to teaching than merely knowing the course content. I had been so concerned with mastering the subject matter and teaching the material that I failed to understand the many roles undertaken by a teacher. One role in particular, that of counselor, presented one of the greatest challenges and bestowed one of the most fascinating blessings.

A predominately Hispanic university had given me the responsibility of teaching oral communication skills to a large proportion of the first-year students. We had co-created a learning environment that encouraged some interesting self-disclosure. Our class discussion centered on the Johari Window. The students were sharing various types of self-disclosure, and it seemed that they were mastering the content. While students engaged the content and began to establish a sense of community, I noticed that one student, Sam, was very quiet.

Sam was a model student. He engaged the material, challenged various assertions, and had apparently won the admiration of his peers. Seeing him behave in this withdrawn, atypical manner caused me some concern. Thinking possibly that he was having a bad day, I did not draw attention to his silence.

No more than 24 hours after that class session had passed, I was doing paperwork in my office. Sam appeared at my door and wanted to know if he was interrupting me. He was polite and acknowledged that his visit was happening during a time that was not my regularly scheduled office hours. I indicated that I was glad to see him and made certain to push my paperwork aside.

Sam stated that the reason for the visit was to explain why he "could not get into the last class discussion." He indicated that his mother and he had engaged in conflict over the weekend, the nature of which could cause him to be "disowned." I thought if Sam wanted me to know, he would reveal the content. I decided to describe what I observed during our last class session and indicated my concern over his lack of enthusiasm.

One of the qualities I liked about Sam was his candor. He decided to disclose what was troubling his academic and personal life, stating that his mother and he had fought about his sexual orientation—Sam was gay.

Hearing Sam reveal that he was gay evoked a variety of reflections. I conjured up stereotypical images of being gay, but Sam did not fit the stereotype. I looked to see if he was teasing. I wondered if I had said or done anything in class that would have encouraged him to approach me with his concern. Without saying a word, I waited for Sam to speak.

Sam elaborated on his mother's religious convictions and how his lifestyle was going against such religious teachings. He did not want to hurt anyone, but at the same time he wanted to be true to himself. I gave no advice. It seemed that Sam needed to talk and had chosen me to be his reflective mirror. As a result of paraphrasing his words, we devised some strategies that he could use to help his mother deal with his gayness. He said that he would seek a support group for himself and would let me know about the status of his relationship with his mom. I hope that Sam found the unconditional affection he sought from his mother.

Michael Elkins, Beginning College Instructor

of detailed information on how to solve a problem or correct an answer is providing an *explanation*. A student who responds with the answer rather than an explanation of how that answer was determined or who simply tells other students that their answer is correct or incorrect is providing *terminal help*. Terminal help does not assist the other students in the process of solving the problem.

Webb's review of cooperative group behavior found that:

1. Not all kinds of help are equally effective.
2. Giving and receiving explanations are beneficial to learning.
3. Giving and receiving terminal help are not beneficial for learning.
4. Exchanging information is not effective for learning.
5. Receiving no response to one's question is detrimental to learning.
6. High-ability students are most likely to give explanations to others.
7. Extroverted students are more successful than introverted students in obtaining explanations when they ask questions.
8. Boys may be more successful than girls in receiving help.
9. Groups with only students of medium ability spend more time explaining, and all students participate in group discussions.
10. Heterogeneous groups with a moderate range of ability demonstrate a high level of explaining.
11. Groups with only low-ability or high-ability students do little explaining.

12. In groups with a wide range of ability, the high-ability students often explain to the low-ability students while ignoring the medium-ability students.

13. In groups with equal numbers of boys and girls, all students are able to obtain help when asked.

14. In groups where boys outnumber girls or when girls outnumber boys, the boys are more successful than girls in obtaining help.

15. In groups of mostly girls, the girls direct many of their questions to the boy, who is not likely to answer all of their questions.

16. White students tend to be more active and influential in groups than minority students.

How does this behavior compare to the behavior exhibited in the cooperative groups in your classroom?

REFLECTION

Reflecting 6.10 Observing Group Work

Purpose: To observe and assess student participation and effort during cooperative group work.

Time required: 30 to 60 minutes

Procedure: The dynamics between individual students can be complex during group work. Observe a small group working in your or a colleague's classroom. As you observe, use the list of questions below to guide your assessment.

1. What students emerged as the leaders or major contributers of the group?

2. Was there any pattern of interaction between students of different ethnic, racial, or cultural groups?

3. Was there any pattern of interaction between boys and girls?

4. If there were handicapped students in the group, how were they integrated into the group?

5. Did the group remain on task?

6. Did the students appear to be prepared to work in groups?

7. Did the group successfully complete its task?

Questions: How do various groups of students interact with each other? What students appear to emerge as the leaders of the group? What patterns of interaction

do you notice? How could you restructure the group in order to improve its interaction and performance?

Reflecting 6.11 Utilizing All of Your Counseling Skills

Purpose: To apply the counseling skills you have attained in this chapter.

Time required: Varies

Procedures: Read the following scenario; then, using the skills you learned from
this chapter, answer the questions below.

> Naomi had been looking tired and pale lately, but you assumed that she
> had the flu that had been going around the school. You knew that she was
> a hemophiliac who often missed school and was periodically assigned a
> tutor; consequently, her appearance did not cause you any undue concern.
>
> Naomi had been absent from school for a week when her mother sched-
> uled an appointment with you and the school principal. You assumed that
> Naomi would now be absent from school for an extended period of time
> and that her mother wanted to discuss how she could keep up with her
> studies. Although she had been absent quite often, she remained one of the
> top students in your third-grade class, so you were confident that she
> would not fall behind the rest of the class.
>
> Her mother shocked both you and the principal when she confided that
> Naomi had contracted AIDS from one of her many blood transfusions.
> She was insistent that Naomi continue to attend school when she was feel-
> ing well and that she be included in regular school activities. Although you
> supported Naomi and her mother's decision, you were concerned about
> your students and how their parents would react to this news.

Questions: How would you support Naomi? What strategies would you use with
the other students in the class? How would you work with your students' parents?
with other teachers? How would you react if you actually had a student with AIDS
in your classroom?

Conclusion

This chapter has attempted only to introduce you to the role of teacher as counselor. You cannot possibly acquire the tools necessary to become an effective
teacher-counselor from one chapter in a textbook. This is a lifetime process. As you
gain teaching experience, you will acquire the skills and knowledge necessary to
become an effective counselor and adviser. You will know when it is necessary to
refer your students to a trained professional counselor. You will learn how to create
an environment where students work cooperatively and gain respect and trust for
each other, and you will learn effective strategies for improving your students' self-
concept. The role of counselor will be one of your most challenging and rewarding
functions as a teacher.

Recommended Readings

Combs, A., Avila, D., & Purkey, W. (1978). *Helping relationships: Basic concepts for the helping professions.* Boston: Allyn and Bacon.

Combs, A., Blume, R., Newman, A., & Wass, H. (1974). *The professional education of teachers: A humanistic approach to teacher preparation.* (2nd ed.). Boston: Allyn and Bacon.

Dembo, M. (1991). *Applying educational psychology in the classroom.* (4th ed.). New York: Longman.

Peterson, R. (1970). *Counseling tips for the beginning teacher.* Dubuque, IA: Kendall/Hunt.

Van Tassel-Baska, J. (ed.). (1990). *A practical guide to counseling the gifted in a school setting.* Reston, VA: ERIC Clearinghouse on Handicapped and Gifted Children and The Council for Exceptional Children.

References

Arends, R. (1988). *Learning to teach.* New York: Random House.

Canfield, J., & Wells, H. (1976). *100 ways to enhance self-concept in the classroom: A handbook for teachers and parents.* Englewood Cliffs, NJ: Prentice-Hall.

Carkuff, R. (1969). *Helping and human relations: A primer for lay and professional helpers. Vol. 1. Selection and training.* New York: Holt, Rinehart and Winston.

Clark, L. (1973). *Teaching social studies in secondary schools: A handbook.* New York: Macmillan.

Cohen, E. (1986). *Designing groupwork: Strategies for the heterogeneous classroom.* New York: Teachers College Press.

DeVries, D., Edwards, K., & Slavin, R. (1978). Biracial learning teams and race relations in the classroom. *Journal of Educational Psychology, 70* (3), 356–362.

Frey, D., & Carlock, C. (1984). *Enhancing self-esteem.* Muncie, IN: Accelerated Development.

Gazda, G., Asbury, F., Balzer, F., Childers, W., & Walters, R. (1977). *Human relations development: A manual for educators.* Boston: Allyn and Bacon.

Gibson, R., & Mitchell, M. (1990). *Introduction to counseling and guidance.* (3rd ed.). New York: Macmillan.

Good, T., Mulryan, C., & McCaslin, M. (1992). Grouping for instruction in mathematics: A call for programmatic research on small-group processes. In D. Grouws (ed.), *Handbook of research on mathematics teaching and learning.* New York: Macmillan.

Hamblin, D. (1974). *The teacher and counselling.* Oxford, England: Basil Blackwell.

Hamilton, C., & Parker, C. (1987). *Communicating for results: A guide for business and the professions.* Belmont, CA: Wadsworth.

Jarolimek, J., & Foster, C. (1989). *Teaching and learning in the elementary school.* New York: Macmillan.

Johnson, R., Rynders, J., Johnson, D., Schmidt, B., & and Haider, S. (1979). Interaction between handicapped and nonhandicapped teenagers as a function of situational goal structuring: Implications for mainstreaming. *American Educational Research Journal, 16,* 161–167.

Meggert, S. (1989). Problems of self-esteem. In D. Capuzzi & D. Gross (eds.), *Youth at risk: A resource for counselors, teachers and parents.* Alexandria, VA: American Association for Counseling and Development.

Munter, P., Blaine, G., King, S., Leavey, J., Powell, D., Sand, J., & Walters, P. (1988). *Counseling students.* Dover, MA: Auburn House.

Simon, S., Howe, L., & Kirschenbaum, H. (1972). *Values clarification.* New York: Hart Publishing Company.

Slavin, R. (1986). *Using student learning.* (3rd ed.). Center for Research on Elementary and Middle Schools. Baltimore, MD: Johns Hopkins University.

Wattenberg, W., & Clifford, C. (1962). *Relationship of self-concept to beginning achievement in reading.* U.S. Office of Education, Cooperative Research Project No. 377. Detroit, MI: Wayne State University.

Webb, N. (1987). *Helping behavior to maximize learning.* Paper presented at the annual meeting of the American Educational Research Association, Washington, DC.

Chapter 7

The Ethicist Role

Chapter Objectives

After completing this chapter, you will be able to

- describe the teacher's role in moral education.
- describe the ethical issues associated with teaching.
- describe the "hidden curriculum" and its role in schooling.
- describe values clarification and how it can be utilized to assist students to clarify their own value system.
- identify your personal value and ethical system and the role it plays in your teaching career.
- describe the role of teacher expectations as it relates to interaction with students.
- explain the changes in the educational goals of society throughout this century.
- identify how changes in society and education will affect your role as a teacher.

$\mathcal{T}$his chapter will introduce you to the role that community, school, and teacher values and ethical principles have in the world of teaching and learning. Of all the roles that you will assume in and out of the classroom, perhaps the most controversial is that of ethicist. Most people identify an ethical teacher as one who possesses a system of moral values that exerts a positive influence on students. How this influence is exerted on students is the source of many heated debates. Should morals and values be taught in the schools? If so, who decides which values or whose moral/value framework is taught in the classroom?

Although the answers to those questions may not be clear, it is certain that you will bring a value system into the classroom and that your students will be influenced

◆ Challenge

The Case of the Caring Teacher

Philomena Rodriquez has taught mathematics at City High School for five years. She enjoys the students and has a good relationship with the administration and other teachers. Lately, however, she feels like she has been hitting her head against a brick wall. Despite attempts to make her lessons motivating and to involve technology in her classroom, her students remain apathetic and unmotivated in their own performances. When Philomena schedules before- and after-school tutoring sessions, very few of her students show up. During parent–teacher conferences, few parents attend. She is beginning to feel as though she should explore a position in another school district or perhaps even a new career.

Given these feelings, Philomena schedules a meeting with her school principal, Mrs. Nelson, who has always considered her to be a valued member of the faculty. After listening to her feelings, Mrs. Nelson tells her that it is not unusual for a fifth-year teacher to begin feeling a bit negative about her career. She counsels Philomena to not take things so seriously and reminds her that her students come from a working-class neighborhood (most of the parents have jobs at the local cannery) and that higher education is not in most of her students' futures. She also states that most of the parents support a "basic" education and believe that "frills" have no place in the classroom. Philomena leaves the meeting more depressed than ever.

to some degree by this system. The manner in which you interact with your subject matter, students, and colleagues, the jokes you tell, and the personal habits you bring into the classroom are all examples of behavior that can influence your students. You must also be aware of how casual decisions about grouping and tracking students, apportioning the domains of knowledge in the curriculum, allocating daily and weekly instructional time, scheduling, and other practices often distribute access to knowledge unfairly and unequitably (Goodlad, 1990).

Strike (1988) stresses three conditions that describe the nature of ethical issues confronted by teachers. First, ethical issues concern questions of right and wrong. They relate to our duties and obligations, our rights and responsibilities. Second, ethical questions cannot be settled by an appeal to facts alone. Knowing the consequences of our actions is not sufficient for determining the right thing to do. We may know that spending more time with the slower readers will increase their reading scores, but is it fair to spend a disproportionate amount of time with only one segment of the class? Facts pertain to deciding what to do, but they are not enough by themselves. Ethical principles also are required in order to judge facts. Third, ethical questions should be distinguished from values. Strike states that values concern what we like or what we believe to be good. Ethical obligations, however, are often independent of what we want or choose. We may want the new sweater in the store, but we are not entitled to take it. Ethical obligations are constant regardless of what we want or choose.

The purpose of this chapter is to help you examine your own and the school's value and ethical systems and their potential impact on your students. The three core competencies of the ethicist role are

Competency 1: School Values and Ethical Principles

Competency 2: Teacher Expectations and Judgments

Competency 3: Role of Education and Schooling in a Democratic Society

---

Competency 1 SCHOOL VALUES AND ETHICAL PRINCIPLES

ASSESSMENT

Assessing 7.1 "I Believe" Statements

Purpose: To assess your beliefs regarding student diversity, knowledge/curriculum items, teacher–pupil relations, teacher roles, the role of the community in the school, and the role of the school in society.

Time required: 20 minutes

Procedure: Complete the following open-ended "I believe" statements. Your answers should reflect your honest beliefs about these important educational relationships. There are no right or wrong answers. After completing the statements, answer the questions at the end of the exercise.

1. I believe that the relationship between teachers and students should be . . .
2. I believe that the relationship between the school and the classroom should be . . .
3. I believe that a diverse student population makes . . .
4. I believe that a teacher's primary role should be . . .
5. I believe that the school's role in society should be . . .
6. I believe that the role of knowledge and curriculum in the school should be . . .

Question: What do your responses tell you about your belief system and its impact on your role as a teacher?

Assessing 7.2 What Are Your Beliefs?

Purpose: Educational ethicists acknowledge the importance of being aware of your own background beliefs. Understanding your own belief system may assist you in defending your actions to students, peers, administrators, and/or parents.

Time required: 20 to 30 minutes

Procedure: It is important that you answer each of these questions as honestly as possible. There are no right or wrong answers. After doing so, go on to answer the questions at the end of this exercise.

1. What are the moral beliefs that are most important in guiding your life? Are there any that you would publicly proclaim? lose a job over? die for? Where do they come from, and how do you know they are valid?

2. What do you view to be your purpose in life?

3. Do you believe that some moral beliefs are more true or right than others? Are there some that all or most people ought to hold and act on? Which ones and why?

4. Is there a moral plan for human lives? Are we affected by a power beyond human control?

5. During those times when people seem to you to be utterly immoral, egoistic, or without even the most basic human scruples, what holds you up or renews your moral hope?

6. Suppose that generosity, fidelity, responsibility, truth-telling, autonomy, or justice is your most precious principle. What evidence makes your claim to these highest moral principles valid?

7. In what ways do these background beliefs, these ideals, find expression in your ethical decision making? What factors block the expression of these ideals? (Nash, 1991, p. 170)

Questions: What do your responses tell you about your awareness of your value system? How will your value system impact your relationship to your students? your subject matter?

EXPERIENCE

Thomas (1990) claims that schools play a large part in a culture's morality. The standards of moral behavior, however, have not remained constant. In the nineteenth century, moral education standards were linked to obedience and conformity to rules (Ornstein, 1990); prayer, Bible readings, and the moral intonations of the *McGuffey Reader* played a major role in a child's daily schooling. Today, moral education is defined more by commitments to inquiry, diversity, knowledge, competence, caring, and social justice (Sirotnik, 1990).

Thomas (1990) believes that schools are both sources of moral instruction and sites of moral struggle and that it is the teacher who is at the center of both. It is the teacher who spends long hours each day with children and youths and whose influence often facilitates the making of moral choices. His argument that teaching is an inherently moral enterprise is supported through his description of teaching:

- Parents entrust their children to school. Trust obliges teachers to be careful. Teachers are to proceed carefully with the work of empowering students.

- Empowerment is remarkable. One human being sets out to make others strong and able. That human being is not to exploit, coerce, or manipulate the others. What is required of such a human being? What kind of person must he or she be? At the outset, we can at least say that the empowering teacher must be powerful, for impotence does not call forth potency.

- Parents entrust their children to teachers. School is mandatory, and that mandate settles on the shoulders of the teacher. The teacher, then, is obliged to care for children and be responsible for their empowerment. (pp. 266–267)

Ethical Issues

Strike (1990) states that there are three ethical issues closely associated with teaching. The first is indoctrination: A democracy presumes that people have the right to determine for themselves what they will believe. This basic right also exists for students in the classroom; thus, an ethical rationale exists for teachers to utilize techniques that promote student reasoning skills, that emphasize evidence and help students develop a capacity for reasoned judgment. On the other hand, teaching techniques that are coercive, manipulative, and require only rote learning should seldom be used.

A second ethical issue regards grading and evaluation. You will be responding to student work on a regular basis. Your comments should be informative so that students can build on their strengths and learn from their mistakes. Your grades should be fair and accurate. One of the most serious mistakes any teacher can make is to assign a grade without a rationale for why that grade has been assigned. As a result, your evaluation process should minimize bias and should be consistent from assignment to assignment and student to student.

A third ethical issue concerns values that are internal to the subject matter. Strike claims that teachers should teach their subject in ways that respect the subjects' fundamental values. He states, for example, that beauty and concern for the human condition are central to the study of literature. A teacher who teaches poetry for the sole purpose of writing advertising and manipulating consumers violates the core values of the subject matter. This argument would seem to indicate that a health teacher whose habits do not promote a healthy lifestyle is unethical in representing the fundamental values of the subject matter.

Hidden Curriculum

Although schools deliver a planned curriculum and instructional program, students often learn much that is outside of this planned delivery system. Although not planned, the hidden curriculum is an important part of school learning and may have a dramatic effect on students. As a teacher, you must be aware of the hidden curriculum and how you might unintentionally influence your students' knowledge, attitudes, and behavior.

Myers and Myers (1990) state a number of dimensions that are related to the hidden curriculum. The first deals with unintended content and includes the unintended ideas, skills, and values students learn in class that were not planned by the teacher. For example, they may gain new insights or formulate values from the comments of other students. It is possible, however, that the values portrayed as negative by the teacher or a student may be received positively by another student.

A second dimension of the hidden curriculum focuses on the school's organization—how the school is organized, how it functions, and how the teachers teach. For example, a chemistry teacher who terrorizes students with unreasonable and unfair rules may have students who score well on tests but who also develop a strong dislike for the subject. A school district that strongly encourages competition for grades and class standing may also unwittingly promote cheating and dishonesty among the students. In his book *Savage Inequalities* (1991), Jonathon Kozol describes schools that do not have enough desks and textbooks for all students, that operate out of old skating rinks, that have holes in the ceilings and walls, and that have none of the equipment or opportunities afforded students in neighboring suburban school districts. What hidden message about their worth is given to these students? What might be the long-term consequences of this message?

Finally, the hidden curriculum is closely associated with the school culture, which consists of the traditions, rituals, student–student relationships, and student–teacher relationships that shape a school experience. These aspects of school life can foster self-confidence or stifle it; promote self-esteem or destroy it. Whether a student receives a kind remark from the teacher or not; whether a student does or does not receive an invitation to a party; whether a student makes or does not make an athletic team—all of these situations can have a major impact on how that student thinks about self, school, and future.

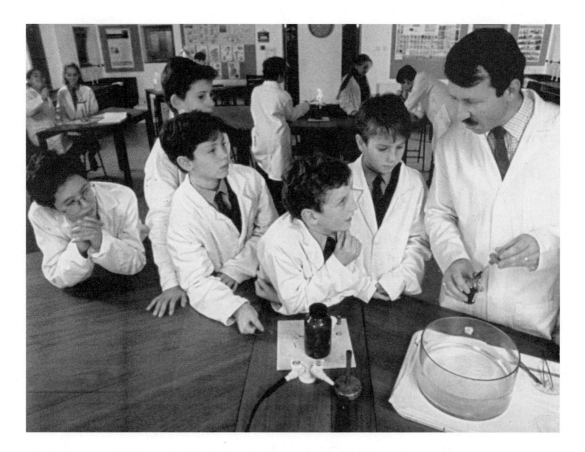

Another aspect of the school culture is how it relates to diversity and human differences. Kurth-Schai (1991) states that human difference is often responded to as a problem, a deviance from the norm. We condemn as disadvantaged or less worthy those who deviate from the norm—whether that deviance be in thought, appearance, behavior, or attitudes. Kurth-Schai believes that since we live in a society where difference often results in segregation and discrimination, teachers must practice a policy of inclusion and must be prepared to confront the challenges of a culturally diverse student population.

None of these aspects of schooling are planned by the administration and teachers; however, you must take them into account because the hidden curriculum is often a more powerful influence on students than the planned curriculum.

Moral Development

Ornstein (1990) states that a person can have moral knowledge and obey secular and religious laws yet still lack moral character. Moral character requires a developed personal philosophy and clear set of values.

Reality Bite

The Purpose of Education

The purpose of education is to give every student a chance to succeed in school, to take the knowledge learned and transmit it into becoming a responsible, productive citizen. To do this, teachers must learn to cultivate certain attitudes and values. They must develop expectations for appropriate behavior to elicit respect and establish ideals. The student is prepared for a social role and the type of education received is largely responsible for that preparation.

Sara Ybanez-Dodson, Elementary Teacher

Lawrence Kohlberg (1964) presented a hierarchy of moral development, a theory based on the belief that morality is a set of rational principles for making judgments about how to behave and that children proceed through a series of stages during which they refine their moral judgment. He grouped these developmental stages of moral judgment into three levels: I, preconventional; II, conventional; and III, postconventional.

During the preconventional level, children have not yet developed a sense of right or wrong. Someone at this level is more interested in the consequences to the individual than in society's laws. For example, a child may follow the instructions of a parent for fear of being punished or may behave a certain way because that action results in rewards. Although this level is represented primarily by children, it can represent adult reasoning as well.

At the conventional level, a person deals with moral issues from the point of view of what others think. For example, a child may behave a certain way in order to obtain parents' approval or to meet society's laws. This level develops during adolescence and remains the dominant level of moral reasoning for most adults.

The third level, postconventional, is reached by only a minority of people. They deal with moral questions from individual principles of consequences. At this level, a person believes that there is a higher moral perspective than society's laws.

You will have many opportunities to raise issues, questions, and dilemmas dealing with moral situations. The examination of these moral situations can encourage students to reflect on their own moral judgments and standards.

Values Clarification

Simon, Howe, & Kirschenbaum (1972) developed a program called values clarification, which is designed to encourage students to examine their own value systems and to have a better understanding of how they make decisions. Values clarification does not emphasize the values a person holds but rather focuses on the process to mold those values.

Louis Raths and his colleagues (1978) developed a model designed to enable teachers to help students clarify their values (Table 7.1). You can use these questions, or similar ones, to frame a discussion that examines values. Remember, values clarification was designed to help students understand and clarify their value systems, not to teach specific values. You need to be aware that parents in some communities might question the use of any classroom activity focusing on values.

Table 7.1 Questioning Strategies for the Valuing Process

1. *Choosing freely:*
   a. Where do you suppose you first got that idea?
   b. How long have you felt that way?
   c. What would people say if you weren't to do what you say you must do?

2. *Choosing from alternatives:*
   a. What else did you consider before you picked this?
   b. How long did you look around before you picked this?
   c. Was it a hard decision? What went into the final decision? Who helped? Do you need any further help?

3. *Choosing thoughtfully and reflectively:*
   a. What would be the consequences of each alternative available?
   b. Have you thought about this very much? How did your thinking go?
   c. This is what I understand you to say . . . (interpret statement).

4. *Prizing and cherishing:*
   a. Are you glad you feel that way?
   b. How long have you wanted it?
   c. What good is it? What purpose does it serve? Why is it important to you?

5. *Affirming:*
   a. Would you tell the class the way you feel?
   b. Would you be willing to sign a petition supporting that idea?
   c. Are you saying you believe . . . (repeat the idea)?

6. *Acting upon choices:*
   a. I hear what you are for; now is there anything you can do about it? Can I help?
   b. What are your first steps, second steps, etc.?
   c. Are you willing to put some of your money behind this idea?

7. *Repeating:*
   a. Have you felt this way for some time?
   b. Have you done anything already? Do you do this often?
   c. What are your plans for doing more of it?

Source: Adapted from Raths, L., Harmin, M., & Simon, S. (1978). *Values and Teaching.* (2nd ed.). Merrill Publishing Company, pp. 64–66. Reprinted by permission of Jan Raths.

COACHING

Coaching 7.3 Assessing the School's Value System

Posner (1993) states that there are six basic issues of teaching: control, diversity, learning, role, school and society, and knowledge. A school's value system, both stated and unstated, often can be viewed through these six basic issues. Over a period of several observations, review the questions in this section as they pertain to each of the issues. What do your perceptions of these issues tell you about the school's value system? Are there areas with which you agree or disagree? Is there a strong hidden curriculum within the school? What types of learners does this value system produce? Share your perceptions with a group of peers, your cooperating teacher, and/or your mentor.

1. *Control*
    Who selects and designs classroom goals, activities, and evaluation standards? Who selects the textbooks? Do the same rules apply to all students? Do all students have an opportunity to participate in classroom discussions?

2. *Diversity*
    How are the students labeled by the school? How are the students labeled by other students? Is there a class system in your school? If so, what determines who is included or not included in the "in group"? Are all students treated equally in the classroom, or are there attempts to meet individual needs?

3. *Learning*
    Does the school promote discovery learning or rote learning? Are the students grouped for learning? Is competition used as a motivation technique for learning? Are students permitted to progress at their own pace?

4. *Role of the Teacher*
    How formal or informal are the teachers in their interactions with students? How do students address their teachers? What types of clothing do the teachers wear? Who determines the rules in the classroom?

5. *School and Society*
    What community groups, if any, have influence in the school/school district? Does the curriculum allow the questioning of society's mainstream values? Is there pressure on new teachers to be socialized into the school's norm? Are diverse points of view included in classroom discussions?

Reality Bite

Cultural Diversity

Cultural diversity has become a very common phrase in education today, yet its commonality does not mean that it is easier for a teacher to incorporate multicultural education in the classroom.

The teacher must become educated in multicultural thinking and employ special strategies to accommodate the different cultures of diverse students. Teachers need effective communication skills (both verbal and nonverbal) and an understanding of characteristics, methods, and traditions involved in students' education.

It is the teachers' responsibility to better understand multicultural thinking. By doing so, they will be better equipped to teach immigrant students and to help all students learn about and appreciate our society.

Sara Ybanez-Dodson, Experienced Elementary Teacher

6. *Knowledge*
   Who decides what knowledge will be taught? Does knowledge represent a multicultural perspective? Do all students have access to the same knowledge? Can the teachers' view of knowledge be challenged by the students?

REFLECTION

Reflection 7.4 The Morally Mature Person

Purpose: To reflect upon attributes that help define a morally mature person.

Time required: 30 minutes

Procedure: The Association for Supervision and Curriculum Development's Panel on Moral Education generated the description of a morally mature person shown in Table 7.2. Using those characteristics, assess your own behavior and develop a framework for interacting with your students.

Reflection 7.5 Code of Ethics

Purpose: To gain insight into your own perspectives regarding ethical issues of teaching and schools.

Table 7.2 **The Morally Mature Person**

I. Respects human dignity, which includes
   1. Showing regard for the worth and rights of all people
   2. Avoiding deception and dishonesty
   3. Promoting human equality
   4. Respecting freedom of conscience
   5. Working with people of different views
   6. Refraining from prejudiced actions

II. Cares about the welfare of others, which includes
   1. Recognizing interdependence among people
   2. Caring for one's country
   3. Seeking social justice
   4. Taking pleasure in helping others
   5. Working to help others reach moral maturity

III. Integrates individual interests and social responsibilities, which includes
   1. Becoming involved in community life
   2. Doing a fair share of community work
   3. Displaying self-regarding and other moral virtues—self-control, diligence, fairness, kindness, honesty, civility—in everyday life
   4. Fulfilling commitments
   5. Developing self-esteem through relationships with others

IV. Demonstrates integrity, which includes
   1. Practicing diligence
   2. Taking stands for moral principles
   3. Displaying moral courage
   4. Knowing when to compromise and when to confront
   5. Accepting responsibility for one's choices

V. Reflects on moral choices, which includes
   1. Recognizing the moral issues involved in a situation
   2. Applying moral principles (such as the Golden Rule) when making moral judgments
   3. Thinking about the consequences of decisions
   4. Seeking to be informed about important moral issues in society and the world

VI. Seeks peaceful resolution of conflict, which includes
   1. Striving for the fair resolution of personal and social conflicts
   2. Avoiding physical and verbal aggression
   3. Listening carefully to others
   4. Encouraging others to communicate
   5. Working for peace

Source: ASCD Panel on Moral Education (1988). Moral education. *Educational Leadership*, vol. 45, 8, p. 5.

Reality Bite

Personal Agendas

I would tell a beginning teacher to do some additional reading on moral development and to discuss this chapter with other teachers in their school. New teachers need to think about how their moral code influences the way in which they relate to their students. I would tell them to be aware of the possible conflicts between their personal moral code and the value system within their school and community. If the two do not coincide, what becomes more important—school values or personal values? When do you fight for what you believe?

I think teachers have to be moral, but I don't think that one's moral code is a personal agenda. School is not the place to push a personal agenda.

Tresa Tolley, Experienced Teacher

Time required: 30 to 45 minutes

Procedure: Complete this exercise with another student(s). Discuss each of the questions from your belief system about teaching, schools, and children. How are you and your partner similar in your responses? How are you different? How would these similarities and differences affect a school's environment? There are no right or wrong answers.

1. Under what circumstances should a teacher not inform a parent of facts about a student? At what age? In particular, should a teacher tell a fundamentalist parent that a child of nine spoke of his loss of faith? In general, what are the ways in which teachers should protect students' right to privacy against their parents?

2. How can the rights of parents who are conscientious objectors be protected in classroom discussions of war, or vegetarians in discussions of farming, or certain religious groups in discussions of certain literature?

3. Should teachers respect without question the right of colleagues to behave as they wish in the classroom? What is the line between collegiality and toleration of inefficiency or immorality?

4. Are there general "discipline-based" rules (those derived from the character of the discipline) that teachers should observe in instruction? Does it matter whether children guess answers in history or science, get the right answer by accident in math, or learn things that are false, even though commonly accepted as true?

5. What should management do to respect the rights of teachers as citizens within schools? To what extent does management undermine a teacher's citizenship by restricting political discussion in classrooms? (Adapted from Sockett, H. [1990]. Accountability, trust and ethical codes of practice. In J. Goodlad, R. Soder, & K. Sirotnik [eds.], *The moral dimensions of teaching*. San Francisco, CA: Jossey-Bass.)

It is important that you be able to identify and understand the values and ethical principles held by the community, the school, other teachers, and yourself. The school's belief systems and your belief system will often be congruent; at other times, however, they will differ. By understanding these belief systems, you will be better able to determine how they might affect your students and how they might affect you, thus helping you become a more effective teacher.

■ *Competency 2* TEACHER EXPECTATIONS AND JUDGMENTS

ASSESSMENT

Assessing 7.6 Checking Your Expectations

Your expectations of yourself and your students can greatly influence your interactions with your students and their academic achievement. Below is a list of variables related to schooling. For each variable, discuss your expectations for yourself and for your students. Share your expectations with your peers, cooperating teacher, or mentor. What do your responses tell you about yourself? How do your expectations shape your teaching? your interactions with students?

Student behavior	Academic rewards
Student achievement	Teacher behavior
Classroom environment	Gifted education
Student gender	Students' homelife
Parents	Community influence
Administration	Corporal punishment
Special needs learners	Multicultural education

EXPERIENCE

Throughout your professional career, you will encounter many types of students in your classroom. They will exhibit different behaviors, different learning styles, and different levels of ability. How you interact with these students can influence your expectations of them and can impact on their performance.

Teacher Expectations

Weber (1986) describes expectations as those perceptions that the teacher and the students hold regarding their relationships to one another. They are predictions of how you and others will perform and/or behave. An effective teacher creates an environment where the expectations are accurate, realistic, and clear.

In 1968, Rosenthal and Jacobson published *Pygmalion in the Classroom,* a study that created much controversy about teacher expectations in the classroom. At the beginning of the school year, all children in an elementary school were administered a nonverbal intelligence test. Teachers were told that the test would be able to predict those students who would have academic success during the school year. In fact, the students were selected at random, not on the basis of the test scores. At the conclusion of the school year, the students were tested again and those "predicted" to do well did demonstrate significant intellectual growth. Thus the teachers' "knowledge" that certain students would likely do well academically caused them to work with those students in a way that enabled the expectations to become a reality.

Brophy (1985) provided a summary of data relating to how teachers may behave differently toward different students in the classroom:

1. Wait less time for low-expectation students (lows) to answer.
2. Give lows the answer or call on another student rather than attempt to improve lows' responses by probing, giving clues, or rephrasing the question.
3. Inappropriate reinforcement rewarding inappropriate behavior or incorrect behavior by lows.
4. Criticizing lows more often for failure.
5. Praising lows less frequently than highs for success.
6. Failure to give feedback to the public responses of lows.
7. Generally paying less attention to lows or interacting with them less frequently.
8. Calling on lows less often to respond to questions.
9. Seating lows farther away from the teacher.
10. Demanding less from lows.

◆ —— *Reality Bite*

Technology

To many students, reading has a bad connotation. They believe that it involves thick books with vocabulary that may be difficult to understand. With the advent of modern technology, however, students are now able to read using other resources. Students can read stories that have graphics and involve interaction between the student and the computer. By employing these means, students understand that reading does not have to be boring but instead can be exciting!

Keith Bryant, Vocational Director

11. General differences in type and initiation of individualized interactions with students; teachers interact with lows more privately than publicly and monitor and structure their activities more closely.

12. Differential administration or grading of tests or assignments, in which highs but not lows are given the benefit of the doubt in borderline cases.

13. Less friendly interaction with lows including less smiling and other nonverbal indicators of support.

14. Briefer and less informative feedback to the questions of lows. (pp. 309–310)

Our expectations of students are communicated both verbally and nonverbally. Many people assume that since there is so much verbal interaction in classrooms, teachers communicate most of their "messages" orally. However, Mehrabian (1969) discovered that over 90 percent of the messages teachers send to students are nonverbal. Teachers often communicate more by how they look at a student than by what they say to a student.

Garrett, Sadker, and Sadker (1986) have developed a list of verbal and nonverbal cues that, if used effectively, can communicate a positive message to students. Nonverbal cues include eye contact, facial expressions, body posture, and physical space. *Eye contact* refers to the eye-to-eye contact with the person you are speaking to or with the person speaking to you. Typically, it is suggested that you look the person in the eye when speaking or being spoken to. To look away from the person may communicate a lack of respect or unattentiveness to their message; however, you must be aware of the individual nuances of your students or fellow teachers in this regard. Some people are very sensitive to eye-to-eye contact, and some cultures may have specific beliefs about eye-to-eye contact that differ from yours.

Your *facial expressions* can relate important information to the speaker; for example, raised eyebrows, a smile, a frown, or a smirk can communicate surprise, acceptance, disapproval, or praise to the speaker. As a result, you must be aware of your facial expressions and their effect on other people. You also need to be aware of the facial expressions of your students when they are speaking to you. What nonverbal messages do you notice when interacting with your students?

Body posture, or body language, can send a strong message to your students. For example, touching a student or leaning toward a student during conversation relates a high level of interest. Leaning away from the student or standing with arms folded communicates a defensive, closed posture that is not open to understanding the student. Try to pay more attention to your body posture during your next interaction with students.

The final nonverbal cue is *physical space*—the distance that people create between themselves. The distance you place between you and your students can communicate your willingness (or lack of) to establish a closeness with or understanding of them. Teachers who sit behind their desks during class discussion are putting a barrier between themselves and the students. Those who walk among the students while teaching are relating their desire to get close to them. Hall (1966) describes an 18-inch distance between speakers as "intimate space," an 18-inch to 4-foot distance as "personal space," a 4-foot to 12-foot distance as "social distance," and beyond 12 feet as "public distance." What is the physical space you create between you and your students? What message does it convey to them?

The verbal cues described by Garrett, Sadker, and Sadker (1986) include silence, brief verbal acknowledgments, and subsummaries. Too often, a teacher wants to respond immediately to a student's answer or statement or wants to interject a comment before the student has completed a response. *Silence* conveys that you are listening to their answers, that you are thinking about what they are saying, and that what they are saying is important to you. When you interrupt students, you are telling them that what you have to say is more important than what they have to say. *Brief verbal acknowledgments,* such as "I see," "That's good," and "Okay," express interest in what the student is saying without interrupting. Finally, *subsummaries,* when appropriate, summarize the essence of the speaker's argument in two or three sentences. The subsummary communicates to the speaker that you are listening and are attempting to clearly understand the message.

Gender and Race Expectations

The previous section establishes the power that teacher expectations can have on the performance, attitudes, and behavior of students. A perfect world would have schools and teachers with similar high expectations for all students. Unfortunately, ours is not a perfect world, and not all schools and teachers believe that all students are equal or can learn equally well. Recent studies reveal that female students and students of different races and cultures are often treated differently by schools and teachers.

In 1992, the American Association of University Women (AAUW) released a report that delineated the following inequitable treatment of females in the schools:

- Girls receive significantly less attention from classroom teachers than boys.
- Sexual harassment of girls by boys—from innuendo to actual assault—is increasing in our schools.
- Girls are less likely than boys to take the most advanced math courses.
- Girls who are highly competent in math and science are less likely to pursue scientific or technological careers than are their male classmates.
- Boys are more apt to receive scholarships than are girls who have equal or slightly better high school grades.
- Girls do not emerge from our schools with the same degree of confidence and self-esteem as boys.
- The contributions of females are marginalized or ignored in many of the textbooks used in our schools.

In order to combat the unequal treatment of females in our schools, the AAUW has issued the following goals:

- Strengthened reinforcement of Title IX.
- Teachers, administrators, and counselors must be prepared and encouraged to bring gender equity and awareness to every aspect of schooling.
- The formal school curriculum must include the experiences of women and men from all walks of life. Girls and boys must see women and girls reflected and valued in the materials they study.
- Girls must be educated and encouraged to understand that mathematics and the sciences are important and relevant to their lives. They must be actively supported in pursuing education and employment in these areas.
- Continued attention to gender equity in vocational education programs must be a high priority at every level of educational governance and administration.

A school or teacher's negative expectations about the potential performance of a certain race or ethnic group can also have devastating results. A 1971 study by Rubovits and Maehr reported that teachers gave less attention to African-American

Reality Bite

Inclusion

Inclusion in the classroom does not apply to special education students, but to all of the pull-out programs, including migrant, Chapter I, and gifted and talented students. Inclusion enhances the self-esteem of all students and emphasizes the strengths and abilities of all students rather than their weaknesses. In addition, it breaks down the walls between students and teachers, it fosters collegiality and collaboration, it causes teachers to look at individual learning styles, and it prescribes that the teacher make the classroom one to all students.

Frank Goode, Educational Specialist
Keith Bryant, Vocational Director

students, called on them less frequently, encouraged them less frequently to continue with statements, ignored a greater percentage of their statements, criticized them more, and praised them less. The AAUW Report (1992) found that African-American girls have fewer interactions with teachers than do Caucasian girls, despite evidence that they attempt more interactions. Also, when African-American girls do as well as Caucasian boys in school, teachers often attribute their success to hard work while assuming that the boys did not work to their potential.

What do these actions tell these students? How do we modify teachers' beliefs and attitudes that perpetuate these negative expectations? What does the future hold if we cannot modify these expectations?

Inclusion

There have been few educational concepts as appealing and as threatening as inclusion. This concept emerged from the Individuals with Disabilities Education Act of 1990, which stipulated that children with disabilities must be provided a free appropriate public education in the *least restrictive environment*. The debate rages around whether inclusion is appropriate for all children with disabilities—learning or physical or both?

What is our ethical responsibility to disabled students? How much adjustment should the school and teachers make for the disabled in the regular classroom? How does inclusion impact the learning of all students in the classroom? Many articles in professional journals highlight the successes and failures of inclusion programs. Baker, Wang, and Walberg (1994/1995) report that recent research demonstrates a small-to-moderate beneficial effect of inclusive education on the academic and social outcomes of special-needs students.

What is your opinion of inclusion? How much experience have you had working with disabled students? Hopefully, your teacher education program has provided you with the knowledge and skills to be effective in an inclusive classroom.

Ethics and Testing

Strike (1990) states that teachers must be aware of and concerned with the relationship of ethics and testing. Student assessment is clearly one of the major responsibilities of all teachers. You are expected to respond to student performance with informative comments and grades that are fair and accurate, but in order to do so, you must be intellectually competent or else your response can be educationally damaging to the student. Also, the purpose of testing is to assess the students' attainment of objectives; therefore, it is ethical to not only teach the students the content related to the objectives but also to test them on this material. To test students on trivial material or on material not covered or assigned by you is unethical.

The grades that you assign the students should have due-process requirements. In other words, you should have clearly stated reasons for the assigned grades, should follow procedures that eliminate bias, and should be consistent between student to student and from case to case. For example, if you are grading a writing assignment, your assessment criteria should be determined and communicated to the students at the time you give the assignment. In this way, the students know what is expected of them.

Teacher Efficacy

It is clear that teacher expectations for student performance and behavior can play a major role in the classroom. Another construct that has interested educational researchers is the notion of teacher efficacy—a teacher's belief in his or her own ability to affect student learning (Ashton & Webb, 1986). Research indicates that teachers who have a greater sense of efficacy produce higher achievement gains in their students. In other words, if you believe that you can make a difference in the classroom, the odds are in your favor that you *will* make a difference!

Dembo and Gibson (1985) report that teacher efficacy results primarily from environmental factors. They state that teachers who are properly educated to deal with the diversity of students found in the classroom, who are supported by their principals, who develop collegial relations with fellow teachers, and who work cooperatively with parents are more likely to develop the belief that they can solve problems and help students to learn. Teachers with a low sense of efficacy who do not have these experiences are less likely to believe that they can help certain students to learn.

COACHING

Coaching 7.7 Characteristics of Successful Teachers

Nearly every text on teaching has a list of characteristics applicable to successful teachers. Jarolimek and Foster (1989) present eight guidelines for successful teachers that are based on a review of research on effective teaching. This research indicates that a dedicated, well-organized, and hard-working teacher can make a difference in the success of children.

Review the following list and apply it to your own teaching practices. Discuss these characteristics with your peers, cooperating teacher or student teacher, and/or mentor. Are there other characteristics that you believe should be included in the list? What can you learn about your own teaching? What modifications can be made in your approach to teaching and learning?

1. *Effective teachers realize their level of responsibility to students.* They have high expectations for their students. Effective teachers are confident in their personal abilities and consider all children as potential learners.

2. *Effective teachers provide children with the opportunity to learn.* Research clearly indicates that the more opportunities students are given to learn any material, the greater the success rate of student achievement. However, increasing instructional time, by itself, does not guarantee increased student achievement. Instead, effective teachers combine increased time with meaningful activities and immediate feedback to provide a high level of student success.

3. *Effective teachers manage their classrooms efficiently.* They clearly explain classroom procedures to the students at the beginning of the school year and are consistent in their implementation throughout the year. Students are held responsible for following these procedures.

4. *Effective teachers pace instruction to ensure that learners will be involved in meaningful tasks.* Student achievement level must be matched with what is to be learned. To ensure success, teachers must be aware not only of students' prior knowledge but also of the required prerequisite knowledge. Effective teachers require more work than do ineffective teachers but do so in small steps.

5. *Effective teachers are active teachers.* They assume responsibility for actively directing instruction. Effective teachers utilize small- and large-group instruction, demonstrate skills, and provide practice sessions before allowing students to work on their own.

6. *Effective teachers have learners master desired outcomes.* Effective teachers reteach material until it is mastered. Students are asked to accomplish lower-level objectives before being asked to master higher-order objectives.

7. *Effective teachers recognize grade-level differences that require different teacher behavior.* Effective teachers utilize more one-to-one interactions with primary age students and more large-group instruction and small-group activities for older children.

8. *Effective teachers provide a supportive learning environment.* Effective teachers create a positive classroom climate that supports an academic focus. These teachers require high standards and provide much positive reinforcement and acknowledgment of academic success.

Coaching 7.8 Philomena Rodriquez and Teacher/School Expectations

The previous Experience section focused on the expectations that teachers have for their students. Reread the Case of the Caring Teacher at the beginning of the chapter. If you were Mrs. Nelson, how would you advise Philomena Rodriquez? How does Philomena translate her expectations into student performance? Do you know of any situations similar to that of Philomena?

REFLECTION

Reflection 7.9 Expectations and Untested Assumptions

The following list illustrates decisions that teachers have made about students. In each instance, the statement was assumed to be true but had not been tested or verified. Examine the list and determine how each untested assumption could impact on a teacher's interaction with that student. How might that untested assumption and related teacher reaction affect the student's performance or behavior? Even when these statements can be verified, they should not be verbalized to the students because of the undesirable incidental learning that may result.

1. The student is not ready for a particular book or problem.
2. The student can't be trusted or believed and is guilty unless proven innocent.
3. The student can't be allowed to use special equipment because he will break it.
4. The student must be isolated from others because she has no self-control.
5. The student can't talk quietly and therefore should not be allowed to talk at all.
6. The student will cheat unless you take precautions to prevent it.

7. The student won't understand the next activity.

8. The student obviously knows the answer since she is in the gifted program.

9. The student will need assistance finding the correct page.

10. The student will cause trouble unless seated next to the teacher.

11. The student will need a lot of help to be able to do this problem and therefore should be given a tutor.

12. The student is daydreaming, not thinking about schoolwork.

13. If Thaddeus doesn't know the answer, no one will know it.

14. The student will fail next week's test.

15. It's Friday afternoon, so the class will be rowdy.

16. This student is just like his older brothers and doesn't like schoolwork. (Adapted from Good & Brophy, 1978)

The expectations that you have for your students and for yourself help determine your effectiveness in promoting student learning. Research indicates that effective teachers believe not only that all of their students can encounter success but also that they can make a difference in these students' lives. We hope that this section caused you to reflect on your expectations of students and on the expectations you have for yourself.

■ *Competency 3* ROLE OF EDUCATION AND SCHOOLING IN A DEMOCRATIC SOCIETY

ASSESSMENT

Assessing 7.10 Reflecting on Your Own K-12 Experience

Purpose: To reflect upon your own K-12 school experience in order to apply your personal perspective to Competency 3.

Time required: 30 to 45 minutes

Procedure: Take a few minutes to reflect upon your own K-12 school experience and jot down some notes that would help describe your feelings. Are your feelings toward your K-12 schooling positive or negative? Who was your favorite teacher? What characteristics made that teacher your favorite? Were all students treated fairly at your school by the faculty, administration, or other students? What are your most favorable memories about your K-12 schooling? What are your most negative memories about your K-12 schooling?

Share your feelings with some of your peers. How are their experiences different from yours? If they are different, what factors contributed to making them different? How do your K-12 school experiences shape your expectations toward schooling, teaching, and students?

EXPERIENCE

The expectations that permeate from our schools often have their origins in the community's perceptions of the purposes schools should play in educating children. However, the purposes of schools have been debated in our communities and across the country for decades. Goodlad (1979) states that goals for schooling emerge through a sociopolitical process in which certain interests prevail over others for a period of time. For example, during the late nineteenth and early twentieth centuries, high schools were viewed as preparatory schools for students who planned to attend a college or university. Responding to the needs of society in 1918, the Commission on Reorganization of Secondary Education developed and published the *Cardinal Principles of Secondary Education,* typically referred to as the *Seven Cardinal Principles.* These principles stimulated an expansion of course offerings in high schools designed to meet the needs of students who would not be attending an institution of higher education, stating that students should receive an education in (1) health, (2) command of fundamental processes, (3) worthy home membership, (4) vocation, (5) civic education, (6) worthy use of leisure, and (7) ethical character.

Times change, however, and schools must adapt to meet societal, economic, and philosophical changes. Much like the *Seven Cardinal Principles* guided the goals and objectives of schooling for decades, the *Goals 2000* (1994) plan was designed to direct the goals and objectives of schooling into the twenty-first century. The educational goals for America's schools as stated by *Goals 2000* are as follows:

1. All children will start school ready to learn.

2. The high school graduation rate will increase to at least 90 percent.

3. American students will leave grades 4, 8, and 12 having demonstrated competency in challenging subject matter including English, mathematics, science, history, and geography; and every school in America will ensure that all students learn to use their minds well, so they may be prepare for responsible citizenship, further learning, and productive employment in our modern economy.

4. The nation's teaching force will have access to programs for the continued improvement of their professional skills and the opportunity to acquire the knowledge and skills needed to instruct and prepare all American students for the next century.

5. U.S. students will be ranked first in the world in science and mathematics achievement.

6. Every adult American will be literate and will possess the knowledge and skills necessary to compete in a global economy and exercise the rights and responsibilities of citizenship.

7. Every school in America will be free of drugs and violence and the unauthorized use of firearms and will offer a disciplined environment conducive to learning.

8. Every school will promote partnerships that will increase parental involvement and participation in promoting the social, emotional, and academic growth of children.

How are these goals different from those proposed in the *Seven Cardinal Principles*? What changes have occurred in American society that have caused these differences? How will these goals affect your life in the classroom?

Citizenship Education

One of the long-standing purposes of schooling has been education for citizenship. It has been the view of many people that schools must prepare youngsters to be good citizens who are able to function in and contribute to a democratic society.

But how do you define a good citizen? One segment of the community might advocate teaching students to strictly adhere to existing social norms. At the same time, another segment might advocate that good citizenship entails the obligation to become involved in community affairs and to question and change existing social norms. How would you reconcile these differences in your classroom?

Remy (1980) lists three conditions that make it useful to consider what constitutes basic elements of citizenship education for today's students. First, citizenship has become more complex because the number and complexity of tasks and responsibilities associated with being a citizen have greatly increased. Societal changes have included the rise of global interdependence, the growth of large-scale institutions (especially government), technological innovation and knowledge explosion, the reemergence of racial and ethnic consciousness, the concern for equal opportunity, and an increase in mistrust of and alienation toward traditional institutions.

Second, as our society becomes more complex, citizenship education becomes more diversified. Today, citizenship education may include not only history and government courses but also coursework in global education, multicultural education, moral education, and community involvement. As we introduce our students to a broader avenue of ideas, their perceptions of what constitutes a good citizen might also change.

Third, citizenship education is a societywide process. Therefore, citizenship is taught and learned both in our schools and through our religious affiliations and our business and labor organizations. These agencies may reinforce each others' ideas or may contradict each other.

In order to define the basic citizenship competencies that would be useful to educators and others when identifying instructional practices and curriculum materials, the Basic Citizenship Competence Project (Remy 1980) identified the following competencies:

1. *Acquiring and using information*—Competence in acquiring and processing information about political situations.

2. *Assessing involvement*—Competence in assessing one's involvement and stake in political situations, issues, decisions, and policies.

3. *Making decisions*—Competence in making thoughtful decisions regarding group governance and problems of citizenship.

4. *Making judgements*—Competence in developing and using standards such as justice, ethics, morality, and practicality to make judgments about people, institutions, policies, and decisions.

5. *Communicating*—Competence in communicating ideas to other citizens, decision makers, leaders, and officials.

6. *Cooperating*—Competence in cooperating and working with others in groups and organizations to achieve mutual goals.

7. *Promoting interests*—Competence in working with bureaucratically organized institutions in order to promote and protect one's interests and values.

Remy (1980) states that these seven competencies should be looked upon as a set of flexible tools or guidelines for identifying what constitutes basic preparation for today's citizen. Although the competencies are not meant to be a curriculum outline in and of themselves, they can serve as a guide for developing content for your lessons focusing on citizenship education.

Personal and Social Development

Closely aligned to citizenship education is education for personal and social development. Armstrong, Henson, and Savage (1993) indicate that accounting for individual differences is so ingrained into the American way of life that it is an unquestioned article of faith. As a result, the quest to meet the individual needs of all students is an almost universal expectation of the schools.

Heck and Williams (1984) believe that academic achievement must be integrated with personal and social areas of development. Personal development includes the acquisition of knowledge, attitudes, and skills that enhance students' confidence in their own and others' dignity and worth. In addition, personal development includes the ability for self-motivation and self-direction to become a "lifelong learner." Social development includes the acquisition of knowledge, attitudes, and skills that reflect respect for cultural diversity and empathy for others' needs and beliefs. Social development also involves the motivation to become involved as a contributing citizen of society.

Heck and Williams (1984) believe that if your goal is the development of the "whole" student, then academic goals must be integrated with personal and social goals. Problem-solving, divergent thinking, and attention to individual learning styles are among several approaches intended to foster different points of view and to develop individual strengths and interests. You need to communicate to your students and their parents how these goals will be integrated and how they will be assessed.

COACHING

Coaching 7.11 Education in the Twenty-First Century

Purpose: To examine your instructional skills and the curriculum used in your classroom in order to determine their effectiveness in preparing students to be citizens in the twenty-first century.

Time required: 20 minutes

Procedure: Review with your peers the seven competencies proposed by Remy as guidelines for identifying what constitutes basic preparation for today's citizen: (1) acquiring and using information, (2) assessing involvement, (3) making decisions, (4) making judgments, (5) communicating, (6) cooperating, and (7) promoting interests. As you reflect on these premises, examine the curriculum implemented in your classroom. How well does it prepare students to be citizens in today's society? How well are you prepared to integrate these premises into the curriculum? What changes need to be made in your instruction and in the curriculum?

REFLECTION

Reflection 7.12 Philomena Rodriquez and Community Expectations

Purpose: To apply the knowledge gained in the preceding Experience section to the Case of the Caring Teacher.

Time required: 20 minutes

Procedures: Philomena Rodriquez was confronted by the conflict between her expectations for her students and those of the school and community. This scenario occurs more often than we would expect, and there are several ways to address the conflict. One is to find strategies for combating low expectations. Another is to realize the tough odds and conform to everybody else's expectations. A third strategy is to find another teaching position in another school district. What would you advise Philomena to do? Do these conditions exist in your community or in a community nearby? Could the converse conditions exist? Can a community hold expectations that are too high or unrealistic for their students? What effect might that have on teachers and students?

Summary

Teachers, administrators, and students enter schools with a system of values, ethics, and morals that have been developed by personal experience and prior formal and informal education. As a teacher, you must become aware of your own personal values and how they affect your students. Your values will greatly influence your expectations as a teacher, and the expectations of your students.

Too often, teachers are unaware of their own values, ethics, and morals and are also unaware that their students may not share their values. It is imperative that you examine your value system as it relates to students, teaching, and learning. How do your values, morals, and ethics influence your classroom and how you relate to students? This self knowledge will help you better understand your behavior and that of your students, and will contribute to making you a more effective classroom teacher.

Recommended Readings

Brophy, J., & Good, T. (1986). Teacher behavior and student achievement. In M. Wittrock (ed.), *Handbook of research on teaching.* New York: Macmillan.

Butts, F., Peckenbaugh, D., & Kirschenbaum, H. (1977). *The school's role as moral authority.* Washington, DC: Association for Supervision and Curriculum Development.

Glickman, C. (1993). *Renewing America's schools: A guide for school-based action.* San Francisco: Jossey-Bass.

Goodlad, J. (1994). Educational Renewal: Better teachers, better schools. San Francisco: Jossey-Bass.

Hirsch, E. (1987). *Cultural literacy: What every American needs to know.* Boston, MA: Houghton Mifflin.

Overly, N. (1970). *The unstudied curriculum: Its impact on children.* Washington, DC: Association for Supervision and Curriculum Development.

Strike, K., & Soltis, J. (1985). *The ethics of teaching.* New York: Teachers College Press.

Tom, A. (1984). *Teaching as a moral craft.* New York: Longman.

References

American Association of University Women (1992). *The AAUW report: How schools short-change girls.* Washington, DC: American Association of University Women.

Armstrong, D. G., Henson, K. T., & Savage, T. (1993). *Education: An introduction,* 4th ed. New York: Macmillan.

Ashton, P., & Webb, R. (1986). *Making a difference: Teachers' sense of efficacy and student achievement.* New York: Longman.

Baker, E., Wang, M., & Walberg, H. (1994/1995). The effects of inclusion on learning. *Educational Leadership* (52)4, 33–35.

Brophy, J. (1985). Teacher–student interaction. In J. Dusek (ed.), *Teacher expectancies.* Hillsdale, NJ: Erlbaum.

Commission on the Reorganization of Secondary Education (1918). *Cardinal principles of secondary education.* Washington, DC: Government Printing Office.

Dembo, M., & Gibson, S. (1985). Teachers' sense of efficacy: An important factor in school improvement. *Elementary School Journal, 86,* 173–184.

Garrett, S., Sadker, M., & Sadker, D. (1986). Interpersonal communication skills. In J. Cooper (ed.), *Classroom teaching skills.* Lexington, MA: Heath.

Good, T., & Brophy, J. (1978). *Looking in classrooms.* (2nd ed.). New York: Harper and Row.

Goodlad, J. (1979). *What schools are for.* Bloomington, IN: Phi Delta Kappa.

Goodlad, J. (1990). The occupation of teaching in schools. In J. Goodlad, R. Soder, & K. Sirotnik (eds.), *The moral dimensions of teaching.* San Francisco, CA: Jossey-Bass.

Hall, E. (1966). *The hidden dimensions.* Garden City, NY: Doubleday.

Heck, S., & Williams, R. (1984). *The complex roles of the teacher: An ecological perspective.* New York: Teachers College Press.

Kohlberg, L. (1964). Development of moral character and moral ideology. In M. L. Hoffman & L. W. Hoffman (eds.), *Review of child development research.* New York: Russell Sage Foundation.

Kohlberg, L. (1976). Moral stages and moralization. In T. Lickona (ed.), *Moral development and behavior: Theory, research and social issues.* New York: Holt, Rinehart and Winston.

Kozol, J. (1991). *Savage inequalities.* New York: Crown.

Kurth-Schai, R. (1991). The peril and promise of childhood: Ethical implications for tomorrow's teachers. *Journal of Teacher Education, 42* (3), 196–204.

Mehrabian, A. (1969). Significance of posture and position in the communication of attitude and status relationships. *Psychological Bulletin, 71,* 359–372.

Myers, C., & Myers, L. (1990). *An introduction to teaching and schools.* Fort Worth, TX: Holt, Rinehart and Winston.

Nash, R. (1991). Three conceptions of ethics for teacher educators. *Journal of Teacher Education, 42* (3), 163–172.

Ornstein, A. (1990). *Strategies for effective teaching.* New York: Harper and Row.

Posner, G. J. (1993). *Field experiences: A guide to reflective teaching,* 3rd ed. New York: Longman.

Raths, L., Harmin, M., & Simon, S. (1978). *Values and teaching,* 2nd ed. Columbus, OH: Merrill.

Remy, R. (1980). *Handbook of basic citizenship competencies.* Alexandria, VA: Association for Supervision and Curriculum Development.

Rosenthal, R., & Jacobson, L. (1968). *Pygmalion in the classroom.* New York: Holt, Rinehart and Winston.

Rubovits, P., & Maehr, M. (1971). Pygmalion analyzed: Toward an explanation of the Rosenthal-Jacobson findings. *Journal of Personality and Social Psychology, 19,* 197–203.

Simon, S., Howe, L., & Kirschenbaum, H. (1972). *Values clarification: A handbook of practical strategies for teachers and students.* New York: Holt, Rinehart and Winston.

Sirotnik, K. (1990). Society, schooling, teaching, and preparing to teach. In J. Goodlad, R. Soder, & K. Sirotnik (eds.), *The moral dimensions of teaching.* San Francisco, CA: Jossey-Bass.

Sockett, H. (1990). Accountability, trust, and ethical codes of practice. In J. Goodlad, R. Soder, & K. Sirotnik (eds.), *The moral dimensions of teaching.* San Francisco: Jossey-Bass.

Strike, K. (1988). The ethics of teaching. *Phi Delta Kappan, 70,* 156–158.

Strike, K. (1990). The legal and moral responsibility of teachers. In J. Goodlad, R. Soder, & K. Sirotnik (eds.), *The moral dimensions of teaching.* San Francisco, CA: Jossey-Bass.

Thomas, B. (1990) The school as a moral learning community. In J. Goodlad, R. Soder, & K. Sirotnik (eds.), *The moral dimensions of teaching.* San Francisco, CA: Jossey-Bass.

United States Department of Education (1994). *Goals 2000: An education strategy.* Washington, DC: United States Department of Education.

Weber, W. (1986). Classroom management. In J. Cooper (ed.), *Classroom teaching skills.* Lexington, MA: Heath.

Chapter 8

The Professional Role

Chapter Objectives

After completing this chapter, you will be able to

- incorporate a proactive problem-solving perspective in your daily teaching environment.
- evaluate effective and ineffective teaching strategies based on the Action Research Framework.
- demonstrate effective preparation for an employment interview.
- develop strategic questioning techniques and answers to achieve interview goals.
- reduce anxiety associated with the interview process.
- identify the mentoring process and key mentoring principles.
- synthesize and evaluate components of the Model for Successful Mentoring.
- develop action plans that focus on beginning teacher needs.

*A*s the Case of the Beginning Professional Teacher on the next page reveals, professionalism in teachers requires a new way of thinking about yourself and teaching. Is teaching truly a profession, like law and medicine? If so, what makes a student teacher become a professional teacher? First, to be a profession, four critical elements must be present: (1) knowledge base (clearly defined and shared professional theories, research, values, and ethics); (2) quality controls (evaluations, assessments, policies); (3) resources (salaries, equipment, facilities); and (4) conditions of practice (autonomy, authority, and resources to act on one's own knowledge in the classroom) (Corrigan & Haberman, 1990).

Challenge

Case of the Beginning Professional Teacher

Gloria wrote the final entry in her student teaching journal on December 12. She described her student teaching experience as rewarding and insightful. During the final interview with her university supervisor and cooperating teacher, both referred to the journal entry and asked Gloria to be more specific. They suggested that she begin by describing something or someone that she felt made a major impact on the quality of her classroom instruction. She did not have to think long before describing an event that occurred early in the semester that changed her attitude and approach toward teaching.

Gloria began by describing her feelings and beliefs about her own experiences in college. She discussed her respect for her professors. She thought that they had provided her with new knowledge about teaching and allowed her the opportunities to apply this new knowledge in early field experiences before student teaching. According to her early thinking, her job was to apply the knowledge of the "experts" in the field of education to real-world classrooms. Gloria was happy and felt that she was truly gaining expertise as a teacher. She felt prepared and ready to begin student teaching. However, during student teaching, she discovered a missing link to the new knowledge-application paradigm she had developed early in her preservice education: teacher thinking and problem-solving skills. Rather than simply applying new knowledge from the educational experts, Gloria began to develop systematic problem-solving skills that encouraged her to synthesize and evaluate information, and thus solve her own problems. She described this revelation in her final interview with her university supervisor:

"I spoke to my cooperating teacher, Mr. McNulty, about my difficulty in motivating my eighth-grade English classes. I told him that I had read several books and articles on motivating students, remembered all of my professors' suggestions and tips, and practiced several strategies in my early field experiences. Unfortunately, the strategies did not seem to be working with my classes during student teaching. Mr. McNulty suggested that I adopt a new way of thinking about problems. This new thinking involved incorporating a problem-solving approach—sometimes referred to as action research—in my teaching. This approach is designed to help me develop my own motivational strategies for increasing student interest. He demonstrated the action research model and encouraged me to use the model in my classes. I began to accurately define and research my problem, set realistic criteria for solutions, brainstorm possible alternatives, choose the best alternative, implement the approach, and continually critique the solution. I found this method extremely helpful in solving my own unique classroom

problems. It focused on my classroom, my students, my teaching beliefs, and my teaching style. I use the method not only to improve motivational strategies but also with other areas of my professional and personal life. For example, I became proactive in such areas as preparing for future employment interviews (many of my fellow student teachers did not even think about interviewing until after student teaching) and gaining valuable information from veteran teachers (through this method, I discovered that I could learn much from other teachers).

I guess the most significant result of incorporating this problem-solving method or way of thinking was to give me confidence in my own teaching abilities. At first in student teaching, I felt uncomfortable and afraid in the classroom, even though I had been well prepared and thought I was ready to teach. After developing problem-solving skills, I felt that making mistakes was acceptable and that I could learn from my mistakes by finding specific solutions to my problems. I felt in control, and that is a great feeling.

Developing authority and expertise in the classroom is not an easy task. The requirements for becoming a professional teacher demand not only new ways of thinking and problem-solving but also the ability to incorporate this new framework into everything that you do. It is not a sometimes, maybe, or when-it's-convenient approach. Becoming a professional requires careful thought and commitment from you. In this chapter, we will discuss three core competencies of the professional role that facilitate professionalism in beginning teachers:

Competency 1: Using Action Research for Problem-Solving

Competency 2: Successful Interviewing

Competency 3: Mentoring: Teachers Assisting Teachers

Competency 1 USING ACTION RESEARCH FOR PROBLEM-SOLVING

ASSESSMENT

Assessing 8.1 Problem-Solving

Purpose: To describe your approach to solving problems.

Time required: 15 minutes

Procedure: Read the following problem, then describe how you would solve it. What can you do to make the beginning of class and the lesson transition smooth and time-effective?

> You have a fifth-period class that is continually behind. The students do not appear to need more time to master the concepts; however, each day as fifth period ends, you notice that students are not finished with the assignments, and you leave class with an uneasy feeling of not having covered the material as effectively as in your other classes. You begin to observe that students returning from lunch appear talkative and are difficult to "settle down"; beginning class takes almost twice as long as it does in other periods throughout the day; you are more talkative and less ready to begin the lesson than in your other periods; and students are in the habit of sharpening their pencils in the class.

EXPERIENCE

Action Research Framework

Action research involves a form of reflective self-analysis developed by teachers to improve teaching practices. It enables teachers to better understand their abilities, beliefs, and attitudes about teaching and learning. Through critical self-analysis, teachers are more in tune with their students, parents, and the environments in which they teach.

The purpose of action research is to put teachers in charge of their profession and its improvement. Action research empowers teachers to make changes ranging from substantive changes to minor fine-tuning when needed. Teachers decide what they wish to change and what they do not wish to change; as a result, they gain control over their own destinies.

What does action research mean to a beginning teacher? How meaningful is it for a teacher who is struggling daily to survive in the classroom? Action research transforms reactive, self-absorbed teachers into proactive, student-oriented teachers by encouraging early investigations of and interventions designed to diffuse potential problems before they reach a crisis state. Teachers who use action research discover that the process allows them to answer difficult questions, alter their teaching strategies, and adapt to the specialized needs of their students.

The objective of this section is to introduce the Action Research Framework and encourage you to incorporate it in your classroom and daily life. This requires you to adopt a new way of thinking or mind-set designed to help solve classroom problems before they interrupt or impede instruction. The Action Research Framework (Table 8.1) consists of eight sequential steps. Each will be discussed briefly and applied to Mrs. Fig's account below.

Table 8.1 **Action Research Framework**

1. Define personal theories and beliefs of practice.
2. Define the potential problem or area for self-improvement.
3. Research and analyze the problem.
4. Establish realistic criteria.
5. List potential alternatives.
6. Evaluate alternatives based on criteria.
7. Select best alternative and implement.
8. Evaluate alternative and implementation process.

Fig's Action Research*

Over the years, my teaching style has changed. After being chosen "Outstanding Future Educator" by my college professors, I began my teaching life realizing my hopes and dreams for providing children with a stimulating, holistic learning environment. The children and I sang, played soccer, learned to do primitive firings in pottery, and also learned the "core curriculum."

Now, eight years later, the types of activities I most wanted to do are performed by "specialists." I have become consumed with making absolutely certain that all of the curricular objectives mandated by our state are drilled into 25 third-grade students. I have become obsessed with the performance of the duties I consider to be the necessary components of "teaching." Each day is an attempt to have the perfect program—classes begin on time, transitions are smooth and quick, lessons follow the seven-step plan, all students are "on task," and procedures are established and evident in the function of the class.

The change in my teaching began about four years ago. I had lost my vision of teaching. My brain was taken over by a notebook full of learning objectives and by numbers that appeared on sheets each spring that were supposed to measure how effective an educator I was.

I have always received great evaluations. Nonetheless, I felt uncomfortable about what was happening in my class. The children were performing well, but I felt the atmosphere was not right. Still, I continued teaching in the same manner, knowing that something would have to give or I would be looking into another profession very soon.

This past year I enrolled in a university action research class. It is a course designed for active educators who want to take a close look at what they are doing in their classrooms, evaluate it, alter it, evaluate it again, and determine its effectiveness given one's goals.

*Adapted from excerpts from Phyllis Ferrell's research reports found in Rogers, D. L., Noblit, G. W., & Ferrell, P. (1990). Action research as an agent for developing teachers' communicative competence. *Theory Into Practice, 29* (3), 177–184.

My original goal was to spend more time with my children. It soon became clear that I first needed to know how much individual time I spent with children during the instructional part of the day. I already spent time with them at lunch, while walking in lines, and after school. My goal was to somehow spend more time with them so that the teachable moment was once again possible, and so that they could have a chance to share their lives with me.

I tried several different methods of collecting data to analyze how much time I spent with each child. Recording in a nightly journal was not effective because I could not remember all of the interactions. I asked the children to keep a record on a special form. As a class, we discussed my goal and what they should consider an interaction to be, but the children never could remember to mark their forms or agree on just what constituted an interaction. I tried wearing a form on my back for children to mark immediately after having an interaction. This worked well at first. They loved writing on my back. The excitement soon faded, however, and I was spending valuable time tracking down someone who had not marked the form.

I decided to try one more method. I made a large wall chart with all the children's names on it. Each time I interacted with a child I would hand out a sticker for the child to place on the chart. I scribbled a few words on each sticker about the nature of the interaction. This lasted about a week. Writing down what the interaction was became distracting to me. However, the chart was revealing. For the first time I had devised a method that was cumulative. Over the course of a week, some children had accumulated 10 or more stickers, while some children had only one, or none.

My research question has been answered. How much time do I spend with my children? Not enough . . . (Through action research) I have come to feel better concerning my own ideas about teaching, but I am still not satisfied. I know more about what teaching should be but there is still a part of me that believes I will never really understand teaching. As changing social and economic forces within our society influence the school's role in helping our children learn to lead healthy, responsible, and enriched lives, I think I will have to be comfortable with a continual questioning of my own values and decisions concerning just what teaching is in order to be the *best* I can be (pp. 179–181).

Discussion, Explanation, and Application of Fig's Action Research

1. *Define personal theories and beliefs of practice.* Articulating your own personal theory of practice is the first step in the Action Research Framework. Teachers develop, through their observations and actions, interrelated sets of beliefs and practices about how students learn, what they should learn, and how motivation occurs. Teachers' personal theories of practice serve as guides to action and are often quite difficult for teachers to articulate. Nevertheless, it is crucial for teachers to articulate what they believe about how children learn best if teachers are going to become fully aware of how personal theories of practice guide their actions. For example, in Fig's Action Research, Mrs. Fig began her teaching career by providing

Reality Bite

Do You Have Time?

Time is a precious commodity in education, especially for teachers. Action research is going to take time; therefore, new teachers must plan their time wisely when implementing this problem-solving method. If new teachers take time during their first year to implement action research, they will save precious time in the long run by solving problems as soon as they occur.

Severo Alvarado, Assistant Principal

students with a stimulating, holistic learning environment. To ensure success in her theory of practice, Mrs. Fig sings and plays soccer with her students as a means of orchestrating the implementation of the core curriculum.

To articulate your personal belief of how students learn, begin by thinking about your teachers and college instructors and your most meaningful learning experiences as a student. Examine each experience for the underlying learning principles represented. As an effective teacher, your job is to provide students with a "connection" of meaningful learning experiences. To be successful in making connections of meaningful learning experiences for your students, you must uncover and articulate learning principles or personal theories of practice.

2. *Define the potential problem or area for self-improvement.* It is important that you understand thoroughly the need and problem area before continuing with this process. If the problem is vague, too broad in scope, or even unknown, then focusing on the observed symptoms and perceived size of the problem may help you determine the specific problem (Hamilton & Parker, 1993). For example, in Fig's Action Research, Mrs. Fig felt uncomfortable with what was occurring in her classroom; consequently, she enrolled in an action research course at a local college. This action research course was designed for educators who want to take a close look at their own classroom practices—evaluate, alter, reevaluate, and make final judgments—in order to determine overall effectiveness. By participating in this course, Mrs. Fig had the opportunity to identify and define her area of concern— the amount of instructional time spent with her students.

3. *Research and analyze the problem.* This step is important to avoid adopting unworkable solutions. For example, Mrs. Fig would need to collect data about how much time she was spending with each student on a daily basis; how much *instructional time* she was spending each day; how to define the "quality" of the time she was willing to spend with her students; how to define the *amount* of time she would be willing to spend with her students (How much time is she willing to afford to her students?); and how to determine the *time of day* she would be affording this time to her students.

In addition, Mrs. Fig needs to gather information on time-management strategies, on streamlining the curriculum, and on the dynamics of classroom interactions. She could do her research in the library, consult her professors or colleagues, or use a computer network system to do a search.

4. *Establish realistic criteria.* Criteria are guidelines, boundaries, standards, or rules by which one evaluates possible alternatives in selecting the final solution to the problem (Hamilton & Parker, 1993). For example, Mrs. Fig needs to develop a set of guidelines, boundaries, standards, or rules by which she can evaluate possible alternatives when considering final solutions to her classroom dilemma. Her criteria might include:

- Set a time limit she will spend with students (a maximum and a minimum amount of time).
- Data collected must be effective (not time consuming, farfetched, or counterproductive).
- Data collected should be relevant to the problem under study.
- Solution must be within school policy.
- Solution must be positive and beneficial for students.
- Solution must enhance and be within the goals and objectives of the school.

Once Mrs. Fig chooses an alternative solution, she will need to test it against all criteria; and if the solution meets the criteria, she can begin implementing the solution.

5. *List potential alternatives.* Brainstorm as many potential alternatives as possible. Ask a colleague or mentor to assist you in developing a list of potential alternatives. Do not stop and evaluate each alternative at this time. Remember to strive for as many creative and unusual alternatives as possible. For example, Mrs. Fig could have tried many more alternatives, but given her time restraints, she decided to implement these four: (1) keeping a nightly journal; (2) having students keep a daily record of the time she spent with them; (3) wearing a notepad on her back so students could write her notes; and (4) utilizing wall charts and stickers.

6. *Evaluate alternatives based on criteria.* This step is designed to help you avoid selecting an alternative that is unrealistic and unworkable. Examine your list of potential alternatives and eliminate those not meeting your criteria. Combine similar alternatives into a single alternative. Continue reducing your list until you have clear and concise alternatives. Prioritize the remaining alternatives. For example, Mrs. Fig had several alternative but had to evaluate (test) each one against her criteria. First, the nightly journal was not effective because it took too much time to complete, and she could not remember all of the interactions with her students.

The second alternative, having students keep a record at school, was ineffective because students were confused about what constituted an interaction. Moreover, many students did not mark in interactions. The "form-on-the-back" alternative was also time consuming, and her students quickly became bored with the idea. In addition, she had to track down those students who had forgotten to write on her back. Clearly, the first three alternatives did not meet at least two of the criteria. They were relevant, positive, and fell within overall school policy, but they were time consuming and ineffective.

7. *Select best alternative and implement.* Select the best alternative and develop a plan for using it in your classroom. Ask a colleague for assistance on plan development and implementation. For example, Mrs. Fig decided that the chart was the most helpful in determining how much time she spent with each student, so she implemented this procedure. Once she found the solution to be effective in helping her solve her problem, she felt more in control of her time in the classroom. She felt satisfied that she had developed a way to spend more time with each of her students.

8. *Evaluate alternative and implementation process.* Collect information on the alternative selected through observations, student interviews, videotapes (tape your classroom for a week), and peer assessment (ask a teacher to observe your classroom). In analyzing the information, you may discover that although the problem has been reduced, it still remains. Keep in mind that the alternative may be sound and effective, whereas the implementation process may be faulty. If you discover that your alternative is not working, select your second alternative and implement. Remember, the Action Research Framework requires continual monitoring and reflective analysis. For example, Mrs. Fig noticed that the chart and the stickers were revealing. She could finally "see" her actions and could evaluate them to make modifications in her classroom. Her final alternative was the solution to her problem; this could help her devise a schedule, or some strategic plan, that allowed each of her students to spend quality time with her. Implementation of the alternative answered her research question, and she used it as an "instructional crutch" to enhance her classroom practice.

COACHING AND REFLECTING

Select a real-world problem that you or another beginning teacher have experienced. Discuss your problem with your cooperating teacher and university supervisor. Use the Action Research Framework to help define the problem, research and analyze the problem, select realistic criteria, list possible alternatives, check alternatives with criteria, select best alternatives to implement, collect data, and evaluate alternatives. Keep a journal of your progress using action research to alter or change behaviors. Ask your supervisors to serve as process evaluators to determine how well you have followed the framework, implemented and evaluated the changes, and responded to feedback from students and colleagues.

Use the Action Research Framework as you tackle the remaining two competencies in this chapter—successful interviewing and teachers assisting teachers.

Competency 2 SUCCESSFUL INTERVIEWING

Is the teacher employment interview really *that* important in securing a teaching position? Absolutely! The interview plays a major role in teacher selection. A survey of more than 250 employers that hire recent college graduates included effective interviewing skills at the top of the list of reasons for hiring. Marcum (1988) asked over 300 personnel directors and principals what characteristics they looked for when hiring new teachers. The results of the survey indicated that the most important quality sought in prospective teachers was enthusiasm. Enthusiasm in this context is defined as the candidate's ability to show their genuine care and concern for children while motivating student achievement. The interview is an indispensable tool for determining teacher enthusiasm. Interviewers want to know if you enjoy teaching, like children, and share the same values and goals as do members of their community and school district.

Whereas the interview may not be the most reliable or valid measure of an applicant's teaching abilities, rarely are teachers hired without a personal interview. Let's begin by examining what you know about interviewing and the interview process.

ASSESSMENT

Assessing 8.2 Preparing for the Teacher Interview

Purpose: To determine your readiness to interview for a teaching position.

Time required: 15 minutes

Procedure: The following sample questions are often asked by interviewers during teacher interviews. Place yourself in the role of the interviewee, and rate how prepared you are to answer each question. Place a W in front of those questions you feel "well" prepared to answer, an S in front of those questions you feel "somewhat" prepared to answer, and a U in front of those questions you feel "unprepared" to answer. During the coaching phase of competency 1, you will have an opportunity to research and confer with your coach concerning possible answers to difficult interview questions.

_____   1.   What do you know about our school district?

_____   2.   What three adjectives best describe you as a teacher?

_____   3.   What is the hardest thing that you have done in the classroom?

_____ 4. What is the best way to communicate with parents? Do you consider most parents as helpful or hostile? How do you handle a hostile parent?

_____ 5. What is your philosophy concerning classroom discipline?

_____ 6. How do children learn? Can all children learn?

_____ 7. What do you like most about teaching? Least about teaching?

_____ 8. Why should we hire you?

_____ 9. What social and cultural issues impact education today? What is the teacher's role in a changing society?

_____ 10. Evaluate effective classroom instruction. What are the key elements involved?

_____ 11. How involved should teachers be with leadership and management issues in schools?

_____ 12. What makes an effective school leader? What qualities would you look for in hiring a school principal?

_____ 13. What professional journals do you read? To what professional organizations do you belong? Why did you choose those journals and associations? How do they make you a better teacher?

_____ 14. What are your short-term (one year) career goals? Long-term (next five years) career goals?

_____ 15. What are the current state and national goals for education?

_____ 16. What will teaching and learning be like in the future? How will our schools look in the twenty-first century?

_____ 17. Describe teaching in a (rural or urban) school. What are the challenges of this environment and how will you meet these challenges?

_____ 18. Name two current educators that you admire. Describe their contribution to education or what makes them special.

Assessing 8.3 Factors Affecting Interview Outcomes

Purpose: To analyze potential factors affecting decisions to hire.

Time required: 15 minutes

Procedure: List five potential factors that may affect interview outcomes. For example, interviewee dress may project a positive or negative image. Discuss your five factors with a colleague. Perhaps the colleague can offer other examples.

Assessing 8.4 Responding to Unlawful Interview Questions

Purpose: To help you recognize unlawful questions and determine effective and ineffective answers.

Time required: Varies

Procedure: Write L for lawful or U for unlawful after each of the following questions. For each question marked U, decide how you would respond to it if asked in a formal interview. Remember, there are two basic guidelines used to determine if a question is lawful or unlawful: All questions must be job related, and the same questions must be asked of all applicants for the position (Hamilton & Parker, 1993, 4th ed.). After responding to each question, check the Answer Key to see if the question is lawful or unlawful.

1. Are you a citizen of the United States?   _____

2. Have you ever been arrested?   _____

3. How old are you?   _____

4. Our school board members play golf. How is your golf game?   _____

5. Do you have any physical handicaps?   _____

6. Discuss your student teaching experience and your GPA.   _____

7. Do you own a home or business?   _____

8. Are you married? If so, is your spouse looking for a job also? _____

9. What personal qualities make you a good teacher?   _____

10. What religious holidays do you observe?   _____

11. What foreign language(s) do you speak, read, or write fluently?   _____

12. Do you have any children? Are you planning to have children?   _____

13. Why did you leave your previous teaching position?   _____

14. How well do you relate with persons of different cultures and races?   _____

Answer Key

1. Lawful.

2. Unlawful.   Arrested does not mean convicted. The question would be lawful if stated, "Have you ever been convicted of a crime?"

3. Unlawful. If all job qualifications are met, the age of an applicant has no relevance to job performance.

4. Unlawful. Playing golf is not job related.

5. Unlawful. This question is unlawful unless the applicant cannot physically function in a classroom. It is better to state the question as "Do you have any physical or health problems that may affect your teaching performance?"

6. Lawful.

7. Unlawful. Owning a home is not job related and may be a form of discrimination.

8. Unlawful. Marital status is not job related and may be a form of discrimination.

9. Lawful.

10. Unlawful. This question may be used as a form of religious discrimination.

11. Lawful.

12. Unlawful. Plans to have children are not job related.

13. Lawful.

14. Lawful.

Adapted from Hamilton & Parker (1993) and O'Hair & Friedrich (1995, 2nd ed.).

If a question is unlawful, the best response is to answer the fear behind the question. For example, an interviewer asks you if you plan to have any children. Rather than remaining silent or saying, "That's an illegal question, and I refuse to answer it," respond to the fear behind the question: "I assure you that if we decide to have children, this decision will not affect my teaching. I will continue to meet all of my teaching responsibilities." Practice answering the fear behind each of the unlawful questions listed above.

EXPERIENCE

To be a successful interviewee, beginning teachers must have some understanding of themselves and the interview process. Successful interviewing is not a hit-and-miss, experience-cures-all process. In other words, depending upon interview experience alone is not enough to ensure success and may result in the loss of preferred job offers. Successful interviewing is a science and requires significant study and dedication by both interviewees and interviewers. In this section, you will examine interview formats and the basic organization of teacher employment interviews. The Coaching section will help you answer difficult questions, understand factors that affect interview outcomes, and develop proactive stances toward

 *Reality Bite*

Ethical/Moral Dimensions

You felt that most of the questions you were asked during your interview were illegal. Follow the necessary steps to rectify this predicament:

1. *Write down the questions that you believe were unethical.*
2. *Take these questions to a supervisor and see what he or she thinks.*
3. *The supervisor can help decide if the questions in the interview were unethical or immoral.*
4. *The supervisor can either assist you in pursuing the matter in a legal sense or give you direction on how to best handle this situation.*

Lisa Cogswell, Experienced Teacher

factors that are advantageous rather than detrimental to the hiring process. Questioning techniques, interview preparation, and résumé writing will be examined in the Reflection section.

Interview Formats

Perhaps we are most familiar with the one-on-one, basic interview format in which one interviewer asks one interviewee questions. However, there are several new interview formats emerging in education.

Melissa, a beginning teacher, encountered a new format during her first interview. When asked to report to an elementary school for an interview, she expected to be interviewed by the principal and given a tour of the building. Melissa was surprised to discover that her interview was with other teachers in a board format. (A *board* interview involves more interviewers than interviewees.) Not being prepared for such a format frightened Melissa and resulted in a significant decrease in her overall performance.

Melissa's experience is not uncommon. We in education are seeing more and more nontraditional interviews conducted. As teachers become decision makers and share authority and responsibility for student success with administrators, it is no surprise that teachers are becoming more involved in the personnel selection process.

Reality Bite

Dress to Impress

First impressions are very important in interviewing. For the best possible interview, it is important to be properly attired. Make sure that your attire is pressed, clean, and fits. To avoid any misconceptions of cultural norms, it is best to dress in the following traditional attire. Conservative attire allows the interviewer the opportunity to concentrate on the most important attributes of the interviewee: you and the strengths you can bring to the position.

Men	Women
Navy blue or black suit	*Navy blue or black suit (Skirts should be no higher than knee level.)*
White shirt (or modest print)	
Conservative tie	*White or off-white blouse*
Simple jewelry	*Natural colored hose*
Modest amount or no cologne	*Modest amount or no cologne*

Stacy Caviel, Beginning Teacher

Some nontraditional formats include panel, board, telephone, and audio- or videotaped interviews. Table 8.2 offers brief descriptions and helpful hints for adjusting to interview formats. Other innovative formats may include student, parent, and business involvement in the teacher selection.

Basic Organization of Interviews

Although different interview formats exist, all interviews have in common three basic organizational stages: the opening, the body, and the conclusion. The success of the interview centers on the smooth exchange of valuable information during each of these stages.

The Opening. Most hiring decisions are made within the first four minutes of the interview (O'Hair, 1989; Springbett, 1958), thus the opening of an interview is perhaps the most significant part. It involves three key components: (1) impression formation (Do I like this person? Can I trust this person?); (2) orientation (What will this interview include?); and (3) motivation (What will I gain from this interview?).

Table 8.2 **Interview Dos and Don'ts**

Format	Dos	Don'ts
Panel Interviews involve more interviewees than interviewers.	1. Participate. 2. Speak and look at everyone, not just the interviewer. 3. Try to be seated where you are not constantly moving your head in order to give everyone direct eye contact; constant head movement is distracting.	1. Don't always speak first. 2. Show original thought; don't always agree with someone's response without elaborating.
Board Interviews involve more interviewers than interviewees.	1. Try not to be the first applicant interviewed. Often, interviewers are uncertain of their roles at first and become more comfortable in later interviews. 2. Make eye contact with all members, not just the person asking the question. 3. Observe each member's nonverbal reactions to your questions.	1. Don't give lengthy answers; each member probably has questions for you. Be concise, sincere, and honest. 2. If your answer is challenged, don't become defensive. State that there are several ways to look at it.
Telephone Interviews involve an audiotaped telephone interview that is usually played back to the interview team. Used for long-distance interviews.	1. Practice answering questions on the phone. 2. Investigate the city and district before the interview. 3. Explain your answers by giving vivid descriptions. (Remember, without nonverbal communication, your verbal communication is all you have.)	1. Don't agree to an interview during a time of the day that you may not function particularly well (i.e., right after lunch, early in the morning). (Remember, the interviewer may be in a different time zone.) 2. Don't plan to read directly from your notes. This will sound rehearsed and unnatural.
Videotaped and Audiotaped Interviews involve videotaping and/or audiotaping a basic interview between interviewer and interviewee for later analysis.	1. Pretend that the tape recorder and/or camera is not there. Relax and give direct, concise, sincere answers. 2. Support answers with appropriate gestures and paralanguage. 3. Increase your enthusiasm a bit for the camera. We often appear less enthusiastic on tape than in real life.	1. Don't look directly at the camera. Focus your eye contact on the interviewer. 2. Don't ask to begin again. As if by asking to rewind the tape, you could actually start over. (It is impossible to erase a shaky beginning. The best way to counter shaky beginnings is to proceed in a confident manner.)

Reality Bite

Accessories for the Interview

Gaudy jewelry is definitely out for this season of interviews, but certain accessories can enhance any interview.

A Philosophy of Education *is definitely in fashion for runway interviews of the nineties. To better enhance this trend, we must not forget our* Position Paper. *No wardrobe would be complete without a* 15-Minute Sample Video of Your Teaching *abilities. To offset your colors, use a* Résumé. *By the way, do not forget to wear your favorite* Sample of Teaching Units *for luck.*

1. *A philosophy of education is a one- or two-page paper that states your personal views about teaching.*

2. *A position paper should be no longer than five pages and should consist of your vision of the instruction and learning process.*

3. *A 15-minute sample video should provide a brief view of your teaching style in a classroom setting.*

4. *A résumé should include experiences that have enhanced your teaching ability.*

5. *A sample of teaching units should include classroom activities that encourage and motivate students of all different backgrounds and educational levels.*

Stacy Caviel, Beginning Teacher

Impression formation occurs during the opening phase of the interview, and first impressions are more important than we often realize. When an interviewer and interviewee meet for the first time, each brings expectations, concerns, and stereotypes to the meeting. For example, when hiring a computer teacher, an administrator may expect to interview a thin, bookworm-type, male teacher; however, when the applicant is a middle-aged, attractive female the interviewer's expectations are violated. The interviewee's credibility as a successful teacher may reside initially with first impressions.

When issues of credibility become important, interviewers and interviewees may wish to adjust to what Burgoon, Buller, and Woodall (1989) and other researchers describe as the major principles of impression formation:

Reality Bite

Technology

Are you aware that some phones have attached monitors that allow you to see the person with whom you are communicating? Will this set a future trend for over-the-telephone interviews?

In future, instead of sending a letter, résumé, or application to the schools, will your résumé and application be on a CD-ROM?

How about conducting interviews by E-mail or other computer networks?

These technological trends may have an impact on the interviewing styles of the future.

Lisa Cogswell, Experienced Teacher

- People evaluate one another from limited external information.
- First impressions are based partly on the stereotypes held by individuals.
- First impressions are often initially based on outward appearances.
- Initial impressions form a baseline of comparison for succeeding impressions and judgments.
- Length of interaction time affects impression formation. Longer interactions help reduce the impact of first impressions.
- Impressions consist of judgments on at least three different levels: physical (age, sex, race), sociocultural (socioeconomic status, education level, occupation), and psychological (maturity, temperament, moods).

Awareness of these key principles is important for both interviewee and interviewer. The unconscious exchange of information based on nonverbal cues alone can be misleading and often harmful. All parties involved in an interview must be cognizant of and sensitive to their own nonverbal liabilities and strengths and to the stereotypes they possess. This awareness may be demonstrated by asking yourself the following questions: What is an interviewer likely to conclude as a result of my physical appearance, enthusiasm level, gestures, voice, eye contact, and so on? Are there any of those characteristics I can modify or improve? Do I want to make any changes? For those characteristics that cannot be changed, is there anything I can do to reduce their impact? For example, it is easy to change one's attire into professional dress (suit, dress, tie, etc.) rather than casual dress (jean, sweats, loafers). What tends to be more difficult is modifying one's vocal patterns to reduce "nasal" sounds, increasing eye contact, and demonstrating active listening skills.

A significant component of impression formation involves establishing rapport with the interviewer. Rapport is described as a comfortable, "I-respect-you-as-an-individual, relaxed feeling that makes both participants receptive to the interview and willing to talk" (Hamilton & Parker, 1993). To establish successful rapport, consider these factors: the *environment* (making the person feel comfortable, reducing distractions); *nonverbal communication* (standing and greeting the individual with a handshake; sitting next to the person rather than behind a desk, leaning forward, and establishing eye contact); and *conversational topics* (discussing mutual acquaintances, unusual weather, school district setting, or immediate reference to the subject of the interview). Perhaps the key to establishing rapport is to encourage talk, thereby reducing initial nervousness and anxiety. Remember, no set rules for establishing rapport exist, but rapport must be established for a successful interview to occur.

The second component in the opening of an interview is the orientation. Applicants need a clear picture, or orientation, of the interview. In this stage, interviewees and interviewers should understand clearly the purposes of the interview and the process involved. It is important for both parties to understand the following information:

- The applicant's name *and* the interviewer's name. Schools are busy places with principals and teachers involved in many different aspects of schooling. It is wise to verify names, especially when several teacher applicants may be interviewed for the same or similar positions by one or more interviewers.
- The purpose or desired outcome of the interview.
- What information is needed and how it will be used.
- The approximate length of the interview.

The third component in the opening phase of the interview is motivation. Interviewers should use motivational strategies that help applicants relax and give honest and complete answers. Interviewers want responses to their questions that reflect careful thought. Here is an example of a motivational strategy:

This interview is an important part of the application process with this district, Ms. Campbell—not just a formality. I feel sure that you are as interested as we are in finding you a position where you will be most successful with students. To place you accurately in the district, we need honest and detailed answers from you, okay?

Remember, the type of motivational approach chosen by the interviewer will depend on the individual being interviewed.

The Body. The second phase of the interview—the body—is sometimes referred to as the question–answer phase. It is the core of the interview and allows the exchange and verification of important information. As an interviewee, you must carefully prepare for this portion of the interview. Rarely do interviewees effectively answer questions that take them by surprise. Careful reflection on potential questions is necessary. In addition, interviewees should carefully outline information depicting their personal and professional strengths, areas of knowledge, and past accomplishments. Much of this information is provided in résumé form; however, some areas are not easily categorized in a résumé (e.g., enthusiasm, love for children). The goal of the interviewee is to communicate pertinent information to the interviewer.

In addition to giving information, applicants should ask pertinent questions about the district, school, community, job requirements, and professional opportunities. At the end of the body phase of the interview, interviewers often ask the applicant if she or he has any questions. Some possible questions are found in Table 8.3.

Most applicant questions focus on three areas: benefits, including professional growth; job requirements; and the district's or school's commitment to teaching and learning. It is wise to avoid the topic of salary in the first interview. The topic of compensation often detracts from projecting the image that one's primary commitment and motivation is to teaching excellence.

The Conclusion. The closing of an interview involves a summary of information gained. Summaries allow interviewers and applicants the opportunity to make sure that important information is not overlooked, misconstrued, or forgotten during the interview. In addition to summarizing, interview etiquette requires that the interviewer and interviewee, when appropriate, agree on what selection steps should follow and make arrangements for the next meeting if one is needed. For example, a teacher interviewing for a teaching position needs to know *when* the interview team or principal is going to make a decision and *how* candidates will be notified of the hiring decision.

Table 8.3 **Possible Applicant Questions for Interviewer**

1. What opportunities exist for professional growth in the district?
2. To what professional organizations do most of your faculty belong?
3. How are instructional decisions made in the district? the school?
4. Is there a mentoring system for new teachers?
5. What will my teaching assignment consist of?
6. What is the district's philosophy concerning the use of new technologies in the classroom?
7. Do any extracurricular student activities need faculty sponsors?
8. Describe parental involvement in the district or school.
9. Describe the district's special education program. Are most special education students placed in regular education classrooms?
10. Describe programs and policies for recognizing and celebrating cultural diversity in your district. How are individual teachers involved?

Reality Bite

Cultural Diversity

What is your experience in working with students of different cultures? This may very well be asked at an interview. Here are some ways to help you become more culturally diversified:

- *Take a class about different cultures.*
- *Read books about different cultures.*
- *Volunteer at places that you can experience working with youths of differing cultures.*
- *Go to events that are culturally based; for example, Cinco de Mayo, German Festival.*

Lisa Cogswell, Experienced Teacher

COACHING

What have teachers discovered about interviewing? Is there a shared body of knowledge concerning successful and unsuccessful interviewing? This section encourages you to discuss interviewing with your peers and with other professionals both in education and in business, and it focuses on two specific areas: factors affecting interview outcomes and questioning strategies. Research findings are incorporated into each topic to serve as a guide or framework for discussion.

Factors Affecting Interview Outcomes

Whereas we would like to believe that employment decisions are based solely on the applicant's teaching abilities, interviews provide a blatantly unreliable means of selecting employees (O'Hair, 1989; Skopec, 1987). Many variables unrelated to the applicant's abilities affect interviewers' judgments. Explore, with your coach, the following intervening variables: atmosphere, communication, enthusiasm, psychological factors, demographic data, and stereotypes. Take the definitions and research findings presented here and begin to analyze, synthesize, and evaluate each variable based on your prior experience and the experience of your coach. See Figure 8.1.

Atmosphere. The interview atmosphere for teaching positions tends to differ significantly from that of business interviews. Most beginning teachers attend job fairs, sometimes referred to as "teacher markets." Teacher applicants usually find themselves in a large, noisy room with more than 100 other people talking and moving around simultaneously. This atmosphere requires that the interview be highly structured, in that each applicant receives the same set of questions in a specified time frame. If an applicant survives the "teacher market" and personnel office interviews, he or she may discover a very different atmosphere when interviewed by principals and teachers. Site-based interviews tend to be less formal and more relaxed with more emphasis on the candidate's personality and strengths.

Communication. Teachers possessing exemplary communication skills are preferred by interviewers. As schools adopt site-based management plans requiring shared decision making, principals recognize the need for effective communication skills within themselves and their faculty. As we approach the twenty-first century, school improvement and reform is less dependent on one person (such as the principal) and more dependent on the relationships among principals, teachers, parents, and community members. Interviewers want to hire teachers who possess interpersonal communication skills (teacher–student, teacher–principal, teacher–parent, and teacher–teacher); small-group communication skills (problem-solving, focus groups, and school improvement planning); and public communication skills (school–community relations and media relations).

The interview is an excellent vehicle for determining communication skills. Nonverbal communication that is inconsistent with verbal communication during the course of an interview affects the overall decision to hire. Body language (including gesture, eye contact, posture, handshake) and paralanguage (including rate, pitch, volume, vocal fillers) send immediate messages about one's enthusiasm for and love of children and teaching. When nonverbal and verbal messages conflict, interviewers tend to remember nonverbal communication, or *how* we say something rather than *what* we say. Mehrabian (1981) found that very little of the message is conveyed by verbal or language codes. He reported that approximately 7 percent of the message is conveyed through verbal codes, whereas nonverbal (including paralanguage) conveyed approximately 93 percent of the total message. Our next topic of discussion, enthusiasm, is a prime example of the importance of nonverbal communication.

Enthusiasm. As stated earlier, district hiring officers and principals wish to select enthusiastic and motivated teachers. They see the interview as an indispensable means to determine these essential teacher qualities. Candidates who demonstrate a sincere love of children and genuine enthusiasm for teaching are more likely to be selected than teachers who do not.

Psychological Factors. Psychological factors affecting the interview process include teaching and discipline philosophies, maturity level, ethics, occupational stress, goal congruency, and collective teamwork. A common thread found in successful schools involves positive staff morale and a sense of teamwork. Interviewers are concerned with matching individual teaching and discipline philosophies with those of the districts they represent in order to enhance the existing atmosphere.

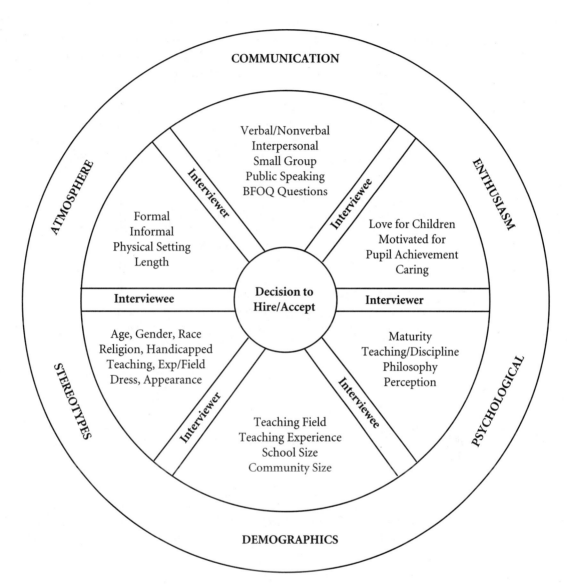

Figure 8.1 **Factors Affecting the Decision to Hire Model**

Source: Adapted from O'Hair, M. J. (1989). Teacher employment interview: A neglected reality. *Action in Teacher Education,* *11* (1), 53–57.

Districts wish to hire ethical and mature individuals with the ability to adapt to district goals, policies, and procedures. John Goodlad (1984) identified goal congruence among teachers, administrators, students, and parents as the greatest predictor of school success. Interviewers wish to determine if teacher applicants have, as described by Carl Glickman (1985), a "cause beyond oneself." "Teachers do not view their work as simply what they carry out within their own four walls. Instead, in successful schools, teachers see themselves as part of the larger enterprise of complementing and working with each other to educate students. For successful schools, education is a collective and not individual enterprise" (p. 20). The interview process is an excellent mechanism to test psychological factors of goal congruency and "cause beyond oneself" orientation.

Beginning teachers must remember that some psychological factors may serve as barriers to effective interviewing. For example, high stress and anxiety may reduce the clarity and effectiveness of an applicant's responses. Stress reduction techniques are available to help reduce contextual stress associated with interviewing.

Demographics and Stereotypes.   Research indicates that stereotypes and demographics affect decisions to hire. Research findings are discussed in Table 8.4.

REFLECTION

Reflecting 8.5 Interview Preparation Plan
Based on the interview tips and suggestions, develop a comprehensive interview preparation plan that follows the Action Research Framework. Keep in mind that each beginning teacher's plan is based on personal strengths and weaknesses and will be different. Share your plan with your supervisors and colleagues.

------- ■ *Competency 3* MENTORING: TEACHERS ASSISTING TEACHERS -------

A mentor for a beginning teacher is as important as a mentor for other professionals. Recent research in psychology and career development has reported that the absence of a mentor in young adulthood is a handicap, parallel to parental absence in early life (Kronik, 1990). School districts and universities are striving to develop successful mentoring programs to ensure the success of beginning teachers.

Our purpose is to help you, as a beginning teacher or protégé, to understand the mentoring process and develop skills necessary for classroom success. As school districts and universities teach exemplary veteran teachers to assume mentoring roles, they often neglect the training of beginning teachers to assume protégé roles. We believe that guidance for *both* mentors and protégés is crucial if mentoring is to be successful. Before we discuss the mentoring process, let's look at two factors crucial to defining classroom successes for beginning teachers: identifying needs of the beginning teacher and understanding key mentoring principles used to address those needs.

Table 8.4 **Stereotypes and Demographics Affect Decisions to Hire**

Research Findings	Implications for Practice	Action Plans
1. Stereotype studies indicate that interviewers have an "ideal applicant" in mind.	For example, a football coach may be stereotyped as an athletic male, whereas an older female may not fit.	Stereotypes tend to decrease as the interview progresses. For applicants who do not fit commonly held stereotypes, the length of the interview is crucial.
2. Candidates' age is found to adversely affect hiring decisions. Interviewers possess inherently strong beliefs about hiring a person of appropriate age for the position.	Applicants who are 22 years old but outwardly appear 16 may experience age biases. Also, older-than-the-norm first-year teachers may experience discrimination based on the fear that older individuals cannot succeed in schools of today.	It is important for younger appearing teachers to dress and act like professionals. Both verbal and nonverbal communication assessment is important. Older candidates must demonstrate flexibility and cooperation to dispel fears of rigidity and "set in one's own way" mentality.
3. Studies report that an individual's handicapped status may affect hiring decisions.	Interviewers tend to rank individuals who are handicapped lower in terms of an overall hiring rating but give handicapped applicants higher ratings in terms of motivational variables.	Individuals who are handicapped must address not only their desire to teach but that their handicap will not interfere with the learning process. Also, people who are handicapped may wish to demonstrate their teaching style to help dispel unfounded fears.

Source: Adapted from O'Hair, M. J. (1989). Teacher employment interview: A neglected reality. *Action in Teacher Education,* *11* (1), 53–57.

ASSESSMENT

Assessing 8.6 Beginning Teacher Needs

Purpose: To synthesize current knowledge, thinking, and experience concerning the needs of beginning teachers and to develop a prioritized list of beginning teachers' needs.

Time required: 30 minutes

Procedure: In a small group, generate a list of needs, prioritize the list, and report back to the large group.

Assessing 8.7 Understanding Key Mentoring Principles

Purpose: To define the mentoring process and to evaluate current mentoring programs operating in school districts.

Reality Bite

Purpose of Education

As teachers, our main professional focus should be on students and teaching these students.

When answering questions during an interview, be positive and keep your answers focused on the students. Try to always bring up students and your concern for them. Do not assume that the interviewer knows that you are really concerned with students. Answer your questions in a way that tells the interviewer that you teach because of the students.

Lisa Cogswell, Experienced Teacher

Time required: Varies

Procedure: (1) Respond to the following list of key statements by defining each italic word or phrase. (2) Write a short statement reporting the presence or absence of each principle in local school districts and colleges of education. (3) Examine ways to improve or maximize the full potential of each principle.

1. Mentoring is a *complex process* and function.
2. Mentoring involves *support*, assistance, and guidance, but *not evaluation.*
3. Mentoring *requires time and effective communication.*
4. Mentoring should *facilitate self-reliance* in protégés.
5. Mentoring is *bigger than teacher induction.*
6. Mentoring programs should involve local school districts in *collaboration* with institutions of higher education, state departments of education, and teachers' bargaining groups.
7. The *structure of mentoring programs* should be *consistent with school district goals.*
8. Mentoring programs should be *evaluated.*
9. Mentors should be *selected based upon identified criteria.*
10. Mentors should be *prepared* (trained) and *offered incentives* for their work.

*Adopted by the Commission on the Role and Preparation of Mentor Teachers at the Annual Conference of the Association of Teacher Educators, New Orleans, February 1991 (Bey & Holmes, 1992, p. 4).

EXPERIENCE

The Mentoring Process

The mentoring process is best understood from within the larger context of teacher induction, which involves the moving from student of teaching to professional teacher (Griffin et al., 1983). The mentoring process found in induction programs is designed to provide beginning teachers with much needed supervision and support. The induction phase involves the smooth transition from preservice teacher education to inservice teacher education and incorporates a program of systematic and sustained assistance for beginning teachers. This type of program requires numerous orientation sessions designed to describe district policy, employee benefits, and teacher appraisal plans. Teacher induction programs focus on meeting specific needs of beginning teachers, and developing positive teaching strategies. Let's examine each area specifically.

Needs. Unless specific needs of beginning teachers are met, we find that as many as 40 percent leave the profession during the first two years, compared to the overall teacher turnover rate of 6 percent a year. It is also estimated that the most academically talented teachers are among the first to leave the profession.

According to Yvonne Gold (1990), the needs of beginning teachers fall into three groups: (1) emotional–physical, (2) psychosocial, and (3) personal–intellectual. Emotional–physical include needs such as self-esteem, security, acceptance, self-confidence, and illness resistance (Gold & Roth, 1993). Controlling emotional–physical needs often requires implementation of a stress-reduction program. Negative side effects of physical and emotional teacher stress include increased teacher turnover and absenteeism, reduced caring for children and academic achievement, and increased physical and emotional health problems for teachers. Kim, a beginning teacher, relates teachers' emotional–physical needs to riding on a roller coaster: "Each day I wake up and dread getting up. Usually, during first period, I have my first discipline crisis, and just as I am recovering from it and life is looking up, a second one occurs. This pattern continues throughout the day. Each day I go home feeling tired, frustrated, and helpless. I keep thinking that I must be doing something wrong. How can teachers go through this process every day and not go crazy?"

Kim, with the help of the teacher next door, a self-assigned mentor, was able to break the cycle and effectively teach her seventh-graders. Many beginning teachers never receive assistance that addresses the emotional–physical needs and choose to leave the profession as the only way to break the cycle. Mentors help beginning teachers meet their emotional–physical needs.

The second area of teacher needs is psychosocial, which focuses on the need for friendships, relationships, collegiality, and interactions. Teaching is often characterized as the second most private act. Beginning teachers need support to help eliminate feelings of isolation and alienation. Mentors and support groups help meet psychosocial needs.

Finally, personal–intellectual needs involve intellectual stimulation, new ideas/knowledge, aesthetic experiences, challenges, and innovative techniques to help avoid boredom (Gold & Roth, 1993). Todd, a second-year biology teacher, described this area: "I thought teaching would be more exciting. It seems that all I do is grade papers and complete paperwork. Seems like my biology teacher in high school had more fun while doing an excellent job motivating students to want to learn biology. Maybe he was just an extraordinary teacher, and I am not." Mentors help beginning teachers have fun and learn to be creative teachers.

Teaching Strategies. Unless they have a mentor, adviser, or peer that they feel comfortable with asking for help, many beginning teachers frequently resort to learning by trial-and-error. The trial-and-error process leads to the development of "coping" strategies that help beginning teachers survive in the classroom (Huling-Austin, 1990). Unfortunately, most of the coping strategies developed are negative and harmful to student learning. For example, a beginning teacher has difficulty maintaining control during cooperative learning, so as a coping strategy she eliminates all group work by students. If beginning teachers are not given the support and assistance during their first years of teaching, these negative coping strategies become ingrained and develop into permanent teaching patterns.

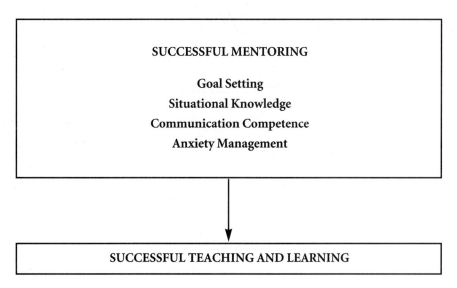

Figure 8.2   **A Model for Successful Mentoring**

A Model for Successful Mentoring

As a beginning teacher, understanding the mentoring process is essential to derive the benefits it affords. Deep understanding of the mentoring process requires the development of the four specific skills presented in the Model for Successful Mentoring (Figure 8.2). Success in the classroom involves achieving your potential in those skills:

1. *Goal setting.* Each teaching episode can be approached as a goal-setting activity. You will be more likely to succeed in your teaching if you set clear and challenging goals for yourself. Sometimes goal setting backfires as a result of setting unrealistic goals. Your mentor is available to help you set reasonable goals for your level of teaching experience and expertise.

2. *Situational knowledge* refers to the extent of your real-world knowledge concerning a variety of teaching and learning contexts. Your mentor can help increase your awareness of particular classroom contexts. By increasing your awareness, you greatly improve your chances of success by knowing what is expected and appropriate for you to do. Many beginning teachers lack the situational knowledge to make informed, strategic decisions in their classrooms.

3. *Communication competence.* After setting goals and developing situational knowledge, beginning teachers must carefully choose the most meaningful communication channel to send messages. Communication competence also involves a number of factors, such as style of delivery, type of channel, word choice, and paralanguage, that demonstrate your understanding of the context and people

Reality Bite

Ask and You Shall Receive!

As a new teacher in a new school, you are surrounded by new faces, and many questions tend to surface. No question is too redundant, inappropriate, or unimportant to ask your mentor. For example:

> *In case of emergencies, what shall I do?*
>
> *What are all these notebooks in my room used for? (curriculum guides, scope, and sequences, etc.)*
>
> *What do I do the first week of class?*
>
> *How do I know if I am following school policies?*
>
> *What should I do when I get ill during the day?*
>
> *To whom do I talk about my immediate supervisor? administrators?*
>
> *What do I do about problems with parents?*
>
> *What are my legal rights as a teacher?*
>
> *What type of discipline plan does the school have?*
>
> *How much of the curriculum do I teach?*
>
> *How much professional growth am I expected to complete each year?*
>
> *What do I do about strangers in the building?*
>
> *What do I do with all the paperwork?*
>
> *How many grades should I put in my grade book for every subject?*
>
> *How much detail do I need in my lesson plans?*

These are some of the most frequently asked questions by a beginning teacher during a one-year period. Never hesitate to ask about any thing you're unsure of. It's safer to ask than to assume.

Severo Alvarado, Assistant Principal

involved. Communication competence involves sending and receiving appropriate verbal and nonverbal communication, and understanding that when verbal and nonverbal messages contradict, receivers believe the nonverbal messages (e.g., saying that you feel great when your voice sounds tired and shallow).

4. *Anxiety management.* Any new situation often produces anxiety. The key is to balance your anxiety at the "threshold of nervousness." This balance serves to energize your teaching rather than diminish your effectiveness. Mentoring is designed to help reduce anxiety and increase self-confidence.

COACHING

Coaching 8.8 Planning a Mentoring Program

Purpose: To strengthen your action plans to include effective mentoring relationships.

Time required: Varies

Procedure: Based on identified needs of beginning teachers, mentoring principles, the Model for Successful Mentoring, and your own experiences, plan a mentoring program for your school that focuses on beginning teacher needs and the achievement of campus goals. After you have planned the program, answer these process questions: Overall, how well did you focus on the needs of beginning teachers? Did you consider all or most of the mentoring principles? How did your plan help reduce anxiety in beginning teachers? To what extent would your program change if the focus was on burned-out veteran teachers rather than beginning teachers? Describe the change.

REFLECTION

Reflecting 8.9 Beginning Teacher Needs and Mentor Support in Identifying Solutions

Critically analyze your needs and the mentoring process for one month. Keep a journal log of each need area you and your mentor identify, whether emotional–physical, psychosocial, or personal–intellectual. Evaluate your goal setting, situational knowledge, communication competence, and anxiety management. Ask your mentor for specific feedback and apply information to improve teaching strategies. Carefully chart your specific need, any progress made toward your goal, and any help you received from your mentor.

CONCLUSION

As a new member of the teaching profession, you have both responsibilities and challenges. As a professional educator, you must focus on "the essence" of school renewal as described by Glickman (1993) as the internal, critical process of studying one's own individual and school practices—looking at one's learning covenant (beliefs about learning), raising critical questions about current educational practices, and then assessing where the greatest priorities abide in preparing students to become productive citizens of a democracy.

Reality Bite

Where's the Boss?

Although surrounded by many helping hands, beginning teachers need to seek assistance and support from school administrators—they often have answers. Make sure you ask an administrator to visit your classroom once a week to informally evaluate your performance by giving you feedback to help you improve instruction. Administrators are there to help you improve your teaching instruction.

Severo Alvarado, Assistant Principal

In this chapter, we have evaluated three professional processes: critical inquiry or action research, interviewing, and mentoring. Each of these requires autonomy, leadership, cooperation, and resources in order to balance one's knowledge in the classroom with the collective knowledge of colleagues. Each requires understanding change and the change process.

Professional teachers must begin to view change as a process, not as an event. Hopefully, teacher isolation will become a past phenomenon. What lies ahead involves teachers who share leadership with administrators through collaborative decision making on all aspects of schooling. Fullan (1993) describes that as we move into the twenty-first century, professional teachers' capacities to deal with change, learn from it, and help students learn from it will be crucial for societal development and improvement. Professional teachers must become agents, rather than victims, of change.

Recommended Readings

Bey, T. M., & Holmes, C. T. (eds.). (1992). *Mentoring: Contemporary principles and issues.* Reston, VA: Association of Teacher Educators.

Darling-Hammond, L. (1990). Teachers and teaching: Signs of a changing profession. In R. Houston (ed.), *Handbook of research on teacher education.* New York: Macmillan.

Glasser, W. (1990). *The quality school: Managing students without coercion.* New York: Harper and Row.

Guyton, E., & McIntyre, D. J. (1990). Student teaching and school experiences. In R. Houston (ed.), *Handbook of research on teacher education.* New York: Macmillan.

Huling-Austin, L. (1990). Teacher induction programs and internships. In R. Houston (ed.), *Handbook of research on teacher education.* New York: Macmillan.

O'Hair, M. J. (1989). Teacher employment interview: A neglected reality. *Action in Teacher Education, 11* (1), 53–57.

Stewart, C. J., & Cash, W. B. (1988). *Interviewing: Principles and practices.* (5th ed.). Dubuque, IA: William C. Brown.

Tom, A. R., & Valli, L. (1990). Professional knowledge for teachers. In R. Houston (ed.), *Handbook of research on teacher education.* New York: Macmillan.

References

Bey, T. M., & Holmes, C. T. (eds.). (1992). *Mentoring: Contemporary principles and issues.* Reston, VA: Association of Teacher Educators.

Corrigan, D. C., & Haberman, M. (1990). The context of teacher education. In W. R. Houston (ed.), *Handbook of research on teacher education.* New York: Macmillan.

Glickman, C. D. (1985). *Supervision of instruction: A developmental approach.* Boston: Allyn and Bacon.

Glickman, C.D. (1993). *Renewing America's schools.* San Francisco: Jossey-Bass.

Gold, Y. (1990, February). Psychological support for beginning teachers: Beyond stress management. Paper presented at the meeting of the Association of Teacher Educator's 70th Annual Meeting, Las Vegas, Nevada.

Gold, Y., & Roth, R. A. (in press). Teachers managing stress and preventing burnout: The professional health (PH) solution. London: Falmer.

Goodlad, J. I. (1984). *A place called schools: Prospects for the future.* New York: McGraw-Hill.

Griffin, G. A., Barnes, S., Defino, M., Edwards, S., Hoffman, J. V., Hukill, H., & O'Neal, S. (1983). *Teacher induction: Research design for a descriptive study.* Austin: University of Texas R & D Center for Teacher Education.

Hamilton, C., & Parker, C. (1993). *Communicating for results: A guide for business and the professions* 4th ed. Belmont, CA: Wadsworth.

Huling-Austin, L. (1990). Teacher induction programs and internships. In R. Houston (ed.), *Handbook of research on teacher education.* New York: Macmillan.

Kronik, J. W. (1990). On men mentoring women: Then and now. *ADFL Bulletin,* 22–27.

Marcum, K. (1988). An unpublished dissertation. New Mexico State University, Las Cruces.

Mehrabian, A. (1981). *Silent messages.* Belmont, CA: Wadsworth.

O'Hair, H. D., & Friedrich, G. (1995). *Strategic communication,* 2nd ed. Boston: Houghton Mifflin.

O'Hair, M. J. (1989). Teacher employment interview: A neglected reality. *Action in Teacher Education, 11* (1), 53–57.

Skopec, E. (1986). *Situational interviews.* New York: Harper & Row.

Springbett, B. (1958). Factors affecting the final decision in the employment interview. *Canadian Journal of Psychology, 12,* 13–22.

The Political Role*

Chapter Objectives

After completing this chapter, you will be able to

- provide a definition of school politics.
- recognize political behavior in schools.
- identify and discuss political strategies that teachers use to influence students.
- identify and discuss the consequences of teacher political strategies of influence on students.
- identify and discuss political strategies that students use to influence teachers.
- identify and discuss the consequences of student political strategies of influence on teachers.
- identify and discuss other important political variables that exist in the school structure that influence the internal political situation of the classroom.

$\mathcal{W}$e continue our study of the Reflective Teaching Model by examining the political role. The teacher's task in the political role is to analyze the political structure of the school and classroom and to respond accordingly. Teaching is a political process. This chapter will focus on the following three core competencies of the political role:

Competency 1: Defining and Recognizing Political Behavior in Schools

Competency 2: Understanding Classroom Politics

Competency 3: Understanding Other Important Political Variables That Exist in the School Structure That Influence the Internal Political Situation of the Classroom

*Chapter 9 was written by Angela McNabb Spaulding, Ed.D.

The Case of Student Political Power in the Classroom

On Wednesday afternoon, Janet Brock, a first-year teacher, informed her eighth-grade class that she had scheduled the science unit test for the following Monday. She further explained that all unit homework was to be turned in by the following day, Thursday, so that it could be graded and returned in time for class discussion and test review on Friday. After receiving and discussing their graded homework on Friday, the students were to spend the weekend studying for the science unit test. Janet made it clear to the students that she was determined to stay on her teaching schedule in order to cover all curriculum objectives by the end of the year; thus, the students would have to be prepared to take the unit test on Monday.

The students, not accustomed to having homework on the weekend, were outraged. According to them, Mrs. Brock was the only eighth-grade teacher to ever assign homework over a weekend. To make matters worse, the upcoming weekend was the date of the final eighth-grade football game. In addition, the school was sponsoring several special activities after the game, such as a barbecue dinner and western dance. As soon as Janet's class was dismissed on Wednesday, students began to group together and discuss their displeasure with the weekend study assignment.

During science class on Thursday, Janet was shocked to see how much trouble her students were having with the assigned homework. The entire class period was spent answering questions about the homework that was to be turned in that day. She could not believe the number of times students requested that she repeat explanations. Each student seemed to want her to explain the concepts just one more time. Furthermore, it seemed that each time she began her explanation, a student changed the subject. Class time came to an end before Janet could answer and explain all of the troublesome areas identified by students. The students hinted that they needed more time to prepare for the test. Furthermore, several students suggested that they take the work home again that night in an effort to better understand the material. After all, as one student mentioned, it would sure look bad if the whole class failed the test.

Janet hesitantly agreed to give the students another day to work out their problem areas. She announced that the test would be moved from Monday to the following Wednesday in order to accommodate more student study time and classroom review. The last thing she wanted was to have the class fail the unit test. Whereas she was glad to see the students' newly found interest and concern about the test, she was disappointed that the extra study days would put her behind in her teaching schedule. The students, however, were very complimentary toward her and commended her on her decision *to move the test. They further expressed their appreciation for her sensitivity to their academic needs.*

If Janet had been watching the students gather in the hall immediately after her class was dismissed, she would have seen a group of students who, from their laughing and backslapping, seemed to be celebrating some sort of a victory.

■ *Competency 1* DEFINING AND RECOGNIZING POLITICAL BEHAVIOR IN SCHOOLS

ASSESSMENT

Assessing 9.1 Defining School Politics

Purpose: To identify your mind-set (i.e., biases, attitudes) and definition of politics.

Time required: 15 minutes

Procedure: You have undoubtedly read or heard the word "politics" many times during your life. What meaning(s) does it conjure up in your mind? List several descriptors that immediately come to your mind when you think of politics, then create and write out your own definition of the word. Compare your responses to the following political definitions found in the professional educational literature; then answer the questions at the end of the exercise.

- The use of formal and informal power by individuals and groups to achieve their goals in schools (Blase, 1991a).
- The strategies taken within the school to acquire, develop, or use power and other resources to achieve preferred outcomes in situations where there is uncertainty, dissension, or displeasure about choices (Pfeffer, 1981).
- The ways in which individuals attempt to influence others through both cooperative and conflictive strategies in order to attain desired goals (Spaulding, 1994b).

Questions: How did your political definition compare to the three listed above? How did it contrast? Were there any surprises? Do politics exist in schools? Should

politics exist in schools? Can political activity be avoided? Is political activity beneficial? harmful?

You should now have identified your mind-set toward politics. Open your
mind to the rest of this chapter, and don't allow any biases or preconceptions to
prevent you from gaining new insights that will help you operate in the political
world of schools.

EXPERIENCE

Defining Political Behavior

A political awareness is crucial to understanding everyday life in schools. Even so,
the political layers of the school are often overlooked. Political behavior is best witnessed through a framework of individual and group relationships and interactions—for example, interactions occurring between and among superintendents,
teachers, parents, administrators, and students.

In recent years significant research has been conducted in the area of school
politics (Ball, 1987; Blase, 1991a). New research in micropolitics has produced
information on how school members (principals, teachers, students, parents, etc.)
use political strategies to influence others and to protect themselves in order to
achieve their desired outcomes or goals.[1]

Micropolitical strategies are a predominant part of life in schools. Studies of
school micropolitical reveal that school members develop and construct micropolitical strategies that have consequences for their work. A micropolitical strategy is
any behavior or action that a school member might take in order to accomplish a
desired goal or outcome. Micropolitics, then, refers to the use of strategies to
accomplish desired goals. Blase offers a more formal definition of micropolitics:

> "The use of formal and informal strategies by individuals and groups to
> achieve their goals in organizations. In large part, micropolitical strategies
> result from perceived differences between individuals and groups, coupled
> with the motivation to use power to influence" (1991a, p. 11).

Perceived differences, as mentioned in Blase's definition, are the result of differing individual or group goals. According to Blase (1991a), goals are the desired
ends or aims pursued by an individual that may result from individual interests,
values, needs, ideologies, preferences, beliefs, motivations, or purposes. Furthermore, schools are composed of members each seeking their own individual
goals. In order to achieve these goals, school members develop political strategies.
Blase also explains that although such micropolitical strategies are consciously
motivated, any strategy, consciously or unconsciously motivated, may have political significance in a given situation. In addition, both cooperative and conflictive

---

[1] See Ball, 1987; Blase, 1991a, 1991b, 1991c; Spaulding, 1994a, 1994b.

Reality Bite

Gender in the Classroom

I was recently asked to observe a new teacher who was having disciplinary problems in a general education college class. While in her class, I noticed not only that all of the student challenges were coming from male students but also that most of the challenges were direct attacks on the teacher's credibility. In addition, I found that the female students in her class rarely spoke. When they did, their comments were usually disregarded by the majority of the male students in the room. After sitting in on a few more classes, I was able to appreciate the significant role that gender can play in the political environment of a classroom.

Marc Rich, Communications Instructor

strategies are part of the realm of micropolitics. Micropolitics, then, describes the ways in which individuals attempt to influence others through both cooperative and conflictive strategies in order to attain desired goals (Spaulding, 1994b).

Recognizing Political Behavior

In order to understand school behavior, you must recognize political behavior. Spaulding (1994b) makes a couple of recommendations that will help you learn to recognize political behavior.

First, beginning teachers should spend time reflecting on their own political behavior and the political behavior of others. For example, as a teacher, you should take time to observe how your political actions are being responded to by students, and to solicit feedback from students about the consequences of such actions on them. You should also reflect on the political behavior of students so you'll know when and how to appropriately respond to student political influence.

Second, beginning teachers should seek opportunities to develop political knowledge. You could develop political knowledge in any of the following ways: (1) as both a producer and consumer of political research, (2) through literature and research presentations, (3) through group discussions, (4) through role-playing, (5) through simulated or real experiences, (6) through sensitivity training, and (7) through mentoring projects.

Looking at schools politically allows educators to explore the reasons behind political strategies and how the strategies affect the classroom and school. When you have finished reading this chapter, you will probably have a new awareness and appreciation for the existence of political behavior that heretofore you may have only sensed. Chances are that you will start looking back over your own school life and recalling certain political experiences that you had. More important, you will begin to understand the impact that political behaviors have on you, your students, and the school as a whole.

COACHING

Coaching 9.2 Student Political Power in the Classroom

In the Case of Student Political Power in the Classroom, it was the power of the students that determined the outcome of the test schedule. The students were successful in their attempt to move the test date in order to prevent weekend homework. Often, as in the case of this scenario, the political influence of a single student is limited; as a result, a political coalition of students emerges. A coalition is a group of people who are committed to achieving a common goal. According to Bacharach and Lawler (1980), a coalition provides maximum mobilization of power and some protection against retaliation. Political coalitions often form shared strategies in order to achieve successful goal outcomes. Did you recognize, based on the information given in the scenario, the political behavior of the students and the consequences of that political behavior on the teacher? Do you think the teacher recognized the students' political goals and behavior?

REFLECTION

Reflecting 9.3 Your Political Power

After reading the Case of Student Political Power in the Classroom, did you begin to recall similar instances of political influence from your own days as a student (pre–high school, post–high school, or college)? Reflect back in time. How *did* you or how *do* you influence your teachers or professors? What individual political strategies do you or did you use? Describe a time when a political coalition was used to influence a classroom goal. Share and exchange your stories with your supervising teacher, your cooperating teacher, and/or other beginning teachers. How important is it for a teacher to be politically aware?

Reflecting 9.4 Scenario and Micropolitics

How does the Case of Student Political Power in the Classroom correspond to the definition of micropolitics given by Blase (see page 290)? Discuss the politics of the scenario with other beginning teachers.

In this first Competency, we defined politics and affirmed that political behavior does indeed exist in schools. In addition, we discussed the importance of recognizing political behavior. The remaining two Competencies will help you recognize the specific types of political strategies that occur in school and the impact these strategies have on school members.

Competency 2 UNDERSTANDING CLASSROOM POLITICS

ASSESSMENT

Assessing 9.5 Conducting Research on Student Use of Political Strategies in the Classroom

Purpose: To create an awareness of the political strategies that students use to influence teachers.

Time required: Varies

Procedure: Over a period of two weeks, observe students in various school classrooms (i.e., in different classrooms, in different content areas within the same classroom, and with different teachers). Using a form similar to that shown in Figure 9.1, research and record:

1. the type of political strategy (you name it) used by the student(s) to influence the teacher;
2. a thorough description of the strategy used;
3. the student's goal in using the strategy (i.e., according to the student; and,
4. the consequences of each strategy (i.e., how did the strategy affect the teacher, the students, or the classroom as a whole?).

Present your findings during a class or seminar. Did you discover any surprises?

EXPERIENCE

Teacher–Student Political Relationships

In order to understand the political relationship that exists between teachers and students, it is important that you understand the nature of the classroom and how the classroom promotes political activity. The following three characteristics are common to all classrooms:

1. Each person in the classroom can affect how the others are treated. Any teacher or student can gain the attention of his or her classmates and impinge on their lives and work; and every person is at the mercy of the other people in the classroom.

2. Teachers and students are exposed to continuous examination by every person in the classroom. Such examination eventually reveals each person's sensitivities and limitations to everyone else in the classroom, thus increasing the person's susceptibility to influence by other classmates.

3. Teachers and students know that their contact with the other people in their classroom will be lengthy and sustained. For the whole school year, the quality of teachers' and students' lives is controlled by a single group of people: those that make up their classroom. (Adapted from Pauly, E. (1991). *The classroom crucible: What really works, what doesn't and why,* p. 40. U.S.A.: Basic Books.)

In other words, teachers and students have many opportunities to influence those around them as a consequence of the lengthy and sustained classroom relationship. It is these characteristics that provide the foundation for political activity in classrooms. In analyzing that activity, researchers have found that teachers and students have political orientations toward each other and develop political strate-

Strategy	Description	Goal	Consequence
1.			
2.			
3.			

Figure 9.1   **Sample Political Strategy Observation Sheet**

gies that promote their own goals.[2] The following section explores the political strategies of both teachers and students, and how these strategies have consequences for the classroom.

Teacher Political Strategies and Student Consequences

One of the most profound changes reported by teachers concerning their professional growth is the development of a political orientation toward their students and other school members (Blase, 1991b). Teachers are political players. According to recent research in the field of micropolitics and related research in teacher–student interaction, teachers use two main types of political influence toward students: political strategies of support and political strategies of control.[3]

The goal of teacher political support strategies, according to teachers, is to promote and develop the academic achievement of students.[4] In order to accomplish that goal, teachers often use the following support strategies to influence students: praise, encouragement, humor, giving attention, reassurance, rewards, seeking student input, protecting student academic work time, and adapting classroom instruction and space to meet individual needs of students.

Teacher political strategies of support, such as those listed above, have positive consequences for students. Students stated that teacher support strategies positively influenced their perception of the teacher. In addition, they linked teachers' use of support strategies to increases in student academic effort, student relaxation in the classroom, and student academic achievement (Spaulding, 1994b).

The goal of teacher control strategies is to regulate and guide student behavior to conform to a set of classroom behavioral rules and procedures. Teachers often use the following control strategies to regulate and guide student behavior: threats, rules, intermediaries, peer pressure, labeling students, withholding privileges, classroom expulsion, sarcasm, bribes, and avoidance.[5]

Strategies of control such as those listed above were found to primarily have negative consequences for students. There was only one exception: In a year-long qualitative case study conducted by Spaulding (1994b), elementary students described teacher control strategies as being either appropriate or inappropriate. Appropriate use of teacher strategies of control, according to students, meant that the teacher used political strategies only when necessary and not as the primary influence. When teachers used political control strategies appropriately, positive student consequences resulted. For example, positive learning consequences occured when teachers used strategies of control to stop student misbehavior from preventing or distracting learning for either individual students or the classroom as a whole.

[2]See Blase, 1991c; Bloome & Willett, 1991; Spaulding, 1994b.
[3]See McCroskey & Richmond, 1983; Pauly, 1991; Richmond & McCroskey, 1992; Spaulding, 1994b; Woods, 1990.
[4]See Richmond & McCroskey, 1992; Pauly, 1991; Spaulding, 1994b; Woods, 1990.
[5]Ibid.

On the other hand, students stated that when teachers used political control strategies in an excessive or inappropriate way, negative consequences resulted. The negative consequences included negative student perceptions of the teacher; student inability to relax in the classroom; student apathy; student anger; decreases in student self-esteem, work effort, academic achievement, and concentration; and increases in student fatigue, fear, inappropriate classroom behaviors such as cheating, feelings of retaliation toward the teacher, and a desire for increased physical distance between the teacher and the student.

Teachers also use political control strategies for self-protection; for example, when they perceive themselves to be vulnerable to students or vulnerable to student criticism, discipline problems, and student coalitions (Blase, 1991b). In addition, many teachers feel that their survival in the profession depends on their ability to control the classroom. Control is necessary because much of student behavior falls outside the school's definition of appropriateness.

Many political strategies may be used unconsciously. Bloome and Willett (1991), in their research on classroom political interaction and from the analysis of a phonics lesson, found that ethnicity, language, class, and gender issues constitute a large part of the micropolitics of classroom interaction. The teacher observed in the Bloome and Willett study was unaware of her use of differing strategies toward students in regard to these issues. Often, political strategies are deeply embedded in the culture of schools and of society in general. You must become aware of these unconscious strategies and how they could potentially affect your classroom.

Remember two important points: (1) Teachers are political players who utilize political strategies to achieve their goals in the classroom, and (2) teacher political strategies have consequences for students, negative or positive, depending on the appropriateness or inappropriateness of the strategy to the classroom situation. As teachers make strenuous efforts to increase their influence in the classroom through the use of political strategies that purposefully alter student behavior, they must become aware of how these strategies affect their students. Teachers must learn how political strategies develop and contribute to teacher–student relationships that ultimately lead to classroom success or failure.

Student Political Strategies and Teacher Consequences

Many people think of political influence in the classroom as something that belongs only to the teacher. According to Pauly (1991) and others, this is an inaccurate description of how classrooms work.[6] Often, what works in the classroom is determined by what students do—for example, students decide how to respond to their teachers' instructions, how to treat their teachers and their classmates, how to respond to a distraction or a whispered comment, and how hard to work. Thus political influence (the ability to shape events toward one's own goals) is used by

---

[6]See Bloome & Willett, 1991; Jackson, 1968; Richmond & McCroskey, 1992; Spaulding, 1994b.

Reality Bite

Ethical/Moral Dimensions of Teaching

I never really understood how much influence I had on my students until the end of my first teaching year. It is powerful and very scary. I feel I have a moral and ethical obligation to carefully and appropriately influence the students in my classroom. Just look at all the horror stories you read in the paper about teachers who have somehow led their students astray.

Cindy Timms, First-Year Drama Teacher

both students and teachers to shape teaching and learning in the classroom. In this manner, teachers know that their teaching success depends on student cooperation, while students know that their classroom success (i.e., grades and acquisition of knowledge) depends on the teacher. Thus students and teachers have a reciprocal classroom relationship—what one does affects the other.

Students of all ages use political strategies to influence their teachers. It begins early in the elementary years when young students come to grips with the socialization of school life. According to Jackson (1968), during these formative elementary years, students develop political strategies that stay with them throughout their school years and beyond.

Students develop political strategies to respond to the behavior of their teachers. Students have also been found to use political strategies of resistance and cooperation depending on the behavior of the teacher.[7] According to Mehrabian (1969), students cooperate with teachers whose behavior they like, and they resist or move physically, mentally, and emotionally away from teachers whose behavior they dislike. Likewise, Spaulding (1994b) found that students use political strategies of resistance and cooperation toward the teacher depending on the behavior of the teacher.

For example, Spaulding found that students use political strategies of resistance in order to delay, distract, modify, or prevent teacher-initiated classroom behaviors that students dislike. To resist teacher-disliked behaviors, students use the strategies of repetition, interruption, topic changes, ignoring, partial compliance, protesting, and the use of intermediaries. Other related research reveals that students also resist disliked teacher behaviors through the use of temper tantrums, coalitions, open defiance, and physical withdrawal from the classroom.[8]

[7]See Kearney et al. 1988; Mehrabian, 1969; Spaulding, 1994b, 1996.
[8]See Bloome & Willett, 1991; Gorham, 1988; Hargreaves, 1979, 1991; Oakes, 1985, Woods. 1990.

Student political strategies of resistance have both positive and negative consequences for teachers. A limited amount of passive student resistance provides teachers with important feedback that they need to redirect their teaching to better meet student needs.[9] However, student political strategies that are excessive, aggressive, and continuous result in negative consequences, including teacher feelings of professional incompetence, personal discouragement, job dissatisfaction, and fatigue.

As previously mentioned, students also use political strategies of cooperation toward the teacher. Spaulding (1994b) found that the goal of student cooperation in the classroom was based on an exchange process. Reduced to a catchphrase, the cooperative exchange process between teachers and students could be expressed as

[9]See Pauly, 1991; Spaulding, 1994b.

"You scratch my back, and I'll scratch yours." Students stated that they cooperated with the teacher in exchange for rewards, which revolve around student preferences. In order to receive preferred rewards from the teacher, students utilized the following eight political strategies:

1. Self-concept confirmation—comments that help their teachers feel good about themselves.

2. Sensitivity—acting in a warm and empathic manner toward their teachers.

3. Nonverbal immediacy—nonverbal cues that communicate an interest and affection for their teachers.

4. Reward association—providing their teachers with special favors, information, and resources.

5. Assuming a teaching role—student instruction or direction aimed at fellow classmates for the purpose of getting fellow students to behave in teacher expected ways.

6. Listening—paying close attention and listening actively to what their teachers say.

7. Following directions—doing exactly what their teachers request, even in cases when teacher directions failed to make sense.

8. Achievement—student accomplishment of their teacher's academic expectations.

Student use of cooperative strategies has positive consequences for the teacher (Spaulding, 1994b). First, it positively influences teachers' personal sense of professional competence and self-esteem. Furthermore, teachers connect their positive professional self-perception to increased professional satisfaction and enjoyment of their teaching jobs. Likewise, teachers' positive self-esteem is linked to their abilities to cope with stress, to pursue self-improvement plans, and to meet personal needs, such as the need to be liked and perceived as important by students.

COACHING

Coaching 9.6 Observing Your Political Strategies

One way become aware of your own use of political strategies is to use video technology. With the help of your coach, videotape yourself teaching. Review the tape several times to discover the political strategies that you used during your teaching lesson.

◆ —— *Reality Bite*

Technology

It is really hard to watch yourself teach on a videotape. I watched the tape twice before I could actually see past the way I looked and sounded! But I am so glad that I made myself do it. I saw myself from a completely different vantage point. I guess you could say it was from my students' perspective. I learned a lot about myself and how my actions affect my students. I even watched the tape with my students and asked them for their feedback. It was a very enlightening discussion. I think we all understand each other better now. Every teacher would benefit from routine classroom videotaping. You aren't always aware of how you are influencing your students. Videotaping will help you see what you are doing and how your students are responding to your influence. It also provides an opportunity to initiate student–teacher conversation about classroom influence.

Aaron Curtis, First-Year Science Teacher

REFLECTION

Reflecting 9.7 You and Micropolitics

Reflect on and discuss your political strategies within the framework of the micropolitics definition (Blase, 1991a). For example, were your strategies utilized for support or control? Were they targeted toward individuals, groups, or both? Are there any strategies that you are now aware of that you previously were using unconsciously? Most important, did the political strategies you utilized have negative or positive consequences on your students?

Reflecting 9.8 Teacher Political Strategies

Review the political strategies of teacher control and support presented in the Experience section. Can you see how these strategies might influence students? Discuss your thoughts with your teaching peers and supervising teacher. Provide examples of how political strategies such as praise, sarcasm, bribes, and rewards could be used by teachers to influence students. What are the possible consequences of these teacher strategies of influence on students?

Reflecting 9.9 Student Political Strategies

Review the political strategies of student resistance and cooperation given in the Experience section. Can you see how these strategies might influence teachers? What other student strategies can you think of? Discuss your thoughts with your teaching peers and supervising teacher. Refer back to the eight student political strategies that were defined earlier. Discuss how each strategy could be used by students to influence teachers. What are the possible consequences of these student strategies of influence on teachers?

Analyzing classroom political activity will help educators to understand the reasons behind political activity and how political activity affects the classroom.

■ *Competency 3* UNDERSTANDING OTHER IMPORTANT VARIABLES THAT EXIST IN THE SCHOOL STRUCTURE THAT INFLUENCE THE INTERNAL POLITICAL SITUATION OF THE CLASSROOM

The political behavior discussed in Competencies 1 and 2 is tied very closely to the school itself, and the same is true for this final Competency. We do not wish to ignore the external political concerns that impinge on the classroom concerns such as how classroom curriculum is affected by national, state, and local initiatives or how federal and state laws impact classroom grouping practices. These external politics are indeed real and of concern to schools; however, it is beyond the realm and intent of this chapter to deal with all of the external variables that have political implications for the classroom. You should nevertheless be aware that countless external political influences exist and that all can affect your classroom.

Although numerous political variables exist in the school structure that influence the internal political situation of the classroom, the discussion in this Competency will focus on only three: parental influence, principal influence, and peer teacher influence.

Parental Influence on the Classroom

Parents play an important role in the life of the classroom. They influence the classroom both through the expectations that they have for their children and through their level of participation in the classroom (Spaulding, 1994c).

Whereas most parents are seen as friendly and supportive, some are viewed as potential problems for teachers. Teacher and parental academic expectations of students frequently conflict. Teachers perceive some parents to have unrealistic academic expectations for their children and to put tremendous pressure on students to live up to these parental expectations. Often, students are punished if they fail to

Reality Bite

Purpose of Education

Most people agree that the purpose of education is to prepare students to be active participants in an ever changing world, but few agree on just how to accomplish the purpose of education. As a result, education is filled with individuals and groups who seek to promote their own goals and methods for educating students. Most new teachers not only feel confused and overwhelmed by these differing goals and methods but are unprepared to respond to the political pressure they feel from these individuals and groups. One can almost hear a new teacher thinking aloud:

"I get really confused. Who's right? I have all these different people—parents, other teachers, and my principal—telling me how and what I should be teaching. Everyone has a different opinion. I don't know who is right or wrong. What am I supposed to do? I know my university professors wouldn't agree with most of what I am doing. I didn't count on having all these people telling me what to do and what not to do. I am going to burn out in my first year of teaching.

Caitlin Cole, First-Year Second-Grade Teacher

achieve parental expectations and are given special rewards if they do perform as expected. In discussing the political ramifications of one parent's expectations, a teacher stated,

> I have a student that missed three items on the practice spelling test last week. She cried and cried. I couldn't believe it. Her mother called to find out what was wrong. The mother told me about all the extra work they were making the child do at home because she had missed three on the practice spelling test. It was ridiculous. I told the mother that I thought missing three words on the practice test was very good. After all, it is the first test and it doesn't even count as far as grades go! I told the mother that I thought she should ease up on her daughter. She didn't take it very well. She will probably go talk to the principal. But, I mean it is affecting the whole class now. Every time she makes a mistake or misses something she starts crying. It takes forever to get her settled down. (Spaulding, 1994c)

The above comment reveals that the parent and the teacher hold differing expectations about the academic achievement of this student. Those differences have consequences for the teacher, the student, and the class as a whole.

Parents exert influence on the teacher for purposes of altering classroom situations that fail to meet their expectations. This type of parental influence is stressful for teachers; so, when parents exert influence on the teacher to make classroom changes, teachers are faced with a dilemma: Do they confront the parent and stand their ground? Do they try to reach a compromise with the parent? Do they give in to the parent's demands? Of course, how the teacher responds will depend on a number of situational factors, but regardless of the action taken by the teacher, it will have political ramifications for the classroom. For example, one teacher modified her preferred method of teaching reading to please a parent who felt that her daughter was bored and unmotivated with the teacher's current method of reading instruction. The consequences of this action for the teacher and the classroom were negative. The teacher experienced both professional and personal dissatisfaction with her action and a growing bitterness toward both the parent who influenced the decision and her new method of teaching reading. As a result, both her teaching instruction and her students' learning were negatively affected. You need to be aware of the potential consequences of your responses to the political influence of parents.

Parents also influence the classroom through their participation or lack of participation in classroom activities (Spaulding, 1994c). Parents who do not participate and support their children in classroom activities (e.g., homework assignments, providing classroom supplies) are generally perceived negatively by teachers. Teachers view unsupportive parents as failing to fulfill their responsibilities as parents. When parents fail to fulfill their responsibilities, teachers take on a "parental role" for the student. While participating within this classroom parental role, teachers provide needy students with mental, emotional, and physical resource support in the classroom. This support often results in teacher costs in terms of their own time and physical, mental, emotional, and financial resources.

Principal Influence on the Classroom

The principal is also a strong influence on the classroom for both students and teacher. For students, the principal's main influence is on student behavior: Thoughts of "getting in trouble" with the principal help to influence student behavior in the classroom. In a recent study (Spaulding, 1994c), students stated that they were influenced through their fear of the principal's authority and power, especially the principal's authority to inflict punishment.

The principal is often recognized by teachers for having the power to evaluate and judge teaching effectiveness. As a result, teachers spend time participating in political behaviors that seek to please the principal and that meet his or her expectations for teaching effectiveness. Pleasing the principal is especially important to beginning teachers who want to make a good teaching impression (Spaulding, 1994c). As a result, they spend a great deal of time visiting with and observing other school members in an attempt to determine exactly what the principal's expectations are and then emulating the perceived expected behaviors.

The principal's decision-making power also influences the classroom; for example, in some schools the principal decides what students will be assigned to what teachers. The type of students assigned to a classroom influence the type and amount of curriculum to be used. The principal also makes decisions that influence

◆ —— *Reality Bite*

Cultural Diversity

Dealing with parental influence in the classroom can be difficult and challenging for the first-year teacher. This is an area that baffles even the most experienced teachers. Predicting parental attitudes and actions is impractical and unwise, especially considering the diversity of the school population. You should strive to understand parents and students from cultural identities and perspectives. One way to accomplish this is to have students write papers at the beginning of the year that describe their families and emphasize their cultural heritage and traditions. This information can provide useful insights into your students' home life and can help you to respond appropriately to both students and their families.

Bob Hand and Janice Muller, Experienced Teachers

I thought that I was the only teacher who was so easily influenced by parents. I now realize how easily I was controlled by influential parents. I could have avoided some of the parental conflicts had I understood the cultural traditions and beliefs of my students and their families, especially in regard to religion.

Cindy Timms, First-Year Drama Teacher

classroom time schedules. For example, elementary principals often schedule certain "pull-out" activities where students leave their teacher and classroom in order to get special instruction in another academic area such as library, computers, art, or music. As a result, teachers must find a classroom schedule that works around all of the pull-out activities. Pull-outs affect not only their academic schedule but also the types and amount of academic content that can be presented to students.

In many schools, the principal also has the power to decide the amount and type of resources (i.e., within the school district's budgetary constraints) that will be available for classroom use. The abundance or lack of resources influences the classroom (Spaulding, 1994c); for example, extra classroom time is often used up when students are required to share classroom resources. Shortage of classroom resources also means that teachers have to modify lessons. Spaulding found that teachers often skipped math pages and sections of the math curriculum because students did not have access to adequate classroom resources such as calculators or computers.

Furthermore, a shortage of classroom resources often results in teachers trying to improvise to find comparable resources and to juggle resources among students.

The shortage of certain resources requires teachers to modify, delete, or lengthen certain instructional lessons and, as a result, often changes teachers' preferred methods of instruction.

The principal further influences what goes on in the classroom by allowing or preventing teachers the freedom to make professional choices (i.e., curriculum choices) about their classrooms (Spaulding, 1994c). When given the freedom to make professional choices, teachers are able to make decisions that best meet the needs of their individual students. The freedom to make decisions about their classrooms results in teacher job satisfaction and enhanced teacher self-efficacy; when not permitted that freedom, the result is just the opposite—job dissatisfaction and decreased self-efficacy.

Peer Teacher Influence on the Classroom

The term "peer teacher" is used to refer to other teachers employed within a school or school district. Spaulding (1994c) found that peer teachers influence the internal political situation of the classroom. For example, teachers are primarily very protective of their students, and unnecessary, negative comments about students made by peer teachers are unwelcome and often result in protective reactions by the teachers of these students. Negative comments are frequently met with a determination by the student's teacher to discredit the peer teacher's remark. As one teacher explained, "I don't like it when teachers tell me negative things about my students. If anything, it makes me want to prove them wrong."

Peer teachers' classroom activities and the appearance of their classrooms also influence teachers, especially beginning teachers. In Spaulding's study of elementary school classrooms, teachers often compared what they were doing in their own classrooms to what peer teachers were doing in theirs. Teachers said that in this way they ensured that their accomplishments in their own classrooms were comparable to those of peer teachers. If the teacher found, as a result of comparison with peer teachers, that he or she was lacking in a specific area, the teacher worked toward improving that area. Teachers knew exactly what peer teachers were doing in their classrooms. One teacher made the following comparison between her classroom and her peer teachers' classrooms:

> I have noticed that the other teachers have more things in their rooms, like learning centers, wall decorations, and even artwork hanging from the ceiling. Their rooms are just wall-to-wall with stuff. I need to do this in my room. My room looks so bare compared to theirs. I am going to start working on it right away. (Spaulding, 1994c)

Thus, as revealed in the above comment, the actions of peer teachers heavily influence the actions that teachers take in their own classrooms. Peer teachers transmit influence through their comments, advice, and actions, through their classroom activities, and through their classroom appearance.

Reality Bite

Politically Correct Principal

My ideal politically correct principal would handle school matters with consistency, treat all staff and students alike, be visible throughout the school, follow through with new agendas, always have an open door, and respect and welcome teachers' ideas with an open mind. These characteristics may be difficult to find or entirely lacking in most principals, but some of the reasons for that lack may not be their fault.

Principals wear a different hat than the one they wore as teachers. As they leave the classroom, they enter a new environment and oftentimes quickly forget the realities of classroom teaching. They must now enforce many of the same policies that, as teachers, they may have felt robbed them of classroom autonomy. Principals must administer these everyday policies as established by their school board and by other state statutes, policies that most teachers feel could be fewer in number. In a society of lawsuits and entitlement programs, the encumbering laws are necessary to protect all school personnel.

Robert Nimtz, High School History Teacher

You should now have a deeper awareness of how parents, principals, and peer teachers influence what happens in the classroom. You should also begin to recognize numerous other influences on the classroom, both within the school and external to the school. With your new political awareness, name some of these influences and state how they potentially influence the internal situation of the classroom.

REFLECTION

Reflecting 9.10 The Influence of Parents, Principals, and Peer Teachers on the Classroom

Interview several veteran teachers, and ask them the following questions:

1. Describe how parents, principal, and peer teachers influence your classroom. Are there other in-school variables that influence your classroom (e.g., school activities)?

2. What external variables (i.e., outside the school) influence your classroom (e.g., business community, legislature, special interest groups)?

Share the results of your interviews with other beginning teachers in a seminar or class setting. What new political insights did you discover? Do the teachers you interviewed seem politically aware? How will the information you have gathered help you as a classroom teacher?

Reflection 9.11 Recognizing Political Behavior

Political behaviors affect all aspects of school life. Reflect and relate what you now know about political behavior to the other roles of the Reflective Teaching Model: organizer, communicator, innovator, professional, manager, counselor, legal, ethicist, and motivator.

Conclusion

In the political role, the teacher's task is to analyze the political structure of the school and classroom and to respond accordingly. Teaching is a political process. This chapter has focused on defining and recognizing political behavior in schools, understanding classroom politics, and understanding other important political variables that exist in the school structure that influence the internal political situation of the classroom. Our purpose has been to create in you an awareness of the often hidden political layers of the classroom and the school. We hope that this awareness will enable you to see how political activity develops and contributes to school member relationships that ultimately lead to classroom success or failure.

The political role is one that you must be prepared to participate in. From the political role you will see that political behavior is a predominant part of life in schools. Whereas it is impossible to recommend exactly how you, as a teacher, should behave in order to be politically effective, we can make some general suggestions.

First and foremost, as a beginning teacher you should make every effort to develop a deep awareness of your self, especially your political values and purposes, as well as the strategies you use to influence others (Blase, 1991a). Examine and determine how your political behavior influences others; for example, do your political classroom strategies result in positive or negative consequences for your students? Take special effort to determine how you may unconsciously and inadvertently influence others through, for instance, inattention, nonaction, or habitual or routine behavior.

Second, in addition to developing an awareness of your political self, you, as a beginning teacher, will benefit from efforts to understand other school members from a political point of view. You should seek school member relationships that are cooperative and that improve the school's effectiveness in serving students.

In summary, political awareness and knowledge will enable you to construct effective ways to respond to the influence of others, to anticipate the consequences of political interactions, and to analyze the political structure of schools. In addition, the political role will help you become more effective in the classroom and more confident of your ability to successfully and positively influence students with whom you interact every day.

Recommended Readings

Blase, J. (ed.). (1991a). *The politics of life in schools: Power, conflict, and cooperation.* Newbury Park, CA: Sage.

Blase, J., & Kirby, P. (1992). *Bringing out the best in teachers: What effective principals do.* Newbury Park, CA: Sage.

Cusick, P. (1992). *The educational system: Its nature and logic.* New York: McGraw-Hill.

Gorham, J. (1988). The relationship between verbal teacher immediacy behaviors and student learning. *Communication Education, 37,* 40–53.

Hargreaves, A. (1979). Strategies, decisions and control: Interaction in a middle school classroom. In J. Eggleston (ed.), *Teacher decision making in the classroom.* London: Routledge & Kegan Paul.

Jackson, P. (1968). *Life in classrooms.* New York: Holt, Rinehart and Winston.

Lortie, D. (1985). *Schoolteacher.* Chicago: University of Chicago Press.

McCroskey, J. C., & Richmond, V. P. (1983). Power in the classroom I: Teacher and student perceptions. *Communication Education, 32,* 176–184.

McNeil, L. M. (1986). *Contradictions of control: School structure and school knowledge.* New York: Routledge & Kegan Paul.

Oakes, J. (1985). *Keeping track: How schools structure inequality.* New Haven: Yale University Press.

Plax, T. G., Kearney, P., McCroskey, J. C., & Richmond, V. P. (1985). Power in the classroom VI: Verbal control strategies, nonverbal immediacy and affective learning. *Communication Education, 35,* 43–55.

Pollard, A. (1985). *The social world of the primary school.* London: Holt, Rinehart & Winston.

Richmond, V. P., Gorham, J. S., & McCroskey, J. C. (1987). The relationship between selected immediacy behaviors and cognitive learning. In M. McLaughlin (ed.), *Communication Yearbook, 10,* 574–590.

Woods, Peter. (1990). *Teacher skills and strategies.* Bristol, PA: Falmer.

References

Bacharach, S. B., & Lawler, E. J. (1980). *Power and politics in organizations: The social psychology of conflict, coalitions, and bargaining.* San Francisco: Jossey-Bass.

Ball, S. (1987). *The micro-politics of the school.* New York, N.Y.: Routledge.

Blase, J. (ed.). (1991a). *The politics of life in schools: Power, conflict, and cooperation.* Newbury Park, CA: Sage.

Blase, J. (1991b). Everyday political perspectives of teachers toward students: The dynamics of diplomacy. In J. Blase (ed.), *The politics of life in schools: Power, conflict, and cooperation.* Newbury, CA: Sage.

Blase, J. (1991c). The micropolitical orientation of teachers toward closed school principals. *Education and Urban Society, 23* (4), 356–378.

Bloome, D., & Willett, J. (1991). Toward a micropolitics of classroom interaction. In J. Blase (ed.), *The politics of life in schools: Power, conflict, and cooperation.* Newbury Park, CA: Sage.

Gorham, J. (1988). The relationship between verbal teacher immediacy behaviors and student learning. *Communication Education, 37,* 40–53.

Hargreaves, A. (1979). Strategies, decisions and control: Interaction in a middle school classroom. In J. Eggleston (ed.), *Teacher decision making in the classroom.* London: Routledge & Kegan Paul.

Hargreaves, A. (1991). The micropolitics of teacher collaboration. In J. Blase (ed.), *The politics of life in schools: Power, conflict, and cooperation.* Newbury Park, CA: Sage.

Jackson, P. (1968). *Life in classrooms.* New York: Holt, Rinehart and Winston.

Kearney, P., Plax, T. G., Smith, V. R., & Sorensen, G. (1988). Effects of teacher immediacy and strategy type on college student resistance to on-task demands. *Communication Education, 37,* 54–67.

McCroskey, J. C., & Richmond, V. P. (1983). Power in the classroom I: Teacher and student perceptions. *Communication Education, 32,* 176–184.

Mehrabian, A. (1969). Significance of posture and position in the communication of attitude and status relationships. *Psychological Bulletin, 71,* 359–372.

Oakes, J. (1985). *Keeping track: How schools structure inequality.* New Haven: Yale University Press.

Pauly, E. (1991). *The classroom crucible: What really works, what doesn't, and why.* U.S.A.: Basic Books.

Pfeffer, J. (1981). *Power in organizations.* Marshfield, MA: Pitman Publications.

Richmond, V. P., & McCroskey, J. C. (1992). *Power in the classroom: Communication, control, and concern.* NJ: Erlbaum.

Spaulding, A. M. (1994a, April). *The politics of the principal: Influencing teachers on school based decision making.* Paper presented at the annual conference of the American Educational Research Association, New Orleans.

Spaulding, A. M. (1994b, October). *The micropolitics of the elementary classroom.* Unpublished doctoral dissertation, Texas Tech University.

Spaulding, A. M. (1994c). *The politics of the school: School member relationships and their influence on the classroom.* Unpublished dissertation, Texas Tech University.

Spaulding, A. M. (1996). The politics of primaries. In A. Pollard, A. Flier, D. Thiessen (eds.), *Children and the curriculum: The perspectives of primary and elementary school pupils.* London: Falmer Press.

Woods, Peter. (1990). *Teacher skills and strategies.* Bristol, PA: Falmer.

Chapter 10

The Legal Role*

Chapter Objectives

After completing this chapter, you will be able to

- recognize some of the legal issues and concerns that confront classroom teachers on a daily basis.

- recognize the personal and professional importance of staying legally informed and up-to-date.

- recognize the value of exercising good judgment and common sense.

- understand the importance of the legal role as an integral component of teachers' professional practice.

- reflect on teaching practices that help minimize risk and reduce the likelihood of becoming embroiled in litigation.

*P*lease remember this scenario as you read and react to the Competencies in this chapter. As you will begin to see, the law and school-related legal issues impact education and teachers in many ways. This chapter will help expose you to the figurative "tip of the school law iceberg" that—unlike the unfortunate helmsman of the Titanic—you will want to circumnavigate as you embark on your career as a teacher.

In many ways, it is unfortunate that today's teachers must constantly be aware of the potential legal ramifications of much of what they do. Some experienced teachers complain negatively that the law (or, perhaps more accurately, the effect of too many lawyers) has taken some of the enjoyment and spirit out of teaching. In addition to what might be construed as contemporary society's perceived inclination to file a lawsuit for every little injustice or injury, it often seems that there is an

*Chapter 10 was written by Fredrick Hartmeister, J.D., Ed.D., and Joseph Claudet, Ph.D.

An Ounce of Prevention or a Pound of Trouble?
The Case of the Legally Uninformed Teacher

In general, Tracy Adams couldn't be much happier after her first two months on the job. As a beginning teacher at Lincoln Middle School, Tracy is teaching three sections of seventh-grade English and two sections of eighth-grade creative writing. She and a veteran teacher in her department named Jerry Davis are also team teaching a literature class for gifted ninth-graders that the school district just implemented this year. Although Tracy is staying very busy and finding that there never seems to be enough time to get everything done that she wants to do, she is thoroughly enjoying her career choice. She approaches each school day with excitement and enthusiasm, and even the occasional student discipline problem doesn't seem to be anything that she can't handle. All in all, being a beginning middle school teacher in a relatively quiet suburban community is proving to be better than she had hoped; however, that is not to say that Tracy's life as a professional educator is completely trouble-free. . . .

Today started out like most other school days in the past several months. Tracy awoke before her alarm sounded. After a shower, breakfast, and quick look at the morning newspaper, she headed to school. Her briefcase was filled with student papers and workbook assignments that she had graded the night before. In addition, she had several novels that she had recently skimmed in anticipation of making recommendations to the principal for instructional purchases for the spring semester. As she usually did, Tracy arrived at school nearly an hour earlier than most of the other teachers and staff. She went to her classroom and began getting ready for her first period class—the ninth-grade "gifted lit" class.

When Tracy and her "team teacher" Jerry Davis met yesterday after school to discuss and plan today's class activities, Tracy had not been too concerned at that time about a suggestion that Jerry had made regarding today's class. The ninth-grade students in the "gifted lit" class were in the midst of reading Born to Cry, *a fictionalized account of life in a poor inner-city high school faced with an all-too-common array of contemporary social problems—racial and cultural disunity, gang warfare, spontaneous violence, teen pregnancy, and indiscriminate drug usage. Jerry had suggested that they should have the students role-play several of the situations presented in the book so that the students could gain insight into some of the social and emotional dilemmas facing the book's leading characters. At the time Jerry made his suggestion, Tracy had favored the idea; now, however, she was beginning to get cold feet.

On one hand, Tracy knew that most of the students were enthralled with the book. Several had made favorable comments about how "real" the book seemed, and they had almost insisted on being given reading assignments that would move the class through the story at a faster pace. On the other hand, this morning Tracy was going to be teaching the class solo since Jerry had been called for jury duty and his substitute would not be coming in until after the first-period classes were finished. Despite feeling that she knew all of the ninth-grade students in this class reasonably well, she was still a little apprehensive about several of the more rambunctious and less reserved "characters" in the class. There were at least three or four students who seemed to take great pleasure in doing and saying things in class seemingly only for shock value rather than to add anything substantive to class discussions. Just as important, Tracy was feeling some uneasiness about the particular reading assignment for today's class. Although by comparison the portion of the book that the students had been asked to read wasn't any more provocative than other sections of the book, the author had included dialogue that used several four-letter words as well as a brief but graphic reference to a sexual act. Now that it was almost time for class, Tracy's confidence was beginning to waver that the students would necessarily handle a role-playing exercise in an educationally appropriate manner. Besides, since her teammate Jerry was going to be absent from today's class, she wasn't totally convinced that she could control the situation if things began to get out of hand. She hadn't yet mastered Jerry's knack for turning awkward situations into "teachable moments."

As she worked in her classroom to prepare for the day ahead, Tracy's first-period class wasn't all that was on her mind. For example, Tracy had decided the previous evening that she wanted to take both sections of her eighth-grade creative writing classes to a traveling exhibit of modern art that was being shown at a museum in a neighboring community. She had tentatively set the date for the field trip to take place two weeks from today; however, she had not yet announced this event to her students nor confirmed the trip with her principal. Tracy hoped that a visual dose of modern art might inspire greater creativity among several of her more sedate and expressively conservative students. Since she had never planned a field trip, she was uncertain about what she needed to do to complete all of the necessary arrangements and comply with her school district's requirements.

Last, but not least, when Tracy was grading papers the evening before, she came across a reference on one of her seventh-grader's English papers that had left her feeling troubled. Written in the margin near the bottom of the last page of a female seventh-grader's workbook assignment was the statement, "Dillon's dad really beat *the crap out of him this time!" Since Tracy has a student named Dillon Booth in one of her seventh-grade classes (although not in the particular section whose workbooks she had been grading the night before), she was concerned about whether she should investigate or "follow up" the comment. After all, as a teacher who takes a sincere interest in the well-being of all her students, Tracy certainly didn't want to miss a cry for help if one of her students was being abused by a parent—or by anyone else for that matter. However, she didn't have a clue where to begin. Dillon had not complained to her of anything being wrong at home, and from what Tracy had observed in class, he did not appear to have been injured or acting any differently than he normally did. Should she talk to the student whose workbook she had graded? Should she confront Dillon and ask him if everything was OK? Should she report the comment to the middle school principal or to the school nurse? She was certain that she needed to do something, but she just wasn't sure as to the best course of action.*

ever expanding body of federal, state, and local laws, rules, regulations, and guidelines that restrict and constrain the educational process— and teachers in particular.

Regardless of whether this portrayal of contemporary education is justifiably subject to criticism, the fact remains that teachers need to be aware of the legal implications of their professional decisions and personal conduct (Pell, 1994). However, at the national level, only a small number of teacher training programs include coursework designed to give preservice teachers a general understanding of educational law; by far the majority of educational law courses are taught only at the graduate level and are usually reserved for prospective school administrators, not teachers (Sparkman & Desrosiers, 1986). Thus it is likely that most preservice teachers have had, at best, only a limited exposure to educational law concepts and implications.

Although this chapter is too small an arena to explore more than a handful of legal issues, it at least provides a starting point from which you may begin to appreciate some of the legal realities that you will encounter in the real world. The intent here is not to frighten you, since "teaching scared" is seldom the best way to achieve sound educational objectives, but to instill a sense of familiarity with and confidence about certain aspects of educational law. Although we recognize that most teachers confront a far greater number of legal considerations on a regular basis, this chapter will examine three fundamental and relatively common areas:

Competency 1: Understanding Academic Freedom

Competency 2: Recognizing Tort and Liability Issues

Competency 3: Complying with Statutory Requirements—
Reporting Suspected Child Abuse or Neglect

Competency 1 UNDERSTANDING ACADEMIC FREEDOM

ASSESSMENT

In this section, you are asked to explore your understanding of the dynamics between a teacher's freedom of expression in the classroom and the various other factions or interest groups involved in the educational setting.

Assessing 10.1 How Much Academic Freedom Will You Have as a Classroom Teacher?

Purpose: To help identify the competing interests that influence the extent of a classroom teacher's academic freedom.

Time required: 5 minutes

Procedure: *Part 1*—Teachers claim that *their* academic freedom gives them the right to speak freely in their classrooms about the subjects that they teach. In effect, teachers assert an interest based on their professional judgment to control class discussion and to choose instructional methodologies. Identify the three other primary interest groups that are commonly thought to compete for classroom control in an academic setting. Also describe the basis upon which each group asserts its power.

Part 2—When asked to compare the scope of academic freedom shared by college and university professors with that of classroom teachers at the elementary and secondary levels, courts have traditionally held that the extent of academic freedom is much greater for those involved in higher education. List three significant reasons why you think this might be so.

EXPERIENCE

During your years as a college student, you have probably come across the concept that teachers and professors have a great deal of control over what is said and done in the classroom. Perhaps this notion arose when one of your college professors claimed a right to lecture on the advantages (or disadvantages) of a particular form of governance (e.g., the merits of a democracy versus other nondemocratic governing structures such as socialism or communism). Maybe you encountered the concept much earlier in your life—for example, when a group of parents in your junior high or high school approached the local school board to complain about why or how a particular subject was being taught (e.g., a newly implemented health or sex education class; the inculcation of values in the school's overall curriculum that certain religious groups within the community found to be objectionable). Regardless of whether you have ever given much thought to the concept, the fact that academic freedom describes an often sensitive focal point of competing interests makes it imperative that you understand what is at stake as well as the extent to which you will enjoy such freedom as a classroom teacher.

Academic freedom gives teachers the right to speak freely in their classrooms about the subjects that they teach (Thomas, Sperry, & Wasden, 1991). However, as suggested in the Assessment section for this Competency, this right is not absolute and does not necessarily entitle a teacher to say *anything* she or he wants, use *any* books or materials, or employ *any* teaching method. Rather, the individual teacher's freedom is balanced against that of at least three other interest groups: (1) the state's interest in providing public education as played out at the local level by a school board's involvement in adopting curriculum and assigning teaching positions that reflect the collective public will; (2) the interest of students in having wide-ranging access to knowledge and ideas; and (3) the interest of parents wishing to have a say in their children's education (Kemerer & Walsh, 1994).

As a rule, local school boards establish school district curriculum. Once the curriculum is set and the school board imposes general regulatory guidelines to which teachers are expected to adhere, teachers are usually vested with substantial discretion to determine the best methods, materials, and, in some cases, the textbooks to use in transmitting the assigned subject matter to students. Within reasonable limits, a teacher usually has the right to discuss controversial topics, ideas, and philosophies with students so long as the discussion is related to the subject matter that the teacher has been assigned to teach (Thomas, Sperry, & Wasden, 1991).

For the most part, elementary and secondary school teachers claiming a right to academic freedom have enjoyed the greatest success (and legal protection within the courts) when they contend that they are "child advocates"—in other words, they depict *their* academic freedom as being a derivative of *their students'* right to know and learn. The critical question then becomes one of whether the information or message that each teacher is trying to convey is something that the particular students in this particular school should be exposed to at this particular time (Hartmeister, 1995).

Although this nation's courts have clearly recognized that college and university professors have a constitutionally protected right to academic freedom and free expression in the classroom, legislative and judicial systems have not seen fit to extend this same broad protection to teachers employed below the college level. This is due in large part to differing missions: higher education scholars are expected to *discover* truth and knowledge whereas public school teachers are charged with *transmitting* knowledge. In addition, the age and maturity of the respective students creates a distinction that, when coupled with compulsory attendance laws, makes it imperative that younger students in a captive setting not be subjected to indoctrination or proselytizing (Thomas, Sperry, & Wasden, 1991).

It is interesting to note that academic freedom is not explicitly mentioned in the United States Constitution. Instead, the concept comes from combining the freedom of speech provision in the First Amendment with a lengthy history of court cases that have considered the importance of free expression in the classroom. Of these cases, courts faced with different facts and circumstances have ruled both in favor of and (with greater frequency) against teachers claiming a right to academic freedom.

Kingsville Independent School District v. Cooper (1980) is an example of a case in which a teacher prevailed in her claim of academic freedom. In *Kingsville,* an American history teacher used a role-playing simulation exercise to introduce her students to the concept of life during the Reconstruction era following the Civil War. After the classroom exercise resulted in controversy within the community, the teacher was told by her principal and other school district administrators not to discuss African-Americans and, for that matter, to avoid discussing anything in class that might serve to generate further controversy in this particular Texas community. However, since the teacher was not told to discontinue the role-playing exercise, she completed the activity with her class. Although she was subsequently recommended for reemployment at the end of the school year by her principal and the superintendent, the school board voted not to issue a contract. The federal appellate court that ultimately decided the case held that the teacher's classroom activities and discussions involved constitutionally protected activity. The court declared that since the school board could not demonstrate that the controversy or disruption that resulted from the classroom activity impaired the teacher's instructional effectiveness, then the teacher was entitled to be reemployed. The court ordered the school district to reinstate the teacher in addition to awarding her back pay and her attorney's fees.

In contrast, a recent Louisiana case involving a high school history teacher who was transferred to a middle school position demonstrates a teacher's unsuccessful claim of academic freedom. In *Moody v. Jefferson Parish School Board* (1993), the same court that decided the *Kingsville* case considered a teacher who divided her history class into groups and assigned each group a project dealing with a different aspect of the First Amendment. One group of students decided to focus on freedom of the press by publishing a newspaper entitled *Your Side.* Although intended as a parody, the newspaper included articles that advocated cheating, mentioned erotic sexual dreams, and recommended that students who are bored should drop out of school. The school board objected to the teacher's methods and issued a written letter of reprimand in addition to transferring her to another building. After the teacher challenged her reprimand and transfer on the basis of an alleged First Amendment right to academic freedom (coincidentally the same constitutional provision that her students had been studying), both a federal trial court and a federal appellate court found that the teacher had failed to rebut the school district's evidence that it had three legitimate reasons to transfer the teacher: inadequate supervision of her students, violations of the school district's financial policies, and willful neglect of her duties. In effect, the courts avoided having to deal with the academic freedom issue raised by the teacher by focusing on other circumstances raised by the school district in its defense of its actions. One factor that worked against the teacher in *Moody* was the teacher's failure to seek and secure the school administration's approval for the class project when she recognized from the outset that the newspaper content might create discontent and other problems for the administration.

Although a general trend toward a more expansive recognition of rights for students and teachers began to take shape in the 1960s, several recent United States Supreme Court decisions appear to have slowed the trend. *Hazelwood School District v. Kuhlmeier* (1988) is probably the most significant example of the Court's contemporary view of the relationship between the school officials in charge of operating a school and the school's students and teachers. In *Hazelwood*, the Court held that a high school principal acted properly within his authority when he unilaterally deleted several potentially controversial articles that had been written and submitted by students for publication in the school newspaper. In holding that the principal's actions did not violate students' First Amendment rights to free speech, the Court found that school authorities were able to establish a connection between their actions and the school's "legitimate pedagogical concerns." Since this case was decided, several lower courts have applied the *Hazelwood* standard in a broader range of circumstances than just those dealing with students and student newspapers. Consequently, if school authorities can satisfy the requirement of demonstrating a "legitimate pedagogical concern," they now appear to enjoy greater control over certain instructional activities that might formerly have fallen under the umbrella of academic freedom (McCarthy, 1993). However, due to the recency of the *Hazelwood* decision and the fact that not too many academic freedom cases have been decided since that time, it is still too early to know whether the concept of academic freedom at the elementary and secondary school levels is truly in decline.

COACHING

In the exercises that follow, you will analyze and broaden your understanding of academic freedom and how it will affect your role as a professional educator.

Coaching 10.2 Identifying the Extent of Academic Freedom in Your School

Conduct informal interviews with at least three experienced teachers in your building to find out how the concept of academic freedom is viewed. You might begin by asking each person to define academic freedom. Does everyone share a common view? Have any of the teachers ever "claimed" a right to academic freedom? If so, in what context? Do any of the persons you interview know of other teachers who have dealt with this issue? (If so, you might want to interview those teachers as

Reality Bite

Controversial Issues

As a social studies teacher, I've found that controversial issues in the classroom are somewhat commonplace. The key is not to avoid controversy but to maximize the learning potential and minimize secondary or nonacademic issues. You can accomplish this by setting the stage both within and outside the classroom. Within the classroom, the teacher should be on target with facts and never substitute for the truth just to make a point or to win an argument. Be honest with students since they can recognize dishonesty a mile away. Allow students to see both sides of an issue in order for "real" learning to take place. Outside the classroom, make sure that your building administrators are aware of what is going on in your classroom. This allows them to field questions and concerns from parents or other community members so that they may be your ally and advocate rather than your opponent. Make sure that you know what your school district's policy is for dealing with complaints about controversial topics. All of these concerns will not eliminate controversy from the curriculum but will make possible conditions that can ensure that quality learning becomes an obtainable objective.

Chuck Keating, Experienced Teacher

well.) Create a list of the major points that you develop from your interviews. Do any of the things you learn from your interviews give you a reason to think ahead to when you might someday be inclined to teach something controversial? In all of this, how significant is it to always consider the age and maturity level of the students involved? Discuss your findings with your coaches.

Assuming that you teach something other than middle school "gifted lit," can you think of instances where academic freedom arises at the elementary school level or in other secondary school subject areas? Identify some of these areas and speculate as to possible issues that might arise. (For example, the discussion of evolution versus the Biblical account of creation frequently comes up in science classes.)

Coaching 10.3 Investigating School District Policy and Practice

Conduct an informal interview with the principal in your school. Find out if the principal's impression of the teachers' academic freedom in the building matches that of the teachers you interviewed in the previous exercise. Ask whether the

school district has specific policies with regard to the relationship between the four interest groups identified in the Experience section. If the school district has a mission statement, does the statement address the school board's role in adopting curriculum while allowing teachers to select appropriate methods to convey knowledge without undue interference from school officials and parents? If so, how? If not, do you think it should?

Coaching 10.4 Textbook and Instructional Material Selection

You will recall from the scenario at the beginning of this chapter that Tracy Adams had been asked to review several books for possible adoption by the school district. Investigate the method used in your school district for the selection and adoption of textbooks and other instructional materials. Is it a formal process with lots of committee involvement, or is it substantially left to the discretion of individual teachers or programs? Discuss with your cooperating teacher and university supervisor how a teacher's input in the textbook/instructional material selection process parallels several of the academic freedom issues presented in this competency.

REFLECTION

Reflecting 10.5 Is Discretion the Better Part of Valor?

Think back to the Case of the Legally Uninformed Teacher at the beginning of this chapter. As you will recall, Tracy Adams was feeling uneasy about the prospect of having her "gifted" ninth-grade literature class role-play scenes from *Born to Cry*. Applying the new Assessment, Experience, and Coaching knowledge you have acquired to an understanding of Tracy's legal role regarding academic freedom, what would *you* do if you were in her shoes? You might begin by trying to identify exactly what the issues are that should be troubling her. Is there anything else about Tracy's particular community, school district, or school that you would want to know before selecting a course of action? As a new teacher, do you think that Tracy should take a chance by having the class proceed with the planned role-playing activities? Can she justify the value of the role-playing experience regardless of the fact that several of the students might take things too far? Would discretion be the better part of valor in this instance? Discuss these and other questions and concerns that come to mind with your coaches. How do their observations and advice fit within a framework of using common sense and good judgment when faced with a challenging classroom dilemma?

■ *Competency 2* RECOGNIZING TORT AND LIABILITY ISSUES

ASSESSMENT

Assessing 10.6 What Constitutes a Safe Environment for Students?

Purpose: To help beginning teachers recognize the importance of creating and maintaining a safe learning environment for students.

Time required: 30 to 45 minutes

Procedure: Prepare an informal "risk assessment audit" for your classroom and other areas of supervisory responsibility (e.g., the playground, hallways, locker rooms) by identifying 15 or 20 different physical or situational characteristics that create a risk of injury to students or others. For purposes of this exercise, an example of a physical characteristic might be something like a worn or frazzled area of carpeting in the classroom, which might cause a student to trip and fall; a situational characteristic could be a particular group of overly aggressive students who, despite school rules to the contrary, tend to engage in rough play (e.g., "tackle" football) during recess or other recreational or noninstructional periods. In effect, by looking closely at the total environment in which you teach, try to create your own worst-case scenario of things that might happen or go wrong.

Next, rank your entire list of potential dangers according to the probability or likelihood of something actually happening. If time and circumstances permit, it might be interesting to ask your cooperating teacher and/or your university supervisor to prepare their own risk assessment audits for the same learning environment. After you have independently finished your respective audits, a comparison of your results might reveal some interesting and enlightening differences.

Assessing 10.7 School Law Close to Home

Purpose: To learn vicariously from the experiences of others.

Time required: Undetermined

Procedure: Interview the experienced teachers in your school to find out if any of them have ever been threatened with or actually involved in a school-related lawsuit. Find out what you can about their experiences if they are willing to discuss the circumstances and events. Is there anything that you can learn vicariously from hearing about their experiences? If a particular teacher's experiences centered around his or her own employment in the school district, it might be possible to learn about the situation from the other side (i.e., interviewing administrators or school board members to get both sides of the story).

EXPERIENCE

Along with school administrators and school board members, teachers have an obligation to provide a safe environment for students while they attend school or when they are engaged in school-related activities. The primary duties a teacher owes students are

- to provide adequate supervision,
- to provide appropriate instruction prior to having students begin an activity that may pose a risk of harm,
- to maintain equipment and facilities in good repair, and
- to warn of hazardous conditions and known dangers.

Because teachers share a mutual interest in minimizing risks and avoiding liability from having to pay damages for causing harm, they must exercise care when teaching and supervising students under their control. Even if a teacher may not be

Reality Bite

Minimizing Liability

Ever since I started teaching I've always been aware that I might have some potential for liability if one of my students got hurt. Still, sometimes things happen that don't give you much of a chance to think about your personal risk and you simply react to the situation before you think about the consequences.

For example, one day about ten years ago, Willie was causing a disturbance outside his classroom as I was walking by. I noticed and walked over to see what was happening. When I got there, Willie was swinging at another student. I grabbed Willie's arm to restrain him. He immediately began shouting and swinging at me. At this point, I thought I might be able to calm Willie down by holding him in a "bear hug." I wrapped my arms around him and sat down on the floor so that Willie was facing from me. Even though I wasn't squeezing him and was simply trying to help him calm down, Willie was yelling that I was hurting him and that he couldn't breathe. In doing so, he was creating quite a commotion and drawing a crowd of other students. In a short time, another teacher came along and she was able to calm Willie so that I could release him.

When I first wrapped Willie in my arms, I thought that I had done a good thing; later I started having second thoughts about what he was yelling and how other students and teachers might have perceived what was happening. While I know that I will always intercede in a similar situation, this incident with Willie will always make me run the risks through my mind very quickly before I do anything inappropriate. I try to make sure that my actions fit the circumstances and that I don't do anything out of the ordinary to endanger or harm a student—even if the student is causing problems and is out of control.

Tom Dickey, Experienced Teacher

personally liable for damages in a lawsuit, there is always a strong *professional* incentive to not contribute to or be partially responsible for someone else's (i.e., the employing school district) liability. Regardless of a teacher's obvious interest in avoiding liability, the strongest motivating factor should always be student safety—fragile bodies and psyches injured through deliberate or unintentional acts can never be made completely whole with any amount of monetary compensation.

Most lawsuits that result when a student sustains an injury involve allegations of teacher negligence. In this context, negligence is defined as conduct in which a teacher fails to exercise reasonable care to protect someone under his or her care—a student—from the risk of foreseeable harm. Whether a teacher will be found negligent in a civil lawsuit will hinge on a variety of factors, including whether a "reasonably prudent teacher" would have acted as this particular teacher did under similar circumstances and whether the possibility of likely injury could have been foreseen and appropriate action taken to avoid the injury (Hartmeister, 1994).

Negligence is one of several types of tort actions that typically arise in a school setting. A tort is defined as "a private or civil wrong or injury, other than breach of contract, for which the court will provide a remedy in the form of an action for damages" (*Black's Law Dictionary*, 1979). Tort law is premised on the legal theory that people are liable for the consequences of their actions that result in injury to others. In addition to negligence (which is generally considered to be unintentional and, in a sense, somewhat like carelessness), examples of other types of torts include such things as defamation (written or spoken communication that harms a person's reputation or exposes them to ridicule), intentional torts (assault and battery or false imprisonment), and constitutional torts (in which a person is deprived of his or her civil rights under either the constitution or other federal laws) (Reutter, 1994).

Another legal concept closely related to liability is immunity. If immunity protection is made available to the teachers in a given state by that state's legislature, it prevents teachers from being liable in traditional negligence action. In other words, even though a teacher's negligence may have caused or contributed to a student's injuries, statutory immunity will prevent the student or the student's parents from recovering monetary compensation from the teacher (or, in some cases, the teacher's school district) for the teacher's negligence. Another way of protecting against liability is through insurance coverage, which may also serve to protect a teacher from having to pay compensation due to negligence. The laws governing torts, immunity, and insurance vary significantly from state to state; therefore, it is extremely difficult to make accurate generalizations about the particular conditions in any given state (Valente, 1994).

COACHING

Coaching 10.8 Planning a Field Trip

For purposes of this activity, presume that you are Tracy Adams in the beginning scenario and that you have two weeks to make all of the necessary arrangements to comply with your school district's requirements for taking a group of students on a field trip. Sit down with your cooperating teacher, your university supervisor, and a copy of your school district's requirements (i.e., school board policies, building or campus-level rules, all necessary approval forms and paperwork, including such things as medical or health forms and releases, parental notification waivers, bus scheduling forms, class sponsor/parental volunteer arrangements, and budget request forms) and plan Tracy's eighth-grade visit to examine modern art. When you are finished, it might be interesting to show your principal what you have done. As an aside, can you make a convincing argument that Tracy's field trip is warranted—in other words, does it have educational merit?

Coaching 10.9 Liability Protection in Your State and School District

In a discussion with your cooperating teacher and university supervisor, identify the extent to which you may be protected from personal liability in a negligence lawsuit. Will your state allow you to claim statutory immunity from a negligence allegation? Another area to explore would include the availability of insurance coverage through your school district and various professional associations or unions. Finally, have you ever thought about your potential liability as a student teacher? This might well be an additional area to explore with your coaches and perhaps the school principal or other central office personnel.

REFLECTION

Reflecting 10.10 Seeking to Minimize Your Risks

Although this competency section presents only a superficial overview of tort and liability issues, it should cause you to reflect on the obvious and not-so-obvious risks that are inherent in the teaching profession. Unfortunately, because of the interactions between those involved within the confines of an instructional area or educational setting, there are usually an ample number of opportunities for accidents and injuries to occur. The risks increase when students are taken out of their "normal" educational environments during field trip–type activities. While this is *not* to say that field trips and other off-campus or out-of-the-ordinary educational opportunities should be foregone due to increased risks, it *is* to advise that the educational benefits should be carefully balanced against the potential risks to ensure that *all* decisions are professionally and educationally justified.

Using the assessment, experience, and coaching knowledge you have gained in this competency, place yourself in Tracy's position within the chapter's opening scenario. What are some of the key factors Tracy should weigh as she deliberates taking her class to the modern art exhibit? Thinking about the teacher's legal role, what are some aspects of the proposed field trip Tracy might investigate *before* finalizing plans to schedule her classes? What are some of the unique teaching and learning advantages that might make this field trip educationally justifiable? As you can see, many of these considerations extend into other competencies and far beyond just what is "legal."

■ *Competency 3*   COMPLYING WITH STATUTORY REQUIREMENTS: REPORTING SUSPECTED CHILD ABUSE OR NEGLECT

ASSESSMENT

In addition to instructing students, today's teachers are burdened with a variety of monitoring requirements and regulations imposed by such diverse groups as federal agencies, state legislatures, and local school boards. You will recall from having read the Case of the Legally Uninformed Teacher at the beginning of this chapter that Tracy Adams had a concern about a possibly abusive situation involving one of her seventh-grade students, Dillon Booth. This section is designed as a self-assessment for you to learn more about your statutory obligations to report instances of possible child abuse or neglect to the proper authorities in your state.

Assessing 10.11 Reporting Suspected Child Abuse or Neglect

Purpose: To help clarify your understanding of when and how teachers in your state are expected to report instances of suspected child abuse or neglect.

Time required: 5 minutes

Procedure: Respond to each of the True/False questions. Check the accuracy of your responses by reading through the Experience section that follows this exercise.

_____   1. Nearly all of the 50 states have enacted legislation (i.e., statutes) that requires teachers to report suspected instances of child abuse or neglect.

_____   2. By most definitions, child abuse and neglect is strictly physical, not mental.

_____   3. As a teacher, you are only required to report child abuse or neglect to the proper authorities if you are absolutely positive that a child has suffered some type of permanent injury; otherwise, you run the risk of losing a lawsuit premised on defamation or invasion of privacy if your report is unfounded.

_____   4. Prior to filing a child abuse or neglect report, you should always question the child to verify whether abuse actually occurred.

_____   5. If you fail to make a timely report of a suspected child abuse or neglect, usually the worst that can happen to you is that you will receive a small fine.

_____ **6.** As a general rule, if you are unsure about whether abuse or neglect has occurred and are torn between reporting and not reporting, you are better off *not* filing a report.

_____ **7.** Since reporting child abuse and neglect is the law in most states, it really doesn't matter what individual school districts do with regard to implementing policies imposing a "chain-of-command" type of reporting mechanism at the building level.

EXPERIENCE

All 50 states have enacted legislation requiring professionals (teachers, physicians, law enforcement officers, social workers, and others) to report instances of suspected child abuse and neglect (McCarthy & Cambron-McCabe, 1992). Although the exact requirements for reporting vary somewhat from state to state, there are several common elements shared by nearly all of the reporting statutes. However, since each state's statutes are unique (thus making it impossible to make too many accurate generalizations), in order to ascertain the *precise* requirements in your state it is necessary to examine the specific statutory provisions that define abuse and neglect and impose penalties for failing to report. You will have an opportunity to do that in the next section of this Competency.

Child abuse and neglect is generally defined as nonaccidental physical or mental injury, sexual abuse, negligent treatment or maltreatment, abandonment, or placing a child at a substantial risk of death or harm. Most states cover children under age 18 and the coverage applies to the child's parents or others responsible for the child's welfare (Alexander & Alexander, 1992).

One of the key elements in child abuse and neglect legislation is that those filing reports are not expected to have absolute knowledge of an abusive or neglect situation; rather, *suspected* abuse premised on the reporter having a "reason to believe" is all that is necessary. If the reporter can justify making a report on the basis of having a "reason to believe" that something is amiss, then that person will enjoy immunity from liability if the report turns out to be groundless. In most states, all that is necessary to being granted immunity is to be able to demonstrate that the report was filed in good faith. Balancing the notion of good faith immunity against the prospects of civil and/or criminal sanctions for failing to report, it should be obvious that it is almost always better to err on the side of caution when faced with a difficult decision of "Do I report—or not??!" In other words, if in doubt, file a report.

Most school districts have enacted their own reporting policies and practices that supplement state legislation and spell out the school district's expectations for the timely and systematic filing of abuse and neglect reports. Ordinarily, teachers

Reality Bite

Dealing with Child Abuse and Neglect

Dealing with personal cases of child abuse or neglect is one of the hardest things about being a teacher. Because of the nature of abuse and neglect, it is often very difficult to get students to talk to you about the problems that they may be having outside of school. Although a few students may be forthcoming and want to talk, many others are reluctant to open up and discuss their problems. Yet, as a teacher, you can tell that something is wrong and you know that you have a duty to report any such problems.

From my experience, a child's poor attendance, lack of attention, or sudden and significant changes in behavior may be signs of possible abuse or neglect. Although it is impossible to say what a teacher should do in every situation, my advice is to be a sympathetic listener when students wish to discuss personal problems of this sort. Let the student do the talking, don't make too many comments, and don't pass judgment too quickly. Then, if you have reason to believe that abuse or neglect may have occurred, don't hesitate to involve your principal or whoever else is the designated report person in your building. It really helps to have a principal who is strong, tactful, and willing to take an understanding but aggressive approach toward handling the situation and making the necessary reports to social service agencies. The bottom line is this: If in doubt, make sure you report. After all, it is always better to be safe than sorry.

Holly Hursh, Experienced Teacher

are expected to comply with their individual district's reporting mechanism. Doing so allows school officials to carefully monitor the frequency of suspected abuse and, ideally, better assist with intervention and abatement practices.

Most states impose criminal sanctions on professionals who knowingly fail to comply with mandatory reporting requirements. Such sanctions usually include fines of up to $1,000, jail sentences of up to six months or a year, or possibly both. Some states also provide for civil liability to be imposed against teachers if they fail to report.

(Just in case you forgot to check, the correct answer to all of the True/False statements in Assessing 10.11 is "False.")

COACHING

Coaching 10.12 What Do the Statutes Say?

Since the requirements for reporting suspected child abuse and neglect vary from state to state, it is essential that you know precisely what your particular state requires of its teachers. Obtain a copy of the current statutory provisions and the specific school district policies and practices for reporting suspected abuse in your state. Your principal (or, in some instances, the superintendent or other central office personnel) can probably help you with this task. Read the statutes carefully and compare them to any school board policies or other provisions for reporting suspected abuse or neglect that might be contained in the faculty handbook. Does it appear that all of the requirements "fit" in the sense that they are clearly defined and easy to understand and follow? Are the definitions of abuse and neglect clearly identified, and do they appear to be enforceable?

Coaching 10.13 How Do Others Perceive Mandatory Requirements for Reporting Suspected Abuse and Neglect?

Interview three or more of the experienced teachers in your building and see what their understanding of child abuse and neglect reporting laws happens to be. How do their interpretations of reporting requirements fit with what you discovered in the previous exercise? Did any of the teachers that you interviewed have personal experiences with filing reports and dealing with the consequences? If so, how do you reconcile their experiences with your understanding of your state's reporting laws?

Coaching 10.14 Corporal Punishment and Child Abuse

Investigate your state and school district's approaches to corporal punishment. Could they best be described as restrictive or permissive, and why? Discuss with your coaches the relationship between corporal punishment and allegations of child abuse in a school setting and how this might affect your approach to student discipline.

REFLECTION

Reflecting 10.15 What Would *You* Do if You Were Tracy?

Review the scenario at the beginning of this chapter one final time using the new Assessment, Experience, and Coaching knowledge you have acquired in this Competency. Suppose for the moment that Lincoln Middle School is in *your* school district and Tracy Adams came to you for advice. What would you tell her to do? Where should she start? Does she have a responsibility to conduct her own investigation of the circumstances before she files a report with her principal (or whomever else is the designated report person in her building or school district)? How reliable must the student be whose workbook contained the comment about Dillon before Tracy takes any action? In other words, should Tracy automatically discount the student's comment if Tracy knows that in the past the student has been a troublemaker or has proven to have less than a sterling character? Can Tracy afford *not* to file a report in this case?

Conclusion

An understanding of and appreciation for the role that the law plays in most aspects of education is vital to contemporary success. Nearly every phase of a teacher's professional life is touched in some fashion by legal constraints and directives. Most successful teachers attempt to gain a working knowledge of educational law so as to be able to operate safely and efficiently; they also recognize the importance of staying current on legal issues affecting education. Above all, keep in mind that the scope of educational law extends far beyond just the three areas highlighted in this chapter (academic freedom, tort and liability issues, and compliance with statutory requirements); additional legal issues range among such broad areas as the separation of church and state, employment and collective bargaining concerns, student rights, special education, desegregation, discrimination, and various constitutional protections for students and teachers.

In addition to all the other things that teachers are expected to do, they also must know how and when to anticipate and avoid unnecessary risks—for themselves as well as their students. In the long run, a proactive and preventive approach to potential legal problems is certainly more conducive to viable risk management and personal peace of mind. Remember, however, that underlying the notion of professional educator competency (in a legal sense) is a substantial reliance on good common sense coupled with sound, practical, and reasonable judgment.

References

Alexander, K., & Alexander, M. (1992). *American public school law.* (3rd ed.). St. Paul, MN: West.

Black's Law Dictionary. (5th ed.). (1979). St. Paul, MN: West Publishing.

Hartmeister, F. (1995). *Surviving as a teacher: The legal dimension.* Chicago, IL: Precept.

Hazelwood School District v. Kuhlmeier, 484 U.S. 260 (1988).

Kemerer, F., & Walsh, J. (1994). *The educator's guide to Texas school law.* (3rd ed.). Austin, TX: University of Texas Press.

Kingsville Independent School District v. Cooper, 611 F.2d 1109 (5th Cir. 1980).

McCarthy, M. (1993). Post-*Hazelwood* developments: A threat to free inquiry in public schools. *Education Law Reporter, 81,* 685–701.

McCarthy, M., & Cambron-McCabe, N. (1992). *Public school law.* (3rd ed.). Boston, MA: Allyn and Bacon.

Moody v. Jefferson Parish School Board, 2 F.3d 604 (5th Cir. 1993).

Pell, S.W.J. (1994). Preservice teachers' lack of knowledge about education law: Ignorance is no excuse. *Illinois School Law Quarterly, 14,* 138–150.

Reutter, E. (1994). *The law of public education.* (4th ed.). Westbury, NY: Foundation Press.

Sparkman, W., & Desrosiers, E. (1986). *School law courses survey, 1986.* Paper presented at the annual meeting of the National Organization on Legal Problems of Education, Las Vegas, Nevada.

Thomas, G., Sperry, D., & Wasden, F. (1991). *The law and teacher employment.* St. Paul, MN: West.

Valente, W. (1994). *Law in the schools.* (4th ed.). New York, NY: Macmillan.

Appendix

Outline of the Basic Problem-Solving Procedure

I. Define the problem.
    a. Discuss symptoms (especially if problem is unknown).
    b. Discuss size (or seriousness) and impact (effect) of problem.
    c. Determine the exact wording of the problem in question form.
    d. Define terms in the question.

II. Research and analyze the problem.
    a. List topics that need to be researched or discussed, including causes and past efforts to solve the problem.
    b. Research the problem if needed.
    c. Discuss the research in an organized manner.
       1. State the first topic to be discussed.
       2. Give all members a chance to cite research or opinion on the topic.
       3. Ask if anyone has anything further to say on the topic.
       4. Summarize the group's findings on the topic.
       5. State the next topic to be discussed and repeat the procedure until all topics have been discussed.

III. Establish a checklist of criteria (rules, boundaries, requirements, or guidelines) that an alternative must meet in order to be selected as the solution.
    a. List all possible criteria (give everyone a chance to respond).
    b. Discuss each criterion.
    c. Reduce the list to a workable length by combining criteria where possible.
    d. Rank remaining criteria from most to least important.

IV. List possible alternatives.

V. Evaluate each alternative based on the established criteria.
    a. Read through the list of alternatives, eliminating those the group feels obviously do not meet the criteria agreed on in the third step.
    b. Reduce the list further by combining any similar alternatives.
    c. Discuss each remaining alternative's strengths and weaknesses (referring to research presented in the second step when necessary).
    d. Determine how well each alternative meets the criteria—number of criteria met and importance of criteria met.
    e. Continue reducing the list until the best alternative (or alternatives) is reached.

VI. Select the best alternative(s) as your solution and discuss how to implement it (or them).

Source: From Cheryl Hamilton and Cordell Parker. *Communicating for Results,* fourth ed. Wadsworth Publishing Company. © 1993 Wadsworth, Inc. Reprinted by permission.

Bibliography

Alexander, K., & Alexander, M. (1992). *American public school law*. (3rd ed.). St. Paul, MN: West Publishing.

American Association of University Women (1992). *The AAUW report: How schools short-change girls*. Washington, DC: American Association of University Women.

Arends, R. (1988). *Learning to teach*. New York: Random House.

Bacharach, S. B., & Lawler, E. J. (1980). *Power and politics in organizations: The social psychology of conflict, coalitions, and bargaining*. San Francisco: Jossey-Bass.

Baker, E., Wang,, M., & Walberg, H. (1994/1995). The effects of inclusion on learning. *Educational Leadership, (52)*4, 33–35.

Ball, S. (1987). *The micro-politics of the school*. New York: Routledge.

Berlo, D. (1960). *The process of communication*. New York: Holt, Rinehart and Winston.

Bey, T. M., & Holmes, C. T. (eds.). (1992). *Mentoring: Contemporary principles and issues*. Reston, VA: Association of Teacher Educators.

Beyer, B. (1987). *Practical strategies for the teaching of thinking*. Boston: Allyn and Bacon.

Black's law dictionary. (1979). (5th ed.). St. Paul, MN: West Publishing.

Blase, J. (ed.). (1991a). *The politics of life in schools: Power, conflict and cooperation*. Newbury Park, CA: Sage.

Blase, J. (1991b). Everyday political perspectives of teachers toward students: The dynamics of diplomacy. In J. Blase (ed.), *The politics of schools: Power, conflict and cooperation*. Newbury Park, CA: Sage.

Blase, J. (1991c). The micropolitical orientation of teachers toward closed school principals. *Education in Urban Society, 23* (4), 356–378.

Bloom, B., Engelhart, M., Furst, E., Hill, W., & Krathwohl, D. (1956). *Taxonomy of educational objectives. The classification of educational goals. Handbook I: Cognitive domain*. New York: McKay.

Bloome, D., & Willett, J. (1991). Toward a micropolitics of classroom interaction. In J. Blase (ed.), *The politics of life in schools: Power, conflict, and cooperation*. Newbury Park, CA: Sage.

Borich, G. (1988). *Effective teaching methods.* Columbus, OH: Merrill.

Borko, H. (1986). Clinical teacher education: The induction years. In J. V. Hoffman & S. A. Edwards (eds.), *Reality and reform in clinical teacher education.* New York: Random House.

Bowen, W. (1981). How to regain our competitive edge. *Fortune, 103,* 74–90.

Brandt, R. (1989). On parents and schools: A conversation with Joyce Epstein. *Educational Leadership, 47* (2), 24–27.

Brophy, J. E. (1983). Classroom organization and management. *The Elementary School Journal, 83* (4), 265–285.

Brophy, J. (1985). Teacher-student interaction. In J. Dusek (ed.), *Teacher expectancies.* Hillsdale, NJ: Erlbaum.

Brophy, J. E. (1987). On motivating students. In D. G. Berliner & B. V. Rosenshine (eds.), *Talks to teachers.* New York: Random House.

Brown, M. A., & Willems, A. L. (1977). Lifeboat ethics and the first-year teacher. *The Clearinghouse, 51,* 73–75.

Bullough, R. V. (1987). First-year teaching: A case study. *Teachers College Record, 89* (2), 219–237.

Calabrese, R., & Anderson, R. (1986). The public school: A source of stress and alienation among female teachers. *Urban Education, 21* (1), 30–41.

Canfield, J., & Wells, H. (1976). *100 ways to enhance self-concept in the classroom: A handbook for teachers and parents.* Englewood Cliffs, NJ: Prentice-Hall.

Carkuff, R. (1969). *Helping and human relations: A primer for lay and professional helpers. Vol.1. Selection and training.* New York: Holt, Rinehart and Winston.

Carroll, J. (1963). A model of school learning. *Teachers College Record, 64,* 723–733.

Clark, C., & Yinger, R. (1979). *Three studies of teacher planning.* East Lansing, MI: Institute for Research on Teaching, Michigan State University.

Clark, E. (1980). An analysis of occupational stress factors as perceived by public school teachers. *Dissertation Abstracts International.* Auburn University.

Clark, L., & Starr, I. (1991). *Secondary and middle school teaching methods.* (6th ed.). New York: Macmillan.

Coates, T., & Thoressen, C. (1978). Teacher anxiety: A review with recommendations. *Review of Educational Research, 51* (2), 159–184.

Cohen, A. (1977). Instructional systems in reading: A report on the effects of a curriculum design based on a systems model. *Reading World, 16,* 158–171.

Cohen, E. (1986). *Designing groupwork: Strategies for the heterogeneous classroom.* New York: Teachers College Press.

Cohen, M. W. (1986). Research on motivation: New content for the teacher preparation curriculum. *Journal of Teacher Education, 37* (3), 23–28.

Cohen, M. W., Emrich, A. E., & deCharms, R. (1976–1977). Training teachers to enhance personal causation in students. *Interchange, 7,* 34–39.

Collins, M. (1978). The effects of training for enthusiasm on the enthusiasm displayed by preservice teachers. *Journal of Teacher Education, 24* (1), 53–57.

Commission on the Reorganization of Secondary Education. (1918). *Cardinal principles of secondary education.* Washington, DC: Government Printing Office.

Corrigan, D. C., & Haberman, M. (1990). The context of teacher education. In W. R. Houston (ed.), *Handbook of research on teacher education.* New York: Macmillan.

Costa, A. (1985). Teacher behaviors that enable student thinking. In A. Costa (ed.), *Developing minds.* Alexandria, VA: Association for Supervision and Curriculum Development.

Cruickshank, D. R., Kennedy, J. J., & Myers, B. (1974). Perceived problems of secondary school teachers. *Journal of Educational Research, 68,* 154–159.

Dembo, M., & Gibson, S. (1985). Teachers' sense of efficacy: An important factor in school improvement. *Elementary School Journal, 86,* 173–184.

Dewey, J. (1910). *How we think.* Boston: Heath.

Doyal, G., & Forsyth, R. (1973). Relationship between teaching and student anxiety levels. *Psychology in the Schools, 10,* 231–233.

Dropkin, S., & Taylor, M. (1963). Perceived problems of beginning teachers and related factors. *Journal of Teacher Education, 14,* 384–389.

Drummond, H. (1964). Leadership for human change. *Educational Leadership, 23* (8), 626–629.

Dunkin, M., & Biddle, B. (1974). *The study of teaching.* New York: Holt, Rinehart and Winston.

Dunn, R., & Dunn, K. (1978). *Teaching students through their individual learning styles: A practical approach.* Reston, VA: Reston Publishing Company, Division Prentice-Hall.

Edmonds, R., Mortimore, P., and Rosenshine, B. (1981). *Teacher and school effectiveness: Leader's guide.* Alexandria, Virginia: Association for Supervision and Curriculum Development.

Eisner, E., & Vallance, E. (1974). *Conflicting conceptions of curriculum.* Berkeley, CA: McCutchan.

Emmer, E. T., Evertson, C. M., Sanford, J. P., Clements B. S., & Worsham, M. E. (1989). *Classroom management for secondary teachers* (2nd ed.). Englewood Cliffs, NJ: Prentice-Hall.

Ennis, R. (1962). A concept of critical thinking. *Harvard Educational Review, 32* (1), 81–111.

Ennis, R. (1985). Logical basis for measuring critical thinking skills. *Educational Leadership, 42,* 44–48.

Eskridge, D., & Coker, D. (1985). Teacher stress: Symptoms, causes, and management techniques. *The Clearing House, 59,* 387–390.

Farber, B. (1984). Teacher burnout: Assumptions, myths, and issues. *Teachers College Record, 86,* 321–338.

Forman, S. (1982). Stress management for teachers: A cognitive-behavioral program. *Journal of School Psychology, 20,* 180–187.

Fox, S. M., & Singletary, T. J. (1986). Deductions about supportive induction. *Journal of Teacher Education, 37* (1), 12–15.

Frey, D., & Carlock, C. (1984). *Enhancing self-esteem.* Muncie, IN: Accelerated Development.

Fullan, M. (1993). *Change forces: Probing the depths of educational reform.* Bristol, PA: Falmer Press.

Fullan, M. (1993). Innovation, reform, and restructuring strategies. In G. Cawelti (ed.), *Challenges and achievement of American education. The 1993 ASCD yearbook.* Alexandria, VA: Association for Supervision and Curriculum Development.

Fullan, M., with Stiegelbauer, S. (1991). *The new meaning of educational change.* New York: Teachers College Press.

Garrett, S., Sadker, M., & Sadker, D. (1986). Interpersonal communication skills. In. J. Cooper (ed.), *Classroom teaching skills.* Lexington, MA: Heath.

Gazda, G., Asbury, F., Balzer, F., Childers, W., & Walters, R. (1977). *Human relations development: A manual for educators.* Boston: Allyn and Bacon.

Gibson, R., & Mitchell, M. (1990). *Introduction to counseling and guidance.* (3rd ed.). New York: Macmillan.

Glickman, C. D. (1993). *Renewing America's schools.* San Francisco: Jossey-Bass.

Glickman, C. D. (1985). *Supervision of instruction: A developmental approach.* Boston: Allyn and Bacon.

Gold, Y. (1990, February). Psychological support for beginning teachers: Beyond stress management. Paper presented at Association of Teacher Educators 70th Annual Meeting, Las Vegas, Nevada.

Gold, Y., & Roth, R. A. (1993). *Teachers managing stress and preventing burnout: The professional health (PH) solution.* London: Falmer.

Good, T., & Brophy, G. (1987). *Looking into classrooms.* (4th ed.). New York: Harper and Row.

Good, T., Mulryan, C., & McCaslin, M. (1992). Grouping for instruction in mathematics: A call for programmatic research on small-group processes. In D. Grouws (ed.), *Handbook of research on mathematics teaching and learning.* New York: Macmillan.

Goodlad, J. I. (1979). *What schools are for.* Bloomington, IN: Phi Delta Kappa.

Goodlad, J. I. (1984). *A place called school: Prospects for the future.* New York: McGraw-Hill.

Goodlad, J. I. (1990). The occupation of teaching in schools. In J. Goodlad, R. Soder, & K. Sirotnik (eds.), *The moral dimensions of teaching.* San Francisco: Jossey-Bass.

Goodlad, J. I. (1994). Educational renewal: Better teachers, better schools. San Francisco: Jossey-Bass.

Gorham, J. (1988). The relationship between verbal teacher immediacy behaviors and student learning. *Communication Education, 37* (1), 40–53.

Goss, B., & O'Hair, D. (1988). *Communicating in interpersonal relationships.* New York: Macmillan.

Granger, R. E. (1989). Computer-based training improves job performance. *Personnel Journal, 68* (6), 116–120.

Griffin, G. A., Barnes, S., Defino, M., Edwards, S., Hoffman, J. V., Hukill, H., & O'Neal, S. (1983). *Teacher induction: Research design for a descriptive study.* Austin: University of Texas R & D Center for Teacher Education.

Guilford, J. P. (1967). *The nature of human intelligence.* New York: McGraw-Hill.

Gunter, M., Estes, T., & Schwab, J. (1990). *Instruction: A model's approach.* Boston: Allyn and Bacon.

Hall, E. (1966). *The hidden dimensions.* Garden City, NY: Doubleday.

Hall, G. (1979). The concerns-based approach to facilitating change. *Educational Horizons, 57* (4), 202–208.

Hamblin, D. (1974). *The teacher and counselling.* Oxford, England: Basil Blackwell.

Hamilton, C., & Parker, C. (1987). *Communicating for results: A guide for business and the professions.* Belmont, CA: Wadsworth.

Hargreaves, A. (1979). Strategies, decisions and control: Interaction in a middle school classroom. In J. Eggleston (ed.), *Teacher decision making in the classroom.* London: Routledge & Kegan Paul.

Hargreaves, A. (1991). The micropolitics of teacher collaboration. In J. Blase (ed.), *The politics of life in schools: Power, conflict and cooperation.* Newbury Park, CA: Sage.

Harlow, A. (1972). *A taxonomy of psychomotor domain.* New York: McKay.

Harris, K., Halpin, G., & Halpin, G. (1985). Teacher characteristics and stress. *Journal of Education Research, 78,* 346–350.

Hartmeister, F. (1995). *Surviving as a teacher: The legal dimension.* Chicago: Precept.

Hatfield, F. C. (1972). Effect of prior experience, access to information and level of performance on individual and group performance ratings. *Perceptual and Motor Skills, 35,* 19–26.

Hazelwood School District v. Kuhlmeier, 484 U.S. 260 (1988).

Heck, S., & Williams, R. (1984). *The complex roles of the teacher: An ecological perspective.* New York: Teachers College Press.

Holmes, T. H., & Rahne, R. H. (1967). The social readjustment rating scale. *Journal of Psychosomatic Research, 2.*

Hord, S., Rutherford, W., Huling-Austin, L., & Hall, G. (1987). *Taking charge of change.* Alexandria, VA: Association for Supervision and Curriculum Development.

Horwitz, E., Horwitz, M., & Cope, J. (1986). Foreign language classroom anxiety. *The Modern Language Journal, 70,* 125–132.

Huber, V. L., & Gay, G. (1985, Feb.). Channeling new technology to improve training. *Personnel Administrator,* 49–57.

Jackson, P. (1968). *Life in classrooms.* New York: Holt, Rinehart and Winston.

Janis, I. L. (1972). *Victims of groupthink: A psychological study of foreign-policy decisions and fiascoes.* Boston: Houghton Mifflin.

Jarolimek, J., & Foster, C. (1989). *Teaching and learning in the elementary school.* New York: Macmillan.

Johnson, D., & Johnson, R. (1984). *Cooperative learning.* New Brighton, MA: Interaction Books.

Johnson, R., Rynders, J., Johnson, D., Schmidt, B., & Haider, S. (1979). Interaction between handicapped and nonhandicapped teenagers as a function of situational goal structuring: Implications for mainstreaming. *American Educational Research Journal, 16,* 161–167.

Jones, F. H. (1987). *Positive classroom instruction.* New York: McGraw-Hill.

Jones, V. F., & Jones, L. S. (1990). *Comprehensive classroom management: Motivating and managing students.* (3rd ed.). Boston: Allyn and Bacon.

Joyce, B., Weil, M., & Showers, B. (1992). *Models of teaching.* (4th ed.). Englewood Cliffs, NJ: Prentice-Hall.

Kaiser, J., & Polczynski, J. (1982). Educational stress: Sources, reactions, preventions. *Peabody Journal of Education, 10,* 127–134.

Kane, P. R. (ed.) (1991). *The first year of teaching: Real world stories from America's teachers.* New York: Walker.

Kearney, P., Plax, T. G., Smith, V. R., & Sorensen, G. (1988). Effects of teacher immediacy and strategy type on college student resistance to on-task demands. *Communication Education, 37,* 54–67.

Kemerer, F., & Walsh, J. (1994). *The educator's guide to Texas school law* (3rd ed.). Austin: University of Texas Press.

Kepner, C. H., & Trego, B. B. (1965). *The rational manager: A systematic approach to problem solving and decision making.* New York: McGraw-Hill.

Kingsville Independent School District v. Cooper, 611 F.2d 1109 (5th Cir. 1980).

Koff, R., Laffey, J., Olson, G., & Cichon, D. (1979–1980). Stress and the school administrator. *Administrator's Notebook, 28,* 1–4.

Kohlberg, L. (1964). Development of moral character and moral ideology. In M. L. Hoffman & L. W. Hoffman (eds.), *Review of child development research.* New York: Russell Sage Foundation.

Kohlberg, L. (1976). Moral stages and moralization. In T. Lickona (ed.), *Moral development and behavior: Theory, research and social issues.* New York: Holt, Rinehart and Winston.

Kounin, J. (1970). *Discipline and group management in classrooms.* NY: Holt, Rinehart and Winston.

Kozol, J. (1991). *Savage inequalities.* New York: Crown.

Krayer, K., O'Hair, M. J., & O'Hair, D. (1984). Applications of cognitive restructuring in the treatment of communication apprehension: Perceptions of task and context coping strategies. *Communication, 13,* 67–79.

Kronik, J. W. (1990). On men mentoring women: Then and now. *ADFL Bulletin,* 22–27.

Kurth-Schai, R. (1991). The peril and promise of childhood: Ethical implications for tomorrow's teachers. *Journal of Teacher Education, 42* (3), 196–204.

Lewis, C. (1973). Clear interpersonal communication. In J. Stewart (ed.), *Bridges not halls: A book about interpersonal communication.* New York: Random House.

Litt, M., & Turk, D. (1985). Sources of stress and dissatisfaction in experienced high school teachers. *Journal of Educational Research, 78,* 178–185.

Lueder, D. (1989). Tennessee parents were invited to participate—and they did! *Educational Leadership, 47* (2), 15–17.

Madlin, N. (1987). Computer-based training comes of age. *Personnel, 64* (11), 64–65.

Marcum, K. (1988). An unpublished dissertation. New Mexico State University.

McCarthy, M. (1993). Post-Hazelwood developments: A threat to free inquiry in public schools. *Education Law Reporter, 81,* 685–701.

McCarthy, M., & Cambron-McCabe, N. (1992). *Public school law* (3rd ed.). Boston: Allyn and Bacon.

McCroskey, J. C., & Richmond, V. P. (1983). Power in the classroom I: Teacher and student perceptions. *Communication Education, 32,* 176–184.

McDonald, F. J., & Elias, P. (1982). *The transition into teaching: The problems of beginning teachers and programs to solve them. Summary Report.* Berkeley, CA: Educational Testing Service. ETS Document Reproduction Contract No. 400-78-0069.

Meggert, S. (1989). Problems of self-esteem. In D. Capuzzi & D. Gross (eds.), *Youth at risk: A resource for counselors, teachers and parents.* Alexandria, VA: American Association for Counseling and Development.

Mehrabian, A. (1969). Significance of posture and position in the communication of attitude and status relationships. *Psychological Bulletin, 71,* 359–372.

Mehrabian, A. (1981). *Silent messages.* Belmont, CA: Wadsworth.

Metfessel, N., Michael, W., & Kirsner, D. (1969). Instrumentation of Bloom's and Krathwohl's taxonomies for the writing of educational objectives. *Psychology in the Schools, 6,* 227–231.

Moody v. Jefferson Parish School Board, 2 F.3d 604 (5th Cir. 1993).

Moore, K. (1989). *Classroom teaching skills: A primer.* New York: Random House.

Munter, P., Blaine, G., King, S., Leavey, J., Powell, D., Sand, J., & Walters, P. (1988). *Counseling students.* Dover, MA: Auburn House.

Myers, C., & Myers, L. (1990). *An introduction to teaching and schools.* Fort Worth, TX: Holt, Rinehart & Winston.

Nash, R. (1991). Three conceptions of ethics for teacher educators. *Journal of Teacher Education, 42* (3), 163–172.

Neagley, R., & Evans, D. (1980). *Handbook for effective supervision.* (3rd ed.). Englewood Cliffs, NJ: Prentice-Hall.

Oakes, J. (1986). *Keeping track: How schools structure inequality.* New Haven: Yale University Press.

O'Hair, D., & Friedrick, G. (1992). *Strategic communication for business and the professions.* Boston: Houghton Mifflin.

O'Hair, M. J. (1989). Teacher employment interview: A neglected reality. *Action in Teacher Education, 11* (1), 53–57.

O'Hair, M. J., & Harmon, S. (1990). Elementary students rank what motivates them to learn in the classroom. Unpublished manuscript.

O'Hair, M. J., & O'Hair, D. (1992). A model of strategic principal communication during performance evaluations. *Journal of Research for School Executives, 2,* 13–22.

O'Hair, M. J., & Odell, S. J. (1995). *Educating teachers for leadership and change.* Newbury Park, CA: Corwin.

O'Hair, M. J., & Wright, R. (1990). Application of communication strategies in alleviating teacher stress. In D. O'Hair & G. Kreps (eds.), *Applied communication and research.* Hillsdale, NJ: Erlbaum.

Orlich, D. (1989). Education reforms: Mistakes, misconceptions, miscues. *Educational Leadership, 70* (7), 512–517.

Orlich, D., Harder, R., Callahan, R., Kauchak, D., & Gibson, H. (1994). *Teaching strategies.* (4th ed.). Lexington, MA: Heath.

Ornstein, A. (1990). *Strategies for effective teaching.* New York: Harper and Row.

Passe, P. (1984). Phil Donahue: An excellent model for leading a discussion. *Journal of Teacher Education, 35* (1), 43–48.

Patterson, J. (1993). *Leadership for tomorrow's schools.* Alexandria, VA: Association for Supervision and Curriculum Development.

Pauly, E. (1991). *The classroom crucible: What really works, what doesn't, and why.* New York: Basic Books.

Pell, S. W. J. (1994). Preservice teachers' lack of knowledge about education law: Ignorance is no excuse. *Illinois School Law Quarterly, 14,* 138–150.

Peterson, P. (1979). Direct instruction reconsidered. In P. Peterson & H. Walberg (eds.), *Research on teaching: Concepts, findings and implications.* Berkeley, CA: McCutchan.

Petrusich, M. (1966). Separation anxiety as a factor in the student teaching experience. *Peabody Journal of Education, 14,* 353–356.

Quinn, R. E., Faerman, S. R., Thompson, M. P., & McGrath, M. R. (1990). *Becoming a master manager: A competency framework.* New York: Wiley.

Remy, R. (1980). *Handbook of basic citizenship competencies.* Alexandria, VA: Association for Supervision and Curriculum Development.

Reutter, E. (1994). *The law of public education.* (4th ed.). Westbury, NY: Foundation Press.

Richmond, V. P., & McCroskey, J. C. (1992). *Power in the classroom: Communication, control, and concern.* Hillsdale, NJ: Erlbaum.

Riessman, F. (1967). Teachers of the poor: A five point plan. *Journal of Teacher Education,* 326–336.

Robbins, S. P. (1984). *Essentials of organizational behavior.* Englewood Cliffs, NJ: Prentice-Hall.

Rohrkemper, M. (1985). Motivational coursework in teacher education. In M. K. Alderman & M. W. Cohen (eds.), *Motivation theory and practice for preservice teachers* (Teacher Education Monograph No. 4). Washington, DC: ERIC Clearinghouse on Teacher Education.

Rosenshine, B. (1979). Content, time and direct instruction. In P. Peterson & H. Walberg (eds.), *Research on teaching: Concepts, findings and implications.* Berkeley, CA: McCutchan.

Rosenshine, B., & Furst, N. (1973). The use of direct observation to study teaching. In R. M. W. Travers (ed.), *Second handbook of research on teaching.* (3rd ed.). New York: Macmillan.

Rosenshine, B., & Stevens, R. (1986). Teaching functions. In M. C. Wittrock (ed.), *Handbook of research on teaching.* (3rd ed.). New York: Macmillan.

Rosenthal, R., & Jacobson, L. (1968). *Pygmalion in the classroom.* New York: Holt, Rinehart and Winston.

Rotter, J. B. (1966). Generalized expectancies for internal versus external control of reinforcement. *Psychological Monographs, 80,* 1–28.

Rotter, J. (1971). External control and internal control. *Psychology Today, 5,* 37–53.

Rubovits, P., & Maehr, M. (1971). Pygmalion analyzed: Toward an explanation of the Rosenthal-Jacobson findings. *Journal of Personality and Social Psychology, 19,* 197–203.

Ryan, K. (1979). Toward understanding the problem: At the threshold of the profession. In K. R. Howey & R. H. Bents (eds.), *Toward meeting the needs of the beginning teacher— Initial training/induction/inservice.* Minneapolis, MN: Midwest Teachers Corps Network.

Samples, R. (1977). *The wholeschool book.* Reading, MA: Addison-Wesley.

Sarason, S.B. (1993). *Letters to a serious education president.* Newbury Park, CA: Corwin.

Sarason, S.B. (1990). *The predictable failure of educational reform.* San Francisco, CA: Jossey-Bass.

Schwade, S. (1985, Feb.). Is it time to consider computer-based training? *Personnel Administrator,* 25–35.

Simon, S., Howe, L., & Kirschenbaum, H. (1972). *Values clarification: A handbook of practical strategies for teachers and students.* New York: Holt, Rinehart and Winston.

Sirotnik, K. (1990). Society, schooling, teaching, and preparing to teach. In J. Goodlad, R. Soder, & K. Sirotnik (eds.), *The moral dimensions of teaching.* San Francisco: Jossey-Bass.

Slavin, R. (1986). *Using student learning.* (3rd ed.). Center for Research on Elementary and Middle Schools. Baltimore, MD: Johns Hopkins University.

Slavin, R. (1987). Grouping for instruction in the elementary school. *Educational Psychologist.*

Slavin, R. (1988a). *School and classroom organization.* Hillsdale, NJ: Erlbaum.

Slavin, R. E. (1988b). *Educational psychology: Theory into practice.* (2nd ed.). Englewood Cliffs, NJ: Prentice-Hall.

Smith, H.P. (1950). A study of the problems of beginning teachers. *Educational Administration and Supervision, 36,* 257–264.

Smith, R. A. (1987). A teacher's views on cooperative learning. *Phi Delta Kappan, 68* (9), 663–666.

Soar, R. (1973). *Follow through classroom process measurement and pupil growth (1970–71): Final report.* Gainesville, FL: College of Education, University of Florida.

Sparkman, W., & Desrosiers, E. (1986). *School law courses survey, 1986.* Paper presented at the annual meeting of the National Organization on Legal Problems of Education, Las Vegas.

Spaulding, A. M. (1994a, April). *The politics of the principal: Influencing teachers on school-based decision making.* Paper presented at the annual conference of the American Educational Research Association, New Orleans.

Spaulding, A. M. (1994b, October). *The micropolitics of the elementary classroom.* Unpublished doctoral dissertation. Lubbock: Texas Tech University.

Spaulding, A. M. (1994c). Paper presentation: *The politics of the school: School member relationships and their influence on the classroom.*

Springbett, B. (1958). Factors affecting the final decision in the employment interview. *Canadian Journal of Psychology, 12,* 13–22.

Stallings, J., & Kaskowitz, D. (1974). *Follow through classroom observation evaluation, 1972–73.* Menlo Park, CA: Stanford Research Institute.

Stout, J. B. (1952). Deficiencies of beginning teachers. *Journal of Teacher Education, 3,* 43–46.

Strike, K. (1988). The ethics of teaching. *Phi Delta Kappan, 70,* 156–158.

Strike, K. (1990). The legal and moral responsibility of teachers. In J. Goodlad, R. Soder, & K. Sirotnik (eds.), *The moral dimensions of teaching.* San Francisco: Jossey-Bass.

Suchman, R. (1966). *Inquiry development program in physical science.* Chicago: Science Research Associates.

Taba, H. (1962). *Curriculum development: Theory and practice.* New York: Harcourt Brace.

Tate, M. W. (1943). The induction of secondary-school teachers. *School Review, 51,* 150–157.

Thomas, B. (1990). The school as a moral learning community. In J. Goodlad, R. Soder, & K. Sirotnik (eds.), *The moral dimensions of teaching.* San Francisco: Jossey-Bass.

Thomas, G., Sperry, D., & Wasden, F. (1991). *The law and teacher employment.* St. Paul, MN: West Publishing.

Torrance, E. (1962). *Guiding creative talent.* Englewood Cliffs, NJ: Prentice-Hall.

Trachtenberg, S. J. (1990). Multiculturalism can be taught only by multicultural people. *Phi Delta Kappan, 71* (8), 610–611.

Tuchman, B. (1985). *Evaluating instructional programs.* Boston: Allyn and Bacon.

Tyler, R. (1949). *Basic principles of curriculum and instruction.* Chicago: University of Chicago Press.

United States Department of Education. (1994). *Goals 2000: An education strategy.* Washington, DC: United States Department of Education.

Vacca, R. T., & Vacca, J. L. (1989). *Content area reading.* (3rd ed.). Glenview, IL: Scott, Foresman.

Valente, W. (1994). *Law in the schools.* (4th ed.). New York: Macmillan.

Van Horn, R. (1987). Laser videodiscs in education: Endless possibilities. *Phi Delta Kappan, 68* (9), 696–700.

Veenman, S. (1984). Perceived problems of beginning teachers. *Review of Educational Research, 54* (2), 143–178.

Wagner, T. (1993). Systemic change: Rethinking the purpose of school. *Educational Leadership, 51* (1), 24–29.

Wattenberg, W., & Clifford, C. (1962). *Relationship of self-concept to beginning achievement in reading.* U.S. Office of Education, Cooperative Research Project No. 377. Detroit, MI: Wayne State University.

Webb, N. (1987). *Helping behavior to maximize learning.* Paper presented at the annual meeting of the American Educational Research Association, Washington, DC.

Weber, W. (1986). Classroom management. In J. Cooper (ed.), *Classroom teaching skills.* (3rd ed.). Lexington, MA: Heath.

Wehr, J. (1988). Instructor-led or computer-based: Which will work best for you? *Training and Development Journal, 42* (6), 18–21.

Wey, H. W. (1951). Difficulties of beginning teachers. *School Review, 59,* 32–37.

Williams, F. (1982). Developing children's creativity at home and in school. *GCT, 24,* 2–6.

Woods, P. (1990). *Teacher skills and strategies.* Bristol, PA: Falmer.

Zepeda, S. J. (1993). *A case study of the problem-solving dialogue between a mentor and a first-year teacher.* Unpublished Ph.D. Dissertation, Loyola University of Chicago.

Index

Photo Credits